Where to Watch Birds in

DEVON
& CORNWALL

SECOND EDITION

David Norman and Vic Tucker

OTHER *WHERE TO WATCH BIRDS* BOOKS
PUBLISHED BY CHRISTOPHER HELM

Where to Watch Birds in East Anglia
Peter and Margaret Clarke

*Where to Watch Birds in Bedfordshire, Berkshire, Buckinghamshire,
Hertfordshire and Oxfordshire*
Brian Clews, Andrew Heryet and Paul Trodd

Where to Watch Birds in Kent, Surrey and Sussex
Don Taylor, Jeffery Wheatley and Tony Prater

Where to Watch Birds in Scotland
Mike Madders and Julia Welstead

Where to Watch Birds in Somerset, Avon, Gloucestershire and Wiltshire
Ken Hall and John Govett

Where to Watch Birds in the West Midlands
Graham Harrison and Jack Sankey

Where to Watch Birds in Wales
David Saunders

Where to Watch Birds in Dorset, Hampshire and The Isle of Wight
George Green and Martin Cade

Where to Watch Birds in

DEVON & CORNWALL

SECOND EDITION

David Norman and Vic Tucker

Illustrations by Peter Harrison and Steve Bird

Christopher Helm

A & C Black · London

This book is dedicated to our wives, Karen and Sylvia, in gratitude for their patience and support, as we toiled over the book, and their tolerance of freezing dawn outings, muddy wellies, bird notes strewn around the house and all the other symptoms of ornithology.

© 1984 David Norman and Vic Tucker
Second Edition © 1991

Line illustrations by Peter Harrison and Steve Bird

Christopher Helm (Publishers) Ltd,
a subsidiary of A & C Black (Publishers) Ltd,
35 Bedford Row, London WC1R 4JH

ISBN 0–7136–8051–2

A CIP catalogue record for this book
is available from the British Library

10 9 8 7 6 5 4 3 2 1

Typeset by Florencetype Ltd, Kewstoke, Avon
Printed and bound in Great Britain by Biddles Ltd, Guildford, Surrey

CONTENTS

Contents

General Map of Main Birdwatching Sites

Note: Numbers correspond to chapters

LIST OF ILLUSTRATIONS

ACKNOWLEDGEMENTS

It is a positive pleasure to thank those people who happily contributed various help and information. Our special thanks must go to Roger Lane, Stan Christophers, Bob Burridge, Perry Sanders, Ian Kendall, Chris Riley (Slapton Field Centre), Peter Chamberlain (Devon Wildlife Trust), Martin Elcoate, Robin Khan (Forestry Commission), Stan Davies (RSPB), Nigel Smallbones (Berry Head), Gordon Vaughan, Wal Towler and Norman Barns, for much help freely given concerning sites less well known to us or those which have special fauna and flora in addition to birds.

The production of this new edition has been a major task, involving sifting through hundreds of pages of notes to check on changes which have taken place at each site and updating bird occurrences; new areas have been included and much information added. This would have been impossible without the co-operation we have had from bird-watchers throughout the region. We owe grateful thanks to Steve Bird, who has so skilfully supplemented the original artwork with his own excellent drawings, which have involved extra painstaking effort to relate many to an appropriate local setting, thus enhancing their interest and relevance still further. Steve also drew all the new maps for the Second Edition and updated several originals. Finally, we thank all Christopher Helm staff involved in the book's production, in particular Robert Kirk.

The authors would be pleased to receive any additional information or ideas which might be incorporated in future editions of this guide and hence benefit future users. Correspondence (s.a.e. if reply needed) should be addressed c/o Christopher Helm Publishers, 35 Bedford Row, London WC1R 4JH and marked for the attention of David Norman and Vic Tucker.

Note

A great deal of the material in this book is extracted from the author's personal logbooks, and from information supplied by the correspondents listed above. The following have also been used: Annual reports produced by both Devon and Cornwall Bird Watching and Preservation Societies; *Devon Birds* Magazine (produced by Devon BWPS); *The Birds of Devon*, R.F. Moore, David & Charles, Newton Abbot; *The Birds of Lundy*, J.N. Dymond, Devon BWPS; *Birds of the Cornish Coast*, R.D. Penhallurick, Truro; *Birds of Cornwall*, R.D. Penhallurick, Truro; *Tetrad Atlas of Breeding Birds of Devon*, H.P. Sitters, Devon BWPS.

INTRODUCTION

The object of this book is to guide the reader to areas of ornithological interest in the two counties of the extreme southwest of Britain, Devon and Cornwall, and their offshore islands. The information contained in the text is the distillation of thousands of hours' birdwatching experience in the region by the two authors. Our aim has been to make this book really useful by including local knowledge, the tricks of the trade, developed over the years with a 'feel' of when and in what conditions an area is most worth visiting. Information on occurrences is based on events over the past two decades, during which birdwatching has developed as a mass hobby, although we have also tried to indicate the latest trends and discoveries.

We have selected areas which have proved consistently worth visiting. Many species occur just about anywhere, but our chosen locations are based on the following rules:

1. Those which hold a high *density* of birds, whether breeding, migrating or wintering.

2. Those which form a *specialised* habitat where bird species occur which might not be found elsewhere.

3. Areas which are *representative* of their type, e.g. a wood with a good range of birds which might also occur in less accessible areas nearby.

It should be noted that a few areas well known to local birdwatchers, e.g. certain smaller South Coast estuaries, have private access, and cannot therefore be included in a book such as this.

There remains ample scope for discovery in the region, however, by visiting little-studied districts, or by visiting well-known bird sites during different conditions or times of year from other watchers. Knowledge of the distribution and movements of birds can progress only if someone is prepared to try out ideas.

It is not enough to know that a locality is good for seeing birds. At most birdwatching sites, factors such as tides and winds, as well as season, are of paramount importance in planning your visit. Much valuable information is obtained from county bird reports, but these assume quite a high degree of knowledge. It is not their function to explain in detail the background behind records, or to cover ancillary factors such as timing a wader-watch for high tide (vital if time and effort are not to be wasted). Birdwatching visitors with limited time to spare will find our treatment of these topics particularly useful in planning their stay.

County bird reports, which list what is known to have occurred within each county during any one year, are produced by the Devon and Cornwall Bird Watching and Preservation Societies (DBWPS and CBWPS), two parallel organisations through which regular birdwatching excursions take place in both counties, with local experts in charge. The national Royal Society for the Protection of Birds also has branches throughout the country, which are particularly helpful to children and to beginners of all ages. The County Naturalists' Trusts (Devon Wildlife Trust, formerly Devon Trust for Nature Conservation, and the Cornwall Trust for Nature Conservation) have areas of land which, although not always primarily selected for their bird importance, form refuges for a variety of species. Membership of any of these organisations has this advantage, in the long run the most important of all: the conservation of birds, by protecting the birds themselves and the habitats in which they live.

'How do I identify the birds I see?' is a question to which the answers are outside the scope of this book. There are good field guides, illustrating several 'action' poses of the same species, in positions most usually seen and in varying plumage stages. Beware of some bird books which confuse the beginner by omitting common British birds and substituting species which would probably not be found in this country.

Features of the region's birdlife

As the mildest part of Britain, the region plays host to many wintering birds which normally move further south, including waders (e.g. Avocet) and regular Blackcap and Chiffchaff; in severe winters, large numbers of birds move across from the east coast to shelter. Frost-sensitive species such as the Cirl Bunting, still resident here although in reduced numbers, are rare elsewhere. Areas of non-intensive farming with overgrown hedges remain, holding a good variety of small birds. Extensive valley woodlands, particularly on moorland fringes, hold many breeding residents and summer migrant songbirds, plus a healthy population of larger birds such as Buzzard, Sparrowhawk and Raven. The higher moors form a southern outpost of several breeding species usually found in Scotland and the Pennines, e.g. Ring Ouzel and Golden Plover. The hundreds of miles of rocky coast with offshore islands still hold a number of seabird colonies, while protruding headlands near seabird feeding and migration routes enable a wide range of these birds to be seen passing in spring and autumn. Our southerly position means that spring often arrives early (from late February) and that autumn birds linger well into November; it also makes the region an arrival point for southern migrants such as Hoopoes in small numbers each spring. As we stand at the side of Britain which faces the New World, American wanderers are noted most autumns after westerly winds. In terms of habitat, we have much running water, but few lowland lakes and reservoirs, although some major new reservoirs have just been completed. Although seabirds are well represented, some species such as Tree Sparrow, common farther east, are almost absent. Resident bird-watchers are still thinly spread over most of the region and we still have gaps to fill in our knowledge of a number of species. Thanks largely to the Isles of Scilly and Lundy, plus a few outstanding coastal headlands on the mainland, the list of passage migrants and rare vagrant species is extremely long; we have not attempted to compile a total list, since it would be out of place in a practical guide where information about typical occurrences is more relevant than that on isolated sightings. Some examples of recent notable sightings have, however, been given (and updated in this Second Edition).

On the debit side, oil pollution at sea is sadly regular, as is river pollution by agricultural and industrial waste products; some lakes and waterways suffer toxic algal blooms caused by high nitrate concentrations. Mass tourism has driven breeding terns and waders off mainland beaches; other large-scale amenity developments from water sports in estuaries to proposed woodland leisure parks all threaten valuable habitats and firm conservation policies are ever more vital.

Climate and geography: some general points

Geographers separate Devon and Cornwall from the rest of southern England by the 'Tees-Exe line' drawn on a map from Teesmouth in northeastern England to the Exe Estuary in South Devon. To the west and north of the line lie upland regions with hills, rocks and deep offshore seas; to the east and south lie mainly lowlands and shallow muddy coasts. The peninsula is therefore classed with Wales, northern England and Scotland as a hill area. The hills and the position facing the Atlantic ensure a mild, damp and windy climate; severe gales are frequent in winter on exposed coasts and high hills, preventing tree growth and leading to boggy ground conditions because of the high rainfall. Snow and ice can occur on the mainland, particularly on the moors where snowfalls are sometimes very large, but thaws usually arrive swiftly, especially in the coastal lowlands. Prolonged hard frosts are uncommon in the far west of Cornwall and very rare on the Isles of Scilly. Most of the region's rivers are short and fast-flowing; the weathered granite masses of Bodmin Moor in Cornwall and Dartmoor in Devon are the origin of most of the larger rivers. High Willhays on Dartmoor (about 627 m) is the region's highest point. Exmoor, which lies across the North Devon-Somerset boundary, falls partly within our scope; we have also included, for completeness of country coverage, the sandy heathland ridges and valleys of East Devon, which are geographically distinct from the rest of the region.

Birdwatching in Devon and Cornwall has given the authors a great many memorable and exciting days. There have been dawn watches at St Ives when the sea was strewn with tens of thousands of migrating seabirds during hurricane-force winds; days when some tiny rare Asiatic warbler was found feeding in a remote cove; days when the moorland woods were full of singing Pied Flycatcher and Redstart in all directions; winter days when swerving wader flocks shimmered silver over the mudflats as a Peregrine hunted overhead. Birdwatchers surely cannot be immune to the interest of seeing other wildlife, and we can well remember occasions when a seawatch was interrupted by a 30-ft (9-m) Basking Shark rolling lazily up to the surface just offshore, or when a magnificent Red Deer ran past during a winter moorland visit. We hope that, by giving you the benefit of our experience, we may give you the chance to see and appreciate these sights for yourself.

HOW TO USE THIS BOOK

We often meet inexperienced but keen birdwatchers who rely heavily on field guides and books listing areas of ornithological interest. Many are frustrated and disappointed by inadequate information; for instance, if a book says, 'Dartmoor: Ring Ouzel', where do you start looking in 400 square miles (1036 km^2) of heather, rocks and bog? They are also given the impression that there will always be birds at a particular area in all conditions – yet very few spring migrants, for example, will be seen arriving at southerly coastal watchpoints in an opposing northerly gale. Birds undertake complex movements influenced by many factors such as weather, tides and seasons; human disturbance may also cause them to change quarters (for example, a group of ducks flying from one lake to another when disturbed by sailing). We have set out to highlight these factors to give you the best chance of success at each area you visit.

Measurements

Throughout the text we have given measurements in those units most readily understood by the majority of English readers. Distances are normally stated in miles, followed by the metric equivalent in kilometres (occasionally metres). Altitudes are given in metres, as on all modern Ordnance Survey maps. For surface areas, we have given the imperial measurement, followed by the metric one.

The Information Sections for Each Site

(N.B. Second Edition: for Additional Sites see Note at end of this description)

Habitat

This section aims to paint a 'word picture' of each area and its scenery. The extent of the area covered and main bird-habitat zones are indicated. Where the birdwatcher is likely to see other easily visible wildlife, such as deer, seals or butterflies, a brief note is included.

Species

This section does not list every species found in an area; for reasons of space, common birds are usually excluded. We have aimed to give a sample of the main species of interest, and what they are doing (breeding, moving through, or turning up in cold weather). Frequency of occurrence and scale of numbers involved will guide the visitor on what to expect – whether single birds, small parties, or flocks of hundreds of a particular species. A few ornithological 'goodies' which might be encountered are also mentioned.

The text is arranged in broadly chronological order to help the reader to follow the pattern of bird events through the year. At the start of the section, some reference is made to the general ornithological importance of the area. No attempt is made to give specific dates, as the 'Calendar' section gives further details on when each species usually occurs.

Timing

How to avoid a wasted visit! How to judge appropriate weather conditions for what you hope to see; bird migration is heavily dependent on weather, and a mass of birds along the coastline one day may all have departed by next morning if conditions change. How to judge when particular groups of species will be most active; a dawn watch, for instance, often yields rich results. How to plan your visit to avoid human disturbance which may frighten birds off or make them difficult to see (do not forget that one form of disturbance is thoughtless birdwatchers!). How to pick tides to see roosting or feeding waders on different estuaries. Accurate use of this section is **essential** if you want best results from the book.

Access

How to get there from main towns and A-class roads, down minor roads, and what paths to take when you arrive. Often a maze of country roads leads to a birdwatching site; we have described one practical route. How far you need to walk around the area. Use this section in conjunction with the map provided.

Note:special access restrictions, such as a military firing range or a wardened nature reserve, may mean that you need to plan your visit in advance, so check this section for possible problems beforehand. If an area includes private farmland, you should in all cases seek permission from the farmer before deviating from public footpaths. To follow detailed directions, a 1:50,000 Ordnance Survey map will be a great help; the number of the appropriate map, and a four-figure grid reference for the particular area described, are given beside the heading for each locality.

Calendar

This is a quick-reference summary section, so all information has been condensed and abbreviated as far as possible. The calendar year has been split into seasons which relate to the majority of ornithological events, although obviously some species will not fit this pattern exactly. *Winter* is December–February as far as the larger numbers of winter bird visitors to our region are concerned; *Spring* is March–May as far as most arriving migrants are concerned; *Summer*, in terms of maximum breeding activity and little migration movement, can be extended only over June and July, with some species starting to move even in the late part of this period; *Autumn* is protracted, with migration from August to November, although different groups of species peak at different periods within this. These are not, it should be noted, the same as normal human definitions of seasons. Many people, for example, might take a 'summer holiday' in late August, but if they visited a Guillemot colony then they would find that the birds had finished breeding and departed far out to sea. To avoid confusion, we have repeated these groupings of months by name in each Calendar section.

Within the section we have included the most likely peak periods for each species or group of species; if no further qualifying comment is made, the bird concerned may be looked for with equal chance of success at any time during the season, or peak numbers may occur randomly whenever conditions are most suitable during these months. Where several species or groups are listed in the same period, we have mentioned them in the order most usual in field guides, to facilitate quick reference to identification points in a suitable book.

Note to second edition: Additional Sites

In the First Edition an Appendix gave a very brief description of a number of sites in the region which were considered less outstanding, or less accessible, than those we picked out to describe fully, yet might be worth visiting. In the Second Edition we have taken the opportunity to give further details of such sites, linking them to the nearest appropriate major site, in geographical sequence as far as possible. Some have now become recognised as major sites and are therefore described in a specific chapter; new Additional Sites have been inserted on the basis of recent ornithological discoveries; in some cases, such as a newly flooded reservoir, observations may well prove them worth a full chapter in the future.

We give a description of the general habitat relating to the areas used by birds, and relating to the visitor's requirements, but make no mention of other flora and fauna. The species section is written in a very concise style, mentioning the typical and more interesting birds for which the site is known. Both timing and access sections are complete as they would be for a major site, recognising their importance as a vital aid to those who are unfamiliar with our selected sites. To save space and enable inclusion of the maximum number of such sites, we have avoided giving a 'Calendar' section, by incorporating into the 'Species' text information on seasons of occurrence. No map or bird drawing is provided, but the relevant O.S. map number and a four figure grid reference are given for each site.

Additional Sites are not mapped on the general map of the region at the front of the text, except for Chapter 45, which describes four widely separated inland sites which have little in common with others. Additional Sites, as well as multiple sites containing several distinct zones (e.g. Exe Estuary), are fully referenced to species in the Index.

Key to maps

MAJOR ROADS	
MINOR ROADS	
DECIDUOUS WOODLAND	
CONIFEROUS WOODLAND	
ROUGH GRASSLAND	
MARSHLAND	
TRACK	
FOOTPATH	
RAILWAY TRACK	station
LIGHTHOUSE	
SPOT HEIGHT (in metres)	e.g. 100

A COMPARISON OF THE
BIRDWATCHING AREAS

To assist the reader in selecting areas to visit, we have drawn up an analysis of the main habitats visited by birdwatchers in Devon and Cornwall. Under each habitat heading we have listed those examples included in this book, and given our assessment of their comparative quality derived from our personal knowledge and experience and from other reports which we know to be reliable. Three stars (***) are awarded to areas which have consistently provided good results, the scale descending to one star (*) for areas of more limited local interest or which less often provide interesting birds. The assessment is relative to other sites in *our* region; we have not attempted to make comparison with national standards. The ratings should be used in conjunction with the relevant instructions on how to watch each area. *Note*: we have not included Additional Sites in this analysis.

The habitat types

Reed-Beds
Otter Estuary*
Exe: Dawlish Warren and Exminster Marsh–Topsham**
Slapton***
Beesands*
Hallsands**
South Milton Ley (Thurlestone area)***
Par Beach Pool*
Marazion Marsh***
Lower Moors, St Mary's, Isles of Scilly***

Seawatch Points
Exe: Langstone Rock, Dawlish Warren**
Hope's Nose***
Start Point*
Prawle Point***
Rame Head*
Bass Point, The Lizard*
Porthgwarra***
Porth Hellick Point, St Mary's, Isles of Scilly**
Peninnis Head, St Mary's, Isles of Scilly**
Horse Point, St Agnes, Isles of Scilly*
North Cliffs, Tresco, Isles of Scilly*
St Ives Island***
Towan Head, Newquay***
Hartland Point*
Morte Point (North Devon coastline)*
Capstone, Ilfracombe (North Devon coastline)*

Seabird Breeding Stations
Budleigh Salterton–Ladram Bay*
Hope's Nose**
Berry Head**
Start Point*
Isles of Scilly***
Tintagel-Boscastle***
Lundy***
Heddons Mouth area (North Devon coastline)**

Lowland Heaths
East Devon Commons***
Haldon***
Lizard peninsula at Goonhilly Downs* and Predannack**

Open Moorland
Soussons area**
Cranmere Pool, North Dartmoor***
Dozmary Pool area, Bodmin Moor**
Land's End Moors***

Coniferous Forest
Haldon Woods***
Soussons*
Bellever (Soussons–Postbridge area)*
Burrator*
Bodmin Moor plantations (Upper Fowey Valley)**

Open Turf: Airfields/Golf Courses
Dawlish Warren Golf Links*
Little Haldon Golf Course*
Thurlestone*
Predannack, Lizard Peninsula**
St Just Airfield, Land's End**
St Mary's Airfield, Isles of Scilly***
Davidstow Airfield***

Sheltered Coastal Bays
Exe Estuary off Dawlish Warren*** and Exmouth**
Torbay**
Start Bay***
Plymouth Sound**
Whitsands Bay**
Par, St Austell Bay**
Gerrans Bay***
Carrick Roads, Falmouth***
Falmouth Bay**
Helford Passage (Falmouth area)**
Mounts Bay***
St Ives Bay***

Shingle Beaches
Slapton**
Beesands*
Northam Burrows (Taw–Torridge)*

Sand Dunes
Dawlish Warren**
Hayle Towans*
Braunton Burrows (Taw–Torridge)**

Passerine Migration Watchpoints
Berry Head*
Start Point**
Prawle Point***
Rame Head**
Lizard area***
Porthgwarra–Land's End valleys***
Isles of Scilly***
Hartland Point*

Woodlands (Deciduous and Mixed)
Stoke Woods**
Yarner Wood***
Dartington*
Okement Woods, North Dartmoor*
Plymbridge**
Chapel Wood, Spreacombe (North Devon coastline)*
Tarr Steps, Exmoor**

Estuary Mudflats
Axe Estuary*
Otter Estuary*
Exe Estuary***
Kingsbridge Estuary**
Avon Estuary*
Plym Estuary (Plymouth area)**
Tamar–Tavy, including St John's Lake and the Lynher**
Fal Estuary**
Hayle Estuary***
Camel Estuary**
Taw–Torridge Estuary*

Water-Meadows
Axe Estuary*
Exe at Exminster Marsh*** and Bowling Green Marsh*
West Charleton Marsh, Kingsbridge*
South Huish (Thurlestone)**
Avon water meadows*
Amble marshes, Camel Estuary**

Reservoirs, Lakes and Pools
Slapton Ley***
Beesands Ley**
Burrator Reservoir, Dartmoor**
Radford Lake*
Siblyback Reservoir**
Colliford Reservoir*
Dozmary Pool*
Crowdy Reservoir***

Par Beach Pool*
Swanpool, Falmouth*
Stithians Reservoir***
Porth Hellick Pool, St Mary's, Isles of Scilly**
Abbey and Great Pools, Tresco, Isles of Scilly***
Tamar Lakes***
Arlington Lake (North Devon coastline)*
Wistlandpound Reservoir (North Devon coastline)*

1 AXE ESTUARY

Habitat

At the eastern corner of Devon, the Axe valley provides extensive grazing
meadows and raised saltmarsh, culminating in a half-mile-(0.8km-) long
open muddy estuary. The mudflats are about 200 metres wide and
further grazing marshes lie on the west side near Seaton, separated from
the estuary by an old railway embankment now used for tourist trams.
To the north of the open estuary are numerous drainage channels and
several small reed-beds. The estuary mouth is narrow and enclosed at
the seaward end, with high chalk cliffs rising to the east. The coast and
'Landslip' area, a National Nature Reserve where large sections of rock
strata have slid towards the sea, is botanically very interesting between
here and the Dorset border. Six miles (9½ km) of coastline contain

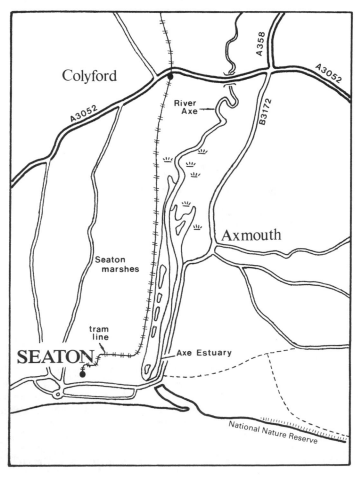

some scarce or local plants including Yellow Archangel, Ivy Broomrape, Narrow-leaved Everlasting Pea and Golden Saxifrage.

Species

The Axe can provide a variety of wintering estuary and marshland wildfowl and waders, although populations of most species are not outstandingly large. Dabbling duck are attracted to the meadows, with over 200 Wigeon and up to 100 Teal often seen. Lapwing, Snipe and Curlew may all exceed 100. One or two smaller, shorter-billed Jack Snipe may also occur near reeds and ditches, although often elusive. Water Rail and Reed Bunting share these habitats. Open meadows may hold small parties of Ruff in winter, although occasionally up to 20 have been found; in prolonged freezing spells they may be joined by Bewick's Swan or White-fronted Geese, although these larger species move on swiftly when conditions improve. Lapwing numbers may also increase to thousands for short periods. On the open estuary Shelduck, gulls and common waders such as Redshank and Curlew are conspicuous, while several Little Grebe, Cormorant and Grey Heron hunt in the main channel. Various other ducks and waders drop in but do not usually stay. Kingfisher, which breed just north of the marshes, are frequently seen darting low across the estuary outside the nesting season. Gull roosts on the upper estuary are worth checking since Little, Mediterranean, Glaucous and Iceland have all been recorded occasionally, once joined by the rare American Laughing Gull.

Shelduck

Spring brings a dozen or so pairs of Grey Heron to traditional breeding woods on the east side of the valley, and perhaps a chance of a rarer relative such as Spoonbill or Little Egret spending a day or two on the estuary. Migrant ducks in ones or twos may include Gadwall or Shoveler on the meadows, while Teal may stay late, perhaps joined by the scarce Garganey, picked out from Teal in flight by its blue-grey forewing. Shelduck prospect nest burrows on nearby hillsides. Common Sandpiper are often seen on the estuary banks, while flocks of 20 or more Whimbrel and the occasional Ruff in breeding dress drop in on the meadows. A few Wheatear are reported, Sand Martin move through to their colonies just upriver, and several pairs of Reed and Sedge Warblers arrive to nest in the reed-beds. Midsummer is not a very active time on the estuary, although Lapwing breed and the other larger resident species are always visible, including Raven, Buzzard and Sparrowhawk soaring overhead. At the end of summer and early autumn the area becomes interesting again, with a good variety of waders, although numbers are never very large, Dunlin for instance gathering only in dozens on the mudflats. At peak periods, both Black-tailed and Bar-tailed Godwits, Greenshank, Spotted Redshank and Ruff may all feed with common waders on the estuary, although repeated visits may be needed to see a range of species as migrants arrive and depart. Several Green Sandpiper are often present, preferring sheltered areas around the head of the estuary, where a paler-backed Wood Sandpiper may join them. Overhead, large numbers of hirundines, thousands at times, gather to feed before migration, perhaps attracting a passing Hobby. Migrant Yellow Wagtail (a species which has bred here in the past) gather in flocks of up to 100 in the meadows, going to reed-bed roosts, with high 'sweep' calls at dusk, but most leave by mid-autumn.

A walk eastward along the Landslip coast footpath could be worthwhile in summer for singing passerines; 20 pairs of Nightingale have recently been found breeding along here, and Lesser Whitethroat are quite common in scrub and thickets, the male birds detected by their rattling song. Both these summer migrant visitors are uncommon in Devon and Cornwall, although more common to the east of our region; indeed Nightingale are only regularly reported here and at Chudleigh Knighton Heath in South Devon. Apart from the loud song, this species can be very skulking and good views are only obtained with luck and patience.

Timing

The marshes are worth checking when wildfowl and open ground species are driven down from further north by ice and snow, particularly when this lasts for more than a few days. Thousands of birds may then shelter in the valley. Most of the unusual wildfowl recorded here come at such times, although periods of extensive flooding can also produce species not normally present. Southerly winds in spring produce the chance of 'overshooting' rarer herons and egrets.

On sunny days, try to avoid looking westward across the mudflats against late afternoon glare. Evening views across the meadows might still produce a view of the scarce Barn Owl. Avoid highest tides for wader watches (half tide may be better) as there is no convenient central roost, although a rising tide pushes waders up towards Axmouth.

As usual, summer migrant songbirds are best sought when active and singing in early morning, or particularly also on fine evenings for Nightingale, although these also sing in the daytime.

Access

The coastal town of Seaton, adjacent to the estuary, lies off A3052 between Sidmouth and Lyme Regis. To reach the eastern bank of the estuary, continue east along the main A3052 to cross the Axe at the northern end of the marshes near Colyford. Beyond the bridge take B3172 south towards Axmouth. Stop and view the meadows at convenient points along this road; there are no public footpaths through them. From Axmouth village the road runs directly beside the mudflats down to the beach, giving easy car-window views all along.

For the western grazing marshes, try viewing with a telescope from minor roads north of Seaton; as on the eastern side, there are no public paths and birds may be distant. Views across the area might, however, be obtained from the Seaton-Colyford tramway, which runs daily between April and October, but weekdays only in winter. To enquire, telephone (0297) 21702. The coast path eastwards towards the National Nature Reserve thickets starts near the bridge across from Seaton at the bottom of the estuary, and is part of the South West Coast Path.

Calendar

Resident: Cormorant, Grey Heron, Buzzard, Sparrowhawk, Partridge, Lapwing, Stock Dove, maybe Barn Owl, Little Owl, Kingfisher, Reed Bunting.

December–February: Little Grebe, maybe Bewick's Swan and White-fronted Goose (hard weather), Shelduck, occasional Gadwall, Wigeon, Teal, occasional Pintail, Shoveler, irregular Tufted Duck, Water Rail, Coot, Oystercatcher, Dunlin, Redshank, maybe a Common Sandpiper, Ruff, Snipe, Jack Snipe, Curlew, gulls, Grey Wagtail, Stonechat.

March–May: winter visitors seen to early April in reduced numbers. Shelduck, Teal, migrant ducks including maybe Garganey, Ruff, Sand Martin, Wheatear (mid-March on), occasional Little Egret or Spoonbill (April–May), Common Sandpipers, Bar-tailed Godwit and Whimbrel (late April on), Yellow Wagtail, Reed and Sedge Warblers, maybe Lesser Whitethroat, on marshes; Lesser Whitethroat and Nightingale on coast walk, end of period.

June–July: rarer 'heron' still possible June. Shelduck, Sand Martin, maybe Lesser Whitethroat or Yellow Wagtail breeding, other waders return from July. Nightingale difficult to locate after June as song finishes.

August–November: maybe Hobby (August–September), wader passage mostly August–September, hirundines and Yellow Wagtail (peak end August), winter visitors arrive from October, when Green and Common Sandpipers still present.

2 OTTER ESTUARY AND BUDLEIGH SALTERTON

OS ref: SY 0782
OS map: sheet 192

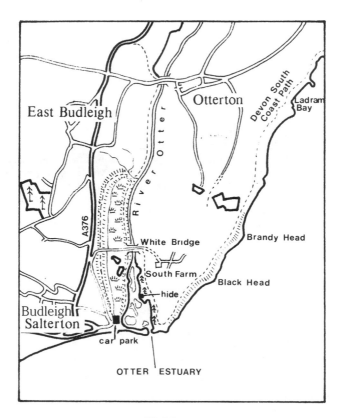

OTTER ESTUARY

Habitat
The East Devon coast between the Axe and Exe valleys is composed chiefly of sandstone cliffs up to 170 m high, with numerous small coves and coastal stream valleys. The only lowland is the Otter, a half-mile (0.8 km) estuary of mud and raised saltmarsh adjacent to the town of Budleigh Salterton. The pebble beach forms a bar across most of the estuary mouth. A narrow strip of meadow, backed by trees and thickets, borders the western side of the river, together with a tiny reed-bed. Devon Wildlife Trust leases virtually the whole estuary as a 57-acre (21-ha) nature reserve. Immediately above the open estuary, moving north towards Otterton village, the river is far narrower, with shallow clear stretches and gravel bars. Budleigh Salterton itself is well wooded, with large mature gardens and ornamental conifers.

Species
This is a well-known area locally for general birdwatching, with a good cross-section of the region's waterside and farmland birds, although

none is restricted to this area alone. Interesting residents include the declining Barn Owl, which might be seen over the meadows at dusk, and Little Owl occasionally perched on a hedge or stump in daytime. Kingfisher are seen regularly, moving upriver to breed but frequenting the saltmarsh channels at other seasons. Grey Wagtail are also widespread here, and Dipper are resident on faster-flowing stretches around Otterton and above. All three species of woodpecker occur regularly in the valley, the Lesser Spotted is possibly seen in the topmost branches of riverside trees.

In winter this estuary usually shelters half a dozen Little Grebe, while Cormorant and Grey Heron stand sentinel along the banks. Ducks are not numerous, but a few Wigeon and Teal fly over from the Exe to feed; the most frequent diving ducks are one or two Goldeneye, but scarcer species such as Long-tailed Duck have occurred, and parties of up to a dozen Red-breasted Merganser turn up irregularly. Canada Geese often graze on saltmarsh islands, and flocks of 40–50 may visit for short periods. Water Rail are heard screaming in the reed-bed. On the narrow mudflats, waders are limited; Dunlin are the only small ones regularly present, except for a single Common Sandpiper which often remains to winter, flying off low with stiff, flickering wingbeats when disturbed. Larger common waders such as Oystercatcher, Lapwing, Redshank and Curlew are generally seen wintering, as are Snipe in neighbouring boggy fields. A watch off the beach can be worthwhile; single divers and Slavonian Grebe are reported in most winters. Shag are present and parties of seaduck may be found. Up to 200 Common Scoter in a tight black raft, together with a dozen Velvet Scoter (uncommon in Devon) and a few immature Eider, have been seen in some winters; they move eastward and sit off rocky coves towards Sidmouth at times. Nearer, look across to Otterton Ledge rocks which project seaward on the eastern side of the river mouth; a few Purple Sandpiper often feed here.

Passerine species by the estuary include Meadow and Rock Pipits in winter, together with several Stonechat perched on posts and fences. Bearded Tit have been found in the small reed-bed, where Reed Bunting are often seen, and town parks or roadside gardens are shelters for Blackcap, Chiffchaff or Firecrest most winters. Another possibility is Crossbill; small groups have occurred in the strip of pines overlooking the eastern bank of the estuary mouth.

In spring, as few other gaps occur in the coastal cliffs, the estuary and surrounding fields and bushes attract passerine migrants. Yellow Wagtail and Wheatear turn up on the cricket field just behind the beach car park, while Blackcap, Whitethroat, Willow Warbler and Chiffchaff follow riverbank path bushes and nearby hedges. The district is not known for rarer migrants, but Hoopoe have occasionally been seen on the cricket pitch, and the extremely rare Blue-cheeked Bee-eater was recently reported nearby. In several recent springs the sibilant, jingling song of a Serin has been heard from ornamental fir trees in Budleigh; this tiny yellowish finch could occur anywhere in the area. As with most of Devon's estuaries, spring may also bring a Little Egret or other vagrant of the heron family. Cliffs east of the Otter as far as Ladram Bay hold breeding seabirds; up to 15 pairs of Fulmar and 30–40 each of Shag and Cormorant, plus hundreds of Herring Gull. Inland, small riverbank Sand Martin colonies, together with resident Kingfisher, Dipper and Grey Wagtail at nest sites, make an interesting upriver walk. Autumn brings less noticeable passerine migration, but waders are more varied, often with two or three Greenshank, their 'tew-tew' flight calls ringing over the estuary, and irregular flocks of smaller species such as Ringed Plover and Turnstone. Offshore, migrant Sandwich Tern move west and other seabirds such as skuas may be driven in by rough weather.

Timing
Wader-watching is easiest away from high tide, as high-water roosts on saltmarsh islands may be concealed. Early mornings following south-easterly breezes are best for spring arrivals, especially on weekdays as many walkers use the riverbank paths on fine weekends. The area is less easy to watch in high winds, except for autumn seawatching which benefits from southwesterly gales. Flattish sea conditions are needed to spot divers etc., from the beach.

Access
Budleigh Salterton, on A376 southeast of Exeter, can be reached via Exmouth along the coast, or inland over Woodbury ridge on minor roads. The estuary mouth car park is at the far eastern end of the seafront, and birds can often be seen from the car. From here, walk along the pebble ridge for views out to sea and up the estuary between the raised saltings. Then take the raised estuary bank path northward; easy walking for ½ mile (0.8 km) up to the minor road at White Bridge at the head of the estuary. On the left, after the cricket pitch, are boggy meadows and a small reed-bed. From White Bridge, either continue upriver towards Otterton (about 1½ miles/2½ km) for riverside birds, or cross the bridge and turn right down the partly wooded eastern bank towards the sea. A bird hide among the trees looks out over the lower estuary. From the seaward end you can continue eastward on the coast footpath towards Ladram Bay (3 miles/5 km) for winter seaducks or summer seabirds.

From White Bridge, turn back left along the minor road to the edge of the meadows, then left again on a public footpath where the trees start; this leads back south towards the car park. For small birds in the town, look for well-timbered parks and avenues; there are many suitable localities. Do not trespass onto private property.

Calendar
Resident: Shag, Cormorant, Grey Heron, Buzzard, Sparrowhawk, Kestrel, Lapwing, Stock Dove, Barn, Tawny and Little Owl, woodpeckers, Kingfisher, Rock Pipit, Grey Wagtail, Dipper, Reed Bunting, Raven.

December–February: maybe Red-throated or Great Northern Diver, Little Grebe, chance of Slavonian Grebe, Canada Goose, Shelduck, Wigeon and Teal (irregular), Eider, Common and possibly Velvet Scoters, Goldeneye or Long-tailed Duck (irregular), Red-breasted Merganser, Water Rail, Oystercatcher, Dunlin, probably Purple Sandpiper, Red-shank, Common Sandpiper (most years), Curlew, Snipe; one or two wintering Blackcap, Chiffchaff or Firecrest in town; Stonechat, possibly Bearded Tit or Crossbill.

March–May: Little Grebe (March), Fulmar, Canada Goose, Wheatear and Sand Martin (mid-March on), Sandwich Tern (late March on); a few migrant waders, e.g. Greenshank, Whimbrel, mostly mid-April–May; breeding gulls and other seabirds on cliffs, chance of Hoopoe or egret;

commoner small migrants peak late April, chance of Serin from mid-April.

June–July: breeding residents and seabirds, Shelduck, Reed and Sedge Warblers, chance of Serin; scattering of waders and Sandwich Tern in July.

August–November: Fulmar mostly August; waders in small numbers mainly August–September, including Turnstone, occasional Spotted Redshank, and often Greenshank; terns and maybe skuas to October; common passerine migrants to end September; winter visitors return by November.

3 EAST DEVON COMMONS

Habitat

This collective title is given to the sand and pebble based lowland heaths on the ridge between the lower Exe and Otter valleys, often known as 'Woodbury area' from Woodbury village and common near the centre. The 7-mile (11 km) stretch of commons reaches a height of around 180 m on the west-facing side, sloping more gently eastward. Width of heath varies from a few hundred metres to nearly 2 miles (3 km), broader in the central and southern parts. Vegetation consists of open heather, gorse and bracken, boggy hollows with birch and willows, stands of pine and larger woods, predominantly coniferous with some beech. The area contains sand quarries, a few small pools, and a reservoir at the south end. This is a good district for lizards, snakes, dragonflies and butterflies; over 30 species of butterfly seen annually at Aylesbeare Common, for example, include Brimstone, Grayling, small Pearl-bordered and Silver-washed Fritillaries.

The RSPB lease 450 acres of Aylesbeare and Harpford Commons as a reserve, principally for summer breeding species, and Devon Wildlife Trust has a 62-acre reserve at Venn Ottery.

For convenience, we have included the geographically related area of Muttersmoor, across the Otter just west of Sidmouth.

Species

Several specialised birds, virtually absent from the remainder of our region, occur regularly in small numbers. Red-legged Partridge is a recent introduction into the commons, which also still hold a number of Common (Grey) Partridge, which have declined badly elsewhere in the region. A few Barn Owls are still believed to live on neighbouring farmland, and there is a fair chance of finding Lesser Spotted Woodpecker in the tops of deciduous trees. Green Woodpecker are a frequent sight by tracks and clearings. A handful of pairs of Woodlark are present in the district; if seen flying up from shelter in bracken, their extremely short tail is conspicuous, but they are more easily detected by the musical spring songflight over woodland edges and clearings. Numbers seem to have been badly affected by prolonged frozen winter periods in the past decade and seem not to have recovered despite recent mild spells. Small numbers of Dartford Warbler have traditionally been present here where deep heather and gorse exists; their ability to reproduce quickly has returned them from the brink of disappearance here and up to twelve pairs have been found, Aylesbeare Common being particularly favoured. Hawfinch and Crossbill are also specialised, scarce breeders perhaps present regularly but overlooked. The stout but secretive Hawfinch, possibly given away by 'tick' calls as it moves through treetops, has turned up, all over the area intermittently, in singles or occasionally family parties; the true population is unknown and many local birdwatchers have never seen them. Crossbill numbers vary annually; after an invasion year, when Continental birds arrive, dozens forage through the pine clumps; in quieter years few are seen, but Hayes Wood is a possible area.

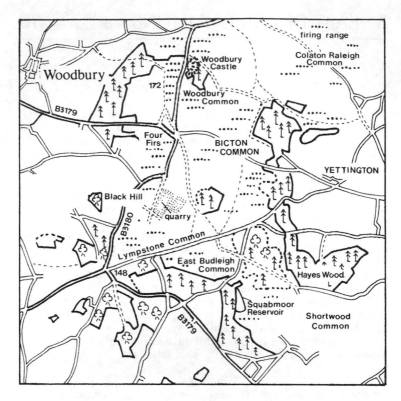

In winter the commons hold several other species of interest; some luck is needed to find them, however. Hen Harrier, including two or three ash-grey males at times, have become regular over larger open stretches, where Merlin also hunt intermittently. Woodcock occur in greater numbers than elsewhere in the region, particularly in cold spells when dozens may arrive. Among a few Snipe in boggy hollows and streamside areas the scarcer Jack Snipe may be encountered; it is probably regular throughout the area in suitable habitat, but most recent detailed observations are of single figures in the north around Venn Ottery. Water Rail occur in similar situations. At least one Great Grey Shrike usually winters on the heaths, pale front prominent as it perches on some vantage point; in early or late winter/early spring it may be seen anywhere, but midwinter sightings are most likely in the southern half, particularly on bushy slopes of East Budleigh Common towards Squab-moor Reservoir. In damp willows and birches flocks of up to 40 Siskin and a few Redpoll probe for seeds together with Reed Bunting.

Siskin are also prominent in early spring, moving up in flocks (sometimes totalling hundreds) into pinewoods as the weather warms. Although a few Hen Harrier and an occasional Great Grey Shrike turn up in new areas early on, most activity is in late spring, when breeding waders, passerines and other specialised heathland visitors have arrived. Sparrowhawk, Buzzard, Kestrel and Hobby may then be hunting over the commons, with a slim chance of migrant raptors such as Montagu's Harrier drifting over in fine weather. Other visitors in recent springs have included a Roller, Bee-eater and singing Golden Oriole. Breeding numbers of Lapwing, Snipe and Curlew are quite small, probably in single figures, Lapwing being the most widespread; Snipe breed at Venn Ottery and might be heard displaying over other wet areas; Curlew nest in deep heather on some larger open heaths. Woodcock probably breed more regularly than in other parts of the region, although only a handful of pairs at best; they could be looked for on 'roding' flights over the northern half of the commons, but may also turn up elsewhere. Turtle Dove are summer visitors to woods in small numbers; flocks of up to 20 arrive in late spring, but not all nest here. Nightjar are well distributed, with churring males on all commons on summer evenings; the slope of East Budleigh Common is a favourite place to watch them float low over the bushes like paper gliders, snatching up moths at dusk. Passerines in summer are not outstanding apart from resident specialities, but large sandpits such as Black Hill near Woodbury hold Sand Martin colonies, and a few pairs of Stonechat, Whinchat and Wheatear nest on larger open heaths. Wood Warbler may be heard trilling in beech woods and

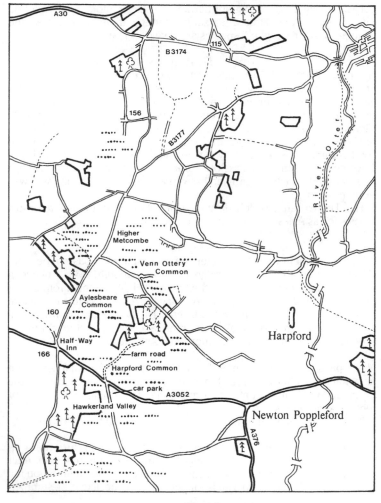

Nightjar

Grasshopper Warbler reel from low scrub and bramble patches on the edge of several heaths.

After the breeding season the area appears relatively quiet. There are occasional sightings of migrant harriers or other raptors, including Red Kite, Goshawk and Honey Buzzard, although in this large area the chances of seeing a 'good' species are not very great.

Timing

Not particularly vital for winter, but avoid wet weather or high winds. Freezing conditions may bring influxes of Woodcock or other winter visitors. In summer, mornings and evenings are best, most specialised heathland visitors being crepuscular; a dusk visit is best for Woodcock, Nightjar or Grasshopper Warbler, but in midsummer Nightjar are unlikely to be active before 21.30 hours. Anticyclonic days with fine southeasterlies are most likely for arrivals of migrant raptors or Turtle Dove flocks. The most accessible commons are heavily walked over on fine weekends, so arrive early unless you are prepared to walk well away from the roads.

Hen Harrier range widely during daytime but return to favoured roost areas such as Aylesbeare as dusk approaches.

Access

From the northern end, A30 Exeter-Honiton trunk road passes the area; B3180 runs south down the ridge towards Exmouth. A3052 between Exeter and Sidmouth cuts across the centre at Half-Way Inn. From Exeter direction, B3179 through Woodbury village gives access to the ridge at Four Firs. A maze of minor roads crosses the commons from east to west, the remotest areas from road access being the centre of Woodbury/Colaton Raleigh Commons and Aylesbeare Common.

Note: parts of the Colaton Raleigh Common in particular are used as a military training area at times; details may be obtained from the Commando Training Centre at Lympstone (tel. Topsham 873781) or local police stations.

Those with limited time will probably go for one of the following:

Venn Ottery: from A3052/B3180 junction at Half-Way Inn, turn north up the B3180 then turn right after a mile (1.6 km) onto a minor road. After ½ mile (0.8 km) park and gain a general view across the common on the left; breeding waders and Grasshopper Warbler are likely in summer, probably Jack Snipe in winter. The fenced-off area owned by Devon Wildlife Trust can only be entered by permit available from their offices.

Aylesbeare/Harpford Commons: from Half-Way Inn go east on A3052 towards Sidmouth. Look immediately for a minor turning on the right marked to Hawkerland. Adjacent to the junction is a car park. Stop here and explore around. The main heath lies on the north side of A3052 opposite the junction. A few Woodlark are still reported here and Dartford Warbler have their regional stronghold in deep heather. A walk down the tarmac track, which crosses the reserve, on a fine spring or summer morning might produce a few sightings of these jerky, active, long-tailed little birds; they are often seen in higher areas of gorse about halfway down on the right. If not in view they might be detected by the scolding 'jee-jit' call. Hen Harrier might be seen in midwinter from this track as they fly in to roost. RSPB sanctuary: open access at all times but please keep to paths. Parties intending to visit should pre-book; contact society for details.

Woodbury Common: half a mile (0.8 km) north of B3180/3179 junction at Four Firs, Woodbury Castle tumulus and pinewood is one of the highest points with views over the surrounding commons and Exe valley; Woodlark and Curlew may be found nearby, while Nightjar are often heard.

East Budleigh: from Four Firs turn south on B3180, passing Black Hill quarries on the left after ½ mile (0.8 km) and drive towards Budleigh Salterton for 2 miles (3 km): the third minor road left leads up past woods and small lakes onto the common. Park in the dirt car park on the right at the hill crest. The bushy slope below overlooks Squabmoor Reservoir, a good summer Nightjar and winter Great Grey Shrike area. Explore left into Hayes Wood and along tracks on the far side of the road.

Muttersmoor: from A3052 into Sidmouth, reach the seafront and turn right; continue along the minor road west from the seafront up Peak Hill, stop in the car park at the crest and walk inland. Nightjar and Grass-hopper Warbler, together with common passerines (Stonechat, Linnet and Yellowhammer) may be found; also a vantage point for a passing migrant raptor if you are lucky.

Access on foot is unrestricted on most heathland, which is crossed by numerous paths, but keep to existing pathways and be careful not to disturb ground-nesting birds.

Calendar

Resident: Sparrowhawk, Buzzard, Red-legged and Common Partridge, Barn and Little Owls, woodpeckers including Lesser Spotted, Woodlark, Dartford Warbler, maybe Hawfinch, Redpoll, Crossbill, Reed Bunting.

December–February: Hen Harrier, possibly Merlin, Water Rail, Wood-cock, Snipe, Jack Snipe, Great Grey Shrike, winter thrushes, Brambling, Siskin, Redpoll.

March–May: most winter visitors leave by late March, but Siskin may stay later. Breeding wader species arrive on sites; Lapwing, Curlew, Woodcock, Snipe from April. Stonechat move up from valleys. Summer visitors arriving; Sand Martin and Wheatear from late March, most others from late April including Hobby, Cuckoo, Tree Pipit, warblers, including a few Wood and Grasshopper, maybe Redstart in woods, Whinchat; Turtle Dove and Nightjar mostly from late May. Occasional migrant raptors, mostly May.

June–July: breeding residents and summer visitors most active singing in June, but Nightjar and Grasshopper Warbler heard all summer. Still a chance of an odd raptor or other migrant, e.g. Golden Oriole into June.

August–November: resident species have parties of juveniles moving about in August. Otherwise relatively quiet, but single raptors may be noted: Hobby or Montagu's Harrier in September, Hen Harrier, Peregrine or Merlin from October. Winter visitors from late October.

4 EXE ESTUARY: GENERAL INTRODUCTION

Habitat

At the west side of Lyme Bay, the Exe has 6 miles (9½ km) of tidal mudflats, over a mile (1.6 km) wide in places, between Exeter and the sea. Dawlish Warren sandspit extends eastward across the mouth. Tidal mud tends to be more sandy in the lower estuary. Extensive *Zostera* (eelgrass) beds grow in sheltered areas. The river is tidal up to Countess Wear on the edge of Exeter. Water meadows up to a mile (1.6 km) wide flank the upper western bank, separated from the tidal channel by Exeter Canal. A tidal reed-bed lies opposite Topsham at the head of the estuary. Both this area and the adjoining Old Sludge Bed area to the north are leased by Devon Wildlife Trust as nature reserves. The RSPB is negotiating to set up a reserve on part of Exminster Marshes. Shooting is banned on the western bank, and Dawlish Warren is a Local Nature

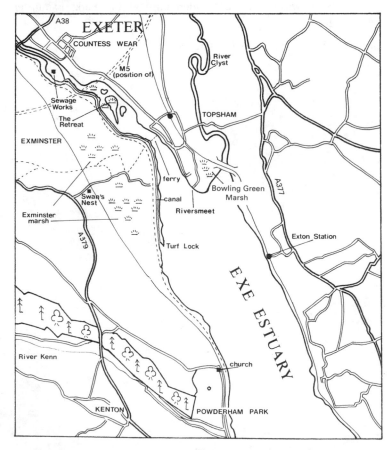

15

Reserve owned partly by Devon Wildlife Trust and partly by Teignbridge District Council. The estuary mouth is heavily used by holidaymakers in summer, and water sports are increasing.

Species

The estuary flats form southwestern England's most important wader and wildfowl feeding area, with up to 20,000 waders of 20 species and several thousand ducks. Numbers of some species, including Brent Goose and Black-tailed Godwit, are recognised as internationally important. Avocet have increased dramatically, forming Britain's largest winter flock. The shallow sea is attractive to passing gulls and terns, and to grebes and seaducks in winter. Together with surrounding farmland, the area holds an extremely wide variety of birds.

Main Birdwatching Zones

Because of the size and complexity of the area, we have split the text into zones with local specialities, concentrating on those with easiest access and most birds, although anywhere around the banks may repay investigation.

West bank: Dawlish Warren; Powderham and the Park; Exminster Marshes and the Canal.

East bank: Topsham and the Clyst; Exmouth.

Habitat

A mile-long (1.6 km) sand dune spit projecting eastward across the estuary mouth, the seaward side heavily used by the public. Offshore lie shallow waters, with extensive sandbars at low tide. The centre of the Warren is a dune slack with bushes, artificially dredged pools and a small reed-bed. The inner (facing upriver) side of the spit is a golf course, with *Spartina* saltings in the bay behind. The tip of the peninsula curves upriver, leaving a sheltered tidal bay behind the dunes, overlooked by a birdwatching hide near the golf course. The area is well known botanically, with rare Sand Crocus and orchids, including Southern Marsh Orchid and Autumn Lady's Tresses; escaped Tree Lupin covers large areas of dune. The Warren also supports a variety of dragonflies. To the west, along the seawall, grass-topped Langstone Rock projects seaward.

Species

This excellent area for waders and waterbirds is much visited by birdwatchers. Winter brings large high-tide roosts of waders and hundreds of Brent Geese often close in front of the hide. Oystercatcher (usually over 1,000 and sometimes over 3,000), Dunlin (hard to count, often 2,000–3,000) and several hundred Bar-tailed Godwit are the principal species, with a couple of hundred Ringed Plover, Grey Plover and Curlew; a few dozen Knot, Sanderling and Turnstone are also likely. Larger species roost in packs along the tideline, while smaller waders mass on mud and gravel near the hide. Generally, waders using the lower estuary are those adapted to coarse, sandy mud. Shelduck and larger gulls also feed in the bay. Goldeneye and Red-breasted Merganser in flocks fish on the estuary behind the Warren, occasionally accompanied by the smaller Long-tailed Duck. Farther in behind the spit, hundreds of Wigeon graze among saltings, and Grey Heron or Kingfisher may be found along muddy Shutterton Creek entering the main channel. Peregrine often take advantage of the concentration of birds by hunting in this section of the estuary.

On shore, a Short-eared Owl often sits in the marram grass among dunes near the point, and a Snow Bunting might be found on the beach in hard weather. A few Reed Bunting are still present in the central bushes, and Water Rail in the reeds. Bearded Tit have occurred several times in this flooded area, and Chiffchaff or Firecrest often winter in the bushes around the edges in small numbers. A party of Cirl Bunting may come down from nearby farmland to feed among low brambles and Tree Lupins; Stonechat and a Black Redstart might be with them, or along the seawall towards Langstone.

The sea off Dawlish Warren is one of the region's main wintering areas for marine waterfowl, with divers, grebes and seaducks regularly present. A typical watch will produce up to 15 Slavonian Grebe, which dive in shallow water just offshore, and probably a Great Crested Grebe or two farther out. In most winters, up to half a dozen Red-throated Diver are dotted across the whole Langstone Rock–estuary mouth area, joined by the occasional larger Black-throated or Great Northern; the relatively shallow sheltered sea here suits Red-throated best, indeed this is their most regular haunt on the south coast of Devon and Cornwall. Small packs of Eider, mostly brown or patchy immatures, are often present, sometimes coming close in off Langstone, where Shag perch on the projecting jetty. Common Scoter are seen in tight packs of 200 or more off Langstone, the occasional white bar on an outstretched wing revealing a few Velvet Scoter in their midst. A dozen or so Red-breasted Merganser often feed across the bay, while less common visitors such as a Scaup or Red-necked Grebe may join them in hard weather. Parties of Razorbill and Guillemot often feed in the area. Check in winter for Turnstone and Purple Sandpiper among the weedy rocks below Langstone at low tide. Watching off Langstone may be long-distance and a telescope is helpful; estuary ducks will also roost offshore, and Wigeon often sit in thousands well out to sea.

Large numbers of gulls use the estuary mouth. After onshore gales, thousands, mostly Black-headed, gather along the shore and seawall to scavenge cast-up marine life; they may be joined by a Mediterranean Gull, or a Little Gull fluttering over the breakers. Occasionally after high winds, when dunes and beach suffer severe erosion, a Great Skua comes into the bay to harry Herring Gulls over the sand bars.

Wheatear arriving along the front are soon followed by the spring's first 'kirrick' calls of Sandwich Tern. Spring tern movement attracts many birdwatchers; later in the season, mixed flocks plunge for fish close off the beach or drop in to roost in the tidal bay among waders. Although Sandwich are always most noticeable, migrant Little Tern, up to 40 hovering over the sea on peak days, are far more numerous here than elsewhere in the region. Common Tern, sometimes joined by darker Arctic, may be briefly numerous according to weather conditions, but soon continue eastward. In the second half of spring there is a good chance of a pale-backed Roseate Tern, often coming to roost among the Sandwich flock; up to ten of these scarce terns have been seen, although two or three are more likely. Other sea migrants may include single Arctic or Pomarine Skua, while Eider and sometimes a flock of Great Crested Grebe remain offshore. Meanwhile, Willow Warbler and other spring migrants sing from sallows in the centre of the Warren; Sedge and Reed Warblers turn up in the reeds, one or two staying to breed. When breezes blow from the Continent, a Hoopoe may be probing among the dunes, or sometimes an Osprey or harrier circling in overhead. Recently a Great Spotted Cuckoo was found feeding on caterpillars, although sadly not surviving long. On such days the wader roost is a colourful sight, with resting northbound birds in breeding plumage including hundreds of chestnut-fronted godwits, silver-backed Grey Plover and scurrying groups of Sanderling. Many Whimbrel fly in off the sea, and it is worth a search among smaller waders for an oddity such as a Kentish Plover. Recently the larger, pale Greater Sand Plover from Asia was a surprise arrival, at the same time as a Broad-billed Sandpiper among the Dunlin. A Stone Curlew, very rarely found on migration, has been seen.

Summer is quieter for birds, although Whitethroat and Reed Bunting will be seen, while a few terns remain offshore, sometimes chased by a skua, and parties of Eider may still occur. Cirl Bunting breed behind the coast near Langstone, and the red sandstone embankment west of the rock has traditionally had several pairs of Sand Martin nesting, although this species has fluctuated greatly in population recently. Even while the

Oystercatchers and Sandwich Terns

beach is still thronged with holidaymakers, the first terns and Arctic-nesting waders return. Several hundred Oystercatcher will probably have summered on the estuary flats.

Autumn is protracted, with large parties of waders and terns staying to feed around the estuary mouth for weeks at a time. Screaming juvenile Sandwich Tern fly in across the dunes pursuing parents which have caught sand-eels offshore; up to 200 of this species are regularly present. Among several dozen 'Commic' terns there may be an Arctic or Roseate, more difficult to identify at this season, and four or five Little Tern. The rare yellow-billed Lesser Crested Tern has been seen. Often a Black Tern joins them for a few days, while Black-headed Gulls may attract one or two Mediterranean Gull which stay for several weeks to moult. This source of food attracts Arctic Skua, which may dive in across the roost to rob arriving birds. Waders number several thousand, with an early passage of Ringed Plover and Sanderling, the former sometimes reaching 500 birds, although Sanderling seldom top 100. Through mid autumn patient watchers may pick out several Curlew Sandpiper or pale, short-beaked Little Stint among teeming Dunlin. After westerly gales, Pectoral Sandpiper have occasionally flown in to join the roost, and Buff-breasted Sandpiper have been seen on nearby turf, but neither species has stayed long. Wheatear are a familiar sight in the dunes, and small numbers of migrant warblers feed in the central bushes.

Most terns move out from mid-autumn, although skuas, Gannet and other seabirds may still gather offshore during gales later in the season. Large numbers have sometimes been seen (100 Arctic Skua, dozens of Great Skua, Pomarine, and hundreds of Gannet in a day), maybe even a Sabine's Gull or Long-tailed Skua. After a really rough autumn spell, check in the lee of Langstone Rock for a sheltering ocean-wanderer – a Grey Phalarope, perhaps, or rotund Little Auk. In late autumn the first Brent Geese drop in; recently they have arrived earlier and in bigger groups. Large wintering packs of plovers, Dunlin and godwits may be chased by both Peregrine and Merlin, although the smaller falcon may find Meadow Pipit on the golf links easier prey. This season might produce a report of a Richard's or Tawny Pipit, both very rare on the Devon mainland. As the last summer migrants pass through, Wigeon reappear in whistling thousands, and birdwatchers search the sea again for divers and grebes.

4B POWDERHAM AND THE PARK

OS ref: SX 9784
OS map: sheet 192

Habitat

The one-mile (1.6 km)-wide central estuary tidal flats are bordered on the west by the wooded parkland and fresh water of Powderham Park, the Earl of Devon's estate. A herd of several dozen Fallow Deer, easily seen, grazes in the grounds near the castle. The small River Kenn runs through the estate into the estuary in two branches, the northern one widened into a shallow mere, often overflowing into nearby fields. North of the park, low-lying meadows behind the estuary seawall slowly widen northward towards Exminster Marsh. The main deepwater channel of the estuary flows close in off the embankment bend.

Species

The park boundary and seawall northward are one of the region's most popular areas for autumn and winter wader-watching. The meadows behind the seawall area are a high-tide roost for waders from nearby mudflats. The balance of species is different from that at Dawlish Warren, with more species adapted to probing soft mud. Curlew and Black-tailed Godwit predominate; the flock of 600 Black-tailed, smart birds in flight with black and white wing-stripes, is one of Britain's largest gatherings. Recently Brent Geese, as they have increased, have spilled over from the estuary to graze in meadows when other food is short. Rich mud off the embankment attracts many waders, including a few Greenshank and one or two Spotted Redshank, the latter often noticed by their 'chew-it' call. Avocet, based farther upriver, sometimes feed down this far and at high tide may float buoyantly in a group among Shelduck, easily overlooked because of their similar colours. Views may be long-distance and telescopes are recommended.

Flocks of up to 1,000 dabbling ducks rest on mudbanks. Among hundreds of Mallard and Teal, the elegant shapes of 40–50 Pintail may be picked out; smaller numbers of Gadwall and Shoveler join them, particularly in severe weather. On deeper stretches there are generally several Goldeneye or Red-breasted Merganser fishing, along with plentiful Cormorant. Grey Heron stand poised along the waterside. Sometimes the whole mass of ducks and waders erupts as a Peregrine dives to make a kill.

The park serves as a roost for Redshank, Spotted Redshank and Greenshank, which usually fly in to the River Kenn or pools at high tide. Greenshank particularly favour the park, although the main flock of 200 or more Redshank may move elsewhere if disturbed. These freshwater habitats hold dozens of wintering Teal and often Canada Geese, up to 100 strong, probably breeding birds from farther up the Exe valley and Crediton; the goose flock is worth checking for an occasional (escaped?) Barnacle Goose. Kingfishers may speed along the waterside, and sometimes a Green Sandpiper stays to winter on a sheltered channel.

Spring brings large flocks of Whimbrel and 'red' breeding-plumaged godwits dropping in on the mud; Sandwich and Common Terns, or sometimes Little, fly up the estuary following the rising tide, and

Greenshank, usually in twos and threes through winter, become more numerous. The park's large trees hold a heronry of up to 40 pairs, and provide nesting territory for many Stock Dove. Kestrel, Buzzard and Sparrowhawk are often seen circling overhead, while Great Spotted and Green Woodpeckers fly across the clearings. Open spaces are frequently dotted with pairs of Shelduck prospecting rabbit burrows to breed in.

In autumn the park is again worth a look for shanks, with up to 40 pale-fronted Greenshank and several Spotted Redshank among scores of Redshank. Two or three Green Sandpiper, and perhaps a Wood Sandpiper, may be present by freshwater pools in early autumn. Passage of Common Sandpiper can be noticeable on the main estuary. Most watchers visit the seawall in hopes of an Osprey fishing off the bend, as this impressive raptor is recorded annually, in some years staying on the estuary for weeks. Sometimes a Hobby comes down from the marshes to try a small wader meal. In the Dunlin flocks you may find other migrant waders, such as Curlew Sandpiper, if close views are possible. American waders such as a Dowitcher have been seen on the freshwater pools in the park after westerly gales.

Most winter ducks do not return until late autumn, but Teal have often been noted in the park from the end of summer; in colder weather flocks of Tufted Duck, found in few places locally, may join them on the pools. Recent observations of gull flocks bathing at the stream mouths just off the park have included a number of Mediterranean Gull visiting over a period.

4C EXMINSTER MARSH AND THE CANAL

Habitat

On the western side of the upper estuary, water meadows intersected by drainage dykes are up to a mile (1.6 km) wide. Beyond lies low rolling farmland. The old Exeter Canal, now used mostly for angling and rowing, runs down the outer marsh edge, entering the estuary at Turf Lock. Beyond here the estuary seawall embanks a smaller area towards Powderham. This top section of tidal flats is particularly soft, and rich in food. No shooting is permitted on the canal banks, but a private shoot operates on the water meadows. Opposite the marsh, between the canal bank and Topsham village across the river, lies an extensive tidal reed-bed through which the river flows before reaching open mudflats.

Species

In winter the grazing marshes' attractiveness to birds often depends on water levels. Floods lying in the fields may attract large flocks of ducks and waders; hundreds of Wigeon, and smaller numbers of Teal, Pintail and Shoveler; Snipe may be present in scores and cold spells often bring thousands of Lapwing from farther afield. Hundreds of Curlew and Black-tailed Godwit fly in off the estuary to roost or feed by floodwater, some godwits penetrating up almost to Exeter bypass road at the top of the marshes; recently a wintering Hudsonian Godwit from America joined them. Two or three hundred Golden Plover and a variable number of Ruff, usually single figures, stay all winter; in snow they may be joined by parties of White-fronted Geese, which soon leave because of shooting, or by a wild swan, usually Bewick's, grazing among Mute Swan. Fieldfare and Redwing can be seen in hundreds. The canal sometimes holds a surprise such as a Red-throated Diver or Long-tailed Duck, watchable at close range from reed-fringed banks; often King-fishers sit by lock gates. Rough fields at the southern end of the marsh towards Turf are likely to harbour a few Short-eared Owl, which rise and beat slowly across dykes on winter afternoons; in years when vole 'plagues' occur, they are very prominent, half a dozen or more patrolling the marsh, sometimes joined by a ringtail Hen Harrier. The declining Barn Owl might still be seen; sometimes they roost in ivy adjacent to Topsham reed-bed, where an occasional Smew or Goosander appears in bad weather and the 'ping' calls of Bearded Tit have been heard. Green or Common Sandpiper often winter here. On mild winter days the far-carrying song of Cetti's Warbler can be heard from tangled vegetation between the canal bank and reed-bed; this species has become well established in recent seasons.

The upper estuary flats are notable for flocks of wintering Avocet which have increased annually in recent years, reaching over 300 at times. Those wintering on the Tamar are believed to pass through at the beginning and end of the season, when extra groups appear briefly. The main Exe flock may move between Turf, Topsham across the river, and Powderham, but by careful timing (see that section) close views can be obtained of these elegant waders sweeping the shallows off the lower

22

Drake Garganey

marsh. Apart from other interesting regulars such as Spotted Redshank, the mudflats are the site of a massive roost of Black-headed (over 5,000) and Common Gulls from the Exe valley farmland. Peregrine are often seen overhead. Goldeneye are frequent on the main channel, reaching 30–40 at times, and small groups of Scaup sometimes winter off Turf.

Spring's earliest arrival is often Garganey, with one or two of these scarce ducks on freshwater channels and pools in the marshes. Sadly they do not stay to breed, as they did occasionally in the past, but Shoveler which often arrive may breed in small numbers if trampling cattle allow. Wheatear and Sand Martin usually pass up the marsh edge soon after the Garganey. From mid spring a variety of warblers, including Sedge, Reed and sometimes Grasshopper, arrives to sing along the canal banks. Several pairs of Cetti's Warbler are now thought to breed, although always elusive. Large flocks of Whimbrel, reaching 100 or more, rest on the meadows before continuing overland. Oddities can include a Spoonbill on Turf mudflats for a few days, or a passing Marsh or Montagu's Harrier quartering the fields. Perhaps unexpected is the passage of tern flocks moving north inland along the outer marsh edge on fine evenings; generally they spiral high over the canal banks before flying north towards Exeter. Groups of Sandwich, Common and even dark-chested Arctic Terns have been seen passing, and this is also a good time for waders such as Whimbrel and Common Sandpiper flying over.

Breeding species in the meadows include a scattering of Lapwing, with one or two pairs of Shelduck in nearby farmland. Over recent seasons the tiny colony of Yellow Wagtail, on the western edge of their breeding range, has become less regular, although a few still turn up each spring. Redshank have recently returned to breed after a number of years' absence. The aggressive Canada Goose is now often present in summer and likely to breed. Common breeding raptors and Grey Heron are frequent hunters in the fields. A more localised speciality is Cirl Bunting, which occurs in farm hedgerows and sheltered valleys behind Exminster village. Swallows and House Martins nest plentifully around local barns and farmhouses; in late summer many feed over the marsh dykes, where they may be chased by a Hobby, and frequently caught by the slim falcon's unerring accuracy. At the end of the breeding season, thousands of Swallows and Starlings roost overnight in Topsham reed-bed, milling around before dropping in at last light. This concentration of birds is an attraction to predators; sometimes two or three Hobbies hunt here, and the endless babble of Starlings is silenced when Sparrow-hawks glide over.

Passage waders on the marshes often include Common Sandpiper and two or three Green Sandpiper, while flocks of shanks and godwits return early to the mudflats. Look also for the odd Little Stint or Curlew Sandpiper feeding off Turf canal exit with Dunlin. Early autumn can be productive around Turf, with a good chance of an Osprey fishing, causing gulls and waders to fly up in great alarm. Black Tern or Little Gull may dip over the canal's wider stretches, and there are various small migrants in reeds and bushes. Late season has produced unexpected 'wrecked' seabirds during gales, such as an exhausted Pomarine Skua by the lock and a tiny Little Auk resting on the canal. It will be the end of autumn before most Avocet return, and ideally a visit to see them should be left until winter.

4D TOPSHAM AND THE CLYST

OS ref: SX 9787
OS map: sheet 192

Habitat

Topsham village lies on the eastern side of the Exe at the head of the main estuary. Wide views over the upper Exe mudflats can be gained from the waterfront. The Clyst river flows into the estuary immediately below the village and the embanked Clyst water meadows, heavily drained in recent years, extend several miles upstream. Bowling Green Marsh, a 36-acre (14-ha) flood meadow leased by the RSPB as a reserve, is immediately adjacent to the Clyst mouth. The mudflats off the Clyst mouth can also be seen from Exton Station on the east bank of the main estuary.

Species

These are mainly shared with neighbouring localities. The southern end of the waterfront, known as the Goatwalk, overlooks the upper Exe flats, where hundreds of Avocet feed in midwinter. Large numbers of other wintering waders may be seen here, including godwits (mostly Black-tailed), while a Spotted Redshank or two may often be found wading in the shallows around the Clyst mouth. The Clyst river banks higher up, and the meadows if flooded, may hold a Green or Common Sandpiper, while Kingfisher are often seen. Ruff and godwits may feed in the Clyst water meadows if water levels are high; RSPB plans to retain floods at Bowling Green Marsh may lead to increased concentrations of birds. Wintering Brent Geese, as their numbers on the Exe have built up in recent years, have taken to feeding in hundreds on Bowling Green Marsh, occasionally joined by a wild swan or White-fronted Goose (once a rare Lesser White-fronted Goose).

The narrow Exe passage between Topsham and Exminster Marsh, on the western side of the village, is a favourite feeding area for Goldeneye, and up to 20 gather in the channel at high tide, often joined by Red-breasted Merganser. Most other species of the canal bank area and the 'Retreat' reed-bed area to the north, can be seen more conveniently by crossing the channel to the Exminster side; Kingfisher are often seen around the old lock gate by the canal footbridge. (See Exminster section).

Spring brings wader passage up both Exe and Clyst. Pools on the Clyst meadows may encourage a Garganey to drop in, plus a variety of waders including Whimbrel and Green Sandpiper. Lapwing breed in the meadows in small numbers and Yellow Wagtail often stop off to feed. Late summer and early autumn bring more Green Sandpiper to the Clyst, together with one or two scarcer Wood Sandpiper, showing conspicuously pale-spotted against the dark-winged Green Sandpiper. Bowling Green Marsh has recently attracted migrant Little Ringed Plover on several occasions in spring or early autumn, a scarce occurrence this far west. A Little Gull, Black Tern or sandpiper may also loiter in the bay to the north of the Exe narrows. The Goatwalk waterfront path can be a good lookout point for Osprey feeding over the upper estuary in autumn, or even perching to digest a fish on one of the larger pine trees over-looking the Exe/Clyst junction.

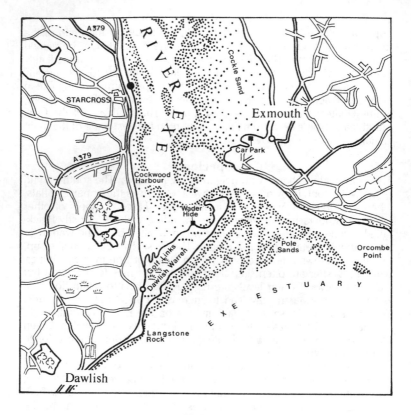

Habitat

At the eastern side of the estuary mouth, Exmouth waterfront gives views out to sea, across the fast-flowing channel to Dawlish Warren, and up the estuary mudflats. High cliffs rise from the eastern end of the seafront. Behind the town lies a wide, sheltered estuary bay with beds of *Zostera* (eelgrass), an important wildfowl food.

Species

In winter the bay at the rear of the town is the estuary's main feeding zone for Brent Goose, Wigeon and Pintail; whistling rafts of up to 5,000 Wigeon are often at close range; Brent Geese, increasing recently, now top 4,000 at times but partially disperse as food runs short; the graceful Pintail can exceed 100 in number. This bay forms the largest wildfowl concentration in our region, and the winter watcher is almost certain to see large flocks. The deeper water of the main tideway is favoured by fishing Red-breasted Merganser; sometimes a Long-tailed Duck stays a week or two, and auks are often present in small numbers. At the seaward end of town, where Orcombe cliff starts, seaweed-covered

26

boulders attract a regular flock of around a dozen Purple Sandpiper, accompanied by Oystercatcher and Turnstone. Groups of Eider in assorted immature plumages often swim near the rocks; farther out there may be Slavonian Grebe, divers and scoters, including a few larger-headed Velvet Scoter, but these move about between Exmouth and the Warren according to wind and tide.

Spring brings large numbers of terns feeding offshore, often picking up sand-eels churned up by the rising tide breaking over sand bars, or moving up past the seafront into the estuary at high tide. They roost on the Warren but dozens may be seen off this side; all commoner sea terns occur here, but Roseate are identified more often from the other side. Terns are also Exmouth's main attraction in autumn, often chased by one or two Arctic Skua; in stormy conditions larger movements of seabirds might be seen off Orcombe cliffs. There have been scattered reports of Little Auk or Grey Phalarope off Orcombe in the autumn.

Timing (All sites)

Most waders and ducks are at great distances from the observer at low tide. Best watching is generally within the two or three hours before high tide, as birds move closer to the banks, and at main roosts such as Dawlish Warren for an hour or so across high tide. Avocet at Turf are best seen when feeding nearest the bank about two hours before high water. They are visible from Topsham at most tides but a rising tide would push some birds closer. All times should be weighed against the height of the tide; spring tides may force birds to abandon feeding sooner, and even to abandon normal roosts (at the Warren they may have to roost on the beach and are frequently disturbed). Terns tend to join the Warren roost when there is some mud left in the tidal bay, two or three hours before or after high tide, or on neap tides; rising tides encourage them to fly upriver as far as Turf. High-pressure weather, with winds from a southerly quarter, is best for all spring arrivals; eastern migrants such as Black Tern arrive mostly in autumn easterlies. Strong southwesterly winds with rain battering the coast in autumn produce concentrations of seabirds off the coast and occasional 'wrecked' birds as far up as Turf. Freezing weather elsewhere brings influxes of wildfowl and open-ground species on the marshes; periods of heavy rain, flooding meadows, may also encourage birds to come from the estuary to feed. Brent Geese and waders at Bowling Green Marsh are seen in highest numbers at high tide. Allow sufficient time to check thoroughly from the roadside as birds can easily be missed. Short-eared Owls on the marshes or Warren Point fly mostly in late afternoons. For raptors such as Peregrine or Osprey, a wait of at least two or three hours at vantage points along the estuary banks is needed. For views of divers and grebes on the sea, choose a calmish sea; in a swell watch from Langstone top. Avoid watching the mudflats from the western bank in early mornings when light glare is against you, and choose days when wind in these exposed spots will not prevent keeping focus on distant birds. Do not try for Avocet in late afternoons, when their white shapes blend with roosting gulls. For ducks or divers on the canal, try weekdays or early mornings (less disturbance).

The reed-bed roost at the Exminster Marsh–Topsham end should be watched from about two hours before dusk, in fine weather, for spring tern and wader movements, or at similar times in early autumn for roosting birds.

Coastal districts are heavily used by walkers at weekends, and by holidaymakers in summer; in July or August especially, early morning visits are best. Windsurfers may disturb wildfowl off Exmouth on fine weekends, especially Sundays, so try other days or early morning if possible (if tides are suited).

Access (All sites)

Dawlish Warren is reached from A379 Exeter–Dawlish road, turning south around Cockwood Harbour bridge, or east at the start of Dawlish town. Go under the railway bridge onto the Warren, then left towards the main estuary, and right for the seawall and Langstone. For sea views, walk right along the seawall to the rock; climb the steps with care and scan from the top. A walk west towards Dawlish should produce winter grebes, or summer Sand Martin if this species recovers in numbers after declines in the past decade.

For the wader roost and estuary mouth, turn into the left car park. Walk along the dune crest overlooking the beach, or past the central marsh and bushes. Walk to the narrowest part of the dunes, then left beside the golf course end to reach the green corrugated bird hide facing the roost bay. A logbook of observations is kept inside. If you continue to the far tip of the Warren afterwards, avoid flushing roosting birds when passing the bay, by keeping to the upper edge of the beach. Short-eared Owl are most likely in the far dunes.

The Warren's sand dunes, seafront and central marsh are managed as a nature reserve by Teignbridge Council, who employ a full-time warden. Golf links and adjacent saltmarshes at the rear of the Warren are owned by Devon Wildlife Trust. Although the golf links can be overlooked from nearby dune and beach paths, there is strictly no access across the greens and the hide must be approached by following the paths skirting the boundary. Access to the rest of the Warren is unrestricted (but please keep off fenced study areas). Large parties should contact the Warden to avoid clashes over use of the hide. Guided walks are available. Contact the Warden via Teignbridge Council Planning Department, Forde House, Newton Abbot, Devon.

Powderham: from A379, travelling north from Dawlish Warren, fork right at north end of Starcross village on the minor road between park and estuary. Stop and look across the park and pools from roadside pull-ins; a telescope is helpful. There is no public access into this side of the park. For the estuary bank, continue to the sharp bend beside the church and park carefully; there is limited parking space here, although more is available around the corner under trees. Walk north along a track leading to the estuary bank. Take great care when crossing the railway line onto the estuary seawall. A footpath leads to Turf Lock (see below), 1½ miles (2½ km) along the bank.

Exminster Marshes: from A379, turn down the lane towards Swan's Nest Inn at the south end of Exminster village. Bypass the inn entrance and continue over a humpbacked bridge across the railway; stop to check fields on either side if flooded. Cross the first major dyke and stop at a small, bumpy area of gravel parking to look around the central marsh. A small path starting at left leads across fields to the marsh edge and views of the tidal reed-bed. From here you can walk down the canal towpath to Turf. Alternatively, continue to the end of the central track, bumpy but driveable provided it is not flooded in winter. Walk up onto the canal bank and south towards Turf, watching adjacent fields for Short-eared Owl in winter. Avocet and other waders are on the estuary opposite you. For better views, cross the lock gates and watch upriver along the outer marsh bank; also look down the estuary channel for diving ducks. (See also Exmouth section for birdwatching boat trips.)

The RSPB hope to arrange observation facilities for birdwatchers, using the old railway signal box which lies immediately to the right after driving across the humpback bridge. This will form a central point for scanning the marshes. Parking facilities will be created.

If access to the eastern bank is needed, a passenger ferry operates between the outer marsh bank and Topsham across the narrow tidal Exe channel. Stand on the slipway and wait; the boatman will come across. The ferry operates from 09.00 to 17.00 hours in winter, extending to 20.00 hours in summer, daily except on extreme low tides.

A rough (often overgrown) path leads up the outer canal bank north past the reed-beds towards Exeter, reaching the A38 Exeter ring road at Countess Wear Bridge.

Topsham and the Clyst: Topsham lies on the main A377 Exeter-Exmouth road. Where the road bends sharply left in the village centre, go straight on into the narrow village streets (parking can be difficult) and down to the waterfront for general views along the Exe. Alternatively, continue left at the bend, on down the main road, then as the road descends on a left curve towards the River Clyst, take a right turn into Elm Grove Road. This road, after passing suburban houses, becomes Bowling Green Road, and gives open views across Bowling Green Marsh meadows to the left. At time of writing there is no access into the meadows, which must be scanned from the roadside, although hides are planned by the RSPB which will overlook the flood areas more closely and also overlook the Clyst estuary mouth. Until this happens, watchers will have to contend with incomplete views of the meadows and some birds may be hidden until they fly up or move feeding area. Continuing to the end of the lane, you reach the Riversmeet area, facing across the main Exe mudflats, a convenient point to view Avocet. Park by the verge; there is limited space in this small lane. Take care not to block house entrances. From the end of the lane the Goatwalk path enables you to walk back right towards Topsham centre. The actual Clyst mouth on your left can only be viewed by walking to the left along the edge of the mud at low tide.

The embanked River Clyst and surrounding fields (which are private, with no access, although open to view) can be seen at the point just south of Elm Grove road turning, where the A377 crosses the river. Views of the upper Exe estuary flats can also be obtained from Exton Station approach lane, 2 miles (3 km) south of Topsham on A377.

Exmouth: Continue south on A377, follow signs through Exmouth centre to the seafront and try various points. For Eider and Purple Sandpiper try the far end; a path leads up onto Orcombe cliffs. For the estuary, drive back past the docks and turn left to Imperial Road car park (past station), which gives open views over the mudflats. Winter birdwatching trips (advertised as 'Avocet Cruises', but also giving chances of seeing a wide range of species) start from the docks, going upriver towards Turf (November–March). Contact RSPB Regional Office, Exeter, for details.

Calendar

Resident: Grey Heron, Eider (some years), Sparrowhawk, Buzzard, Pheasant, Coot, Lapwing, Oystercatcher (non-breeders summer), Stock Dove, Barn Owl, woodpeckers, Cetti's Warbler, Stonechat, Cirl Bunting, Reed Bunting.

December–February: Divers, especially Red-throated, Slavonian and Great Crested Grebes offshore, Little Grebe, Cormorant, Shag, occasional Bewick's Swan and White-fronted Goose, Brent Goose, Shelduck, possibly Gadwall, Wigeon, Teal, Pintail, Shoveler, probably Tufted Duck, maybe Scaup, Common and perhaps Velvet Scoters, Goldeneye, probably Long-tailed Duck, Red-breasted Merganser, occasional Goosander or Smew, Peregrine, occasional Hen Harrier, Water Rail, Avocet, Ringed Plover, Golden Plover, Grey Plover, Turnstone, Dunlin, Knot, Sanderling, Purple Sandpiper, Redshank, Greenshank, Common and Green Sandpipers, probably Ruff, Curlew, Black-tailed Godwit, Bar-tailed Godwit, Snipe, Jack Snipe, rarely Great Skua, gulls, including probably Mediterranean; Short-eared Owl, Kingfisher, Chiffchaff, possible Black Redstart, winter thrushes, maybe Bearded Tit, occasional Snow Bunting.

March–May: Wheatear first seen on coast, probably Garganey on marshes; first Sandwich Tern offshore by end of third week. Avocet and most wildfowl leave by mid March. Slavonian Grebe flock in March before leaving, a few stay to mid-April. Passage divers (most Red-throated) through May. Whimbrel and Common and Green Sandpipers move up through marshes; migrant shanks pass from mid-April, peak end April. Reed and Sedge Warblers and Yellow Wagtail arrive mid-late April. Short-eared Owl occasional to early May. Main tern passage mid-April–May, mostly end April and first half May, when Roseate usually seen. Occasional Arctic or Pomarine Skua early May. Occasional scarcer migrants e.g. Osprey, Marsh or Montagu's Harrier, Kentish Plover, Hoopoe, or rare heron, late April through May. Shelduck and occasional Shoveler breed. A few Great Crested Grebe, Common Scoter and auks on sea, passing Fulmar, Gannet and Kittiwake.

June–July: a few Sandwich or Common Tern summer, maybe Common Scoter. From end June–early July, first waders returning, a few terns arrive staying off-passage until autumn, including one or two Arctic and Roseate, chance of Mediterranean Gull. Adult Shelduck fly north to moult from end June.

August–November: Common, Green, maybe Wood Sandpipers August–early September on marshes, migrant warblers, Wheatear and wagtails; hirundines and Starling roost in reed-bed, with Hobby and other raptors in pursuit, from August, hirundines leaving through September. Terns feeding in large numbers August–early September, a few Black Tern through September, Arctic Skua frequent, chasing terns from mid-August. Small numbers of Little Stint and Curlew Sandpiper through September, maybe Little Ringed Plover, maybe Pectoral or other American sandpiper, often Osprey staying. Peregrine, Merlin and Short-eared Owl mostly October–November. Arctic, Great and maybe other skuas, or Sabine's Gull, offshore in gales September–October. Maybe Little Auk or Grey Phalaropes October–November. Divers and grebes arrive from mid-October, mostly late November. Snow Bunting occasional on beach and Black Redstart often arrive, late October–November. Wildfowl return from late September, but mostly November. Few Avocet until late November.

5 STOKE CANON MEADOWS AND WOOD

OS ref: SX 9397
OS map: sheet 192

Habitat

Approximately 2 miles (3.2 km) of low-lying river valley north of Exeter, bordered along the eastern flank by Stoke Woods, a mixed wood on a steep hillside, designated as a Country Park. The River Exe meanders through meadows liable to flood. Above Stoke Canon, towards Brampford Speke village, the river is faster and shallower, with shingle bars. Below Stoke Canon village, the Exe and Culm rivers converge; willow and alder trees line the banks, and at low river levels mudbars are exposed.

Species

This is a convenient area close to Exeter to see woodland and waterside birds. The attractiveness of the valley meadows to different species depends on water levels. Flocks of up to 100 Canada Geese drop in to graze outside the breeding season. Winter floods bring varying numbers of dabbling ducks, mostly Wigeon with 200 most years and over 500 at times. The slender Pintail is less common but there are often ten or more in midwinter, usually in larger flood patches. Teal occur in

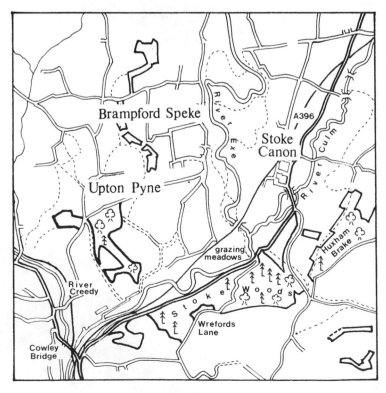

scattered parties generally totalling under 100, but are less affected than other ducks in dry winters. Shoveler are seen sporadically in twos and threes. On the river, up to five brownhead Goldeneye are sometimes joined by Tufted Duck. Freeze-ups may bring a Goosander or other unusual displaced duck. Hundreds of Lapwing and dozens of Snipe feed in damp fields, while Common and Green Sandpipers winter in ones and twos on sheltered riverbanks and pools, the Green Sandpipers looking like large House Martins as they fly up. The riverside is always worth watching, with Dipper bobbing in shallows near Brampford Speke, while Kingfisher and Grey Wagtail feed all along. Parties of up to 40 Siskin forage in overhanging trees, and mixed flocks of other finches feed on stubble fields near Stoke Canon village. Woodcock are sometimes flushed from quieter parts of the wood. Woodland species such as woodpeckers (with a regular pair of Lesser Spotted), thrushes, tits, Nuthatch and Treecreeper are encountered; visit a cross-section of habitats, including mature beeches for woodpeckers and undergrowth for small passerines.

Lapwings

Spring arrival can be noticeable as birds funnel up from the Exe Estuary. Garganey sometimes drop in on remaining flood pools. Greenshank stop off on shingle bars beside teetering parties of Common Sandpiper, and large groups of Swift and hirundines follow the waterway. A pair of Canada Geese often tries to breed, while pairs of Shelduck and Great Black-backed Gull, unusual this far inland, have been present in several recent springs. Lapwing are regulars with two or three usually tumbling over meadows in display flight. Kingfisher generally nest in one of the bigger riverbanks and Sand Martin can be watched entering nest holes below Brampford, where 20 or more pairs may breed, although numbers have fluctuated greatly in recent years owing to problems in the species' winter quarters in Africa. Sometimes they lose their nests here if the river rises unexpectedly. One or two Sedge Warbler sing in damp thickets. Little Owl occur in small numbers on neighbouring farmland, but are easily missed; a pair or two of Cirl Bunting may still be present, although this attractive bunting has now become rare away from the coast. The wood is worth a visit when summer visitors have arrived, with commoner warblers such as Blackcap, Garden Warbler, Willow Warbler and Chiffchaff in good numbers. Several trilling Wood Warbler can be heard, particularly in beeches. Less common for Devon are one or two Turtle Dove, and, in some years, Nightingale have skulked in dense undergrowth in the lower wood, near the bottom of Wrefords Lane. A pair of Raven often raises young in the upper part of the wood near the hill crest.

Early autumn, with low river levels leaving exposed mud, is good for waders. Greenshank and Common and Green Sandpipers, as in spring, are most frequent; twos and threes are usual but sometimes up to ten Green Sandpiper rise from the mud with loud 'tluee' calls. A Wood Sandpiper might also occur. Lapwing and Common Gull flock in the fields, where various small migrants such as Yellow Wagtail and Whinchat are often found. Apart from frequent Sparrowhawk, predators hunting over the riverside may include Hobby or Barn Owl.

Timing

Duck numbers increase greatly when meadows flood after heavy rain; partial floods are present most winters. Flood pools at migration periods may also attract waders, or occasional Garganey. Frozen conditions can bring scarcer wildfowl in winter. Evening visits in late summer/early autumn can be good for waders moving. Disturbance by public use can be a problem in the wood on fine summer weekends; try mornings for songbirds in spring.

Access

A396 Exeter-Tiverton road runs north from Cowley Bridge on the edge of Exeter. For the water meadows continue 1 mile (1.6 km) and park beside the wood, in a small lay-by on the right after passing two signposted woodland entry points. Cross the main road and take the gated public footpath left across fields to Staffords Bridge; scan around from here. Alternatively, several roadside pull-ins on the left further up the main road give views over likely flood areas. Park near the foot of Wrefords Lane, which joins from the right halfway along the wood (do not park on main road), and look left across the Culm-Exe meeting point. In summer check the wood near the lane; the small valley behind is good for most woodland birds. Try also turning right up the lane and stopping at car parks on the right for more mature stands of trees.

The north end of the valley can be viewed by continuing up the A396, crossing the River Culm at the start of Stoke Canon village. Turn immediately left down the lane past a bungalow estate; look across nearby fields. Follow the lane around to a railway signal box and gated crossing point, then take the public footpath for ¼ mile (0.4 km) to Brampford Speke riverside.

Calendar

Resident: Sparrowhawk, Buzzard, Lapwing, Stock Dove, Little Owl, Kingfisher, woodpeckers including Lesser Spotted, Grey Wagtail, common woodland passerines, Dipper, maybe Cirl Bunting, Raven.

December–February: Cormorant, Grey Heron, Canada Goose, Wigeon, Teal, Pintail, Shoveler (irregular), maybe Tufted Duck, possible Goosander or Smew (hard weather), Goldeneye, Common and Green

Sandpipers, Woodcock (Stoke Wood), Snipe, Stonechat, winter thrushes, Brambling, Siskin, Redpoll, other finches.

March–May: Most ducks leave by early March. Chiffchaff and Sand Martin arrive by late March. Canada Geese start nesting. Shelduck may be present. Migrant Greenshank, Common and Green Sandpipers, other passing migrants and summer visitors peak late April–May.

June–July: Breeding residents and summer visitors; Canada Goose probable, Turtle Dove, Cuckoo, hirundines, common warblers, Wood Warbler, maybe a Nightingale. Waders and gulls return from July.

August–November: Greenshank, Common, Green, and occasional Wood Sandpipers, peaking August; Common Gull; Yellow Wagtail and other small migrants pass August–September, maybe also Hobby. Most winter visitors return from late October, but duck numbers low until winter.

6 HALDON WOODS AND LITTLE HALDON

OS ref: SX 8885
OS map: sheet 192

Habitat

West of the Exe, Haldon is a conspicuous ridge extending about 6 miles (9½ km) north to south, rising above surrounding farmland to a height of 260 m. The eastern slope is particularly steep. The flat, sandy top is covered largely by coniferous Forestry Commission plantations, with small stands of beech and other deciduous trees. Many small clearings, with a rich summer growth of ferns, vary the woodland habitat, and a few areas of natural heath remain. The largest open area is the horse racing track and surrounding heath in the centre of the ridge. Little Haldon is a smaller, detached block of similar terrain 2 miles (3 km) farther south, with areas of open heather and a golf course. Both hills afford panoramic views over lowlands and coastline, with Dartmoor tors on the northwestern horizon.

The area harbours Fallow and Roe Deer, often glimpsed in quieter woodland areas at dawn or dusk, and extensive Badger setts may be found. Adders and Common Lizards may be seen basking on heaths in warm weather. The area is well known for butterflies, especially on the Forestry Commission's managed 'Butterfly Walks' at the northern side of the hills, an area of cleared glades under power pylons. Grizzled Skipper, Wood White, White Admiral and High Brown Fritillary can be expected among 35 butterfly species. Common Spotted Orchid and Greater Butterfly Orchid may be seen flowering in early summer.

Species

The large area of mature conifers means that most birds are those adapted to this specialised habitat, including an outstanding variety of both breeding and passing birds of prey. In winter the woods can appear lifeless, although the plentiful local Buzzard soar overhead on fine days, occasionally joined by the longer-tailed Goshawk, and Woodcock may be flushed beside the tracks. A thorough search is likely to reveal parties of Siskin and Redpoll moving through treetops. Crossbill can also be found in scattered flocks, swinging silently beneath pine cones or detected by repeated 'chupp' flight calls as parties move about; up to 100 may be present but are hard to locate. In two or three areas of the wood male Crossbill may soon be heard singing, this species being an early breeder, but numbers of pairs are small and irregular, depending on pine cone crop. Assorted finches feeding on fallen seeds or beech mast often include Brambling. Occasional Great Grey Shrike are seen on open slopes, and icy weather on higher ground elsewhere may drive down one or two Hen Harrier to hunt over one of the open heaths.

As spring comes, resident raptors dive in display overhead, and woodpeckers of all three species seek out nest holes in old timber. Other residents in such habitats include a small population of sooty-headed Willow Tit, while Coal Tit and Goldcrest are common in dense conifers. Siskin form pre-migration gatherings of up to 200 birds. After most of these agile little finches have departed northwards, there is a gap before many summer visitors become established. Later spring

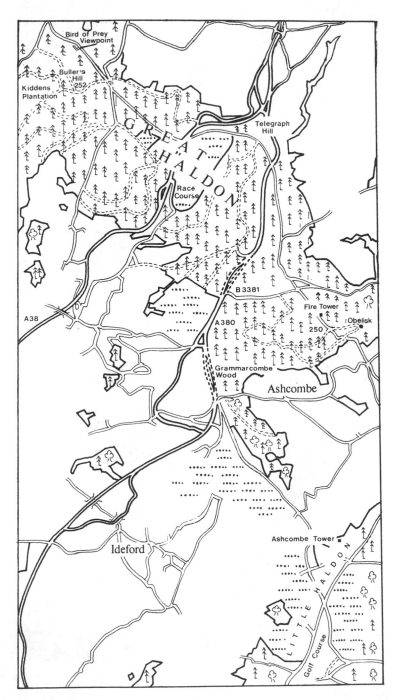

brings a wide variety of breeding species, especially at woodland edges or where clearings or a mixture of tree species give habitat variety; the centres of densest plantations harbour very few species. Apart from commoner warblers such as Willow, there are usually Wood Warbler trilling, especially in beech groves, while the Grasshopper Warbler occurs on some open heaths and larger clearings. Redstart are likely in areas with mature deciduous trees, or old pines with clearings and decayed wood, while Tree Pipit are seen in songflight in many areas, particularly over younger trees. Redpoll chatter in flight between high nests in mature conifers and the low bushes where they feed. Siskin also tend to stay increasingly into summer, with evidence of a number of breeding pairs. Woodcock, a rare breeder in southwestern England, have recently been seen on territorial 'roding' flights. On the heaths, where Cuckoo are fairly common, both Stonechat and Whinchat may be encountered perched on gorse sprigs; Wheatear have been known to nest but are not regular. Dartford Warbler have recently spread into the district after a series of good breeding seasons, although their survival here will depend on a run of mild winters, and numbers are perilously small.

Regular watching in recent years has shown this area's potential for viewing raptors. A pair of Honey Buzzard has arrived annually to breed from late spring, the male often performing its wing-clapping 'butterfly' display flight high over the wooded slopes. Birdwatchers from all over Britain have gathered to see this well-publicised spectacle. At this season additional migrant Honey Buzzard have joined the breeding pair for a few days; the long neck and fuller, longer tail give the species a distinctive silhouette to the experienced watcher. Individual birds may be recognised as plumages vary greatly. Common Buzzard often look short-tailed and tubby in comparison. A Hobby might be seen circling over the heaths, catching insects and eating them in flight, while a heavier-built Peregrine may pass over. Goshawk join the soaring

Honey Buzzard and Hobby

Buzzard occasionally, while Sparrowhawk and Kestrel are frequently overhead. In suitable arrival conditions a migrant Osprey, Montagu's Harrier or other raptor is possible; the sky can be dotted with circling raptors of up to six or seven species, a rare sight in Britain. Close views cannot always be expected, however, as most raptors cover a wide area, and may soar up to a considerable height. Knowledge of shape and outline can be critical in identifying more distant birds.

It is usually the end of spring before the most distinctive breeding species are all present. Up to 50 pairs of Nightjar, possibly the largest concentration in the region, have just arrived. Males are active each evening, 'churring' loudly to establish territories in fern-covered clearings and clapping their wings together to deter intruding males; close views can be obtained by a silent watcher as they glide low overhead in pursuit of moths. Another late arrival is Turtle Dove, for which Haldon is one of the westernmost regular breeding sites.

When the breeding season is in full swing, dense woods do not permit close views of passerines and few birds still sing. Nightjar continue to churr, however, and the cooing of Turtle Dove may be heard to late summer. Breeding raptors may be seen intermittently circling over their territories on fine days throughout the summer. At the end of the season, large assorted parties of tits and warblers search the woods for food. Family parties of raptors may be on the wing. The breeding Honey Buzzards soon depart southward, but Haldon's prominent position may encourage other passing raptors to circle over, including groups of Honey or Common Buzzard, both probably Continental migrants.

Timing

Most species keep under cover in poor weather, especially larger raptors; fine conditions without strong winds are best. Mornings and evenings are easier for passerine activity; larger raptors do not soar until mid-late morning, when the land has warmed and they can use thermals. By midday on a warm summer day they may be too high to watch satisfactorily, however. Late afternoon as thermal currents decline may also provide views. Hobbies stay active later towards sunset. High pressure weather with light east or southeast winds can bring soaring migrant raptors across from the continent. Warm summer evenings with moths and insects on the wing are best for Nightjar (not usually heard churring before 21.30 hours).

Those particularly keen to see raptors should be prepared to sit for 3–4 hours at a time to gain good views.

Access

From Exeter, A38 to Plymouth and A380 to Torquay cross the top of Haldon in parallel. Birds of interest are scattered widely in the extensive woods. The following provide chances of some of the more distinctive species:

Racecourse: at the crest of the ridge beside A38. Turn left just before the course if approaching from the Exeter side. The lane which passes the racecourse entrance gate gives views across the course and adjoining woods. Raptors circling up over the steep eastern side of the ridge may pass over here and Hobbies may hunt overhead. Stonechat, Tree and Meadow Pipits are common. From here, return to A38 junction and use the underpass road north towards Dunchideock. Stop by any gate leading into forest on the left, and listen for Nightjar around clearings at last light.

Buller's Hill: a mile (1.6 km) farther along the Dunchideock road is the Forestry Commission office on the left. Leaflets and general information about the area are available. The next entry track on the left leads to a public car parking area and access to the various marked trails, including walking down the western hill slope to the power pylon line and Butterfly Walk.

Dartmoor View – Bird of Prey Viewpoint: continuing north on the Dunchideock road you reach an open hillside on the left with extensive views. Look for Dartmoor View gravel track and picnic site on the left. The Forestry Commission has recently erected signs to the 'Bird of Prey Viewpoint'. Drive down the track and park. Follow signs to the viewing point on the adjoining hillside. Honey Buzzard can be seen from here most days when present, together with many of Haldon's other characteristic species; constant presence of keen watchers in spring and summer has also led to observations of unusual migrants including recently Black Kite, Woodchat Shrike and Red-rumped Swallow. The open hillside below the watchpoint can provide good views of Nightjar. *Note:* because of the security measures sadly necessary for breeding raptors, birdwatchers are strongly requested to view from the watchpoint and not cause disturbance by walking through woods away from the paths.

Thorns Valley and the Obelisk: from Exeter, take A380 across the ridge and turn left on B3381 towards Starcross and Mamhead. Turtle Dove breed most years near the road junction. Stop by gates to look right across the valley for soaring raptors. Continue ¼ mile (400 m) and turn right at a small crossroads towards Ashcombe. Hillsides on the right have breeding warblers and Tree Pipit. Taller trees left of the road may have Redpoll, Siskin or Crossbill. At the end of the level stretch, park under trees; walk left through woods to Obelisk lookout for extensive views of the eastern flank of Haldon and the Exe valley.

Little Haldon: continue south on A380 beyond Starcross turning. Take B3192 towards Teignmouth. Continue 2 miles (3 km) to a minor road junction with woods to left. Stop and explore along woodland edges. The minor road towards Ashcombe Tower often has Crossbill, and Nightjar are quite numerous in clearings. Try also continuing along B3192 to the heath and car park opposite the golf course, a good vantage point. At migrant seasons look across golf course from roadsides; Wheatear, pipits and open ground species may occur, Dotterel have been reported rarely.

Calendar

Resident: Sparrowhawk, Buzzard, Great and Lesser Spotted Woodpeckers, Stonechat, Dartford Warbler (rare), Willow Tit, common woodland passerines, Crossbill, Siskin, Redpoll.

December–February: occasional Hen Harrier, Goshawk, Woodcock, Snipe, occasional Great Grey Shrike, Brambling and other finches. Crossbill may sing from January when present.

March–May: Siskins flock (March); from late April Cuckoo, Tree Pipit, common woodland warblers, Wood and Grasshopper Warblers, Whinchat, Redstart; Honey Buzzard from mid-May, Hobby, chance of other migrant raptors through May. Nightjar and Turtle Dove from late May.

June–July: breeding summer visitors as above – Honey Buzzard, Hobby, Nightjar, Turtle Dove, Tree Pipit, warblers, Whinchat, Redstart, etc. – plus residents singing in June, quieter in July, but Nightjar churr. Possibly breeding Woodcock. Peregrine and Goshawk seen occasionally.

August–November: Nightjar may still sing to mid-August. Most small migrants leave by late August. Family parties of raptors, Honey Buzzard present to early September, chance of other migrant raptors especially August–September, Woodcock and winter finches return from November.

6A ADDITIONAL SITE: CHUDLEIGH KNIGHTON HEATH AND HENNOCK

OS ref: SX 8477
OS map: sheet 191

Habitat

Between the southeastern fringe of Dartmoor and the Teign Estuary, the Teign/Bovey basin is a low-lying poorly drained inland zone of heath, thickets and copses. The habitat has been fragmented by industrial development, including extensive open claypits; Chudleigh Knighton heath is the best remaining example of the original sites. Devon Wildlife Trust has a 148 acre (59 ha) reserve covering much of the heath, on lease from the clay company. The area is well known for butterflies and orchids. The land rises northward from the heath edge towards Hennock ridge, reaching 250–300 metres between the Teign and Bovey valleys. Three deep narrow reservoirs (Kennick 45 acres/18 ha, Tottiford 35 acres/14 ha and Trenchford 33 acres/13 ha) are surrounded by forestry plantations; the rest of the ridge is occupied by small mixed farms.

Species

Although not visited by large numbers of birds, these areas are known for a few specialities, mostly breeding species. In winter the heath appears bleak, with few birds except for Meadow Pipit, a Stonechat or two, and seed-eaters such as Yellowhammer and Reed Bunting. Occasionally, at the beginning or end of the season, a transient Great Grey Shrike may spend a week or two perched atop bushes on Chudleigh Knighton or neighbouring heaths. This species has also been seen near the reservoirs in winter, particularly in larger clearings between plantations; reports may refer to the same individual seen on the heaths. Although the reservoirs hold very few ducks (single figure counts of Tufted or Pochard being normal), and a few Canada Geese, colder weather can bring a Goosander, Smew or Goldeneye. Such visits are usually brief, the narrowness of the reservoirs and frequent presence of bank anglers creating disturbance. Kennick Reservoir, the widest, and the wider central bay of Trenchford, are most likely to hold visiting ducks. The conifer plantations may be more interesting, although as usual in this habitat, variety of species is limited. In more mature sections, or by Rhododendron cover, a Woodcock may be flushed. Small parties of Siskin and Redpoll roam the treetops, while on fine days even early in the year, a red cock Crossbill may sing from a high branch. Two or three pairs of Crossbill are likely to breed, although larger passing flocks arrive to tackle pine cone crops, with sporadic counts of over 100 in winter. As warmer weather arrives, Siskin gather in chattering pre-migration flocks, counts again sometimes reaching hundreds; a few are seen in summer and probably breed, numbers remaining in territories having increased in recent seasons. By the time migrant Siskin move off, young Crossbill may already be on the wing.

At the same time, another local speciality becomes noticeable; the mellow descending notes of the Woodlark's attractive and distinctive song might be heard around plantation edges, on slopes above the reservoirs or in meadows adjoining the woods. This uncommon decreasing resident is usually present, particularly on the eastern slopes and towards the Teign valley, but if not singing can be difficult to find. There may also be one or two around the edges of Chudleigh Knighton heath.

Later spring brings summer migrants, the main ornithological attraction of Chudleigh Knighton heath. Cuckoos are prominent, gathering to parasitise Meadow Pipit nesting on boggy ground. Several Tree Pipit perform 'parachuting' songflights over the edges of the heath, and one or two Whinchat join chacking Stonechat on low thickets. Telephone wires stretching across the heath are used as songposts by many small passerine species, including Yellowhammer and Willow Warbler. A wide range of warblers includes numberous Whitethroat, and several pairs of Lesser Whitethroat, more common here than in most parts of the region. Woodpeckers and common woodland passerines are seen in trees bordering the heath. Redstart breed in small numbers both here and in the reservoir plantations.

On fine evenings in late spring and early summer birdwatchers visit the heath to hear, or occasionally see, its small colony of Nightingale, the area's main claim to fame. For many years this was the only area in the region where they were known to occur (a colony is now known in the extreme east) and it is certainly their most westerly site in the country. With increased pressure and habitat damage from fires, erection of power pylons and development, the population has decreased, but still up to seven males may arrive to sing from dense tangles of bushes on the central heath; some appear to be unmated, probably three or four pairs actually being present. When first arrived, males sing loudly at times in daylight, but once established they can be hard to see, often only revealed by harsh churring alarm calls or the flash of a rufous tail in the undergrowth. As dusk falls they are occasionally spotted emerging to feed on small tracks next to the bushes. The same areas have recently attracted up to two pairs of Nightjar, which circle out over adjoining heathland to feed. Sometimes a Hobby hunts insects overhead, and the thin trilling of a Grasshopper Warbler might be heard.

Later summer is perhaps more difficult for locating birds, although parties of fledged young passerines move about the plantations and heath. A Quail might have turned up in the farmland between Hennock and the Teign valley, and still be singing from tall cover. As autumn approaches, young birds bred on the higher ground such as Wheatear and Redstart filter down across the heaths. An odd visitor at this period is the occasional Common Scoter, normally a strictly seafaring duck, which arrives on the reservoirs presumably through following an overland migration route; Common Sandpiper are more expected migrants along the stony banks.

Timing

Fine days without strong winds are needed to cover areas mentioned properly, especially for passerines. Ducks are most likely to be watchable on Hennock reservoirs in cold weather, when numbers and variety may increase, or when anglers are fewer, e.g. midweek. Late afternoons and evenings are often most productive at the heath; best chance of seeing Nightingales is in the last two hours before dark, preferably on warm dry evenings, also most likely conditions to see Nightjars at last light; the Nightjar population here is tiny compared with that on Haldon and those wishing to see this species particularly may do better there. Woodlark and, if present, Quail, are also likely to sing in early mornings and evenings; Woodlark may even sing at night.

Access

From A38 Exeter–Plymouth road, turn off to Chudleigh and continue through to Chudleigh Knighton village. Take B3344 towards Bovey Tracey, which crosses the heath, and stop at roadside lay-bys to walk down footpaths. Do not damage plants and birds' nests by walking across vegetation away from paths. The best place to spend time is near the road junction at the centre of the heath (Dunley Cross). Turn left at the junction to park by the roadside on a wider stretch, and explore the paths through the thickets opposite you beside the minor road. Most of the Nightingale sing in this area. Birdwatchers confined to their cars will certainly hear Nightingale from the roadside in the right conditions; stops at other roadside pull-ins may enable views of other characteristic local birds without leaving the car.

For Hennock, turn right (east) at the central crossroads instead of turning left to park. Drive north for 3 miles (4.8 km) to Hennock village. In the village turn left uphill, following signs for another two miles (3.2 km) to the reservoirs. A network of roads crosses the three lakes and plantations adjoining, although the narrow curving shape of the lakes makes overall views difficult. For Crossbill and Siskin, or Redstart in summer, try a walk along forest tracks (public bridleways) on the eastern side of Kennick Reservoir, signposted from the banks. Access to reservoir perimeters is only by permit available from the Recreation Office of South West Water (see address section of book).

Exploration of the Teign valley slopes can be done by continuing east past the foot of Kennick Reservoir and following narrow minor roads towards Christow or Bridford villages.

7 TEIGN ESTUARY AND NEWTON ABBOT DISTRICT

OS ref: SX 8772
OS map: sheets 191/192/202

Habitat

The shallow east-facing estuary basin is three miles (4.8 km) long and up to half a mile (0.8 km) wide, with extensive sandy mudflats at low tide. Teignmouth, a small port and holiday town, lies at the mouth, where a natural sandbar extends south across the estuary. A bridge crosses the lower estuary to Shaldon on the southern bank. The middle and upper estuary, flanked by fertile farmland especially on the less steep northern side, is more muddy. A sewage works and outfall are situated beside the upper southern bank. The estuary narrows sharply at Passage House Inn at the head, where stretches of raised saltmarsh project into the mudflats, leaving sheltered channels between.

Inland from the estuary, the town of Newton Abbot is surrounded by low-lying land used extensively for quarrying clay, especially eastward. Old quarries now form several lakes with overgrown perimeters. Main habitats are:

Rackerhayes, a series of pools and thick tangled waterside trees and bushes, a popular angling area, surrounded by rough pastures, with the River Teign flowing behind, lined by willows and alders.

Jetty Marsh, a reed-bed and clumps of bushes along an old overgrown canal complex immediately east of Newton Abbot town centre.

New Cross Pond, behind the adjoining village of Kingsteignton, a deep 7-acre (3-ha) pit lake with patches of dead flooded trees, and extensive gorse and bramble on the slopes; a Devon Wildlife Trust reserve of botanical interest, with Corky-fruited Dropwort, Southern Marsh Orchid and Common Spotted Orchid; Great Crested Newt breeds.

Decoy Pool, on the opposite (southwestern) side of town, a deep pool used for recreation and sailing, with a wooded hillside behind.

Teigngrace, a riverbank walk where the Teign is shallower and faster-flowing just north of the built-up areas.

Species

This is not a major birdwatching centre, but has a range of estuary, freshwater and woodland birds; the lakes are variable in attraction, often best in midwinter.

At the start of the year rakish Red-breasted Merganser, spiky-crested drakes most conspicuous, fish in the lower estuary or middle reaches above Shaldon Bridge, where close views of 20–30 might be gained. Some also feed at sea off Teignmouth, joining dozens of Shag which gather to catch flatfish off the estuary mouth. Occasional divers, Eider and Common Scoter, or a few Razorbill, might also be diving offshore. The lower estuary is popular with Oystercatcher which peak at 300–400

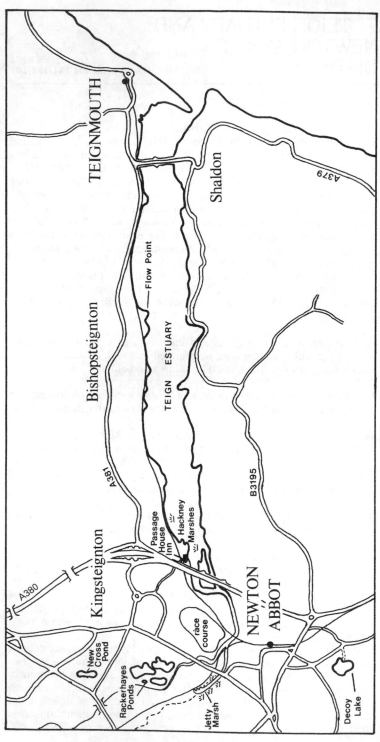

in the area, but little used by other waders except a few dozen Turnstone. On the upper estuary flats off the sewage works, several hundred Black-headed and Herring Gulls roost at low tide, with a few Lesser Black-backed and Common Gulls. Other gulls such as Mediterranean, Glaucous and Iceland have been found among them; with regular reports of scarcer gulls at Hope's Nose just down the coast, it is worth checking the Teign flock especially at gull migration periods (late winter-early spring). On high tides many gulls fly down to rest on the river off Shaldon Bridge. A proposed deep-water sewer outfall off the coast may change future gull feeding patterns.

On the middle and upper estuary Cormorant and Heron feed. Dabbling ducks find little food here, although a few Mallard, Wigeon and Teal call in. Parties of Red-breasted Merganser range up to the estuary head at high tide, joining up to five or six Little Grebe and Goldeneye (usually brownheads) which dive on the main channel. Wild geese are not usual, but a party of Brent may fly across from the Exe to feed. Dozens of Shelduck (peaking around 50) and many Carrion Crows forage over the mud as the tide recedes. A few Oystercatcher feed at the Passage, but roost flocks of up to 300 Lapwing and Redshank, together with perhaps 100 Curlew, are most noticeable. Redshank are joined by a wintering Greenshank or two, often a Spotted Redshank stays through. An American Lesser Yellowlegs once wintered with Redshank; occasionally a Ruff or a party of Godwit drops in. Apart from 100 or so Dunlin, smaller waders are limited. Sheltered saltmarsh creeks around Passage area, where waders roost at high tide on grassy islands, hold a Common Sandpiper most winters, flying off with characteristic stiff wingbeats if disturbed; a Kingfisher is often encountered. Bushes near the river may hold wintering Chiffchaff.

Inland on the pools, Great Crested and Little Grebes may be seen, plus several Cormorant which commute out to the estuary. Black-sterned drake Gadwall have turned up with their drabber brown mates on the larger pools in cold weather. Up to 30 Pochard and several Tufted Duck are regular at Rackerhayes and New Cross, flying between the two when disturbed, smaller numbers occurring at Decoy. One or two brownhead Goldeneye usually occur on Rackerhayes, and in cold weather a Goosander may arrive. Rackerhayes attracts a stray duck with the diving ducks most seasons, such as a Scaup or Long-tailed Duck, staying for several weeks. Feral visitors include small groups of Canada Geese all over the district, sometimes a party of Ruddy Duck arrives from the West Midland reservoirs after hard frosts. Beware also of exotics such as Egyptian Goose and Ruddy Shelduck which wander the district from a wildfowl collection. Fieldfare and Redwing feed around lakesides in flocks, while parties of Siskin (often numbering 40–50 around Rackerhayes) and a few Redpoll, chatter in the alders. The loud calls of Cetti's Warbler have been heard at Jetty Marsh at this season, and an occasional Willow Tit, scarce in South Devon, is recorded by lakesides. With leafless branches, views of resident woodpeckers, which include a few Lesser Spotted, may be obtained more easily than in summer.

In spring a range of commoner waders visits the estuary, including passing Whimbrel flocks; Sandwich Tern fish off Teignmouth seafront, sometimes joined by Manx Shearwater and maybe skuas in rough weather. Shelduck fly up from the estuary to nest burrows in nearby farmland, where thinly scattered pairs of Cirl Bunting breed. Buzzard and Sparrowhawk often soar overhead. The attractive Great Crested

Grebe, a rare breeder in our region, has raised young on New Cross Pond in recent years. Mute Swan and Coot breed at Rackerhayes. Kingfisher move up to breed in the Teign banks towards Teigngrace, where Sand Martin arrive to breed in riverbank holes, while Grey Wagtail and Kingfisher may be seen by those prepared to take a longer walk upriver. In late spring Lesser Whitethroat give their brief rattling song from thickets, and several pairs of Reed and Sedge Warblers arrive to breed in Jetty Marsh reeds. One or two pairs of Turtle Dove might be found in areas of thickets and damp woodland. On the upper estuary Spoonbill have been recorded more frequently than on most of the region's estuaries, while Little Egret have been reported several times.

In summer strings of young Shelduck are led across the estuary mudflats by volunteer 'aunties', and soon flocks of Curlew gather, joined by a few migrant Whimbrel. In late summer up to 30 Common Sandpiper and six or seven Greenshank, with other returning waders, gather at the estuary head roost. Autumn may bring a Curlew Sandpiper among the Dunlin, or a Green Sandpiper in creeks, with Greenshank and Spotted Redshank mingled with the Redshank. Sandwich and Common Terns forage well up the estuary, Common particularly staying to feed off Passage marshes, although less than half a dozen are usual. Kittiwake, terns and a few skuas move southward off the seafront. Raptors are not really a feature of the area, but a Peregrine may wander over outside the breeding season, and occasionally an Osprey has been sighted.

Timing

Variety of species increases sharply in hard weather, when Rackerhayes and Decoy come into their own. For the estuary, the last two hours of rising tide bring waders close enough to watch from Passage shore as they gather to roost; some Oystercatcher and Curlew remain on roadside fields at Bishopsteignton on the northern bank. Passage marshes (also known locally as Hackney) can be visited at other tides to check saltmarsh channels but both waders and gulls will be distant, necessitating a telescope. Strong winds onshore, especially southerlies and easterlies with poor visibility, may bring seabirds off Teignmouth seafront. At Decoy try to avoid sunny Sundays when sailing and public use make watching more difficult.

Access

Newton Abbot lies just off A380 Exeter–Torquay road, which bypasses the town and crosses the estuary head on a flyover near Passage marshes. Turn off the bypass at the Teignmouth (A381) sign from the dual carriageway just north of the flyover. From this roundabout:

For *Teignmouth*, follow A381, stopping in winter e.g. at Bishopsteignton where on the right before the garden centre is a public footpath to Flow Point, overlooking the middle estuary. Park carefully on verges. Roadside pull-ins towards Teignmouth give further estuary views. Stop near Shaldon Bridge (no parking on bridge) to check gull flocks. For estuary mouth and offshore, drive right along Teignmouth seafront to a car park at the end.

For the *upper estuary*, turn back from the roundabout into Kingsteignton village. Take the left turn at mini-roundabout and watch for a lane on left after 100 metres to Passage House Inn. Follow lane and park to the left on rough ground near the estuary; the car park is part of

Passage House Inn property and the owners have kindly agreed to allow birdwatchers to park here.

For *Rackerhayes*, continue left from the mini-roundabout and turn left at next roundabout towards Newton Abbot. At small roundabout, turn right into Tesco supermarket entrance, then down a drive on the right of the building to car park at rear. The muddy lakesides and bushes can be walked from here; the largest, furthest lake is often best for ducks. Access is **only** by permit from Watts, Blake, Bearne Clay Company, who own the land; contact their property department at Park House, Courtenay Park, Newton Abbot for details. In the next few years extension of quarry operations may radically alter this site.

For *Jetty Marsh*, continue along main road to Newton Abbot, take 'ahead' lane at next roundabout, then turn right swiftly. Park nearby along roadside and walk back a few metres up the main road, crossing the reedy channel, then left through gateway onto a rough, often overgrown path between the bushes. This is a public footpath although not signposted. Warblers, including wintering and perhaps breeding Cetti's, use the area and sandpipers are seen around muddy areas; the reed beds may attract passage warblers and are used as a roost by Pied Wagtail later on.

For *New Cross*, go back to Kingsteignton village centre junction, turning left along Broadway Lane. Drive to a junction at the end near a working quarry; the pool is on the right, concealed by a spoil heap overgrown with bushes. Devon Wildlife Trust lease the pool from the quarry company as a nature reserve. Access by permit only; enquire from DWT.

For *Decoy*, go back onto A380 flyover southward, continue across the estuary, then turn right into Newton Abbot at large roundabout. Take first left on entering Newton Abbot into Keyberry Road. Drive through an urban area to next junction on right. Fork right here; the lake entry (green gates) is a few metres along on the left. Park in car park and take signposted lakeside walks.

For *Teigngrace*, turn left at the junction at the far end of Broadway Lane in Kingsteignton; continue until you have passed over a bridge, then park along roadside and take a public footpath on the right (northern) side adjacent to the bridge.

Calendar

Resident: Great Crested and Little Grebes, Shag, Grey Heron, Canada Goose, Sparrowhawk, Buzzard, Coot, Moorhen, woodpeckers, Kingfisher, Grey Wagtail, Cetti's Warbler, common woodland passerines, Cirl Bunting.

December–February: Cormorant, Shelduck, Tufted Duck and Pochard, other diving ducks at times, Red-breasted Merganser, possibly other sawbills in hard weather, common waders, Greenshank and Common Sandpiper, probably Spotted Redshank, Turnstone, gull roost possibly including scarcer species, auks on sea, winter thrushes, maybe Chiffchaff, Siskin, Redpoll, maybe Willow Tit. Peregrine may visit estuary.

March–May: Most winter visitors left by end March. Sandwich Tern and Sand Martin arrive from late March. Gulls continue to pass through. Terns and other seabirds late April–May. Whimbrel and other wader passage from late April. Lesser Whitethroat, Reed and Sedge Warblers from late April; chance of Spoonbill or egret later in season. Shelduck peak late spring.

June–July: Young Shelduck and passerines about, still chance of over-shooting Spoonbill or egret, wader movements start again from late June, especially shanks and sandpipers. Curlew flocks on mud.

August–November: Most activity on estuary, with terns, maybe skuas offshore, flocks of passage waders with chance of less common species, most migrants moved on by mid October. Winter visitors in low numbers in November unless cold.

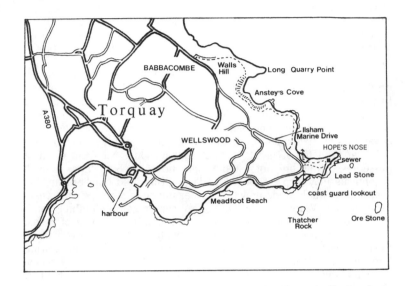

Habitat

At the north end of Torbay, Hope's Nose is the first promontory beyond the Exe Estuary mouth, and the low spit at the end curves north into Lyme Bay. Cliff ledges and a small disused quarry face the bay northward. Offshore lie the rocky islets of Lead Stone (nearest, small), Ore Stone (½ mile/0.8 km out, over 30 m high) and Thatcher Rock (peaked, 45 m high, to the south). The peninsula is covered in bracken, bushes and scrub, with a small pine copse. A sewer outfall is situated near the tip of the point, in front of a disused Coastguard lookout hut.

Species

Hope's Nose is known mainly as a seawatching point. Birds moving along the coast pass close inshore at times, especially in reduced visibility or when blown by onshore winds; most movement is south out of Lyme Bay. Gulls often stop to feed at the sewer outfall, allowing time for good views, and may remain for several weeks, feeding at the outfall when it is discharging. Other species flying past require swifter identification, unless conditions force them close.

The early part of the year brings least variety, but large flocks of Black-headed Gull gather at the outfall. It is worth checking for occasional unusual gulls, such as a Little dipping over the sea or a slightly larger Mediterranean Gull among the Black-headed. Gulls not actively feeding may roost on Lead Stone or the rocky beach right of the sewer, where often a dozen Oystercatcher or Turnstone probe the weeds; Purple Sandpiper might also be seen in small numbers. Rock Pipit are always present near the shore, and some years a wintering Black Redstart. Offshore, a few Gannet and Kittiwake pass; rough weather can bring hundreds of moving auks, and sometimes a burly Great Skua. One or two divers, grebes and seaducks feed in the area, often in the bay on the northern side. The most likely diver on the sea is the hardy Great Northern, told by its steep domed forehead; Red-throated Diver fly past, although passages of both species can occur. Single Great Crested and Slavonian Grebes come out from Torbay to feed off the end. A local speciality is the stout, long-billed Red-necked Grebe, seen in most winters, especially after easterly winds. Ducks include a Red-breasted Merganser or two in the north bay and, very often, several brown immature Eider near Lead Stone.

The start of spring brings several hundred Kittiwake calling excitedly on the water below nest ledges, and often unusual gulls as migration begins; Mediterranean and Little Gulls usually appear, with a chance of an Iceland or bulky Glaucous dropping in very briefly. Small numbers of Chiffchaff, Wheatear and perhaps Black Redstart arrive on land. Later a variety of small migrants feed in the thick bushes, while usually a Lesser Whitethroat gives its brief rattling song. Numbers of most passerine arrivals are not usually high, however. Sometimes a cock Nightingale may stop off for a few days, giving loud bursts of melody from impenetrable undergrowth. Scarcer migrants seen over the years have included Woodchat and Ortolan. At sea, migrant Whimbrel, Sandwich and a few Common Terns pass north, with a chance of skuas. Northward movements in spring are generally small and not very close to shore; best watches are when onshore winds bring in south-moving birds as in autumn. Such conditions occasionally bring packs of skuas, including thick-tailed Pomarine, accompanied by scores of Fulmar, Manx Shearwater, Gannet, terns and auks.

Summer brings thousands of breeding Herring Gull, especially on Ore Stone and Thatcher Rock, with one or two pairs of Lesser Black-backed. Several pairs of Shag breed, white-thighed Cormorant choosing the highest pinnacles. Up to 500 pairs of Kittiwake on Ore Stone and mainland cliffs form one of the largest colonies in mainland southern England. Careful inspection of Ore Stone ledges (telescope useful) will reveal up to 30 pairs of Guillemot and probably two or three Razorbill. Puffin in groups of up to six are seen on the sea or flying past at intervals in late spring and summer, but are not known to nest. Fulmar are not yet established here, but frequently glide past.

Out at sea, parties of dozens of Manx Shearwater regularly feed low over the waves at dawn and dusk through summer. Very occasionally, rough weather will drive a group of tiny Storm Petrel within view of shore; they may even gather to feed off the sewer mouth if conditions are severe. Gannet and parties of two or three dozen Common Scoter are frequent in midsummer, with a chance of a passing skua. From late summer an increased variety of birds occurs; this season often produces a Mediterranean Gull, which may stay for weeks to moult. Manx Shearwater are slowly replaced by smaller numbers of other shearwaters, including a few records annually of the dusky Balearic race. One or two of the large Sooty and Cory's Shearwaters are seen most years, in late summer to early autumn.

As autumn progresses, a steady flow of terns moves south past the Nose in early mornings; Sandwich Tern are most evident at close range, up to 100 passing on good days. Common Tern passage fluctuates more, depending on weather, but up to 300 may pass in a morning, often bunching in large groups farther out; on other mornings hardly any at all pass. Arctic or Roseate Tern are sometimes identified among closer groups by skilled observers. Black Tern, appearing irregularly in small parties, may stop and feed at the sewer. When terns are passing, there will usually be a skua twisting in high-speed aerial pursuit; over 20 Arctic Skua pass on good autumn days, and a peak of over 100 has been reported rarely. Small numbers of Great Skua are regular, single figures being usual, and one or two Pomarine can be expected; the rare Long-tailed has been seen in several recent years. After most terns have departed, skuas may still be blown in by adverse weather, along with a stray oceanic migrant such as a Grey Phalarope, Sabine's Gull or Little Auk; although virtually annual, these last species are seen in smaller numbers than at watchpoints in the far west. Sabine's Gulls are as regular here as anywhere in Devon, however; sometimes three or four have passed in a day. Prolonged gales have very occasionally brought in a dozen or more pale Grey Phalarope, difficult to watch as they fly a few metres before dropping on the sea to feed; Little Auk are far scarcer, however. Parties of Brent Geese and Wigeon flying in to local estuaries, plus a few passing divers, mark the approach of winter.

Adult Arctic Skua and immature Long-tailed Skua

On shore, a few commoner warblers move through the scrub; later in the season a Firecrest may be detected. Wheatear and sometimes Ring Ouzel flit around the rocks in small numbers, replaced later by Black Redstart. Overhead, circling local Raven are often noticed, while Peregrine stay for long periods in autumn, occasionally flying out to attack passing migrants over the sea.

Timing

Seabird movement depends heavily on weather conditions, but largest numbers usually pass in the first three or four hours' daylight; some continue to pass all day if it stays dull, wet or misty but swing away from land once visibility has improved. Days when the horizon is clear and the coastline is seen well will not produce many seabirds. If mist or rain suddenly lifts, such as when a front passes over, there may be a large movement of seabirds out of Lyme Bay past the Nose. Onshore winds (between east and south) give best birdwatching, but strong south-westerlies may sweep birds up into Lyme Bay which then seek to pass back southward. Evening watches may prove worthwhile at migration times, and can bring summer sightings of Manx Shearwater as they move up to feed overnight in Lyme Bay; try the last two or three hours' light. In fine high pressure conditions, skuas and terns also tend to move right up to nightfall. For gulls and terns feeding offshore, choose a falling tide when the sewer is discharging. Gulls may commute between here and the Teign Estuary to the north, although this requires further study. After winter gales, check the bay on the northern side for sheltering waterbirds.

Access
From the top of Ilsham Marine Drive in Babbacombe district of Torquay. From Torquay harbour, turn inland up Torwood Street then right at first traffic signals to Meadfoot Beach. Follow the beach and turn sharp right onto winding, scenic Marine Drive at far end. Park by the road at the highest point. In winter check the bay below for divers and grebes. From the road take the public footpath, steep and muddy in places, down the Nose. Check bushes halfway down for warblers at appropriate seasons. Near the bottom, look left into the quarry and bay behind. Wintering grebes may shelter close under the cliff in rough weather. Continue to the end of the spit, where seabirds come in from the north parallel with the coast; a few pass directly overhead. To see gulls feeding at the sewer, watch from in front of the Coastguard lookout; in wet weather find shelter under rocks. Try also walking right, overlooking the shore, for gulls and waders; this path leads back eventually to the top of the Nose.

Calendar
Resident: Shag, Sparrowhawk, Green Woodpecker, Rock Pipit, Stone-chat, Raven.

December–February: Great Northern, Red-throated and occasional Black-throated Divers, Great Crested, maybe Red-necked and Slavonian Grebes. Gannet, Eider (irregular numbers), Common Scoter, Red-breasted Merganser, Oystercatcher, Turnstone, maybe Purple Sandpiper, Black-headed Gull, possibly Little or Mediterranean Gull, a few Kittiwake, rarely Great Skua, auks passing, maybe Black Redstart.

March–May: Fulmar, Cormorant, Kittiwake, larger gulls and auks start to breed. Gull passage (March) with chance of Little, Mediterranean, Glaucous or Iceland, diver passage starts; Chiffchaff, Wheatear, and sometimes Black Redstart late March, Sandwich Tern arriving. Manx Shearwater, Whimbrel and most terns after mid-April, diver passage and most chance of Arctic or Pomarine Skua in first half May. Whitethroat, Lesser Whitethroat and other warblers end April–May.

June–July: Breeding seabirds, Manx Shearwater feeding movements, Gannets pass, chance of Storm Petrel. Common Scoter flocks, often a few Puffins feed offshore; skuas and terns may occur. At end of period, a Little or Mediterranean Gull may arrive with returning Black-headed, and tern passage starts. Whitethroat breed, Lesser Whitethroat may still sing.

August–November: Shearwater passage mainly August–September, with Balearic race, maybe Sooty or Cory's. Terns August–mid October, mostly Sandwich and Common, maybe Arctic, Roseate or Black, peak end August–mid-September; Arctic, Great and Pomarine Skuas to early November, most end August–early October; Little and Mediterranean Gulls intermittent, mostly August–October; Peregrine from September; warblers, including Blackcap, Willow, Chiffchaff, mostly September; occasional Firecrest from end September, Wheatear stay to October, maybe Ring Ouzel. Possible Storm Petrel, Long-tailed Skua or Sabine's Gull September–October; first divers, generally Red-throated, end September, maybe Grey Phalarope October, Little Auk singles November, Black Redstart and probably Purple Sandpiper from end October.

9 TORBAY AND
BERRY HEAD

OS ref: SX 9060
OS map: sheet 202

Habitat

The sea off Torquay, Paignton and Brixham, mainly shallow and sandy, is sheltered from prevailing southwesterly winds, with Berry Head protruding at the southern end. The sea is particularly shallow off Preston–Paignton–Goodrington, a 2-mile (3 km) urban seafront backed by public lawns, with small Roundham Head in the centre. Clennon Valley, behind Goodrington beach, has several sheltered pools, fringed with natural vegetation, which have been dredged out by Torbay Council to encourage wildlife. Brixham, under the lee of Berry Head, has a substantial trawling fleet and fish quay. Berry Head itself, a limestone mass 65 m high, is flat-topped, with a disused quarry facing the sea on the northern side. The top, a Country Park much used by walkers, has

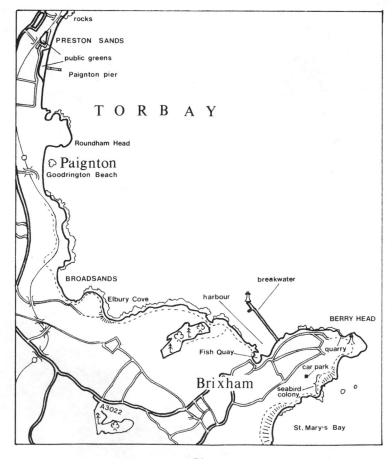

rocks

PRESTON SANDS

public greens

Paignton pier

T O R B A Y

Roundham Head

◊ Paignton
Goodrington Beach

BROADSANDS

Elbury Cove

harbour

breakwater

BERRY HEAD

quarry

Fish Quay

car park

Brixham

seabird
colony

St. Mary's Bay

A3022

grass and low thickets. At the end is a small lighthouse, and behind the cliffs lie ruined fortifications. The Head is botanically important, with White Rock Rose, Small Hare's Ear, Honewort, Small Rest Harrow and Aster Goldilocks among rare and local species. Orchids are well represented, with Bee, Greenwinged, Pyramidal and Early Purple. Butterflies include Small Blue, and Adonis Blue has been recorded; the very local Jersey Tiger Moth is also present. Greater and Lesser Horseshoe Bats use the caves in the quarry and can be seen especially in late summer.

The whole area is heavily used by tourists during the summer, and water sports are increasing throughout the year off the beaches.

Species

The bay is one of the best in the region for a variety of wintering grebes. Berry Head is known mainly as a seabird breeding colony, but has recently produced some good records of migrants, involving both land birds and passing seabirds.

Divers are fairly regular on the sea, with two or three Great Northern usually wintering in the southern half of the bay between Paignton and Brixham, while single Red-throated and Black-throated occur sporadically. Grebes are more widespread, although a telescope is helpful for detailed comparisons between species. Up to 30 Great Crested, scattered widely at times but favouring Broadsands–Elbury Cove end, form the region's largest regular winter population; the dusky Red-necked, with a yellowish bill, is seen only once or twice most years, although prolonged gales may increase sightings. Preston–Paignton is particularly recommended for Slavonian and Black-necked Grebes on the sea together; Slavonian appear slim and contrasted, while Black-necked have a smaller, rounded head and more grey-sided hue; up to ten of either may occur, but five or six is more normal. This is the only bay in our region where Black-necked always winter. Small groups of Eider and Common Scoter also occur here, while half a dozen Red-breasted Merganser fish off Elbury or Brixham harbour. Long-tailed Duck have been regular visitors in single figures in recent winters. All species may be forced to move around by wind, tide or water sports. Torquay end is usually less frequented than the centre and south. Oystercatcher, Turnstone and Purple Sandpiper are seen mostly from Preston south, with small numbers of Purple Sandpiper regular on rocks at the northern end of Preston front and similar numbers (perhaps the same birds?) on Brixham breakwater at times. Gull roosts on Preston Rocks when the tide falls may include a Mediterranean or Ring-billed Gull, in addition to a number of Common Gull among the Black-headed. The same species might be seen in Hollacombe Cove immediately to the north, or roosting in the adjoining Hollacombe Gardens at high tides. A Pied Wheatear and a Short-toed Lark have been surprise arrivals on Preston front, although few other small migrants occur. Rock Pipits, sometimes joined by a Black Redstart, feed on tidewrack in sheltered coves. Peregrine occasionally patrol the beaches in winter. After severe blizzards, when most of Devon is snow-covered, the greens behind Preston–Paignton, usually kept free of snow by salt spray, may provide temporary haven for hundreds of Lapwing, Skylark, Fieldfare and Redwing.

Clennon Valley Ponds form this mainly urban district's only habitat for freshwater duck; Gadwall, Teal, Pochard and Tufted Duck generally winter in single figures, although icy spells can bring influxes of larger

Red-necked, Black-necked and Slavonian Grebes
– winter plumage

numbers for short periods. Lying at low level and only a few hundred metres from the sea, the ponds are only likely to freeze over in exceptional conditions. Dozens of Coot, several Moorhen and two or three Little Grebe are also usually present and a Chiffchaff may be located in waterside bushes. The larger ponds are used extensively by gulls from nearby beaches coming to drink and bathe, with the chance that a less common gull might one day be spotted.

Unfortunately, Brixham fish dock has been little watched for birds, but must also attract interesting gulls and rarer species, as do the Southwest's other fishing ports. Comparison with the list of species seen at Plymouth and the Cornish trawler ports suggests that Torbay birdwatchers with time to spare might do well to make regular observations here. Offshore, feeding parties of Gannet, Kittiwake and auks move about all winter, coming closer in poor weather. Guillemot are often found on Torbay beaches as oil pollution victims (contact RSPCA if live injured or oiled birds are found); the rare northern Black Guillemot has been seen offshore several times.

In early spring, although most divers and grebes soon leave, parties of Black-necked Grebe may occur, shaking golden plumed cheek-tufts in display on warm days. Seabirds gather to breed on the southern side of Berry Head; Guillemot may have returned to ledges on mild winter days, but from now to mid–late summer up to 300 pairs are present on the overhanging cliffs. Several pairs of nesting Fulmar (plus numerous others patrolling past), Shag and Great Black-backed Gull, over 100 pairs of Kittiwake and perhaps two or three of Razorbill, less adapted to open cliff ledges, complete the summer scene. This is now the largest auk colony on the English Channel coast, and birds are easily viewable as they fly to and fro. Herring Gull breed abundantly around the cliffs and quarry, where they are joined by additional noisy pairs of Fulmar; off Torbay beaches a few Sandwich Tern often fish, even in midsummer.

A few pairs of Cirl Bunting are found on open farmland around the edges of Torbay, often within a few yards of encroaching building development.

Berry Head has recently been proved to attract a number of migrants, and a few rarer species have occurred, mostly those characteristic of open rocky terrain; a magnificent white Greenland Gyrfalcon spent ten days roosting in the quarry one spring, while an Alpine Swift frequented the area in early autumn. Wheatear, Redstart, Whinchat and commoner *Phylloscopus* and *Sylvia* warblers are likely in small numbers in spring and autumn, joined by a few flycatchers. Occasionally a shrike might be seen on a prominent thorn bush lookout; Red-backed, Woodchat and even the vagrant rufous-tailed Isabelline have been seen. Shearwaters, petrels, skuas and terns have been seen passing off the cliffs through autumn; continued watching could reveal many of the seabirds which pass Hope's Nose. Incoming fishing vessels may attract marine species; a group of Great Shearwater was recently seen following an incoming trawler.

In later autumn hundreds of pipits, larks and finches may pass over the Head some mornings on coasting movements, while orange-tailed Black Redstart flit around the quarry and ruined fortress.

Timing

Grebes and other waterbirds in the bay are best picked out when cloudy skies cast pale grey 'flat' light on the sea. High tides with little wind and calm sea are helpful; easterly winds usually churn up the surface and make birds hard to watch. On fine Sundays, water sports may cause disturbance unless you arrive early. Heavy blizzards with easterly winds produce arrivals of sheltering birds on Preston–Paignton greens; the bay is very exposed to such conditions and, if these are prolonged, waterbirds may move off to areas farther west. Preston Rocks gull roost is best watched at lowish tide; at high tide birds sit on the sea or move to adjacent Hollacombe beach and gardens. An early morning or weekday visit might provide more chance of seeing gulls settled; they are frequently disturbed by walkers at weekends.

Clennon Valley Ponds are best visited in the early morning or on weekdays when public disturbance is less. A visit during a cold spell might bring increased numbers of all species.

At Brixham, a weekday visit when trawlers are unloading is likely to be best for gulls. Strong southerly winds can force divers to shelter near the breakwater. Try a seawatch for passing seabirds off Berry Head in easterly, southerly or southwesterly winds with mist or rain, particularly early in the morning when birds are first moving, or late afternoon/ evening when returning trawlers approaching Brixham may attract flocks of Gannet, Kittiwake, gulls and other seabirds looking for scraps. For passerine migrants, especially in southeasterly breezes, try early mornings on the Head before public disturbance is too great. There is very limited cover and small passerines are hard to see on windy days. The auk nesting colony can be seen at any time in the breeding season. Autumn coasting movements of finches, pipits, larks and other day migrants are usually in the early to mid-morning, and against a light to moderate headwind (here, a wind with an easterly element).

Access

A379 runs south from Torquay seafront through Paignton, via Preston, with frequent signposts to seafront and beaches; at the hilltop cross-roads beyond Goodrington, A3022 is signposted to Brixham. All seafront areas may be worth checking, but main bird viewpoints are:

Preston, between Torquay and Paignton. Follow main road southward, left past traffic lights and under the railway bridge. Turn left immediately onto a small promenade road. You can watch from car windows in bad weather. Slavonian and Black-necked Grebes are regular. Rocks at far left end often have Turnstone and Purple Sandpiper, plus resting gull flocks. A Black Redstart is often nearby in winter. The public footpath across the small headland to the northern side leads to Hollacombe Cove and gardens (300 m away), where gulls may roost when disturbed from the main beach.

Paignton Pier can be reached by turning left across public greens off the main seafront road. Black-necked Grebe are seen particularly off here. You can walk left along the front to Preston (ten minutes) if desired. Car window views are possible here. No access onto pier itself in winter. Try elsewhere if watersports are in progress, as birds usually move well out or feed in other parts of the bay.

Goodrington is signposted left off the Paignton–Brixham road, at mini-roundabout opposite the sports and leisure complex. Grebes and Eider are often present.

Clennon Valley Ponds are reached by turning right (north) opposite Goodrington entrance. Go left into the large car park by the sports and leisure centre (parking fee in summer). Take the path from the rear of the car park across the full length of the sports fields; the pools are at the far end.

Brixham Harbour, obvious from the town centre, is worth a look at the left (northern) corner near the fish quay, especially when trawlers are unloading, attracting hundreds of gulls. Roadside parking is very limited, but there is a multi-storey car park just before you reach the harbour. Entry into the fish dock is not allowed but you can walk round the quayside path to the right of the dock entrance. From here you can look across the boundary fence to the fish quay a few dozen metres away, although boats coming in at the rear of the quay can only be seen from Freshwater car park further along the road. Beyond the dock entrance the main road curves sharply uphill; a right turn at the bend takes you to Freshwater car park, which overlooks much of the harbour and part of the fish quays. For divers and auks in winter, try also driving round the southern side of the harbour (back from the fish quay to the top of the harbour, then turn sharply left instead of entering the main shopping street). Drive ½ mile (0.8 km) to the breakwater car park and walk along; good views of passing and sheltering birds can be obtained from the end, a few Purple Sandpiper are often present in winter.

Berry Head can be reached by continuing along beyond the breakwater; the road swings up through a sheltered valley to the hilltop car park. If entering the town from Paignton direction on the main road, the Head is signposted to the right as you approach the built-up area. From the council-run car park, walk right at the far end to see the auk colony; an information display on the colony is included in the visitor centre building as you enter the car park. For small migrants check walls and bushes around the edges of the Head, which can be rather windswept on top. Bushes and thickets behind the visitor centre, reached by a network of signposted public paths, can be productive especially in a northerly or easterly wind; try also the sheltered hedgerows and fields towards St Mary's Bay on the southern side of the Head, reached by the same footpath network. Cirl Bunting might be seen in this area on either side of the road between the car park and holiday camp.

For passing seabirds, walk ahead from car park towards the end of the Head, then turn left down a gravel track before reaching the fortress wall. Follow this track around the perimeter fence of the disused quarry until you reach a metal gate and stile; you can walk down an old tarmac road towards the edge of the quarry, immediately below the tip of the Head, and seawatch, where you are often sheltered even in strong southwesterly winds.

Parties intending to visit should write to the Warden, The Bungalow, Berry Head, for additional information; reports of any unusual bird sightings would be welcomed.

Sharkham Point: beyond St Mary's Bay at the southern side of the Head lies this little-watched area with bushes which might hold passerine migrants; a sewage outfall near rock outcrops 100 m off the end has attracted Iceland Gull several times in late winter. Walk south along the coastal path from Berry Head (about a mile (1.6 km) walk) or drive back from the Head down to the crossroads with the B3205 Brixham–Dartmouth road, turning left at traffic lights, towards Dartmouth for ½ mile (0.8 km) and following signs turning left to St Mary's Bay through narrow lanes; turn right to a rough car park near the clifftop signposted to Sharkham Point and follow the gravelled paths to the right. When the path splits, fork left and down towards the tip of the Point. The narrow path can be muddy. Just over the last ridge, a sheltered grassy slope about 40 m above sea level gives views over the sewer. A telescope is advisable to scan the gulls from here.

Calendar

Resident: Shag, common raptors, Great Black-backed Gull, Raven, Stonechat, Rock Pipit, Cirl Bunting.

December–February: Great Northern, Red-throated and sometimes Black-throated Divers, Great Crested, Slavonian, Black-necked, maybe Red-necked Grebes, Little Grebe, Gadwall, Tufted Duck, Pochard, Coot and Moorhen (Clennon Ponds), Gannet, Eider, Common Scoter, Long-tailed Duck, Red-breasted Merganser, Oystercatcher, Turnstone, Purple Sandpiper, gulls including possibly Ring-billed, Mediterranean or Iceland, Kittiwake, Razorbill and Guillemot at sea; irregular Black Redstart. Lapwing, Skylark, winter thrushes after snow. Wintering Chiffchaff in sheltered areas.

March–May: Black-necked Grebe to early April some years, Fulmar on cliffs from start of period, breeding Shag, larger gulls, Kittiwake, Guillemot, Razorbill, Stock Dove from late March. Migrant passerines on headlands late March–May; passing seabirds mostly from mid-April, e.g. Fulmar, Manx Shearwater, maybe skuas, terns.

June–July: bay quiet except for odd Sandwich Tern. Berry Head has breeding Fulmar, gulls, Kittiwake and auks most active to mid-July; Manx Shearwater and Gannet pass.

August–November: Fulmar and gulls still on cliffs in August. Chance of migrant Manx, Balearic and maybe larger shearwaters (mostly August–September), skuas to late October, passerine migrants on headlands August–October, Black Redstart from mid-October. First divers and grebes in bay from mid-October but often scarce until November.

10 DARTINGTON AND THE LOWER DART

OS ref: SX 7962
OS map: sheet 202

Habitat
The River Dart flows south in a loop past attractive mixed woods, park and farmland of the Dartington Estate near Totnes. On the northern side, the river is shallow with gravel bars in places, but on the southern side a wider slow-flowing stretch lies above Totnes weir. The estuary between Totnes and Dartmouth is scenic and winding, with wooded banks and sheltered creeks used extensively for boating.

Species
The shallower stretches of the river are a regular haunt of Dipper and Grey Wagtail bobbing on waterside stones. Early in the year most birdwatchers focus on wider stretches towards the weir. This area is used by a flock of diving ducks, in cold weather among the largest in Devon; they probably move between here and Slapton. Tufted Duck are in the majority, well over 100 at times, but the flock attracts small numbers of related species – usually a few Pochard, often Goldeneye, occasionally scarcer visitors such as American Ring-necked Duck. A

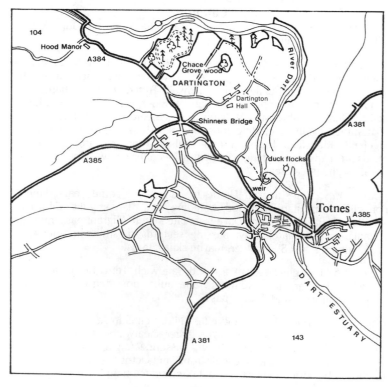

scattering of dabbling ducks has included one or two Gadwall, a species which often frequents diving-duck haunts. When disturbed, flocks may fly to south of the weir, near the town. Little Grebe are also usually seen. The varied habitat and sheltered position ensure a wide variety of farm and woodland species, such as woodpeckers, tits, Nuthatch and finches. The district is noted for a few pairs of Woodlark around copse edges; the males sing their musical descending notes in circular songflights over the meadows from early spring. Summer migrants include wood and hedgerow warblers, e.g. Blackcap, Garden Warbler, Whitethroat, Willow Warbler and Chiffchaff, with Spotted Flycatcher and hirundines around buildings. Goosander have bred farther up the Dart in recent summers and a redheaded female with a brood of ducklings might be seen in the area. At the end of summer, Kingfisher often spend periods on this part of the river before moving down to the estuary to winter.

The tidal estuary, although scenic, is not rated highly for birdlife. Lack of extensive mudflats or bordering marshes means that wildfowl and waders are never numerous, although small numbers of common species occur. Winding stretches make viewing points difficult. The upper sheltered stretches may hold overwintering Common Sandpiper. Outside the breeding season, Kingfisher are often seen along over-hanging trees, and Cormorant usually fish in the waterways. There is a heronry near Maypool on the eastern bank. Shelduck breed, and dozens are seen in spring and early summer; Buzzard and Raven soar over the wooded banks. In autumn, a few Common Tern follow the tide up the estuary, and there have been several sightings of Osprey fishing in the middle reaches up to Duncannon.

Timing

Not too critical at Dartington but duck numbers are highest in cold weather, especially when lakes elsewhere are frozen. Spring and summer early mornings are best for songbirds. The estuary has no central high-tide roost for waders; for these, visit at lower tide.

Access

Dartington Estate is just east of A384 Totnes/Buckfastleigh road. To view the south side, turn right to the estate on leaving Totnes northbound, immediately after Swallowfields, the last houses. Stop by estate gates and walk right to the weir along a muddy public footpath. Alternatively, continue by car to the second gateway on right along lane. Park and cross stile to continue on foot upriver for ducks. This is not a public path but visitors are permitted by Dartington Estate provided they observe the usual country codes. Parties should check with the estate manager before visiting.

The network of footpaths which previously gave access to the northern side of the estate and woods is not open at present; to hear Woodlark singing, however, try a stop up one of the side roads to the north off the main A384, e.g. by turning left near Hood Barton, 2 miles (3 km) farther north; drive up the narrow lane for 200 m and listen but take care not to block farm gateways.

The estuary is difficult to cover from the banks; many visitors take scenic boat trips between Totnes and Dartmouth, available mainly from April to October (contact local tourist information offices for details).

Calendar

Resident: Grey Heron, Buzzard, woodpeckers including Lesser Spotted, Kingfisher, Woodlark, Grey Wagtail, common woodland passerines, Dipper, Raven.

December–February: Dartington – Little Grebe, Gadwall, Teal, Wigeon, Tufted Duck, Pochard, Goldeneye, maybe Scaup or other diving ducks, winter thrushes, Siskin, Redpoll.
Estuary – Cormorant, Shelduck, Water Rail, Common Sandpiper, maybe Green Sandpiper or Greenshank, Redshank, Curlew, Snipe, Kingfisher, maybe Chiffchaff.

March–May: most ducks and waders leave by mid-March. Singing warblers mostly from mid-April, perhaps Wood Warbler at Dartington. A few migrant waders on estuary, Shelduck plentiful.

June–July: Woodlark all summer; common breeding residents and summer visitors, Shelduck breed, Goosander might be seen with young.

August–November: post-breeding flocks of tits and warblers (August), perhaps an Osprey, terns and a few waders on estuary (mostly mid-August–early September), winter visitors from end October.

11 SLAPTON LEYS AND DISTRICT (INCLUDING BEESANDS AND HALLSANDS)

OS ref: SX 8344
OS map: sheet 202

Habitat

Sheltered from prevailing winds by Start–Prawle promontories and high farmland behind, Start Bay faces eastward. Slapton shingle beach, facing the bay, runs south for 2 miles (3 km). The freshwater lagoon of Slapton Ley lies behind the beach, parallel to the coast; halfway along, it is divided by a narrow neck into the northern Higher Ley, reed-choked with encroaching *Salix* scrub and other bushes, and open-water Lower Ley on the southern side. Reeds fringe the Lower Ley and shallow bays at the rear have more extensive reed-beds where streams enter. Opposite Torcross at the southern end are water-lily pads. Along the inland side of the shingle ridge, facing the lake, runs a strip of thickets and brambles; the top of the beach is sandy turf, and the main road runs down its length. A ringing hut owned by DBWPS overlooks the bridge between Higher and Lower Leys; a bird logbook is kept in a tin under the left side of the hut. The Field Study Centre in Slapton village manages the Leys as a nature reserve on behalf of the owners, the Herbert Whitley Trust.

The Leys, beach and surrounding area boast many rare and local flora and fauna, attracting both professional and amateur naturalists. Strapwort grows nowhere else in Britain, Flowering Rush is another Ley-side rarity, while along the beach Yellow Horned Poppy and Viper's Bugloss may be found. A wide variety of dragonflies and damselflies includes Migrant Hawker, Hairy Dragonfly, Downy Emerald Dragonfly and Southern Damselfly. Many other unusual insects are found, including Jersey Tiger Moth. Otters, although notoriously difficult to see in the wild, are present, and can sometimes be seen from Slapton Bridge; beware confusion with feral Mink, now also unfortunately resident. Both Grass Snake and Adder live here, along with a wide range of other British wild animals.

The shingle beach extends south beyond Slapton towards Start Point, blocking the small, deep stream valleys of Beesands and North Hallsands. At Beesands an open lagoon, backed by reeds and bushes, forms a sheltered miniature of Slapton Ley; at Hallsands a semi-dry reed-bed with scattered bushes extends ¼ mile (400 m) up the valley. Beesands beach is used as a caravan park.

Species

Slapton is well known regionally as an easy area to see winter wildfowl, marsh species and a variety of other birds, especially at migration seasons. Beesands and Hallsands are much less watched.

In winter one or two Great Northern Diver, Shag, Eider and Common Scoter are seen regularly from Slapton and Beesands beach, together with a Slavonian Grebe most years and sometimes a Red-necked; a few Grey Plover and 200–300 Dunlin from nearby estuaries often roost on the shingle at high tide. Large gull flocks, often including hundreds of Great Black-backed and a few Kittiwake, collect on quieter stretches of beach, flying over into the Lower Ley or the stream entering the sea just

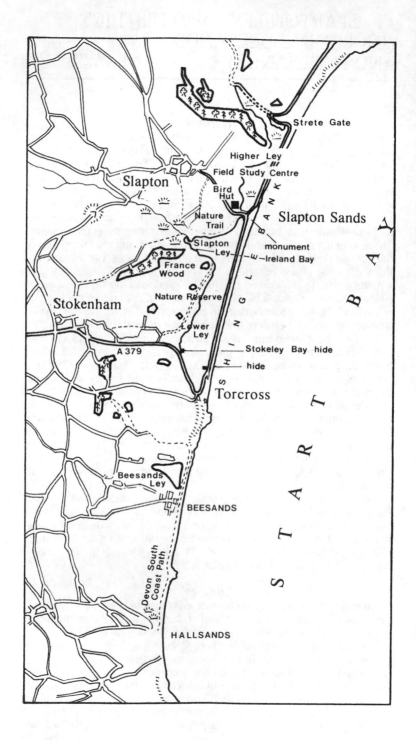

beyond Torcross cliff at the southern end, to drink and bathe; single Little and Mediterranean Gulls are found among the flock in most years. Several hundred ducks, chiefly diving ducks, use the leys in winter, with largest flocks of well over 100 each of Tufted and Pochard on Lower Ley near Torcross. Up to 30 Goldeneye are scattered along the lake, and at least one Long-tailed Duck is usually present. Single Goosander and Smew may turn up briefly on sheltered parts of the Ley. Small groups of feral Ruddy Duck have moved down from Somerset reservoirs in recent winters, and odd ornamental waterfowl compete for scraps with Mute Swan and Mallard at Torcross corner. Apparently wild wanderers to this area, the best in the region for diving ducks, have included several Ring-necked Duck (standing out slightly larger among the Tufted) and Ferruginous Duck (tending to skulk in Torcross reeds or sometimes the Higher Ley). Dabbling ducks are less regular, but parties of Wigeon moving between estuaries often drop in, and small packs of Teal may be flushed from reedy bays; Gadwall are increasing, with five or ten usually present, and up to 50 occasionally, with one or two breeding pairs now present. Great Crested Grebe have become established; this is one of very few sites in the region where they breed, although they spread out to neighbouring areas in winter. Single Slavonian and Black-necked Grebes also occur on the Ley itself in most years, sometimes joined by a diver after gales, and generally half a dozen Cormorant. Coot are abundant (flocks of up to 1,000 at times on open water). The Higher Ley is more difficult to watch, but Cetti's Warbler have become very noticeable among damp vegetation, their loud song carrying far across the ley on mild winter days. Colder weather, which may bring a party of geese or northern ducks, usually produces a skulking Bittern flushed from the reeds, and the metallic 'ping' calls of Bearded Tit are heard irregularly. Up to ten Chiffchaff and two or three Firecrest often stay through the coldest months in sheltered corners at the back of both leys, and many (concealed) Water Rail squeal.

Beesands has similar birds to Slapton; two or three Great Crested Grebe, dozens of Coot feeding on grassy banks, and parties of Tufted Duck and Pochard which fly across from the Lower Ley to feed. Close views are possible on this relatively small lake, where a few Goldeneye are also likely. Rarer ducks such as Ring-necked, which visit Slapton occasionally, may also feed here; try checking Slapton for birds reported at Beesands or *vice versa*. Cirl Bunting breed in the valley, moving nearer to the beach in winter. Cetti's Warbler are present in waterside vegetation both here and at Hallsands; the latter has no major attractions in winter, but often a Black Redstart flycatches on the beach.

Spring soon brings a sprinkling of shoreline Wheatear, with the chance of an early Hoopoe on sandy turf near the road at Slapton beach. Their arrival may coincide with a Scaup, joining the Tufted Duck temporarily, and several Sand Martin circling over the reeds. Garganey may appear in marshy bays, and stay for a week or two; this scarce summer duck has bred in the past. Packs of migrant Common Gull join flocks of other species roosting on the beach. Less usual gulls may be recorded; a Glaucous, perhaps Little or Mediterranean, and once a Ring-billed. Later on a trickle of terns, mostly Sandwich, passes northward, and divers of all three species, mostly singles or pairs, may be seen in breeding plumage off the beach.

From mid-spring, migrants are often numerous. Large numbers of hirundines and warblers feed around the leys, many Reed and Sedge

Warblers staying to breed in reed-beds, and some Grasshopper Warbler reeling in song from thickets may stay to nest. Falls of migrant passerines cannot always be detected in the thick bushes, but two Little Bunting were found one recent spring and lucky observers saw an American Eastern Phoebe, a flycatcher-like bird, in sheltered vegetation at the back of the ley; this was Europe's first sighting. Warblers and flycatchers may be seen in Hallsands valley as they filter off nearby Start Point.

Warm winds, which bring the main arrival of summer migrants, also regularly carry overshooting marsh species from the Continent to Slapton. An egret, or more often, a Purple Heron, arrives most springs, the heron often staying for a week or two although tending to skulk among vegetation. Various southern exotics, such as Squacco Heron, Little Bittern, Whiskered Tern and Great Reed Warbler, have turned up; the deep reeling of Savi's Warbler has been heard in the reeds for weeks. In most springs, a brown immature Marsh Harrier quarters the marsh for a few days; Montagu's Harrier and Black Kite have also passed at this season. Warmer weather encourages three or four pairs of Great Crested Grebe to nest, often performing elaborate 'weed-dance' displays; they have raised very few young in recent seasons, however, probably owing to water pollution and predation by Mink. Remaining Goldeneye on the lake head-jerk in display, and Gadwall often stay late. Water Rail, although common in winter, are scarce breeders (only one or two pairs in recent years) but Coot generally rear young. Raven nest in France Wood.

Out at sea, seabirds, including strings of Manx Shearwater, groups of Gannet and Kittiwake, feed through summer; Kittiwake often fly in to bathe in the lagoon. Fulmar inhabit the cliffs south of Torcross. Late summer may bring a Sooty Shearwater, feeding with the Manx, and Sandwich Tern fish off the beach. Thousands of Swift mass over the leys on humid days; a Little Swift recently joined them briefly. Early autumn may produce an Arctic Skua pursuing the sea terns, and several Black Tern dipping to catch insects over Torcross lily-pads, perhaps accompanied by a Little Gull or Common Tern. Waders such as Common Sandpiper and Greenshank feed on lagoon fringe mud if the water level is low. Thousands of Swallow and Starling roost among Torcross reeds at dusk, swirling flocks forming an attractive target for Sparrowhawk or Hobby as they gather before dropping in. A pale juvenile Rose-coloured Starling recently stayed for weeks among its commoner relatives. Ringing studies have shown that large numbers of warblers pass through the insect-rich reed fringes at this season, including rarely Aquatic Warbler with prominent 'badger-striped' heads, and other uncommon migrants such as Wryneck and Bluethroat have also been recorded. Owing to the dense vegetation, few of these have been seen without being trapped.

Migrants continue to pass late in the year, with regular sightings of Swallows in November. Meanwhile, gales in the Channel may force a tired phalarope, skua or other stray seabirds into the bay. Cold winds later may bring Snow Bunting, or a passing Hen Harrier.

Timing

Slapton's southerly position encourages large numbers of birds to shelter in winter freeze-ups; Bittern, Goosander and large numbers of winter thrushes might be expected. Strong easterly winds, although they probably bring birds, create difficult viewing conditions; a seawatch from the beach car park might pay off. Easterlies in autumn will bring Black Tern, and maybe an Aquatic Warbler or other scarce passerine. The area is sheltered from most other winds. Sea conditions need to be calmish to spot divers and grebes from the low beach. For ducks on the ley, avoid high winds, when many shelter among reeds. Feeding movements of shearwaters are most visible during mist with light southerly winds; strays such as phalaropes (which have included Red-necked and a Wilson's) arrive with prolonged southerly or southwesterly gales and rain. Spring migrant arrivals are most noticeable on cloudy, humid days with winds between southeast and southwest; most rarer heron types have arrived in mild southwesterlies. Ducks disturbed by high winds or boat anglers may fly to Beesands. For the autumn hirundine roost, about an hour up to darkness is best, with a chance of a Hobby attracted.

Slapton beach is very heavily used by the public on fine weekends at any season.

Access
Along coastal A379 between Dartmouth and Kingsbridge. Main areas to watch:

Strete Gate, at northern end of Higher Ley. Park on corner and look off beach for divers or seaducks in winter. Cross road to view Gara Valley reed-bed for possible harrier or herons.

Monument, halfway down the bay, opposite the bridge between Higher and Lower Leys. Suitable seawatch point, or alternatively watch from beach car park nearby. Check scrub and gorse across the road for small passerines. Walk south along beach crest for gull roosts and spring Wheatear, maybe Hoopoe.

Ringing Hut: cross bridge from Monument and check logbook for recent news (please insert details of any sightings you make).

Higher Ley: take path in front of ringing hut **with permit from Field Centre** and walk along back of reed-bed; for rails, Cetti's Warbler, maybe Bittern, a chance of other warblers and migrants at appropriate season. DBWPS members are allowed to use this path.

Ireland Bay: across road opposite ringing hut, take path through gate past fishing boat moorings. Continue on bank path, checking scrub on right for warblers and flycatchers at migration times. View across bay for bathing gulls, and ducks including Goldeneye or Long-tailed in winter. If water level is high, continue along higher path; do not stray into private farmland above. After about 300 m, watch across reeds on left for herons, harriers or warblers. Follow lake-shore path until a gated track turns left across the marsh towards France Wood. Check the pool ahead for herons, rails and ducks, including migrant Garganey. Look in the small overgrown quarry on corner for wintering Firecrest and Chiffchaff. **With permit from Field Centre**, continue down gated track for herons, harriers, rails and waterside warblers, perhaps including Savi's. Cross the boardwalk towards the wood, which has Buzzard, wood-peckers and Raven.

Scrub behind beach: at migration times, try walking the length of the leys between road and marsh for scattered passerine migrants.

Torcross, at southern end of the leys. Ducks are numerous and area is also best for grebes, Little Gull and Black Tern. Divers are seen off the beach, and gulls pass along the shore to drink from the stream beyond the rocks. Fulmars nest farther on. In wet weather the ley can be viewed from roadside car parks. A public bird hide, also suitable for the disabled, overlooks the open ley from the rear of the main car park. Walk from here down around the lower end of the ley, following A379 road verges, for views of ducks at the rear of wide Stokeley Bay; at the point where the road climbs away from the lakeside, a path leads to a small hide. By following the road for another 100 metres you can scan over Stokeley Pond, a farm pool which often attracts Gadwall and other ducks; the surrounding land is private.

At low tide you can walk south ½ mile (0.8 km) on shingle to Beesands from Torcross front.

Beesands: on A379, drive to Stokenham south of Torcross, turn left towards Start Point then left down a steep, narrow road signposted Beeson and Beesands. Walk left to the lake.

Hallsands: continue past the Beesands turn, towards Start. Turn left to North Hallsands valley; check beach and nearby reeds, and bushes along length of valley.

Calendar

Resident: Great Crested Grebe, Grey Heron, Mallard, Sparrowhawk, Buzzard, probably Water Rail, Coot, perhaps Barn Owl, woodpeckers, Cetti's Warbler, Stonechat, Cirl Bunting, Reed Bunting, Raven.

December–February: Great Northern Diver, Slavonian and maybe Black-necked Grebes, occasional Red-necked, Shag, Cormorant, Gadwall, probably Wigeon and Teal, maybe Shoveler, Tufted Duck, Pochard, Eider, Common Scoter, Goldeneye and probably Long-tailed Duck, rarer ducks. Bittern, Goosander, maybe Smew in hard weather; gulls; Kingfisher, Chiffchaff, Firecrest. Waders on beach.

March–May: migrant gulls including uncommon species (March), Wheatear, Sand Martin, maybe Scaup, Garganey and Hoopoe from mid March; early arrivals of a few summer migrants; Fulmar nesting; divers passage April–May, terns and Whimbrel mostly from mid-April, auks feed offshore. From mid-April, wide range of migrants including Yellow and probably White Wagtails, hirundines, warblers; chance of a rarer heron or raptor, especially Marsh Harrier; chance of other southern 'overshoots'.

June–July: seabirds feeding, including Manx and in July maybe Sooty Shearwaters; breeding residents, Reed and Sedge Warblers; Sandwich Tern return July.

August–November: Sandwich, Common and occasional other sea terns to early October, Black Terns and maybe Little Gulls from late August–October; possible skuas to end October, Sooty Shearwater to September, maybe Sabine's Gull off beach September–October, phalaropes end September–October (rare). Heavy migration of Swallow, warblers and other passerines including rarer species, mostly August–September, peaking end August. Swallows and other migrants to early November.

Note: Slapton can easily be combined with a visit to the Start–Prawle area (see Chapter 12) at migration seasons, giving a chance to see a very wide range of birds.

12 START AND PRAWLE POINTS

OS ref: SX 8337 Start;
SX 7735 Prawle
OS map: sheet 202

Habitat

This southernmost projection of South Devon comprises coastal farm-land, rocky outcrops, bracken and cliffs, with sheltered coves into which flow brooks lined by overhanging bushes. The coast includes several National Trust stretches with some of the county's best cliff scenery. Jagged, bracken-covered Start promontory, with a lighthouse, and rocky islets at the tip, projects southeast into Start Bay; the ridge is a spine of rocks, one side of which is usually sheltered from wind. Among high, open farmland behind the point lies Start Farm valley, sheltered from easterly winds, with trees and bushes. West from Start to Prawle (about 5 miles/8 km) a low strip of fields borders rocky Lannacombe Bay, often visited by marine biologists. Within a few hundred metres inland, the land rises steeply, with rock outcrops, to flat farmland at about 140 m.

Prawle Point projects southward, reaching slightly farther seaward than Bolt Head cliffs, visible to the west. Most of the eastern flank is farmland, with stone walls and tall hedges; overgrown rocky outcrops and wartime bunkers clad with brambles overlook the shore. The National Trust car park lies in a sheltered hollow surrounded by thickets, hazel and ash bushes; adjacent to it is a 1½ acre (0.6 ha) DBWPS reserve consisting of a weedy field slope, sheltered bushes and small pool. There is a dense sycamore wood on the steep hillside below East Prawle village, and a tangle of damp vegetation grows behind the duck-pond beside the road into the village. The top of the point, and superb vista of cliffs and coves westward, are largely covered by rough grass, gorse, bracken and boulders. A mile (1.6 km) west is a deep valley, with a stream, trees and thickets, known as 'Pigs Nose' valley by birdwatchers. A small part of the thickets is owned by DBWPS. Inland, west of the village, lie flat fields once used as an airfield.

The sea can produce spectacular sightings of larger creatures such as massive, but harmless, Basking Sharks, which show triangular back fins when circling lazily just below the surface on summer days. Grey Seals often peer up at the intruder from rocky coves, especially on the western flank of Prawle. Rank vegetation in coves in summer and autumn encourages concentrations of butterflies; residents include Green Hair-streak, and migrants include Clouded Yellow; even the spectacular orange and black American Monarch has visited.

Species

Prawle district has recently been recognised as one of the region's top migration watchpoints. Most watchers have concentrated on Prawle rather than Start, partly for convenience of access and partly because birds often stay longer than at Start, where shelter and cover are limited. All counts given below are based on Prawle; anyone watching carefully at Start would probably see many of the same species.

A major attraction for visiting birdwatchers is the resident Cirl Bunting, perhaps commoner here, in thickets and hedges near sea level, than anywhere else in Britain; the flat trilling song of males, at times confus-

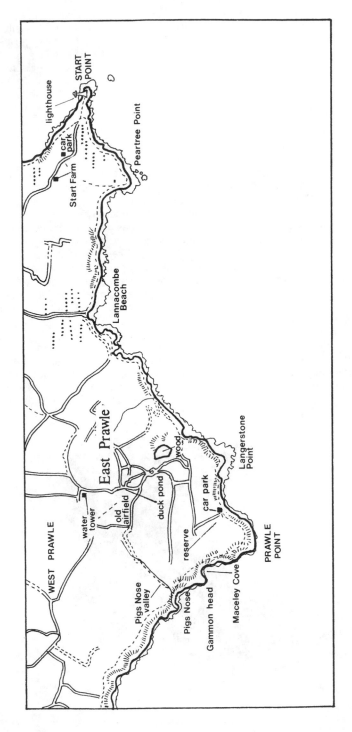

able with Lesser Whitethroat song, is a familiar spring sound and up to eight pairs breed in sheltered fields around Prawle, with further sites along the coast to Start. Outside the breeding season, parties can be detected as they perch in hedges or feed in field edges, giving quiet 'sipp-sipp' notes; a dozen or more may join together. Recent evidence suggests they may be joined by birds from other parts of Devon late in the year; occasionally they mix with Yellowhammer, causing identification puzzles. Female and immature Cirl usually appear smaller and duller than Yellowhammer, with less white in the tail and lacking the orange rump; males with black-lined heads present no problems. *Note*: in view of the increasingly endangered status of this species, it is vital that birdwatchers avoid disturbance, especially in the breeding season. The network of lanes and paths across the area provides regular opportunities to see Cirl Bunting and there is no reason to seek them by trespassing elsewhere. Remember that the species is protected by law and deliberate disturbance of breeding sites constitutes an offence.

Corn Bunting, rare in Devon, are found occasionally and may breed; they prefer high, open fields near the village. Tree Sparrows have bred at Start, and may still be present nearby. Little Owls are seen frequently around Prawle Point, often perched in daytime on rock outcrops or stone walls. Towards sunset they are often active around derelict farm buildings at the edge of East Prawle village. Buzzard and Raven are common, but large Buzzard-like raptors are worth checking for scarcer species at migration times (beware frequent oddly plumaged Buzzard).

In winter, large numbers of Gannet, Kittiwake and auks pass at sea, with a few divers, mostly Great Northern. Westward movements of thousands of Great Black-backed Gull have been seen in gales. Parties of Eider appear irregularly. Flocks of up to 30–40 Turnstone and smaller numbers of Purple Sandpiper feed on the rocks, together with plentiful Oystercatcher and a few Grey Plover, Redshank and Curlew. In sheltered

HARRISON 83

Hoopoe

bushes and coves, a Chiffchaff, Firecrest or Black Redstart may remain from the previous autumn. Overhead, a wintering Peregrine often patrols along the coast. Larger fields near the village are worth checking for lark and finch flocks, with occasional Twite among Linnet on the ground. Flocks of Golden Plover, which may be joined by other waders, particularly Lapwing, appear irregularly on the 'aerodrome' fields and, in hard weather, large flocks of open-ground species arrive from farther north.

Spring can bring large arrivals of migrants, first usually being Wheatear or Black Redstart around the beach, rock outcrops or buildings. Chiff-chaff, Goldcrest and often a Firecrest work their way up hedges and away inland, unless held up by poor weather. The highly distinctive Hoopoe could be encountered from the first warmer March days, probing short turf on Start promontory or the top of Prawle Point near the coastguard lookout. Later, mixed falls of warblers and other small migrants occur in suitable weather, with birds singing and feeding in every bush at dawn, although most soon move on. Willow Warbler are predominant (up to 500 at times), with lesser numbers of Chiffchaff; up to 50 Blackcap and Whitethroat may accompany them, with a scattering of Lesser Whitethroat. Close study of migrant warblers can reveal racial differences, such as the occasional larger pale-fronted Willow Warbler of Scandinavian origin. Three or four Grasshopper Warbler 'reeling' in damp scrub may stay to breed, but Reed and Wood Warblers which sing briefly in sheltered trees are purely migrants; one or two Sedge Warbler may nest near streams. A check of either headland on a good spring day is likely to reveal scattered Redstart, flycatchers and other summer visitors. From mid morning in fine weather, diurnal migrants including hirundines and finches may be seen arriving from France over the cliffs, with a chance of a raptor such as a Hobby. Prawle has an exceptional list of raptors; sometimes a Honey Buzzard with barred wings and tail circling over, maybe a harrier or Goshawk, even rarities such as Black Kite which have become virtually annual between Slapton, Start–Prawle and Bolt Head. Late spring is best for Turtle Dove, with parties of up to 20 in the fields, and many other interesting migrants such as Tawny Pipit, Bee-eater, Common Rosefinch and Great Reed Warbler have turned up. Serin and Woodchat Shrike have been recorded on a number of occasions. Poor visibility and onshore winds can bring large parties of commoner seabirds, with a few divers, waders such as Whimbrel or Bar-tailed Godwit, skuas and Sandwich Tern moving through. Manx Shearwater are present most days, parties sometimes resting on the sea, and hundreds on fine evenings banking low over the waves as they fly up the Channel to feed overnight. The considerably larger Cory's Shearwater from warmer climates has been seen almost annually in late spring or summer, generally single birds. Storm Petrel, often reported by boatmen around Skerries Bank north of Start, may be driven near head-lands by rain or wind.

Other summer birds include breeding Shag, Great Black-backed Gull and a colony of about 30 pairs of Kittiwake at Start tip, while one or two pairs of Lesser Black-backed Gull breed somewhere in the district in most years. Shelduck and Oystercatcher also nest, the former choosing rabbit burrows near Lannacombe Bay. A walk along the coast footpaths through gorse and bracken is likely to produce sightings of cock Stonechat sounding a warning from protruding sprigs, while cock Yellowhammer sing, often from rock outcrops. Density of breeding birds on land, apart from resident specialities, is relatively low, making migrant passerines easy to detect; many common woodland nesters are not normally resident in this exposed area. Late summer brings Sandwich Terns moving westward in twos and threes, often totalling 60 in a morning, while Manx Shearwater are largely replaced by the Balearic race; this Mediterranean race, slightly stouter and lacking the black and white contrast of British birds, is probably as frequent at Prawle as anywhere in Britain, and dozens have appeared on peak days, together with the occasional longer-winged Sooty Shearwater. When major depressional gales start, hundreds of Gannet and other common seabirds pass west, with a variety of shearwaters and skuas; Sooty Shearwater are seen more regularly than elsewhere in Devon, with frequent sightings in rough weather (once over 70 in a day). Skuas have exceeded 100 in a day exceptionally, Great Skua appearing on most watches, with small numbers of Pomarine. Other pelagic species such as petrels may be seen, and scarcer migrants such as Grey Phalarope or Sabine's Gull may beat past. Most seabirds move straight past against the wind, so views are brief. Later in autumn Kittiwake and auks may pass in thousands, often accompanied by Great Skua. Most seabird reports come from Prawle, as it is hard to find a convenient sheltered watchpoint at Start. Recent seasons have featured a number of reports of Black Guillemot, usually singles, often passing on days when few other seabirds were seen, and in varying months; very occasionally a summer-plumaged bird has been seen swimming off a rocky cove.

Early autumn brings peak numbers of migrant passerines, such as warblers, Pied and Spotted Flycatchers and Wheatear, feeding in coves and sheltered farmland. On fine days Yellow Wagtail and Tree Pipit call frequently overhead, with up to 100 of each passing. Warblers and flycatchers often remain several days feeding in bushy hollows and overgrown hedges, occasionally flicking out to snap up a passing insect; often more birds are present than first appears, so wait near suitable cover. Looking stocky among *Phylloscopus* warblers, scarce migrant Icterine and Melodious Warblers, particularly the shorter-winged Melodious, are seen intermittently in most autumns. A seldom-seen visitor is the Corncrake, sadly found dead on roads some autumns. Wryneck and Red-backed Shrike are found most years, usually single individuals.

The small beach in the cove below Prawle Wood, and surrounding rock pools, may hold a few passing waders, including Curlew, Whimbrel and Bar-tailed Godwit in ones and twos; a Pectoral Sandpiper has visited, and a Desert Wheatear was once seen. The hedgerows bordering the cove often hold post-breeding parties of Cirl Bunting.

From mid-autumn, when temperatures start to decline, many diurnal migrants coast overhead. Movements of hundreds of hirundines can attract a Hobby, which might patrol the area for weeks to pick off passing birds. Meadow Pipit also move west in hundreds, stopping to feed on open fields and frequently harassed by dashing Merlin. The Merlin may stay all autumn, attracted later by hundreds of Linnet and Goldfinch which swirl in pre-migration flocks on weed and stubble fields. Grey Wagtail, picked out by hard 'chizz' calls, pass southwest, with up to 30 on some days. Among the pipits, wagtails, Skylark and finches which pour southwest over Prawle on late autumn days, often totalling thousands, calls of northern immigrants such as Brambling and Siskin can often be heard, Serin, picked out by high stuttering calls, small size and pale rump patch, have been detected among feeding finch flocks most years. Peregrine circle over the coast daily, and a passing Hen Harrier or Short-eared Owl might be seen with luck.

As warblers start to thin out, the lively Firecrest is often present on later autumn mornings; usually two or three at favoured locations such as Prawle car park and reserve, and up to 30 in the area on peak days. Blackcap and Chiffchaff, some of the latter apparently of greyish eastern races, still move through, and Ring Ouzel pass in small groups, favouring rocky outcrops. When strong Atlantic gales blow, there is a chance of sighting a vagrant American passerine such as Blackpoll Warbler, Black-and-white Warbler or Red-eyed Vireo; Prawle is the only mainland headland in Devon where these very rare birds have been found. Prawle Wood might hold a few sheltering migrants, or a rarity such as the recent Black-and-white Warbler, in such conditions. Later, one or two scarce eastern birds including Yellow-browed Warbler and Red-breasted Flycatcher are found in the lanes; Black Redstart are frequently seen around coves and coastal buildings, while a few summer visitors put in late appearances. When cold winds bring thousands of Woodpigeon and Starling across from the Continent, there may even be a tiny yellow-rumped Pallas's Warbler hovering to pick insects from the hedges. Late finch movements sometimes include a Lapland Bunting.

Timing

Dawn and dusk are generally productive for passerines; warblers especially are most active in the morning. After a fall of migrants along the cliffs, warblers may continue to work their way up into areas of cover for another hour or two, so check main patches of vegetation again after this. At Start tip, migrants which have dropped in on barren terrain near the lighthouse on cloudy nights should be watched at first light, as they soon move off the promontory; the valley near the farm holds small birds later. In spring diurnal coasting migrants such as hirundines and finches arrive from across the Channel four or five hours after daybreak; raptors take longer and may not make landfall until after midday, or up to late afternoon. Departing diurnal migrants in autumn move southwest out to sea, particularly in light to moderate westerly or southwesterly winds, and movement often finishes by mid-morning. Warblers are most numerous in typical fall conditions; overcast days with cool easterlies can produce rarer species in late autumn. Light southerlies with haze often produce varied migrants, including occasional southern over-shoots. Seawatching is usually worthwhile when the horizon is obscured by mist or drizzle, and when gales occur. In the teeth of a really strong southwesterly wind and rain seabirds do not pass, tending to stay east of Start, moving west past the points when wind or rain slackens. Try also fine high-pressure spring evenings for shearwaters and skuas moving up-Channel. Force 9–10 westerlies in mid-late autumn give best chances of an American vagrant, but little chance for more usual migrants to appear. Short-eared Owl and raptors in late autumn often come on northeasterlies.

To check Prawle car park and Reserve area, avoid sunny midday periods at weekends or main holiday times, when disturbance by the public occurs. In strong easterly winds, the sheltered lowest part of Pigs Nose valley often holds interesting migrants; try also Start valley. Try to avoid seawatching in strong sunlight; glare off the water can be a problem.

Access

From A379 Dartmouth–Kingsbridge road, south of Slapton Ley, both points are reached down narrow lanes.

For Start Point, turn sharp left in Stokenham village, just past Slapton area. Drive to car park at top of Point, passing Start Farm valley on right. Walk back and check roadside trees and field edges for migrants; Cirl Bunting are often present. Go through gate into Start lighthouse access lane beyond car park, turning immediately right down the coastal public footpath. Follow the valley down towards the sea. For the Point tip, walk ½ mile (0.8 km) down the lighthouse lane, looking among boulders for rock-loving birds such as Black Redstart at correct seasons. Kestrel and Raven are usual overhead. The lighthouse compound is open only in daytime public visiting hours. Try a seawatch, or dawn migrant search, from the wall by the compound. Walk up over the ridge to see nesting seabirds. Recent sightings at Start have included Subalpine Warbler, Richard's Pipit and Red Kite; more rare migrants might well turn up.

Some energetic watchers do the Start–Prawle walk by coastal path, with spectacular scenery, rock-pool waders, scattered migrants and Cirl Bunting en route, but most migrants occur near the headlands.

For Prawle Point, from A379, turn off at Frogmore or Chillington down minor roads to East Prawle village. Approaching the village, the duck-pond and thick bushes lie to the right. For the Point, continue into the village, past the green, and keep right down 'no through road' to National Trust car park at the bottom. *Car Park and Reserve:* check surrounding bushes very thoroughly; many species occur here, the easiest spot to find warblers, Firecrest and flycatchers. Most observers base themselves here and check again at intervals. Also look overhead for diurnal migrants moving towards the Point. The Reserve is open only to DBWPS members; others may view from the gateway area.

Lower fields: walk down from Prawle car park and turn left. Walk east along coast path. Check beach for waders, and gullies for sheltering migrants. Look in scrub around overgrown crags and bunkers on left for warblers and Cirl Bunting. Little Owls or raptors may use crags as vantage points.

Prawle wood: continue east around corner into next cove, checking for waders sheltering on the beach. Walk up to wood edge, a very sheltered area for warblers and Cirl Bunting. Watch the edges; the interior is dense and often birdless. This may be a productive area for sheltering migrants after a strong westerly gale.

Top fields: from the wood turn left, back up to the lane. Walk back to the Point past open fields with overgrown stone hedges. Look in fields for dove flocks and other seed-eaters. Raptors may pass over. In windy weather, Redstart and other migrants shelter behind stone walls; Little Owl also sit on them.

Top track (Ash Lane): at the first corner of the lane below the village, a track branches off right past a large house. Bushes along right of the track are sheltered from northeast winds and often hold warblers; this track leads eventually to Pigs Nose valley.

Point and coastguard cottages: from car park, walk down towards the sea and turn right uphill past Coastguard cottage gardens. Warblers may shelter here and Black Redstart sit on buildings. Also try a cliff gully just before the headland for sheltering birds. Cross stile onto heath top and check for pipits, Wheatear and maybe Hoopoe. Daytime migrants pass low overhead here on autumn mornings. *Sea watch:* from near the memorial seat halfway down the right flank of the Point, or shelter under rocks and in nearby gullies if it rains. (Alternative in bad weather; instead of coming up onto top of Point, follow edge of cliff gully before headland, crossing stile beside gully then following path out to grass slope in the immediate lee of the Point.)

West cliffs: from the heath, follow the scenic coastal footpath west to Gammon Head and Pigs Nose valley. Good for small migrants in strong easterly winds, Raven and maybe raptors. Also Grey Seal and spring flowers.

Aerodrome fields and Pigs Nose valley walk: at top end of East Prawle village, take small lane between village corner and duck-pond, turning right if approaching from the north. After 100 m, scan fields either side for plover flocks, finches and buntings. Stop after another 200 m near a sharp bend. Park on the right-hand side grass verge. Walk down the tree-lined public footpath towards Moorsands Cove, watching for warblers in the trees and possibly raptors passing over. Thickets near the stream can hold numerous warblers but need patient observation.

Calendar
Resident: Shag, Sparrowhawk, Buzzard, Oystercatcher, Great Black-backed Gull, Stock Dove, Little Owl, Green Woodpecker, Rock Pipit, Stonechat, possibly Corn Bunting, Cirl Bunting, Reed Bunting, maybe Tree Sparrow, Raven.

December–February: Divers (mostly Great Northern), Eider (irregular), Common Scoter; offshore movements of Gannet, gulls, Kittiwake, auks. Residents flocking on land, Peregrine, Grey and sometimes Golden Plovers, Turnstone, Purple Sandpiper, Curlew, maybe Chiffchaff, Firecrest or Black Redstart, lark and finch flocks, Twite rarely, occasional hard-weather influxes.

March–May: Chiffchaff, Goldcrest and Firecrest, Wheatear, Black Redstart arrival from mid-March, most Firecrest and Black Redstart passing by April, occasional Hoopoe; chance of migrant raptors from late March, but especially April–May including rarer species, Hobby late April–May; wide range of passerines peaking late April–early May; Manx Shearwater and Fulmar commonest May, Storm Petrel and Puffin possible May; diver migrants of all three species, Eider, Common Scoter, Red-breasted Merganser, Whimbrel, Bar-tailed Godwit, a few Great, Arctic or Pomarine Skuas, Sandwich Tern, all mostly late April–May although odd terns from late March; Turtle Dove (May), possibly Serin, maybe Woodchat Shrike or other rarities.

June–July: feeding parties of seabirds, Manx Shearwater, maybe Cory's, occasional Storm Petrel, Gannet, Fulmar, breeding Shag, Kittiwake (Start), occasional late southern overshoots (June), breeding specialities; Shelduck; from mid July, Balearic and maybe Sooty Shearwaters, a few waders, Sandwich Tern.

August–November: seabirds moving throughout; Balearic Shearwaters mostly August–September, Sooty peak mid–late September; odd Arctic and Great Skuas August but most September–mid-October, some Pomarine; a few terns to mid-October. Yellow Wagtail, Tree Pipit, warblers, flycatchers, Wheatear, Whinchat, Redstart peak late August–September; occasional petrels, Grey Phalarope possible mid-September–October; chance of larger raptors September, from late September usually Peregrine and Merlin to November, Hobby to mid October; Firecrest (late September–early November), coasting hirundines, pipits, wagtails, (late September–October), possibly Yellow-browed and other scarce warblers or Red-breasted Flycatcher late September–early November, with late Melodious or Icterine to mid October; lark and finch passage October–November, including scarcer species. Occasional Hen Harrier and Short-eared Owl; Black Redstart arrivals and winter thrushes (late October–November), chance of Pallas's Warbler especially early November, large pigeon and Starling flocks, divers, ducks, seabird passage including many auks, odd late Swallow and summer visitors through November.

12A ADDITIONAL SITE: BOLT HEAD TO BOLT TAIL INCLUDING SOAR AREA

OS ref: SX 7037
OS map: sheet 202

Habitat

On the western side of Kingsbridge estuary mouth (near Salcombe), opposite distant Prawle Point, lies this 5-mile (8 km) -long rugged stretch of coast, extending from Sharpitor west to Bolberry Down. High cliffs owned by the National Trust form a plateau 130 metres above sea level especially between Bolt Head and Bolt Tail, giving spectacular coast views. In the centre of the area, Soar Mill Valley cuts down through the high cliffs to form relatively sheltered Soar Mill Cove.

Around Soar Mill Valley are rocky escarpments, partially clothed with bushes and bracken, while small trees are scattered throughout. A brook runs down the lower part of the valley, and in the wettest part there is a tiny reed-bed, plus a stand of willows. Other parts of the area offer less cover, being rough sheep pasture or dense bracken. Located near Bolt Head and East Soar is a narrow belt of level, tightly sheep-grazed pasture, the Warren. Running parallel and adjacent to the clifftop, it extends for about 1 mile (1.6 km) before reaching the edge of steep-sided Soar Mill Cove. A National Trust-owned farm allows a network of public paths throughout Soar district, including the Warren, also taking in arable fields, and a small farm pool at the head of craggy Starehole Valley. Through this valley flows a small brook with further bracken, trees and bushes scattered throughout. The National Trust gardens at Sharpitor (Overbecks) have sheltering trees, fringed by hedges.

Species

The area's resident speciality is the Cirl Bunting. Two or three pairs breed here, while parties of ten or more can be seen outside the breeding season, often among 80 or so Yellowhammer. One or two Little Owl can often be seen around farm buildings.

Birdwatchers chiefly visit the area searching for migrants, in the main the same species which occur at nearby Start and Prawle, and are seen at the same times, in the same conditions. This venue, however, often produces larger numbers of those same species.

Wheatear are not only among the first spring migrants, but a pair or two may breed. In autumn especially, up to 100 in a day is not unusual, and recently over 500 were seen; often the flocks contain examples of the larger Greenland form. The Warren area is particularly favoured by this and other open-ground species, such as wagtails and pipits. Other migrants which may also breed include Grasshopper and Sedge Warblers (two or three pairs of each), with higher numbers of Blackcap, Whitethroat, Willow Warbler and Chiffchaff. In spring normally migrants are less consistently present, the staying time much shorter, than in autumn. Frequently high numbers are confined to early mornings; even so, good numbers can occur. Apart from expected commoner passerine migrants, less common species have been seen; Hoopoe are regularly recorded in the area. Along the cliffs Kestrel, Fulmar, Stock Dove and Raven breed.

From Bolt Tail you can look into Thurlestone Bay, from which moving seabirds pass the headland. Little seawatching takes place here, which may prove a serious omission; in light southerly winds with poor visibility, terns, skuas and Manx Shearwater, for example, pass in good numbers in both seasons; similarly try from Bolt Head.

In autumn, both valley and clifftops have provided high numbers of diurnal migrants moving along the coast or flying out to sea. Most often numerous are Meadow Pipit, Yellow Wagtail and, later, Chaffinch and Linnet. Among later finch movements Brambling, Siskin and sometimes Redpoll are recorded in smaller numbers. From mid-autumn, high numbers of migrant Goldcrest use Soar, peak numbers exceeding 100 (good numbers pass through in spring, too). Brighter Firecrest are annual visitors, with ten or more sometimes occurring together. Black Redstart, always later arriving than Common, sometimes number over ten. They favour perching on rooftops and farm buildings, including houses and masts at Bolberry Down. Migrant Robin can also easily exceed 100. Ring Ouzel often fly from deep cover, giving harsh 'chack' calls; ten are not unusual, recently 46 were counted. This district is South Devon's best site to look for them on migration.

Scarcer migrants occur regularly, such as Red-breasted Flycatcher, Red-backed Shrike, Melodious and Icterine Warblers. During earlier autumn, one or two Wryneck are anticipated, now recorded annually here. Several Dotterel have favoured the short turf of the Warren. Hen Harrier, Peregrine, Merlin and Short-eared Owl are likely but brief visitors in mid-autumn. The area's outstanding rarities have included Black Kite, Alpine Swift, Pallas's and Bonelli's Warbler, while Red-footed Falcon have visited in both spring and autumn. The few regular watchers patiently await the arrival of the first American rarity here!

Timing
Much as for Start/Prawle area; refer to that entry.

Access
From A381 at Malborough, between Kingsbridge and Salcombe, take the Bolberry road for Bolt Tail, and continue through the village, following signs to headland car park. Public footpaths extend along the clifftop from Bolt Tail to Bolt Head at the eastern end of the ridge, all under National Trust control. For Soar (sign reads Soar and Bolberry), the same exit is taken from Malborough, following signs to East Soar or Soar Mill Cove along narrow lanes.

You can follow public footpaths from Inner Hope to Bolberry (interesting migrants can be seen from this path around Hope Cove; a small wood contains a large Rookery). Car parking facilities are offered by Soar Mill Hotel. A public footpath runs through Soar Mill Valley to the tiny cove. Paths through high, steep grassy slopes near the cove connect the valley to Bolberry Down above, and eastwards towards Bolt Head, via the Warren. From the large car park at East Soar, public footpaths lead out to the Warren area, or towards and through the National Trust-owned farm, where further signs show paths leading to Sharpitor and Starehole. Parts of this site have only recently become accessible for the public, thus increasing the watching area.

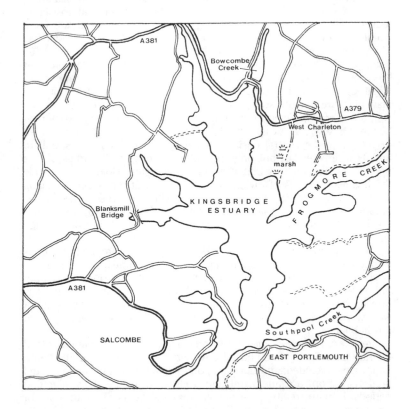

Habitat

This large South Devon estuary extends from Salcombe at the mouth to Kingsbridge town at the head. Several large, sheltered creeks extend up to a mile (1.6 km) on either side. The central basin of the estuary, over 1 mile (1.6 km) wide in places, is about 2 miles (3.2 km) long. The waterways are flanked by farmland or houses; this, together with its shape and poor access points, makes easy checking impossible. The estuary is muddy rather than sandy, with weed-covered rocks bordering in places. Some parts are shot over (except on Sundays) during winter. Adjacent to the northeastern side of the basin lies West Charleton Marsh, a small area of brackish marshy land, set in a large low-lying field separated from the estuary by a seawall. A drainage ditch flows through into the estuary. On high tides seawater can flow back up the ditch, overflowing onto this very low-lying area, killing off the grass and creating shallow muddy pools. There is a very small stand of *Phragmites* reeds.

Species

Because of access difficulties, this estuary is best known for bigger, more easily seen species, especially grebes, ducks and larger waders. This makes it attractive chiefly in winter, unlike most estuaries where passing waders are seen. An unusual feature is the number of sea-going waterfowl which appear on this estuary system, which is almost land-locked, with a narrow mouth. Divers, mostly Great Northern, are seen, usually singly, perhaps sheltering from bad conditions at sea; a few divers and grebes may occur near the estuary mouth, where up to 100 Shag gather. On the creeks the most numerous grebe is Little, with over 20 commonplace, peaking in mid to late winter. An annual scattering of Great Crested occurs, with ten or more not unusual; three or four Slavonian are usually seen, and one or two Black-necked. Ducks are well represented, Wigeon most numerous with an average peak of over 800 in the New Year, when Shelduck reach about 200; most ducks feed in a mass in the central basin. Other dabbling ducks such as Mallard and Teal are regular, but only in double figures; small parties of less regular species such as Pintail might be expected. Goldeneye provide the highest numbers of diving ducks, up to 50 at times but averaging about half this, mostly females, perhaps with only one or two males among them. Red-breasted Merganser average about 15, sometimes reaching 25; there are proportionately more males of this slim-bodied sawbill.

An interesting assortment of further diving ducks, in small numbers throughout the winter period, again includes unexpected species. Pochard, Tufted, Scaup and Goosander might be found and after prolonged rough seas, Eider, Long-tailed Duck and Common Scoter may turn up inside the estuary, even up narrow muddy creeks, and stay for weeks. Velvet Scoter and twice the American Surf Scoter, have visited this habitat.

Grey Heron breed in adjacent woods, and there are spring records of the rare Little Egret, which has also wintered. Other visitors of the heron family have included a number of Spoonbill sweeping the shallows, and brief visits from a Cattle Egret and a Great White Egret at migration periods. In hard weather, geese will graze the fields of winter corn or grass pastures, where human disturbance is minimal; Brent and White-front are most often recorded. Apart from common resident raptors, a Peregrine might appear overhead outside the breeding season, perhaps attracted by flocks of up to 1,000 Golden Plover which may mass on the central estuary, also feeding in nearby fields. Very hard weather causes plover numbers to rise dramatically. Up to a couple of hundred Oyster-catcher and over 400 Dunlin frequent the mudflats; Curlew are generally conspicuous, but numbers are not usually over 150. Small numbers of commoner estuary waders are recorded annually, as passage migrants or winterers. Quiet areas in sheltered creeks regularly produce one or two wintering Spotted Redshank, Greenshank and Common Sandpiper. These same areas are favoured by Kingfisher.

West Charleton Marsh does not have a large bird population, but from time to time attracts those waders which prefer marshy rather than estuarine habitat, such as Ruff. With more regular watching in recent years, however, occurrences of Little Ringed Plover, a scarce wader throughout our region at any season, have been annual, at least two or three passage birds being seen each spring and autumn. Other interesting waders use the marsh intermittently, including Wood and Green

Sandpipers, and Little Stint. A Black-winged Stilt has visited the marsh. A few duck such as Teal are attracted; Water Pipit often visit, usually in early spring, sometimes four or five together, possibly attired in subtle toned pink summer plumage.

The estuary is situated in the midst of the Cirl Bunting's stronghold; thickets and hedgerows around the estuary fringes are home to this decreasing species.

Timing

To watch waders on the estuary, the tide must be at least partly out. An incoming tide pushes them towards observation points near Kingsbridge. An ebbing tide allows waders to alight on freshly exposed mud in the same areas, enabling you to watch them; at low tide they may be too distant. A neap tide facilitates watching, as the area of exposed mud is less. With scattered high-water roosting areas, however, only a portion of waders present will actually behave in this way. High tides may induce some waders to leave the estuary in favour of the marsh. When the tide is fully out, there still remains a substantial main channel stream, used by divers, grebes and diving ducks, although they may drift downstream with the tide.

Any daylight hours will suffice for winter visits to the estuary, but the marsh is open to much disturbance especially from dog walkers; very early mornings or evenings might prove quieter. During or after prolonged periods of gales and high seas, more sea species may shelter. When severe winter weather is worse in other regions of Britain, and in the 'Low Countries', many birds arrive here seeking milder conditions. Rarer herons and other unusual visitors can be looked for in spring southerly winds.

There is much disturbance from people and boats on the estuary in summer.

Access

A379 runs alongside the estuary adjacent to the town, and crosses Bowcombe Creek by a narrow stone bridge. This same road later, going east towards Slapton, passes through West Charleton village and skirts the tip of Frogmore Creek. To check this side of the estuary you can start in the town, although little apart from commoner gulls and a few Redshank and Dunlin can be expected here. Bowcombe Creek Road is on the left immediately before crossing the bridge from Kingsbridge. In winter quite a good mix of ducks can be seen at close range, and there may be Blackcap, Chiffchaff or Firecrest in roadside bushes.

Just past the bridge the estuary suddenly widens considerably alongside the main road, but there are no vantage points other than the roadside, where stopping is dangerous. Apart from nearby verges, there are no parking facilities. When the tide is out, one can walk along this side of the estuary for a considerable distance. Take care that the tide is ebbing when setting out; there are low, sandy cliffs in many places bordering the mudflats, and if caught by a rising tide it may not be easy to find a route back up.

For West Charleton Marsh, turn right in the middle of West Charleton village, into very narrow unmade Marsh Lane; past the last house there is limited parking towards the lower end near the sewage plant (be very careful not to block entrances). A public footpath runs through the flat grassy field which contains the marshy land towards the far end. From this path the marsh is easily overlooked. Continuing a short distance along this path brings you to the estuary, another site from which to check it.

Off A379 at Frogmore, take the Southpool road to look at the South-pool Creek area. From this village at the head of the creek, the road then continues to East Portlemouth near the estuary mouth, running along much of the creek's edge *en route*, giving intermittent views. The opposite side of the estuary is reached by A381 from Kingsbridge to Malborough, but access is more difficult still. The best checking point is probably from Blanksmill Creek; walk out along the beach until able to see the main estuary. Only roadside parking is available. Checking the area from Salcombe town is easy, as roads run beside the waterfront; since there is more traffic, fewer birds occur, but divers, grebes, seaducks and terns are seen in small numbers.

Calendar

Resident: Cormorant, Shag, Grey Heron, Shelduck, Oystercatcher; in adjacent country, common raptors, Grey Wagtail, Stonechat, Cirl Bunting, Raven.

December–February: divers, particularly Great Northern; Little, Black-necked, Slavonian and Great Crested Grebes, probably geese (hard weather); ducks can include Teal, Gadwall, Wigeon, Pintail, Shoveler, Pochard, Tufted, Scaup, Eider, Common Scoter, Long-tailed, Goldeneye, Red-breasted Merganser, occasional Goosander. Peregrine, Coot, Golden and Grey Plovers, Turnstone, Dunlin, Common Sandpiper, Spotted Redshank, Greenshank, Bar-tailed Godwit, Kingfisher. Maybe wintering warblers, Firecrest or Black Redstart, maybe Water Pipit (West Charleton Marsh).

March–May: most of the above depart by end March; apart from a few regular migrants such as Whimbrel, little happens. More watching could produce better records. April–May has produced rare herons and could produce wader passage.

West Charleton: Chance of Little Ringed Plover end April–May, with Water Pipit earlier part of season. Possible Ruff.

June–July: breeding species. Heavy human disturbance.

August–November: the estuary is not usually watched until the later part of the season. Better coverage would almost certainly turn up more interesting species among commoner returning waders.

West Charleton: Possible Little Ringed Plover August–September; also Wood or Green Sandpiper, possible Ruff, with duck such as Teal later in season.

Habitat

Situated in a mild and locally drier part of South Devon, three major habitat zones are found in this interesting area: at South Milton Ley, South Huish Water Meadow, and Thurlestone Bay.

South Milton Ley is a DBWPS reserve, comprising over 40 acres (16 ha) mostly of *Phragmites*, the second largest reed-bed in Devon; there is no open standing water. Facing east-west, the reed-bed lies in a shallow

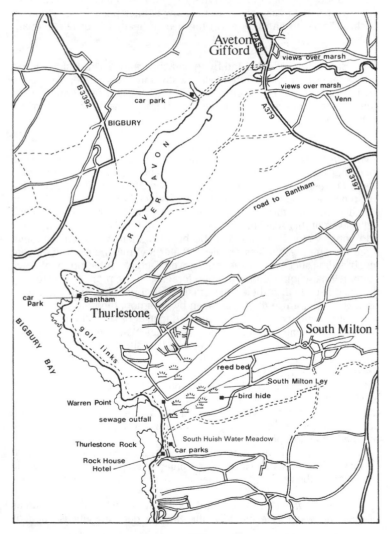

valley, the narrow mouth of the marsh at the west and facing Thurlestone Bay. The ley is regularly flooded by very high tides, especially during winter storms. When sand is piled high over its entrance by wave action, the sea water is not released until either internal water pressure or further storms break open the sand barrier. The highest reaches of the ley remain as fresh water at all times. It is surrounded by arable farmland and, apart from narrow strips of hedgerow and some larger trees at its upper end, supporting cover is minimal. The uncommon Harvest Mouse uses unkempt growth on the side of the ley to build its summer nest.

South Huish Water Meadow is at least 40 acres (16 ha) of flat, easily flooded rough pasture, lying in a shallow open-sided valley among arable farmland. Running east-west and facing the sea, parallel to South Milton Ley which lies over the ridge to the north, it is separated from the bay by about 20 m of low sand dunes, recently reclaimed by the National Trust for use as a car park. The meadow is interspersed with drainage ditches, linked to an outflow on the beach; heavy winter rain partially floods it.

Thurlestone Bay is dominated by remarkably-shaped Thurlestone Rock, which projects from an otherwise mostly sandy shoreline. Two other areas worth checking at certain times are trees and hedgerows in the general area, and the golf course. All summer the beach is a major tourist venue.

Species

South Milton Ley: because reed density is great, many species present, including occasional rarities such as Aquatic Warbler and Bluethroat, are often seen only when removed from a mist net by ringers. Bearded Tit sometimes visit the ley in winter and, especially on calm days, can be watched moving through reed tops giving their distinctive twanging calls. Even at this season, one of the resident Cetti's Warbler may burst into song. Water Rail may also be heard, rather than seen, although Reed Bunting present less problem. Water Rail may be present all year and breeding success was recently proved. During winter, up to five Jack Snipe regularly join Common Snipe foraging in the more open areas of the reed-bed. If disturbed, this smaller, shorter-billed snipe normally rises at a lower angle than that taken by Common, then drops back into cover after a flight of only a few hundred metres or so, without calling.

Through the later spring, Reed and Sedge Warblers sing from reed tops. Cuckoos, which parasitise reed-bed dwellers, are evident during the day, even in the height of summer, as are first-brood fledglings of Reed and Sedge Warblers.

In autumn the reed-bed becomes a major roost site with thousands of Swallow and Starling forming the bulk, joined by wagtails, several hundred Pied and its Continental form, the White Wagtail. Less predictable are Yellow Wagtail, but early autumn normally witnesses several hundreds for short periods.

Rarer raptors have flown over the Ley, including Red Kite, Osprey and Goshawk. Several Marsh Harrier have lingered on their migrations, while hunting over the reed-bed for a day or two, particularly in spring.

South Huish Water Meadow: a hard spell in winter when there are areas of standing water is especially attractive to dabbling ducks such as

Mallard, Teal and Wigeon; numbers vary but 500 Teal and 1,000 grazing Wigeon are not infrequent, and two American Wigeon were recently found with the flock. Geese, usually White-fronted or Brent, sometimes visit in hard weather, and often stay for several weeks. Gulls come to rest, bathe and preen by pools; unusual species should be looked for (see Thurlestone Bay for likely visitors). Migrant Lesser Black-backed Gull often number 100 or so in mid–late winter, and may include individuals of the darker Scandinavian race. Peregrine are frequent, and an occasional Hen Harrier or Merlin stops briefly, attracted by the large numbers of prey.

In spring, returning waders such as Bar-tailed Godwit, seen in small groups of three or four, are often in summer plumage. Similar numbers of Whimbrel may stay several days, although flocks of up to 50 pass over. If water is lying on the meadow in late spring, even if only shallow pools, two or three Garganey may be attracted. Early Wheatear can be looked for from the first spring days. When the meadow dries out, there is little of unusual interest.

Thurlestone Bay: the bay is exposed to westerly winds. A sewer close to the shore off Leysfoot beach, below the golf course, is attractive to gulls: Little, Mediterranean, Sabine's, Glaucous and Iceland have all been seen. Along the winter shoreline, Turnstone and a few Purple Sandpiper are present, while Rock Pipit and Pied and Grey Wagtails feed together among the tidewrack. Grassy cliffs and buildings near Rock House Hotel are favourite haunts of Black Redstart. Divers, mostly Black-throated or Great Northern, or grebes, particularly Slavonian, occur occasionally offshore.

From early spring, Fulmar pass by the bay and the first Sandwich Tern are usually noted, often pausing to fish. Later, substantial numbers of Common Tern, and sometimes flocks of Arctic or Little, may do the same. One or two Black Tern are seen regularly with the passing tern flocks. These prey species often attract a few skuas, generally Arctic. Easterly-biased winds encourage tern flocks to follow the coastline closely, when they may be joined by up-Channel northbound waders such as Whimbrel and Bar-tailed Godwit. Occasionally hundreds of terns and waders move through per day. Stronger easterlies further increase numbers, when a proportion of all migrants may not fly around very exposed Bolt Tail headland, but instead veer inland heading high overland from Thurlestone–perhaps not rejoining the sea again until reaching Lyme Bay?

By late spring, the colony of some five or so pairs of Sand Martin is nesting in the low, sandy cliffside, usually at the entrance of the ley. In autumn unusual waders may use the beach, but are usually frightened off by disturbance; Kentish and Little Ringed Plovers have been seen. Gales can produce unusual gulls off the sewer, especially Little or Mediterranean. Autumn's westerly gales quite often produce Grey Phalarope; sometimes a small group bobs over the waves.

The golf course, although busy, is a specialised habitat used regularly by a few waders, pipits, wagtails and Wheatear, particularly in spring and autumn; a Buff-breasted Sandpiper has been seen. Hedgerows and trees hold small numbers of passerine migrants, as well as Cirl Bunting, and barns in the area may well hold Little Owl. Interesting species turn up in the whole complex around Thurlestone; for example, Hoopoe is recorded nearly every spring, and both Great Reed and Icterine Warblers

Grey Phalaropes

have been found exceptionally late in the year in sheltered vegetation. Spring records have included a Whiskered Tern feeding over a flooded field and a Subalpine Warbler, which has also been recorded here in autumn. Several Wryneck and Woodchat have visited the area, while a Black Stork rested briefly on South Huish Water Meadow.

Timing
Not critical during winter. The sewer operates only on outgoing tides. In spring and autumn an early morning visit is best, partly because there is less disturbance and partly because bird movement is usually greater, or at least more observable, then. East winds are best in spring for tern and wader movements in the bay. Late afternoon and evening checks have been productive, especially for seabirds and waders; at dusk in early autumn, hirundines and wagtails fly in to roost at the South Milton reed-bed. In summer, most breeding birds in the reed-bed are active in early mornings. Try the water meadow when flooded, or containing pools, after rain.

Access
Approaching from the Plymouth side, follow A379 to the top of steep Aveton Gifford hill, then follow Thurlestone signs at the roundabout a few hundred metres after the hilltop. Take the first right off B3197 after the roundabout, down narrow minor roads to the village. Either park beside the road in Thurlestone (often congested at popular times), or preferably drive through it, past the golf course. On the brow of the hill towards South Milton, the road curves left; at this point there is a sharp right turn (about 1 mile (1.6 km) after Thurlestone village). This entrance leads to a car park overlooking the bay, a good place for checking it.

If approaching from Kingsbridge, take A381 towards Salcombe then branch off to Thurlestone (this same road is also initially taken from South Milton or South Huish); either route will bring you to the car park overlooking both water meadow and bay. From here, for South Milton Ley or Thurlestone village and golf course, walk north along the car park; a public footpath opposite public toilets leads across a footbridge over the mouth of the ley. From this point there are good views of the reed-bed. The path continues past a small area of sand dunes before meeting the road which adjoins the first-mentioned Thurlestone car park.

Access into South Milton Ley reserve is normally by permit obtainable from DBWPS. There is no access onto the water meadow, but birds can be seen well from the National Trust car park, especially with a telescope. The perimeter of the golf course has open access, and closely overlooks the sewer.

Calendar

Resident: Sparrowhawk, Buzzard, Water Rail, Little Owl, Rock Pipit, Cetti's Warbler, Stonechat, Cirl Bunting, Reed Bunting, Raven.

December–February: possibly one or two divers, grebes, auks on sea. Geese may visit the water meadow, large numbers of Teal and Wigeon, a few Pintail, Shoveler and Gadwall. Snipe in hundreds, Ruff in ones and twos. Bearded Tit in ley (some years); sheltered places may have wintering Blackcap, Chiffchaff, Firecrest. Hen Harrier, Peregrine, Merlin may hunt over area. Unusual gulls, e.g. Glaucous or Iceland.

March–May: Garganey may visit water meadow from April, also Whimbrel and godwits. Sandwich and other terns from April. Possibly Hoopoe from March, Wheatear from mid-March; Sedge and Reed Warblers in ley from mid-April. Mediterranean Gull may pass through early in period. Commoner migrants may include unusual species.

June–July: Breeding species include Sand Martin; reed bed roost begins to be used by hirundines, wagtails and Starling late July.

August–November: Roost still heavily used to mid-September, when White Wagtail become more evident. Yellow Wagtail often roost in reeds August–early September. Return passage of migrants represented by all main families: raptors, waders, seabirds, passerines, and always species of unusual interest. Grey Phalarope and Snow Bunting irregularly from October, Black Redstarts arrive late October. Mediterranean, Little or other unusual gulls.

15 AVON ESTUARY AND WATER MEADOWS

OS ref: SX 6947
see map 14
OS map: sheet 202

Habitat

A narrow, basically sandy estuary in the South Hams of Devon, flanked by trees, including many oaks. Muddy areas towards the estuary head include saltmarsh. Adjacent to the head of the estuary, water meadows extend inland for about a mile (1.6 km), and are up to half a mile wide (0.8 km). The River Avon meanders through their length. Although potentially extensive, few areas remain permanently marshy.

In winter on high tides and after prolonged heavy rainfall, the entire valley is liable to flood. This situation normally only lasts for a few days at a time, but leaves the soil completely waterlogged with many standing pools throughout winter up to early spring. Along the riverbank grow clumps of alder; other riparian trees such as willows are scattered along this wide shallow valley.

Towards the river mouth (leading out into Bigbury Bay) is the more easily observed part of the estuary at Bantham. The central section of estuary has difficult access, while its narrowness makes it less attractive to many species. Spring comes early to this part of South Devon, and among the hedgerows wild Daffodils and Snowdrops are found. Primroses are plentiful here. Among the sand dunes at Bantham grow Pyramidal Orchids. A wide range of animals lives in the area, from Badgers to the scarce Dormouse.

Species

The sheltered head of the estuary, with most fresh water, attracts typical wintering species found on the region's south coast such as Greenshank, Spotted Redshank and Common Sandpiper, usually in ones and twos. Kingfisher, which have probably only undertaken a local movement from breeding sites further up the Avon, are common in winter, and may be seen resting on a stranded log in midstream, or dashing from tree-lined banks. Cormorant and Grey Heron, like Kingfisher, may be seen up the river as well as the estuary. Up to ten wintering Little Grebe are usually present around the tidal road area, staying in the main channel when the tide is out.

At the head of the open estuary, gulls often congregate to bathe and preen in fresh water discharging from the river. Mostly Black-headed, a couple of hundred may gather, joined in winter by 50 or more Common Gull, and perhaps a Mediterranean Gull.

Waders on the estuary tend to be in small flocks. Ringed Plover in autumn are most numerous, with up to 100, but only a dozen remain through the winter. Oystercatcher and Curlew number about 50, Redshank, Dunlin and Turnstone usually 20 or so. An American rarity was an elegant Lesser Yellowlegs. Duck are mostly Shelduck and Mallard with about 50 of each. Teal vary in number, usually 40 or so, with fewer Wigeon. Mute Swan exceed 50 in winter and several pairs breed, but lack of suitable habitat means success rates are low.

Towards the estuary mouth it widens somewhat, its proximity to the sea encouraging gulls to loaf or shelter, and sea-going birds to wander into its sheltered entrance. Most species occurring around the estuary head will also occur around the mouth, but when small parties of Brent Geese arrive they seem only to favour the mouth, likewise occasional single divers or grebes. Diving ducks tend to remain lower down. Goldeneye are regular in smaller numbers, while both Red-breasted Merganser and Smew have appeared.

Lesser Black-backed Gulls congregate in late winter–early spring, a hundred or more strong. Check through them for examples of the black-backed Scandinavian races (but beware Great Black-backeds mustering flocks sometimes exceeding 500). Later in spring Whimbrel often gather around the mouth or on the beach if not disturbed, before migrating on. The shallow sandy bay itself is less used by interesting seabirds, although certainly worth a look if visiting the general area. Terns can occur in good numbers, and will enter the estuary mouth to fish or rest; among the commoner tern species, scarcer Roseate and Little have been seen.

The water meadows in winter attract various dabbling ducks, irregularly in small numbers, including Pintail and Gadwall. Over 100 Snipe are usually present in harder weather. Water Rail are frequent but impossible to see, their squealing calls betraying their presence. Green Sandpiper have wintered in ones and twos, although half a dozen at a time can pass through in autumn. Difficult to identify, Water Pipit favour this type of habitat, and are seen here from time to time in early spring. When hard weather forces birds to change from their traditional wintering grounds elsewhere, wild geese, perhaps a group of White-fronted, may visit for a short while, or wild swans might be seen, mostly Bewick's, although Whooper have also been recorded. Among the alders a party of Siskin could be feeding on the tiny seeds, or a Barn Owl, still a breeding bird here, might be watched quartering the meadows in early mornings and later afternoons. Most years, by late in the winter period, 'spring' weather arrives sufficiently for the regular ducks to depart, taking with them any other remaining wildfowl, which have included a wintering Blue-winged Teal.

From early spring the first Chiffchaff are already singing among the hazel catkins in the hedgerows. Because the area offers shelter, the first songsters might be overwintering birds. Blackcap may also winter here. The flash of a white rump around the sand dunes heralds the arrival of a true migrant, the Wheatear. Sand Martin, now recovering from a recent crash in numbers caused by severe droughts in their wintering areas, are seen early on, following the river course inland. Exotic-looking Hoopoe sometimes visit from early spring; a check around the dunes may be worthwhile. Just after the first influx of Chiffchaff, Willow Warbler begin to appear, and soon hedgerows are full of their musical descending notes. Above the incessant cawing of Rook, a solitary sonorous croak from a Raven may be heard while doing mid-air rolls over its territory, and Buzzard, thankfully still common in the region, are gliding, mewing and 'skydiving' in display. Soon the first Swallows and House Martins are skimming in over the meadows. There is a chance that a rare heron such as Little Egret may arrive; a Squacco Heron has also been noted. Recently a Marsh Sandpiper, the region's first, touched down briefly on the mudflats.

In summer there is little to be found on the estuary, with persistent disturbance from small boats and water skiers. The heronry midway down the estuary in the woods is active, and a few Mallard and Shelduck breed, along with high numbers of common woodland passerines.

Some waders return early at the start of autumn, and may still wear colourful summer plumage. Hirundine numbers build up steadily in this favourite gathering area. Small flocks of migrant Yellow Wagtail intermingle with up to 100 Pied and White Wagtails. Passing raptors spending a few days hunting have included Hen and Marsh Harriers; further down towards the estuary an Osprey may fish, but none of these raptors is annual.

Timing

The upper part of the estuary cannot be checked until the tide is out, owing to access problems. During autumn and winter any time of day will probably suffice. When the tide has just dropped birds are less likely to be disturbed, and very close views can be obtained, using your car as a hide along the tidal road. Visiting the water meadows at any time of day would suit. Checking during hard weather, especially if worse elsewhere, could well produce more and different birds. When there is little or no standing water, the meadows are unattractive to wading birds. In spring, a visit on a quiet morning to either the water meadows or dune areas in particular, might be successful for newly-arrived migrants.

When the surf is running, surfers may be present all year round, pushing seabirds further out into the bay.

Access

The uppermost part of the estuary can be checked via the narrow tidal road, located off the A379 roundabout adjacent to the Ebb Tide Inn at the southern end of Aveton Gifford village. Several pull-in spots along its length allow close views, ideal for disabled drivers. A small car park is sited at its further end. This road is totally impassable at high tide.

The water meadows are best checked by following either of the minor roads opposite one another at the southern end of the road bridge, or one which starts in the village. On the southern side (towards Kingsbridge) a minor road runs adjacent to the meadows downstream for a few hundred metres; park your car tightly beside the road when checking this area. This same minor road continues to follow the watermeadows (now upstream) across the other side of the main road and is signposted to Venn, running the length of the water meadows, although they are often not in view. An unsignposted steep turning in the middle of Aveton Gifford village (opposite the Post Office) leads to several points where the road overlooks the meadows; about halfway up their length is a good area for ducks and waders.

Public footpaths run either side of the estuary, one starting near the car park area at the bottom of the tidal road, the other on the far side of the road bridge at Bridge End. Although running the full length of the estuary, they lead some way off it in places, affording superb vistas.

Access for the estuary mouth and bay is from the A379 roundabout near the top of steep Aveton Gifford hill south of the river. Take the minor road to Bantham. At Bantham where the road ends, there is ample car parking, except during summer months when the privately-owned car park will be crowded, as the mouth of the estuary, beach and bay all form part of a major tourist area. This lower part of the estuary is easily watched over from the elevated roadside.

Note: A bypass now avoids Aveton Gifford village.

Calendar

Resident: Grey Heron, Shelduck, Mallard, Mute Swan, Sparrowhawk, Buzzard, Kestrel, Moorhen, Stock Dove, Barn Owl, Meadow Pipit, Rock Pipit, Grey Wagtail, Stonechat, Goldcrest, Raven, Reed Bunting. All three woodpecker species.

December–February: Little Grebe, possible Brent or 'grey' geese. Teal, Wigeon, Goldeneye, possible wild swans. Water Rail, Oystercatcher, Ringed Plover, Turnstone, Dunlin, Redshank, possible Greenshank, Spotted Redshank, Green and Common Sandpipers, Curlew, Snipe, possible Mediterranean Gull. Kingfisher, possible Water Pipit and Siskin. Occasional divers, other grebes or sea duck, such as Common Scoter.

March–May: possibly a rarer heron, e.g. Little Egret from mid-April. Whimbrel, hirundines, possible Hoopoe. Commoner migrant passerines include *Phylloscopus* and *Sylvia* warblers, e.g. Chiffchaff, Willow Warbler and Blackcap from April. Lesser Black-backed Gulls gather from end of previous period through this one. Terns, mostly Common and Sandwich, may include scarcer species especially towards end of period.

June–July: breeding species, mostly common woodland passerines.

August–November: Returning waders, possible migrant raptors, e.g. Osprey, possible Mediterranean Gull, Yellow Wagtail. Terns, mostly Sandwich, but occasional other species, all above mostly August–September. Later in period ducks return, first gales may produce sheltering seabirds. Harder winter weather encourages the first less usual species of the season to visit.

15A ADDITIONAL SITE: STOKE POINT AREA

OS ref: SX 5646
OS map: sheet 202

Habitat

A narrow coastal strip of mostly exposed land stretches between two river mouths, the Yealm and Erme, in South Devon. Backed by arable farmland, the greater part of the area is rough sheep-grazed pasture, sloping to a rocky coastline. At Carswell, near the eastern end, cliffs are high and precipitious. The open sward is interspersed with patches of gorse. There is a small wood of mostly chestnut growing at Stoke Point, adjacent to the caravan park, which has further trees and bushes. A tiny, sallow-lined valley runs down from the bushy gardens at Warren Cottage. A relatively level coast footpath runs for virtually the whole length of the area, mostly along its highest points, allowing panoramic views of coastline and open sea.

Species

Up to 30 pairs of Cormorant, and a dozen each of Shag and Fulmar, breed on Blackattery and Carswell cliffs near Battisborough. Several pairs of Shelduck also nest in burrows along the coast. Kestrel are commonly met, perhaps also a passing Peregrine; in autumn a Merlin may chase flocks of larks, pipits or Linnet. A few pairs of Oystercatcher nest on suitable sea-circled rocky outcrops.

At migration seasons a variety of commoner passerines may be seen, such as flycatchers and warblers, chiefly in small numbers. Birds of open country regularly visit, including Meadow Pipit, Skylark, Whinchat and Wheatear. Resident Yellowhammer also like this exposed habitat, but not so Cirl Bunting, which should be sought near either river mouth, and among sheltering trees and hedgerows around Stoke Point or Warren Cottage.

During later autumn especially, the area around Stoke Point attracts more species requiring shelter, funnelling warblers such as Blackcap to feed from elder or blackberries. Thrushes, too, take advantage of this food supply, perhaps a departing Ring Ouzel mingling with incoming Redwings. Foraging flocks of Goldcrest often contain a few Firecrest; recently one such flock with attendant Chiffchaffs produced a Yellow-browed Warbler.

Timing

Birdwatchers will find most interest during migration periods. If the visit is specifically for migrants, as usual favourable weather conditions are required, although Stoke Point itself is sheltered from northerly winds, so may be worth a check then for delayed migrants. Winds from southerly quarters can also produce some interesting seabirds such as Manx Shearwater, terns and skuas passing Stoke Point; misty conditions, even if winds are light, seem more productive than strong westerlies.

Access

Nearest A road is A379 from Plymouth to Kingsbridge, towards Yealmpton from Plymouth. Turn off the main road right, signposted to Kitley and Puslinch. Continue past Noss Mayo village until about ½ mile (0.8 km) past Netton Farm, reaching a National Trust car park, with public access paths to coastal walks. There is no access restriction throughout the total walk of over 5 miles (8 km) from Ferry Wood at Noss Mayo east to Battisborough Cross.

Alternatively, follow signs to Stoke and Holbeton from Noss Mayo, when at a crossroads take a very narrow road signposted to Stoke Beach. There is a small visitors' car park at the entrance of a caravan park. Public footpaths from this car park allow you to walk westwards through the top part of the woods (an important area to check), skirting the more sheltered lower edge of the wood through the caravan park, or eastwards past often productive bramble patches and hedgerows, before either route returns to open land.

16 WEMBURY AND BOVISAND

OS ref: SX 5048
OS map: sheet 201

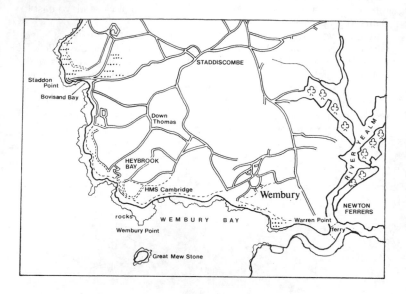

Habitat

This section of the South Devon coast follows from near where Plymouth coast walk (Jennycliff) ends. The Wembury site of the Yealm estuary has quite high cliffs, quickly losing height westward, dropping almost to sea level near Wembury village. From then until Bovisand Bay, cliffs remain mostly only 4–5 m high, rising at Bovisand in one place (for a short distance only) to about 20 m. The low soft-soil-structured cliffs are prone to erosion; recently very high tides combined with storm force winds have caused major damage, requiring the public footpath to be moved several metres inland through much of its length. As the immediate coastal land is low-lying, the vegetation is generally taller. Bushes and trees away from the shoreline are abundant, offering good cover. Among a wide range of commoner butterflies with good populations are Green Hairstreak, Marbled White and Dark Green Fritillary.

The whole coastline is rocky and holds a varied shoreline and rock-pool fauna; it is a marine sanctuary. This walk can offer something of interest all year, with hedgerows, brakes and arable fields forming an intermittent backdrop.

Species

Probably the most interesting area along this walk during autumn and winter is that used by waders at Wembury Point. Owing to high tides and wind motion, large quantities of rotting seaweed are washed ashore, providing rich feeding areas for myriads of tiny animals. Among waders foraging here, Turnstone are found not only during winter, hundreds strong, but unusually as 'residents'; non-breeding individuals attain full summer plumage, numbers dropping to 30 or so in midsummer. During autumn, 30–40 Ringed Plover may be present. Purple Sandpiper are winter regulars, usually about 15 around rocks at the Point. Waders seen occasionally, particularly in autumn, include Little Stint and Curlew Sandpiper, but only ones and twos. Sanderling, Common Sandpiper and Bar-tailed Godwit are regular in slightly larger numbers. Whimbrel pass through in spring and autumn in small groups.

Leaving the immediate shoreline, a third speciality is the resident Cirl Bunting among brakes and hedgerows, or feeding perhaps in the company of Yellowhammer in stubble fields, especially near the Point. A wide variety of migrant birds often arrives when time of year and conditions allow, the habitat encouraging them to linger, common warblers especially. Black Redstart are frequent from later autumn, feeding in sheltered coves, particularly near Bovisand, and also around Wembury church. Less usual later autumn visitors have included a pale sandy Isabelline Shrike on thorn bushes, and a Richard's Pipit. Hoopoe, more likely in spring, have also been recorded. Small numbers of wintering Firecrest are not unusual in the brakes around Wembury Point, where a winter roost of up to 100 Magpie is found. Few interesting species are seen on the sea, although Cormorant, Shag, Fulmar, Shelduck, Herring and Great Black-backed Gulls breed on Great Mew Stone, 1 mile (1.6 km) off the Point. This rock also acts as the major winter night roost for thousands of Herring Gull which scavenge the tips and estuaries of Plymouth, and hundreds of Greater Black-backed which share their routine. Five or six pairs of Fulmar breed on the higher cliffs at Bovisand. Occasional divers, grebes and seaducks visit in ones and twos, very sporadically.

Scarcer visitors to the bay have included Iceland Gull and Black Guillemot.

Cirl Bunting

Timing

A rising tide is required to force waders off rocks and coastline, concentrating them onto the beach at the Point; on morning high tides there is less human disturbance. The naval gunnery school, HMS Cambridge, situated at the Point, causes disturbance to birds unused to firing; a reg flag warns of the danger of approaching within several hundred metres either side (thus interrupting the cliff walk) while firing is in progress. Firing is infrequent, and not undertaken at all at weekends. Disturbance by the public can be a problem on sunny weekend afternoons.

Access

A379 Plymouth–Kingsbridge road is the best starting point. From Plymouth, turn right at Elburton roundabout on the edge of the city (opposite Elburton Inn), through the village, along narrow country lanes. Head towards Staddiscombe for Bovisand and Wembury Point, or direct from Elburton to Wembury village. Continue through village to National Trust car park.

At Bovisand there is a car park, then walk left towards Wembury. At Wembury Point, parking may be more difficult at weekends, as the public road to HMS Cambridge stops at its entrance, with no real parking facilities. Limited parking is allowed along roadside verges. A public footpath opposite the gunnery school entrance leads down through a brake (thicket). This area is often very good for birds. The brakes are best checked either by walking along their edges or by penetrating narrow paths through them. The Green Hairstreak butterfly favours areas near the bottom. The path continues beside a field to the coast path. Views from the roadside are magnificent, the Mew Stone taking your eye seawards.

The main wader area at the Point is viewed very easily from the public footpath which runs adjacent to the cliff edge throughout. Total length of the walk is about 2 miles (3 km); access is unrestricted at any time. Eastward, the coast path leads towards the Yealm estuary.

Strictly no access is allowed on Great Mew Stone without special permission from HMS Cambridge.

Calendar

Resident: Cormorant, Shag, Shelduck, Sparrowhawk, Buzzard, Oyster-catcher, Turnstone, Rock Pipit, Meadow Pipit, Stonechat, Cirl Bunting, Raven.

December–February: Grey Plover, Purple Sandpiper, Curlew, occasional Black Redstart and Brambling.

March–May: March often produces early Chiffchaff and Wheatear, first Sandwich Tern often late March, also Willow Warbler. From April, other passerine migrants, waders, e.g. Whimbrel from mid month, Hoopoe possible.

June–July: Breeding species including Fulmar, Cuckoo, Grasshopper Warbler, Blackcap, Whitethroat, Spotted Flycatcher.

August–November: Possibly a moving Peregrine. Waders, including Ringed Plover, Whimbrel (especially September), Dunlin, Redshank, Sandwich and Common Terns, less frequently other terns, August–September. General passage of departing summer migrants such as warblers, Wheatear, then Black Redstart October–November and early morning coasting movements of Skylark, Chaffinch, Linnet.

17 DARTMOOR AREA: GENERAL INTRODUCTION

OS map: sheet 191/202, or National Park Map

Habitat

Dartmoor is the only major area of high open moor in southern England, with about 400 square miles (1,036 km) of rough grassland, heather, stones, bog, streams and woodland, standing out above surrounding fertile Devon lowlands. Underlying granite shows through character-istically as 'tor' rocks on exposed moorland hilltops. The moor forms a steep-sided plateau from which many rivers and torrents flow, running down through deep scenic wooded valleys around the fringes of the area. The highest hills and main peat bogs, from which most of Devon's rivers originate within a few miles of each other, are on the northern half of the moor, with High Willhays (627 m) and Yes Tor forming a twin high point near Okehampton. The southern moors, south of Princetown, are characteristically 100 m lower than those in the north, with less peat bog and more rough grassland. Gorse grows freely on better-drained slopes, with extensive bracken in summer. Most open ground on the central moor is relatively gently sloping, with broad marshy valleys and rolling hillsides.

Rainfall on high ground averages 80 inches (2,030 mm) per year, substantially higher than in the lowlands, resulting in waterlogged acidic soil. A light covering of snow is common in midwinter, although it often thaws in a day or two as mild depressional air arrives from the sea. Gales are frequently recorded on open hillsides in autumn and winter, combining with cold and damp to give a high 'exposure factor', preventing natural deciduous tree growth over 400 m altitude. A few hawthorn and rowan bushes, often stunted and twisted by winds, grow along sheltered stream banks; the Forestry Commission has well-matured conifer plantations on the centre and southwestern moor. Some rivers have been dammed on the plateau edge to form reservoirs. Parts of the moor, particularly on remoter northern sections, are used as Army firing ranges for a portion of the year.

This whole open area, and much high farmland and valley woods on the flanks, is incorporated into Dartmoor National Park. The moor acts as a centre for relatively undisturbed wildlife, with many Badger setts on better-drained and wooded slopes, while Foxes are met even in high bog zones. Adders are often encountered on sunny hillsides among gorse and bracken in summer. Feral moor ponies are widespread (*note:* do not attract ponies near roadsides as serious accidents can occur), and hardy sheep and beef cattle range over the unfenced hills. Many visitors come in summer and hiking activities have increased in recent seasons; parties now visit even the remotest areas. The National Park authorities arrange guided walks over more accessible sections in summer.

Species

Open moorland holds many small breeding passerines in summer, although the number of species is limited. Skylark and Meadow Pipit sing constantly overhead and Wheatear are seen on many rocky slopes; Stonechat and Whinchat are encountered on gorse and bracken tops.

Raven

Highest moors have very small, scattered numbers of specialised birds such as Red Grouse and Ring Ouzel, with a few breeding waders such as Golden Plover. Steep valley woods on moor fringes hold many breeding summer visitors, including widespread Wood Warbler, and Pied Fly-catcher are becoming firmly established, especially where nestboxes are provided. Moorland conifer plantations have encouraged specialised feeders such as a few Crossbill, Redpoll and Siskin, although the peaty waters of adjacent reservoirs are too barren to attract much birdlife except a few fish-eating Goosander, which have stayed on to breed in small numbers by moorland rivers in recent years. Dipper and Grey Wagtail feed along many swift-flowing streams running off the moor, while Buzzard and Raven sail overhead. Migration times can bring large flocks of Golden Plover, halting on open slopes, and sometimes a passing raptor; even lost seabirds (once a Long-tailed Skua) have turned up. In winter, hardy Red Grouse, occasional crows, Raven or raptors such as Hen Harrier and Merlin may be encountered on open moors. Winter visitors such as Fieldfare and finches tend to feed in less exposed moor valleys and fringes of high farmland.

Of the many sites on Dartmoor, the major birdwatching areas are given below.

17A HAYTOR AND YARNER WOOD

OS ref: SX 7879
OS map: sheet 191

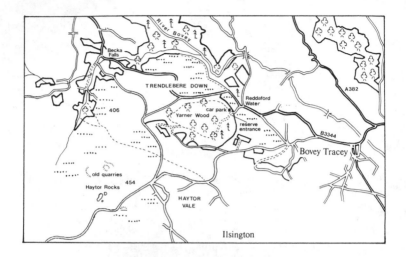

Habitat

At the southeastern edge of Dartmoor, the land rises very steeply from coastal lowlands. The most prominent landmark is Haytor Rocks (459 m), with wide views over South Devon. The down in front of the rocks is heavily eroded by tourists, but behind lie old mining gullies and relatively undistrubed open heath with scattered bushes. On the eastern flank, overlooking Bovey valley, lies Yarner Wood, a mixed woodland National Nature Reserve with many oak trees above a ground covering of bilberries. The wood is particularly rich in wildlife, including butterflies such as Brimstone, Purple and Green Hairstreaks and White Admiral in open glades in summer; massive wood ant nest heaps can be seen beside the paths. Adjacent Trendlebere Down to the north, with bracken and bushes, has unusual butterflies such as Silver-studded Blue, and basking Adders in warm weather. Attractive boulder-strewn Becky Falls lie in the wooded valley below the down.

Species

Yarner is exceptionally rich in summer woodland birds. The area is relatively quiet early and late in the year, but single wintering Woodcock may be found in woodland rides, and sometimes a flock of Golden Plover or a passing Hen Harrier or Merlin may be seen around Haytor. Yarner can provide views of woodland resident birds perhaps more easily in winter than in summer, when leaf cover is thicker, with Lesser Spotted Woodpecker as regular as anywhere in the region. Spring migrant warblers arrive relatively late in these high woods, but the first good migration days may bring in Wheatear or Ring Ouzel on the moor around Haytor. The prominence of this latter viewpoint makes it an attraction to soaring birds and apart from local species, migrant

Pied Flycatcher

raptors such as Goshawk have been seen several times circling north overhead. Recently a Black-winged Stilt fed on a moorland bog by the tor, an extraordinary out-of-place record, and Hoopoe have been seen occasionally on nearby turf slopes.

In late spring Yarner abounds with bird activity, a high density of small passerines singing and feeding overhead in the tree canopy. The trilling song of the Wood Warbler comes from all directions, while other warblers such as Blackcap, Willow and Chiffchaff can also be found. A major attraction is the easily watchable colony of over 40 pairs of Pied Flycatcher which has flourished through provision of nestboxes; the smart black and white males are particularly noticeable in sheltered parts of the wood, looping through the branches to catch tiny insects or singing their short scratchy series of notes from twigs above occupied nestboxes. Males may be polygamous, mated with females from two or three boxes. This species has increased annually in Dartmoor oakwoods in recent years, with hundreds of young produced. Spotted Flycatcher are also present. Redstart, up to 20 pairs, and commoner tits have also made good use of boxes. More open areas at the top and edges of the wood attract a different range of species, with Tree Pipit frequently song flighting from the treetops while larger species such as Buzzard and Raven circle overhead.

The semi-open heathland bordering the wood has its own distinctive birds. In most years a pair or two of Nightjar can be found, although their neighbour, the Grasshopper Warbler, is very variable in numbers from year to year; Stonechat, Whinchat and Tree Pipit are also regular here. Higher up, there could be a pair of Ring Ouzel in old quarry workings behind Haytor, although some old nest sites are now occupied by Blackbirds. Three hundred metres below, characteristic hill-stream birds such as Dipper and Grey Wagtail may be seen close to tourist paths past Becky Falls.

Timing

For migrants arriving at Haytor, fine high-pressure conditions with light easterly or southeasterly winds are needed. Yarner Wood can be watched in most weathers, owing to its sheltered position and thick summer leaf canopy, but sunny mornings are best for watching small birds, as leaf cover cuts down available light on dull days. For Nightjar and Grasshopper Warbler a late dusk visit to Trendlebere on a warm evening should be planned.

Avoid Haytor when heavily congested with tourists on peak summer weekends and holiday periods, unless an early morning start is planned.

Access

From A38 Exeter-Plymouth road, turn north on A382 to Bovey Tracey. Take the first major road left when you reach Bovey Tracey, heading towards Haytor and Widecombe on B3344. After 1 mile (1.6 km), fork left for Haytor, or continue on B-road towards Manaton for Yarner Wood. From this fork directions are as follows:

Haytor: after about 5 miles (8 km), stop in roadside car parks below the tor and walk up to the right; cross to rear of hill for heathland and old quarries.

Yarner: after about 2 miles (3 km), the road dips through Reddaford valley, then climbs sharp right onto the moor. Turn left immediately on the bend, on a tarmac lane into the wood. Pass the warden's cottages and park beyond. There are prepared nature trails and ecology displays (see notice board beside car park).

The wood is wardened full-time by the Nature Conservancy Council. Free access is given to individual visitors, provided that they abide by the instructions posted and keep to the paths. Parties should book with the warden to avoid clashes; May and June weekends are often booked well in advance. Contact the Warden, Yarner Wood NNR, Bovey Tracey, TQ13 9LJ (send s.a.e. for reply), tel. Bovey Tracey 832330.

A minor road through Reddaford, just below the reserve, connects with Haytor route. Trendlebere Down can be watched from roadsides on the moor above the wood entrance, or by taking paths leading out from the wood itself. For Becky Falls continue up Manaton road for another 2 miles (3 km), park and walk down to falls on the right.

Calendar

Resident: Sparrowhawk, Buzzard, Kestrel, woodpeckers including Lesser Spotted, Tawny Owl, Dipper, common woodland passerines, Grey Wagtail, Raven.

December–February: possibly Hen Harrier or Merlin over open land, Golden Plover, Woodcock, feeding parties of small birds.

March–May: occasional migrant raptors, Wheatear and Ring Ouzel (mid March on); from late April many summer visitors, e.g. Cuckoo, Pied and Spotted Flycatchers, warblers including many Wood and probably Grasshopper; Redstart, Stonechat, Whinchat, good numbers of Tree and Meadow Pipits; late May, Nightjar.

June–July: Nightjar active, singing passerines in wood, mainly June, quieter in July when busy feeding young. One or two pairs of Ring Ouzel near Haytor.

August–November: most summer visitors leave in August. Generally quiet period.

17B SOUSSONS AND POSTBRIDGE DISTRICT

OS ref: SX 6780
OS map: sheet 191

Habitat

Near Warren House Inn on the eastern side of the moors, West Webburn River runs south down a sheltered valley overlooked by 450-m heather-covered hillsides and old overgrown tin-mining gullies. Scattered hawthorn bushes and ruins of old settlements stand along the stream banks. The lower valley is occupied by Soussons forestry plantation, and the mine-furrowed hillside is known as Vitifer. Mine gullies extend east across the ridge to Grimspound in the next valley. Unpolluted brook water contains abundant aquatic life in summer, and deep heather on

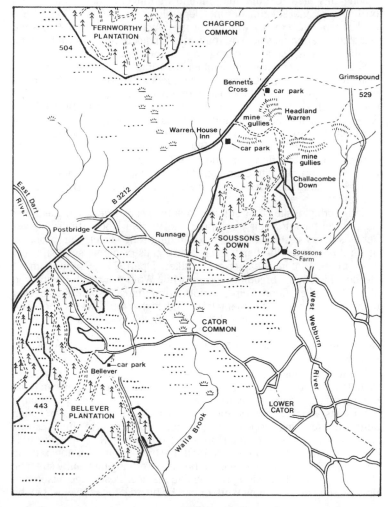

nearby slopes provides cover for wild animals such as Foxes and Stoats.

West of Soussons lies Postbridge, a small community on the upper East Dart River. North and west of the village are boggy riverside pastures, overlooked by high moorland behind. Sundew plants grow in the wet soil and beech and *Salix* trees line the riverbanks. Across the river is the large mature Bellever forestry plantation.

Species

Soussons area is one of the most productive moorland birdwatching sites in winter, valley and plantation acting as a central gathering ground and roost for many species. Woodpigeon, Fieldfare, Redwing and finches pass the night here in large numbers; Sparrowhawk and Merlin often chase roosting flocks as they arrive. Hen Harrier (often ashy-grey males) hunt widely over the hills, and some years they glide to roost in deep heather near the top of the valley; three or four use the valley in some winters, but in others they range further and roost elsewhere, visiting this area to hunt intermittently during the day. Along thorn bushes near the stream, or on telegraph wires, a Great Grey Shrike might be perched alertly waiting for prey. Walking eastward across the Headland Warren hillside, you may flush a pack of Red Grouse from the heather; there is a small breeding population in the district.

Soussons plantation is often quiet on winter days except for a few Goldcrest and Coal Tit. Occasional Woodcock may rise from the side of tracks, or flight out near dusk to feed on open boggy ground, while Snipe can be flushed near the stream. Larger residents such as Buzzard and Raven are usually visible circling overhead. On farmland edges south of the plantation the population is more varied, with flocks of Chaffinch and Brambling often appearing. Bellever can usually be relied on for parties of Crossbill, flying around high treetops above the visitors' car park or nearby rides with characteristic hard 'chip' calls. In winter, Short-eared Owl and other predators sometimes hunt boggy pastures behind Postbridge.

Early spring, while snow still lies in some years, brings Wheatear and Ring Ouzel back to their territories. The Warren House–Vitifer area is perhaps the easiest on Dartmoor for finding Ring Ouzel, with probably half a dozen pairs, the harsh 'tack' alarm calls or piping song showing their presence along heather-clad gullies. Open slopes support many Meadow Pipit in the breeding season, while Whinchat perch on bracken along the valley floor. Snipe perform drumming display flights over rushy pasture below the plantation, and higher up towards the main road a pair of Curlew may be found. Both species, together with Lapwing, also nest in the Dart valley pastures above Postbridge, and Grey Heron, Dipper and Grey Wagtail can be seen along the Dart river; a pair or two of herons often nest nearby, an unusually high site.

Migrants passing up Soussons valley in later spring have sometimes included a raptor such as Montagu's Harrier. A slender Hobby can quite often be seen circling above the heather slopes on a warm day, hunting for insects which it plucks and eats on the wing. Cuckoos are often abundant, scouring slopes for pipit nests to parasitise. In Soussons wood clearings Redstart occur in small numbers, while metallic trills overhead draw attention to Redpoll nesting in fir tree tops; these diminutive finches fly out to feed in bushes overhanging nearby streams. Redstart are also likely along riverbank trees near Postbridge, where the rippling song of the Willow Warbler can be heard. Stock Dove nest in the

Male Ring Ouzel

rocky areas and old mines, and in some years Siskin, increasing in Dartmoor woods, breed in Bellever.

Late summer sees parties of young birds foraging along Soussons valley, while occasional post-breeding flocks of Crossbill from Bellever visit the taller trees. When most other species have departed, Ring Ouzel may still be feeding on rowan berries beside the stream; by the time frost returns to open slopes, Hen Harrier are being seen in the valley again.

Timing

On fine days, most winter roost species spread widely to feed. Although a Great Grey Shrike might be present at any time (perhaps moving up the hillside telephone wires if disturbed), most birdwatchers concentrate on afternoons to see birds gathering in Soussons valley before roosting. Hen Harrier might be seen over the valley or adjacent slopes and farmland, at any time of day. If roosting in the valley, they tend to hunt the area above the plantation in the last two hours' light. In the last hour before nightfall, especially on frosty evenings, pigeons, thrushes, and other mass-roost species fly to the south end of the plantation behind Soussons Farm; at this time Woodcock may fly out. Short-eared Owl, erratically present some years of high rodent population, are most likely to hunt near Postbridge in the afternoon. Breeding waders call and display over territory in early mornings, also the best time for songbirds. Hobbies are most likely feeding over the hillsides in later spring on dry fine days.

On fine weekends and at the peak summer season, there is often disturbance by walkers over all the Soussons–Vitifer area.

Access

B3212 Moretonhampstead–Postbridge road crosses the head of West Webburn valley above Soussons. Birdwatchers seeking Hen Harrier often park by Bennett's Cross (ancient stone monument), in the dip immediately east of Warren House Inn, for pre-dusk views down the valley without needing to walk. To cover the valley and Vitifer gullies, walk down across the moor from here, or down the gravel track near the Inn. Where telephone wires cross the stream halfway along the valley is a good starting point to check for a shrike if about. If energetic, follow the wires east across the ridge for grouse, or in summer for Stock Dove and Ring Ouzel; alternatively, continue to Soussons plantation and explore clearings. If Ring Ouzel have not been seen, try the hillside in front of the Inn when returning. For the lower end of the plantation, continue west towards Postbridge by road, turning very sharply left just before the village; this minor road follows the plantation side. At the minor crossroads near Soussons Farm, turn left to watch over boggy ground to the wood edge.

At Postbridge, cross the river on B3212 westward and park near road for views right over boggy pastures. There are footpaths along riverbanks south past the stone clapper bridge. To reach Bellever, take the sign-posted lane left adjacent to the plantation, following this for 1 mile (1.6 km) to the car park; park under trees and wait nearby for Crossbill calling.

Calendar

Resident: Grey Heron, Sparrowhawk, Buzzard, Kestrel, Red Grouse, Stock Dove, Grey Wagtail, Goldcrest, Coal Tit, Dipper, Crossbill.

December–February: Hen Harrier, Merlin, Woodcock, Snipe, perhaps Short-eared Owl (Postbridge); roosting Woodpigeon, Fieldfare, Red-wing, Starling (some years), finches including Brambling.

March–May: most winter visitors leave by mid-March, Great Grey Shrike may stay to mid-April. Breeding Lapwing, Snipe and Curlew arrive. Wheatear and Ring Ouzel by end March. Cuckoo, Whinchat and Redstart late April. Redpoll active in May, possibly Siskin (Bellever). Occasional migrant raptors late April–May, Hobby likely.

June–July: breeding residents and summer visitors as above, family parties in July.

August–November: summer migrants move out during August. A few Wheatear and Ring Ouzel to October. Passing Hen Harrier, Merlin, sometimes Peregrine from October, winterers become established from late November.

17C ADDITIONAL SITE: FERNWORTHY RESERVOIR AND PLANTATION

OS ref: SX 6684
OS map: sheet 191

Habitat

This reservoir is adjacent to high moors on the eastern side of Dartmoor; to the west and northwest behind the reservoir lies some of the highest peat bog. The 77–acre (31–ha) reservoir is typical of the region's moorland waters, with brown peaty acidic water which sustains limited flora and fauna including, consequently, limited birds. The upper end, furthest from the dam, is fairly shallow, but still lacks muddy margins. A large forestry plantation (mostly spruce) of mature age surrounds much of the lake; the trees are now being felled in places and large clearings created in the centre of the wood, which are replanted with young trees a metre or less high. Within the afforested area, near the lake, is a small area of deciduous trees, mainly beech. From the dam end, views are panoramic, as sloping moorland gives way to farmland, towards the town of Chagford.

Species

The most numerous waterbird using the reservoir regularly in winter is Teal, with up to 30–40 often present around the boggy sides furthest from the dam, where also a dozen or so Mallard usually reside. Tufted Duck usually number fewer; Goosander visit in ones and twos. Cormorant call in to feed, as do Grey Heron. Small numbers of Common Gull join flocks of Black-headed Gull. During winter small flocks of Siskin and Crossbill may be seen, often first heard calling in the high conifer tops, in many parts of the plantation; both species have bred, their numbers depending on the amount of cone crop available for feeding. Redpoll sometimes join the winter flocks and probably also breed. The 'buzzing' calls of a few pairs of Willow Tit might, with luck, be heard.

Migration does not usually bring many passing visitors, but an Osprey has occasionally called in to fish in spring or autumn, when low water levels might tempt Common Sandpiper or a Greenshank to feed. Hobbies are occasionally seen overhead. Golden Plover wheel in hundreds over nearby tors at passage periods.

Among the summer breeding migrants, Tree Pipit are noticeable and common. Several pairs of Wood Warbler breed among the beeches, and a few pairs each of Redstart and Spotted Flycatcher nest in suitable habitat. Chiffchaff and Willow Warbler are also plentiful. Wheatear nest on the adjacent moors, where Lapwing may be seen tumbling in display. A noteworthy summer visitor to the clearings in the wood is the Nightjar, at least two pairs of which are usual. Grey Heron have also recently stayed to breed at this unusually high site.

Timing

This site is far less visited by the general public than Burrator Reservoir at any season, permitting an interesting and scenic walk in comparative solitude. The only special timing needed is to watch Nightjar; less than an hour before sunset the first churring will be heard and views may be obtained. Still evenings from late spring to late summer are the times to try.

Access

From A384 at Two Bridges, near Princetown in the centre of the moors, take B3212 eastward until signs show Fernworthy left on minor roads, just before you descend the eastern edge of the moor. Alternatively leave A382 at Moretonhampstead, travelling west on B3212 until signposted minor roads northwards are again found. Car parking areas are provided by the reservoir, which can be seen from the car windows. A wooden bird hide overlooks the top (inlet) end of the reservoir, where a small area of shallow water and marsh is kept as a nature reserve; this facility is provided by DBWPS but there is open access. A logbook of sightings is kept in the hut. From the main car park, walk on to the forestry huts on right-hand side of road, then down through a gate with DBWPS sign.

There are open access paths throughout the plantation area. Try, for instance, parking at the far end of the reservoir perimeter road, then walking left uphill, which will lead you past some of the larger clearings.

17D OKEHAMPTON AREA: HIGH MOORS AROUND CRANMERE, AND OKEMENT VALLEY WOODS

OS ref: SX 5993
OS map: sheet 191

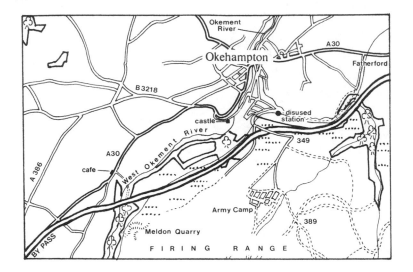

Habitat

The highest part of Dartmoor forms a unique area in southern England. Uninhabited terrain stretches for over 10 miles (16 km) south of Okehampton. Rolling open moorland and peat bogs form a desolate landscape, relieved by a few protruding tors and the white tufted seed heads of bog cotton in summer. The ground, mostly 550–600 m in altitude, is wet and uneven to walk over. Most of Devon's rivers originate here. The 'Pool' itself is a small hollow in the centre, forming a landmark for hikers. A number of shaggy long-horned Highland cattle graze in the shelter of peat banks. On the edge of the high moor plateau, steep escarpments have rock scree and gorse thickets. The open moor is used as an Army firing range for part of the year. Foxes are often encountered in early mornings. Common Lizards and snakes inhabit drier areas.

At the foot of the northern escarpment, the East and West Okement Rivers flow close past Okehampton, through a deep, sheltered valley with oak woods, and carpets of Bluebells in spring.

Species

Both the high moor and the valley woods are best known for specialised breeding birds in late spring and summer. The desolate winter moorland environment, with frequent heavy rain or snow, supports few species except for hardy Red Grouse, which may shelter along roadside banks by Army-range roads, and a few Raven or Carrion Crow. Migration has been little studied, but large passing groups of Golden Plover wheel over the tors at times, and other open-ground species such as Dotterel, or occasional passage raptors, have been reported. Wheatear and Ring

113

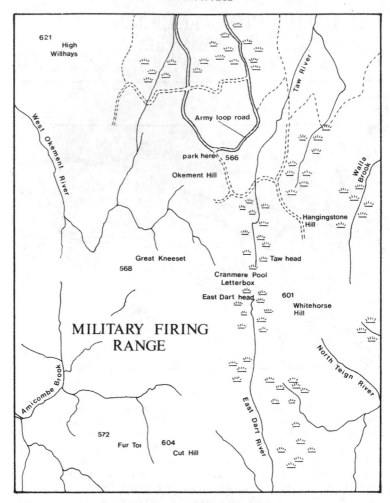

Ouzel arrive early to breed on the high tors, with later Whinchat on gorse thickets lower down near the moor edge, where Redstart breed in stone walls.

In the breeding season, the moors abound with breeding Skylark and Meadow Pipit, sometimes pursued in low, twisting flight by a Merlin; this little raptor formerly bred and single birds still occur from time to time. A Hobby may circle overhead catching insects. Buzzard, Kestrel and Raven patrol the area regularly. The walker is greeted by harsh gobbling calls of breeding grouse as they whirr off low across the slopes; some dozens of pairs breed, widely scattered, and four or five birds may be met in a morning's walk. A handful of pairs of Golden Plover and Dunlin nest each year in extensive bogs around the river sources, this being their southernmost breeding site in Britain. Snipe and Lapwing inhabit rushy valleys a little below the sources, their presence revealed by display flights overhead; although the Lapwing is a fairly widespread breeder, these boggy moorland valleys form the Snipe's main summer home in the region and its distinctive 'chip-per' call is often heard.

On the banks of open running streams, a pair of Common Sandpiper may stay to breed, although this wader, again on the edge of its range, is no longer expected regularly. A Curlew's bubbling song may be heard, and one or two pairs breed on slopes with good heather cover, although the main Dartmoor population is lower down near Postbridge. Dipper and Grey Heron may visit the high streams, but breed at lower altitudes.

Down in Okement woods, a nestbox scheme has encouraged a substantial summer population of the attractive little Pied Flycatcher, with over 50 successful nests in recent seasons, now the largest colony in the region, although some nests are disturbed by Dormice. Other summer migrant songbirds include many Wood Warbler and a scattering of Redstart, while Dipper and Grey Wagtail can be found along the riversides.

Breeding species, apart from a few larger birds, soon abandon the open moors once young have been reared, and summer woodland visitors move back towards the coast. Although high moors are generally quiet at this period, passage birds might be seen, including a wandering Peregrine, moving flocks of Ring Ouzel, or as in spring, waders such as Golden Plover flocks. There is a chance of other strays such as Snow Bunting on open, rocky stretches in late autumn.

Timing

Fine weather is essential to cover the moors properly; accurate weather forecasts should be sought. Do not attempt to walk across the moor in severe winter conditions or fog; every year walkers become ill with exposure (some die), and emergency rescues are needed. Allow sufficient time to reach civilisation before nightfall. Most birds on high ground can be seen at any time of day, but waders are most easily seen in the first three or four hours of daylight when display flights occur. The moor is best avoided on days when large-scale hiking events such as 'Ten Tors' (unfortunately around mid-May) are planned. See also Access section for Army-range restrictions.

Mornings are best for singing Pied Flycatcher and other breeding birds in the valley, which can be fitted in after an early moorland trip.

Access

From Okehampton, which can be reached by turning off the A30 bypass, turn north at traffic lights (left if approaching from Exeter) in the town centre along a minor road signposted 'Dartmoor National Park' and 'Battle Camp'. For the moors, drive up a steep hill, forking right at signposted junction near the church, past the Army camp and through a gate onto the roughly tarmaced military road. (*Note:* Army firing ranges operate some weeks; red flags fly from tors when firing commences. Do not continue beyond the gate before checking. Advance-warning notices are published in local newspapers or at police stations. Do not touch metal objects found on the ranges.) Continue to the farthest point of the 'loop' road at Okement Hill, then explore southward across the bogs. Carry a compass and let someone know where you are going. Try also walking up larger tors and screes for rocky-ground species. Boots and waterproof clothes are needed. The best area to cover for a range of species is between Okement Hill and Fur Tor (south of Cranmere), and around the upper Taw and Dart. A circular walk around these points could be interesting, although very arduous. Try to avoid flushing birds from nest sites. *Note:* severe winter conditions have recently caused considerable damage to the tarmac surface of the moor road; the eastern side of the loop should be avoided. The western side is passable with care. (Turn right at fork in road south of Army camp.)

For woodland species, several access points lead to paths through the East and West Okement valleys. Coming into Okehampton from the east, Fatherford viaduct is a good starting point; turn left down a poorly marked minor road immediately after 'Welcome to Okehampton' sign, opposite Exeter Road Industrial Estate, just before the 40 mph speed limit sign and motel on left. Drive ½ mile (0.8 km) along the narrow lane to the corner where the footpath starts and park carefully on the verge. Footpaths lead both up and down river; by walking right, you can walk through to the access point near the disused railway station (about 1 mile (1.6 km)). If driving up to the high moor, *en route* you can visit either Okement Castle (National Trust propery) on the West Okement, or the East Okement near the old railway station. To reach the castle, start off from Okehampton centre along the Army-camp road, soon turning right with National Trust signposts. Try wooded slopes behind the castle ruins and the woodland edge. For East Okement, continue up the moor access road for ½ mile (0.8 km), turn left along the residential street leading to the disused station and park (unrestricted) before the houses finish on the left. The public path, signposted back to Fatherford viaduct, starts to the left just before the station entry. West Okement woods can also be entered to the west of the town; leave up the main road hill to the west from the town centre, towards Launceston. After 2 miles (3.2 km) you reach Betty Cottles Cafe and a petrol station; turn left on a minor road to Meldon Quarry and Bluebell Wood opposite the cafe. After ½ mile (0.8 km), take signposted paths to the right into the woods, before the lane crosses the new bypass.

Calendar

Resident: Red Grouse, Carrion Crow, Raven on moors, Buzzard and Kestrel range over area. Dipper, Grey Wagtail and common woodland passerines in valley.

December–February: generally very quiet. Possibly Woodcock in woods or a passing raptor on moors.

March–May: Wheatear and Ring Ouzel return from late March. Most other migrants from late April – Whinchat and breeding waders (Lapwing, Golden Plover, Dunlin, maybe Curlew, possible Common Sandpiper, Snipe), passage plovers and maybe Dotterel (latter most likely May), passing Merlin or Hobby; in valley woods, Pied Flycatcher, Wood and other warblers; Redstart arrive same period.

June–July: breeding species as arrived above, active through June but most finished song and display by July when young being fed and post-breeding flocks start to form.

August–November: summer breeding visitors departing. Possibly passing Peregrine or other raptors, e.g. Hen Harrier and Merlin (mostly October on). Chance of Snow Bunting near end. Passing plover flocks again.

17E ADDITIONAL SITE: TAVY CLEAVE, WEST DARTMOOR

OS ref: SX 5583
OS map: sheet 191

Habitat

The boulder-strewn River Tavy runs down through a picturesque gorge off the high moor plateau. The valley floor contains scattered gorse and hawthorn bushes, while higher slopes are covered by rock screes from tors above, with isolated rowan trees. An artificial leat carries drinking water from the Tavy across the lower moor slopes to nearby villages; Brown Trout can often be seen at close range in the clear water. Farmland with rough pasture, surrounded by high stone walls and small trees, lies adjacent to the open moor, Willsworthy firing range used by the Army lies to the north.

Species

This is a convenient area to sample typical moorland species in pleasant surroundings in the breeding season. Farmland fringes hold Redstart, while Wheatear dip off along the valley slopes and Whinchat perch on gorse sprigs. Other summer migrant visitors include Cuckoo and Tree Pipit. The fast-flowing river is a regular haunt of Dipper and Grey Wagtail, while Buzzard and Raven soar over the slopes. Stock Dove nest in small numbers in the valley. Higher valley sides are worth checking for a Ring Ouzel singing, as one or two pairs usually nest among the screes. The higher moor above the valley might harbour an occasional breeding pair of Golden Plover. In autumn, when migrant Golden Plover flocks arrive on open slopes, Ring Ouzel might be found in pre-migration flocks feeding on rowan berries, and raptors occasionally pass over, perhaps a Peregrine or Merlin. There have been reports in some past winters of Red Kite hunting over nearby farmland.

Timing

Fine mornings produce maximum activity, but most breeding species might be seen at any time of day. As usual with moorland sites, those making a long hike should check weather conditions beforehand.

Access

From A386 Plymouth-Okehampton road, north of Tavistock, turn right up minor roads signposted to Peter Tavy and Mary Tavy. From either village continue along narrow lanes up the Tavy valley towards Willsworthy firing range and park near the gate onto the open moor. Walk to the right beside the leat and up into the valley, about 2 miles (3 km).

Note: As usual with firing ranges nearby, watch out for red warning flags and avoid metal objects on the moor. Consult police or local newspapers for Army timetable. Weekends in summer are usually free.

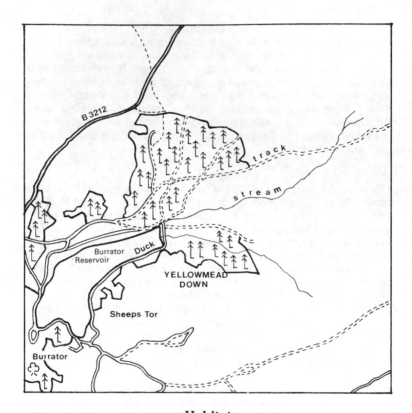

Habitat

Near Yelverton, on the southwestern edge of Dartmoor, this 150–acre (60–ha) reservoir lies in a steep-sided valley, overlooked by scree-covered tors reaching over 300 m altitude. The lower slopes are tree-clad, mostly with Forestry Commission conifers; many trees are now reaching maturity, and large tracts are being felled. Small areas of broadleaf, mostly beech, remain, and many rowan (Mountain Ash) trees are found, with bunches of scarlet fruits in autumn.

None of the Dartmoor reservoirs is very attractive to plant or animal life, being steep-sided and exposed. They lack muddy margins, unless water levels are exceptionally low, and peaty acidic water prevents many plants from growing. Burrator, however, has more varied habitat than other moor reservoirs, and also attracts more public visitors.

Species

Ducks are the main birds found on the lake in winter; this is Dartmoor's best reservoir for ducks, although no other unique specialities occur. Mallard (a few of which breed) and Teal often exceed 50, while Tufted and Pochard remain fairly constant at about 20 each, and Goldeneye visit in twos and threes. Goosander are the most interesting ducks seen regularly. This attractive sawbill has reached over 20 on occasions, although about half that number is more usual. The ratio of males to females has also been much higher than normal recently; often an equal proportion or even a majority of males, conspicuous with pinkish-white sides, occurs. Goosander use the lake as a night roost, flighting in late on winter afternoons from scattered feeding places elsewhere on the moors. Other ducks, including several of the rare American Ring-necked Duck, have visited.

Wild swans might drop in for a short stay, usually in severe weather. Windblown or stray divers or grebes have come, but are very rare. Coots assemble in small groups, and ten or more Grey Heron may line the banks; there is a small heronry at nearby Meavy. Gulls use the reservoir to a greater extent in rough weather, as a sheltered place to rest and preen. All the commoner species visit, but apparently do not roost overnight. Common Gull regularly exceed 100, and sometimes 300 or more are present.

Because the conifers (mostly spruce) are maturing, cones are freely produced. Their seeds are eaten by Crossbill, whose presence is indicated by hard 'chip' calls, and shredded cones littering the ground below. Siskin are also specialised feeders on conifers; their high pitched 'klee' calls help you locate them. Two or three pairs of Siskin now stay to breed. Brambling mix with flocks of Chaffinch foraging among fallen beech mast; on rare occasions Hawfinch join them. Redpoll can be seen in small flocks. Portly Woodcock breaking daytime cover may be an added bonus while waiting for the last Goosander to flight in just before dusk. Dipper are more easily found along the streams in winter, when disturbance is less, sharing the habitat with Grey Wagtail.

When wildfowl depart northward as spring commences, there is normally little to see on the reservoir save for a rare visit from the odd duck, late diver or grebe. Recent seasons have produced summering records of one or two Goosander, however, and on occasion a female has been seen leading a brood of young. This coincides with breeding starting on some of the moorland edge rivers. Apart from this, attention now centres on surrounding woodlands. By mid-spring both Chiffchaff and Willow Warbler are singing, the latter the commonest local warbler. Blackcap and Garden Warbler breed, and up to ten pairs of Wood Warbler inhabit the tall deciduous trees. Pied Flycatcher have increased enormously on Dartmoor in recent summers and a few pairs are now usually present in deciduous woodland here. A population of some 20 pairs of Redstart can be found nesting among dry-stone walls and ruined farm buildings. Cuckoos call, and Tree Pipits song flight from perches on small moorland-fringe trees. These more open areas have held a small population of Nightjar in most seasons. The sparrow-sized, scarce Lesser Spotted Woodpecker may be heard drumming; it is much less easy to see than the commoner Great Spotted or abundant Green Woodpecker.

Summer finds both Sparrowhawk and Buzzard soaring overhead, ever watchful for prey. Family parties of residents such as Coal Tit and Nuthatch may include Siskin and their broods. These roving flocks are soon joined by earlier-breeding summer visitors and their first-brood fledglings. Goldcrest can be abundant, especially if winters have been mild and their stocks have remained high. An irruption of Scandinavian-bred Crossbill may occur, when restless groups arrive.

After a long dry spell in early autumn, the area farthest from the dam may have exposed mud. Very small numbers of waders such as Common and Green Sandpipers may then pass through. Ring Ouzel, moving off the high moor, can be watched feeding on rowan and hawthorn berries. By late autumn, waterfowl are returning.

Timing

Human activity around perimeter roads and verges on fine weekends, even in winter, can be substantial; in late spring and summer, worse still. Fortunately, the vast majority of trippers do not wander far from their cars. The few anglers are not a real disturbance.

In winter, mornings or late afternoons are not only quieter, but there is also a better chance of seeing larger numbers of Goosander.

Nightjar are, as usual, most likely to be noticed when active at dusk.

Access

Leave A386 at Yelverton and take B3212 to Dousland, 1 mile (1.6 km) or so farther. At the village crossroads, follow signs to Burrator, taking a minor road. Roads surround the lake and there are several car-parking and pull-in spots. Permits are required if you wish to enter the reservoir banks; these are obtainable from an office near the dam. There is, however, no need to buy them as the water can be checked from the roadside (at least when leaves are off the trees). Best views are from the road running along the south (Sheeps Tor) side; about halfway along is probably best for Goosander.

Surrounding woods and moorland have open access. Dogs must be kept on leads to prevent them chasing sheep. Tracks at the top end of the lake (farthest from dam) lead off left and right. The right-hand track is probably better. Along this track, among walls and ruined buildings, watch for Redstart. Most other species present in the area can be seen along here.

Calendar

Resident: Grey Heron, Mallard, Sparrowhawk, Buzzard, Kestrel, Barn Owl (a pair may breed), Tawny Owl, Dipper, woodpeckers including a pair of Lesser Spotted, Grey Wagtail, Goldcrest, Coal Tit, Raven, Redpoll, Siskin, Crossbill (some years).

December–February: possible appearance of a diver, grebe or wild swan. Teal, Pochard, Tufted Duck, Goldeneye, Goosander; singles of other ducks, especially in severe weather. Gulls including Common. Brambling.

March–May: by mid-March, most wildfowl have departed except for stragglers or passage birds; Goosander may stay to breed. Maybe a diver or grebe. Cuckoo, House Martin, Tree Pipit, Redstart, Wheatear, Garden Warbler, Blackcap, Wood Warbler, Chiffchaff, Willow Warbler and Spotted Flycatcher arrive to breed, most from late April but Spotted Flycatcher mid-May.

June–July: breeding species; possibly Crossbill influx in July.

August–November: if any exposed mud, waders include Green and Common Sandpipers. September–October, Ring Ouzel. Waterfowl begin to return by end November.

18 PLYMBRIDGE WOOD

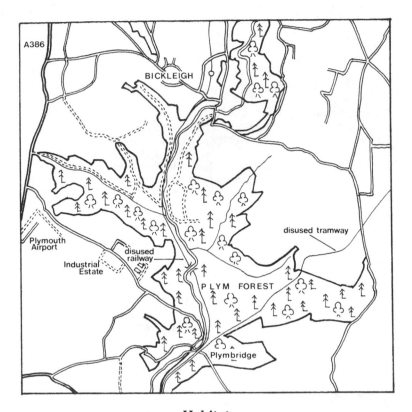

Habitat

On the northern outskirts of Plymouth, this large mixed (mainly broad-leaved) woodland, through which the River Plym flows, is owned by the National Trust. Adjoining the Trust land is a conifer plantation owned by the Forestry Commission. The National Trust's part of the wood, particularly the lower section at Plymbridge, is an extremely popular picnic and recreation area for local residents. The woods, although dense in parts, have open glades and border onto rough meadows. The mixture of trees is great, with good numbers of oak and beech supporting many forms of wildlife. Other fruiting trees, such as chestnut, hazel and rowan are abundant. Open glades with bushy fringes, the river and its banks and damp meadows ensure a range of specialised natural history subjects to study.

Commoner wild animals are present in very good numbers and include those associated with water, such as Water Voles, toads and frogs. Both Grass Snake and Adder are present. Deer are best seen very early in the morning or at dusk. There are several species of bat, and one of the authors has seen 30 species of butterfly here, including Purple Hairstreak, Silver-washed Fritillary and White Admiral.

121

Species

This is a good area to 'learn your birds' as all the commoner passerine families are represented. During winter the so-called 'winter thrushes' can be watched stripping rowan and other berries from trees, or searching among the understorey for food. Woodcock and Snipe may be flushed from wetter areas, and white-rumped Brambling identified among a flock of Chaffinch feeding on fallen beech mast. Among conifers, there is a possibility of wintering Crossbill. Along the river-banks, Redpoll and Siskin swing upside-down on alder trees, while on the river Dipper and Grey Wagtail are commonly seen. The less turbulent stretches are favourite haunts of Kingfisher,which with luck may be seen for more than the usual few seconds of blue and orange blur. Spring brings the return to the wood of less common migrants, such as Garden and Wood Warblers. In summer, especially if an early start is made, breeding species can be watched feeding young, offering a further chance to widen your knowledge. At the end of summer, the phenom-enon of irrupting Crossbill has resulted in flocks of these fascinating and colourful birds frequenting the woods. Autumn provides increasingly less hindered views of resident species, as deciduous trees reveal birds among them.

Dipper

Timing

During summer, all woodland birds become more secretive, as they have nests and families to protect. Early morning is far the most produc-tive time. Later in the day, places where many birds were seen earlier may now appear almost birdless save for the occasional call. Human disturbance can be chronic around the bridge area on fine summer days, but a mile (1.6 km) or so upstream lies a wealth of interesting flora and fauna, relatively free of disturbance.

During winter, there is more or less constant daylight activity by birds, and far less disturbance by humans.

Access

At Estover roundabout, Plymouth (situated near Wrigley company factory), take the narrow, rather steep Plymbridge Road. At the bottom of the hill at the bridge area there is ample parking. Approaching from Plympton, you can pick up Plymbridge Road from either Plymouth Road or Glen Road. Your starting point for the walk will again be the bridge.

From here, follow the woodland path or disused railway track, usually heading north. Length of walk from the bridge to Yelverton Halt is about 4 miles (6½ km).

Calendar

Resident: Sparrowhawk, Buzzard, Kestrel, Stock Dove, Tawny Owl, Lesser Spotted and other woodpeckers, Grey Wagtail, Dipper, Goldcrest, common woodland passerines, Raven.

December–February: Grey Heron, Woodcock, Snipe, Kingfisher, winter thrushes, Brambling, Siskin, Redpoll, possibly Crossbill.

March–May: Late April, first migrant Cuckoo, possibly Tree Pipit; Garden Warbler, Blackcap, Whitethroat, Wood Warbler and Redstart returning.

June–July: possibly Nightjar towards the moors; maybe irrupting Crossbill end July.

August–November: maybe Kingfisher; Redwing and Fieldfare return from October; feeding parties of small passerines (mixed species) move through woods.

19 PLYMOUTH AREA

OS ref: SX 4753
OS map: sheet 201

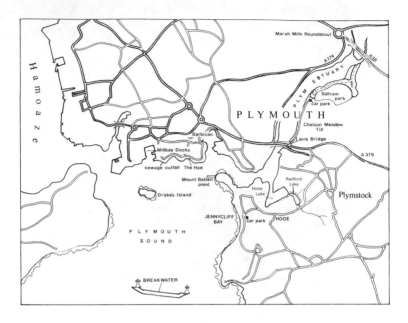

Habitat

Plymouth city lies on the Devon/Cornwall border, on the confluence of four rivers: Lynher, Tamar, Tavy and Plym, all discharging into Plymouth Sound. The city's waterfront has a rocky foreshore, enclosed in a large bay (the Sound), protected from all but roughest seas by a breakwater across the bay mouth; at several points along the waterfront are sewage outfalls. Tiny Drake's Island is situated in the Sound, surrounded by shallowly submerged rocks covered in seaweed. Trawlers unload fish catches at several points, main quay being the Barbican.

On the coastline at the eastern side of the bay, at Jennycliff, rocky cliffs and brakes reach a height of some 90 m. The bay here is sheltered from north and east winds. Nearby Radford Lake is a suburban, Plymouth City-owned brackish lake, in a parkland setting, and located at the head of Hooe Lake, a wide tidal creek leading towards the Plym Estuary on the city's eastern boundary. Fed from one end by a stream, 2½ acre (1 ha) Radford Lake (also known as Radford Pond) is separated from Hooe Lake by a sluiced dam; at higher tides, sea water enters the pond. Hexton woods are adjacent, with Radford woods about 1 mile (1.6 km) away. Jennycliff coastline, bordered by housing, lies about 1 mile (1.6 km) off. No fishing or water sports are allowed on Radford Lake. This enclosed body of water is the only such habitat within the city boundaries capable of producing interesting water birds. Chelson Meadow, the city rubbish tip, is situated adjacent to the Plym estuary. The Tamar and Tavy unite at their mouths, forming extensive mudflats, and are less disturbed than the Plym.

124

Species

The coastal areas produce most of the interesting and rare birds. Every winter, through to early spring, one or two divers and grebes are found in the bay. After prolonged gales or in very harsh icy conditions, numbers and variety often increase as sheltering birds arrive. Up to ten or more divers (mostly Great Northern) and similar numbers of grebes appear. Normally Slavonian is the most regular grebe, with one or two present, but cold-weather influxes are mostly of Great Crested and up to three or four Red-necked Grebes; favourite areas are around Jennycliff and Drake's Island, especially Jennycliff in easterlies and the lee of the island in westerlies. During very mild winters the bay is virtually ignored by these species, but occasional sightings are made of Eider, Common Scoter and Long-tailed Duck, which may stay for weeks.

Severe weather conditions do not really influence the occurrence of uncommon gull species, for which Plymouth has an enviable record. Thousands of gulls gather throughout the area in winter. The presence of a large rubbish tip at Chelson Meadow near the Plym, and the nearby fishing fleet, are added attractions. Plymouth ranks as high as any conurbation in Britain for variety of gull species (in season). During one recent period of only a few weeks, 13 species and four subspecies were present, with a Ross's, Bonaparte's, Ring-billed and Mediterranean Gull standing side by side! Plymouth has recorded 15 species of gull to date. One of the best places to watch them is at the sewer off West Hoe, where they scavenge for edible waste. The fish quays, especially when trawlers are offloading, attract them like magnets. Among their swirling, noisy hordes may be one or two of special interest. Patience and expertise have resulted in many sightings of uncommon, and a few rare, kinds being made. Mediterranean, Little, Iceland and Glaucous Gulls are now seen annually, the two latter mostly between late winter and early spring. Within the last few seasons, expert birders have been finding the once unexpected, exceptionally difficult-to-identify, Ring-billed Gull; these are usually among flocks of migrant Common Gull, from late winter. Other American rarities found have included Franklin's and Kumlien's Gulls.

Iceland Gull and Glaucous Gull – first winter

The Radford and Hooe area can be good for migrant and wintering species, although there are many commoner residents present, including common woodland passerines in the two wooded areas. From autumn to spring are the most productive periods. At Radford Lake small numbers of Little Grebe, Coot, Pochard and Tufted Duck winter, although several Tufted have summered. Other diving species visit irregularly in ones and twos. The pond is unsuitable for most dabbling duck; Mallard feed well on copious scraps and several pairs breed. Ten or more Shelduck winter on Hooe Lake. Moorhen and Mute Swan are resident and breed, while Kingfisher and Grey Wagtail winter. At low tide in winter, several hundred Herring and Black-headed Gulls feed across Hooe Lake's mudflats, joined by smaller numbers of Common Gull. Among the gull flocks, rarer Glaucous and Iceland Gulls have been recorded. More frequent on Radford have been Little Gull, including summer-plumaged spring arrivals. The gulls commute to Radford's fresher water frequently, especially at high tide. Waders are few on the mudflats, but Redshank and Turnstone are regular, with several Dunlin and Curlew. During hard or stormy winter weather, occasional visitors to Hooe Lake may be a diver, scarcer grebes, or seaducks. Radford Lake and its surroundings are quite sheltered, and freshly arrived passerine migrants (especially in early spring) often work through from the exposed coastline, pausing here until able to move on. There could be considerable numbers of hirundines, Chiffchaff, Willow Warbler and Goldcrest gathered here, mixed with lesser numbers of other migrants. A very wide variety has been noted over the years. A recent spring movement brought a Night Heron to the lakeside, while a Woodchat Shrike appeared among a fall of migrant passerines at Jennycliff.

Few waders are able to inhabit the bay's narrow, rocky shoreline. Oystercatcher commonly feed on limpet-strewn rocks, accompanied by Turnstone and a few Purple Sandpiper, and small parties of Whimbrel are brief spring visitors.

Among the bay's first spring migrants are Sandwich Tern, the most numerous tern species here. Terns use the bay in small numbers, pausing to rest and feed on both migrations. Spring sightings of other terns are unpredictable, usually only in ones and twos. On return passage, Sandwich are often first to arrive again, now accompanied by their still semi-dependent juveniles. Common Tern are usually next, Arctic, mostly juveniles, are latest to arrive (as in spring); numbers are always higher than in spring. Black Tern are seen in ones and twos, while Roseate and Little are very irregular.

The Plym estuary, open to frequent disturbance, does not regularly attract interesting waders or ducks. Teal are present in very small numbers; other ducks, perhaps a few Wigeon or one or two Goldeneye, are only spasmodic visitors. Mallard and Shelduck, which both breed, are the commonest wildfowl, the former reaching 100 at times outside the breeding season. Black-tailed Godwit can reach 30 or 40, and flocks of several hundred Golden Plover may visit. Dunlin flocks may exceed 1,000. Small numbers of Common Sandpiper and Greenshank pass through in autumn and one or two often overwinter, recently accompanied by a Spotted Sandpiper, but there is generally a very poor autumn passage of the more interesting waders; other common species overwinter in unremarkable figures. Grey Heron and Kingfisher, both breeding locally, are resident.

The Plym is very good for gulls, many using it to loaf during the day when the tide is out. In winter, over 1,000 Great Black-backed Gulls may assemble. Several hundred Common Gull may include a Ring-billed Gull, this being a favourite haunt. Glaucous, Iceland and Mediterranean Gulls are all relatively frequent visitors, usually singly. Recent sightings have included a Gull-billed Tern. The wide Tamar–Tavy estuary is more difficult to watch, but many of its birds are similar. Ducks are more numerous, with a few Goldeneye, Tufted and Pochard annually. Occasional grebes visit, usually Slavonian or Great Crested, more rarely Black-necked or Red-necked. Sometimes a small group of Avocet breaks away from the upper Tamar population, and may stay for much of the winter. One or two Spotted Redshank, Greenshank and Common Sandpiper regularly overwinter. Every winter, at irregular intervals, a Peregrine spends time hunting in the area, concentrating over the estuaries.

Timing

Tides are of little consequence if checking the bay and waterfront, but an outgoing tide is essential for discharging sewers. Trawlers unloading in winter attract clouds of gulls to the fish quays. Otherwise, times of day are normally unimportant in the bay. Low winter sunlight, however, can make a check of the main sewers very difficult; an overcast day with good but flat light is ideal. Prolonged northerly winds, especially from midwinter onwards, often produce Glaucous Gulls. Gale-force southerly winds in spring or early autumn can cause numbers of terns to shelter in the bay, perhaps accompanied by Little Gulls.

To check the estuaries for waders, it is essential that mud is exposed. The main channels always flow, attracting ducks or grebes. The head of the Plym is less disturbed, although boating and bait-digging are year-round activities. Gulls in particular gather here, where they bathe and preen in fresh river water when the tide is out. Waders on the Plym cluster in the same upper area when an incoming tide pushes them up the estuary; it is also a good time to check just as the tide is ebbing, as birds are again forced to congregate in a restricted space. There are no central high-tide roosts on either estuary. Severe weather can increase all populations.

Visiting the Radford and Hooe area on quieter mornings avoids public disturbance pressure. Foggy or inclement weather and cold winds force tired migrants to move short distances from the coast, seeking shelter, when afternoon or evenings could be productive especially if such conditions persist. Hard winters cause dispersal of unexpected species to new areas, such as the arrival of a Smew here once (although in very harsh conditions the pond can freeze over).

Access

The seafront is well signposted throughout the city centre, from which it is less than ½ mile (0.8 km). Barbican fish quay is a tourist spot. Apart from gulls, occasional divers, grebes or seaducks venture into this area, where very close views can be obtained. Several sewage outlets can be watched for gulls. The best and largest, at the western end of the Hoe, is only some 200 m offshore; it is easily watched from a public walkway off the road, where it bends down towards nearby Millbay, and is also a good place to check the sea for divers and grebes around Drake's Island.

To reach Radford and Jennycliff from Plymouth city, take A379 to Plymstock, where you take the Hooe road (pronounced 'who', a southeastern outlier of Plymouth, not to be confused with the Hoe). This is also signposted to RAF Mount Batten. At Radford just before Plymstock merges with Hooe, at the bottom of a hill (Radford dip), you can turn off right into Meyers Way, where there is limited car parking for visiting Radford and Hooe Lakes. Walk through the adjoining parkland over good footpaths to Radford Lake, continuing on to overlook Hooe Lake, by itself of little merit but worth checking if you are visiting Radford. Continuing on along the road, a left-hand fork at Hooe takes you up to Jennycliff, where there is a large car park. From here, a scan of the sea takes in the whole eastern part of the Sound. Divers, grebes and seaducks can often be best seen from here. Passerine migrants might be seen along the clifftop in spring and autumn.

Plym estuary is very accessible, easily watched, and can be checked from both sides. Immediately across Laira bridge on A379, in Plymstock direction, is a sharp left-hand turn marked to Saltram. Chelson Meadow rubbish tip is immediately adjacent to this road and gulls can be seen flying in to feed. There are parking places along from the turning to the Saltram House entrance, allowing you to walk the entire length of the estuary, taking in the edge of the National Trust wood at Saltram. Kingfisher may be seen sitting on branches overhanging the estuary, or a Lesser Spotted Woodpecker among the trees if you are very lucky. Sunlight is always at your back, and the surroundings are more pleasant than on the opposite bank. If checking from the Embankment side, there are several car pull-in spots, and a pavement runs along its length.

To reach the Tavy estuary at Warren Point, take A38 to St Budeaux then the Budshead road on your left. Walk between factories on an industrial estate, along public footpaths to the point area. Access at Warleigh Point, opposite across the creek, is restricted.

Calendar

Resident: Mute Swan, Mallard, Shelduck, Moorhen, Sparrowhawk, Buzzard, Stock Dove, Lesser Spotted Woodpecker, Kingfisher, common woodland passerines, Grey Wagtail, Stonechat, Raven.

December–February: Waterfront and Sound: occasional Black-throated Diver especially towards end of period, Great Northern annually, Red-throated rarely; all grebe species occasionally, Slavonian most frequent; occasional seaducks. Gulls, including rarer species. *Estuaries:* apart from gulls, also Goldeneye, Pochard, Tufted Duck, Goosander and Red-breasted Merganser, probably Peregrine, Golden Plover, Black-tailed Godwit, possible Avocet on Tavy. Black Redstart in coastal gardens. Tufted Duck, Pochard, possibly other diving ducks at Radford Lake.

March–May: all above seabird species may be present in gradually reducing numbers, except Fulmar arriving and Black-throated Diver possible through early part of period; waders and ducks depart from early March. Uncommon gulls still pass through in March–early April, particularly Iceland and Ring-billed. Sandwich Tern from end March. Chiffchaff and Wheatear from mid-March. Early April on, in favourable conditions, passerine migrants at Jennycliff and Radford. Common Tern may pass. Breeding summer visitors arrive in woods, where Blackcap and Chiffchaff might have overwintered.

June–July: mostly only breeding species.

August–November: mostly waders reappear on estuaries early August onwards, gradually increasing in number and variety. Possible Osprey August or September on Tavy. Terns reappear in the bay; Sandwich from early August, Common a little later, Arctic and Black from September. Passerine migrants at Jennycliff. Black Redstart from October. Uncommon gulls, especially Little and Mediterranean, can occur throughout period.

20 ST JOHN'S AND MILLBROOK LAKES, LYNHER AND TAMAR ESTUARIES: GENERAL INTRODUCTION OS map: sheet 201

Habitat

This complex of tidal waterways is situated at the extreme southeast of Cornwall. All are interconnected by the wide, ill-defined Hamoaze channel, between Torpoint on the Cornish bank and Devonport naval dockyards on the eastern bank. The Devon side of the Tamar–Tavy confluence is described under Plymouth. All sites form mudflats at low tide, with St John's Lake nearest to the sea, directly linked to Plymouth Sound. Both St John's and the Lynher are wide and difficult to observe thoroughly.

All these sites are essentially interesting for waders and waterfowl in autumn and, particularly, winter, with relatively little bird activity in summer. Together they form the region's most important estuary habitat after the Exe.

Main Birdwatching Zones

As these sites are close together, it is usual for birdwatchers to check several of them in one day. Each site has its own interest: ease of viewing, particular species expected, etc. We have split them into three headings: St John's Lake and Millbrook Lake; The Lynher; The Tamar.

20A ST JOHN'S LAKE AND MILLBROOK LAKE

OS ref: SX 4254
OS map: sheet 201

Habitat

St John's Lake is a large area of open water and mudflats, forming a semi-sheltered basin between Plymouth Sound and river estuaries upstream; Millbrook Lake is an estuary backwater providing further shelter from the wind.

Species

Because of the proximity of the sea, St John's Lake tends to harbour more marine species, perhaps when blown in by rough weather, while Millbrook is used more by strictly estuarine birds and marsh birds. Divers are annual and regular, mostly Great Northern in ones and twos; single Black-throated may also occur, but Red-throated are very irregular. The most common grebe is the Little, but small numbers of Slavonian and Great Crested are also seen. Mute Swan number over 50 in autumn, more than anywhere else in Cornwall, although only a pair or two breed locally. Parties of Brent Geese, seen most winters, rarely exceed ten. Shelduck are scattered across the mudflats, 200–300 each winter. The most numerous dabbling duck is the Wigeon; the rafts of up to 5,000 which occur here are by far the largest in the county; the flock may move to the Lynher if disturbed. 200–300 Teal winter, and first-class views can be obtained of this tiny duck, along with other estuary birds, at Millbrook. A wide range of other ducks in small numbers, including less common visitors such as Velvet Scoter and Long-tailed Duck, is noted annually.

Outside the breeding season, Peregrine are occasional lone visitors. Waders are well represented, with an interesting spread of species. Very small numbers of Little Stint and Curlew Sandpiper normally visit Millbrook in autumn. Turnstone are common, with groups totalling 100 or so; good views are obtained beside roads at Torpoint. Both godwit species are seen, usually more Black-tailed, but both normally only attaining 50–60. Flocks of about 300 Redshank and Knot can also be expected. Whimbrel, passing northward in spring, may rest for a day or so; they are seen again in autumn on their return journey, numbers being highly variable but averaging ten. Spotted Redshank, Greenshank, Green and Common Sandpipers all use the area, chiefly in autumn, although every year a couple of each elect to see winter through. Millbrook is popular with them. Rarer wader visitors have included a Black-winged Stilt and a Semi-palmated Sandpiper.

Among Black-headed and Common Gulls, one or two Mediterranean Gull may be present, although they are hard to pick out, especially in immature plumage. Even more difficult to identify are several Ring-billed Gull now reported here. Little Gulls are more obvious visitors in ones and twos, largely in autumn or early winter, juveniles being most usual. Terns frequently feed here, all the British sea terns being noted most years in spring and/or autumn. Roseate and Little are seen the least, mostly in autumn. Higher tern numbers are expected in autumn, but not usually over ten of any single species; Sandwich and Common are most numerous, with a scattering of Arctic, mostly juveniles, and an occasional Black Tern, which favours sheltered areas such as Millbrook. Auks drift in from the Sound, usually in late winter when they begin to come closer to shore, instinctively, at the start of their breeding cycle.

Habitat

This estuary is wide at its mouth into the Hamoaze, narrowing sharply farther upstream near Antony village. There is a small saltmarsh on the opposite bank to Antony, together with several narrow creeks. The main river, forming a long, narrow tidal creek above here, itself splits into three; the first creek ends at Polbathic, the second at Tideford, and the third near Trematon, just outside Saltash. All these creeks have saltmarsh, mostly towards their heads, little visited by birdwatchers.

Species

In the main estuary in winter, small numbers of divers and grebes, including an occasional Red-necked, may be seen; possibly the same birds move up from St John's Lake. Ducks certainly move from site to site, notably Wigeon flocks, and at times of disturbance there may be wholesale interchange between sites. Pintail, however, are the Lynher's speciality; the flock, usually located around the main estuary saltmarsh, reaches about 50 birds. Occasionally a Spoonbill favours this area, and may remain through winter. Migrating Spotted Redshank and Greenshank find the creeks ideal, and may overwinter in above-normal numbers, the former reaching ten or more. Green and Common Sandpipers are also passage migrants which spend winter here in ones and twos. Recently a Forster's Tern visited from America, only the second ever British record. Commoner species are the same as at adjoining St John's Lake, but generally in lower numbers.

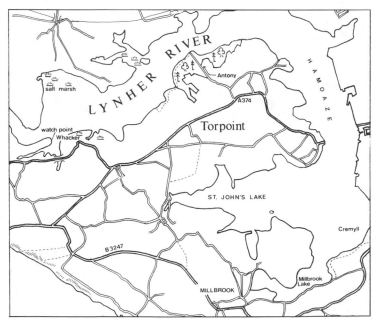

OS ref: SX 4364
OS map: sheet 201

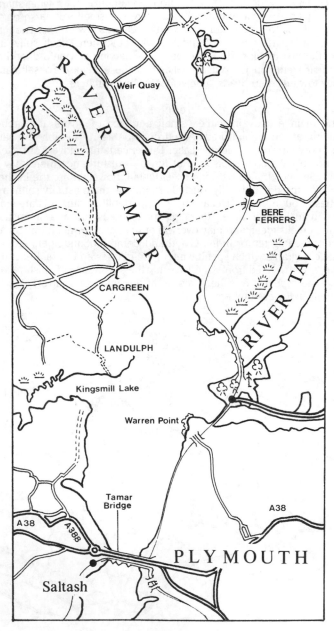

Habitat

This estuary forms the boundary between Devon and Cornwall. From the Tamar road bridge upstream to Kingsmill creek is a wide area of rather unproductive mudflats. From Landulph on the Cornish side, the estuary becomes narrower, but more productive. It is mostly flanked by pasture farmland, and groups of trees meet near the water's edge.

Species

Above all else, the mudflats of the Tamar are best known for that graceful wader the Avocet, adopted and made famous by the RSPB as their national emblem. Evidence exists linking at least some Tamar birds with those raised on RSPB reserves; some chicks marked with coloured plastic leg-rings have been seen later as adults on the Tamar. Avocet begin to arrive from early winter, numbers generally peaking in mid-season with over 100 present.

Avocets

During winter, other regular species include a few Little Grebe. Small flocks of Mallard, Wigeon and Teal are regular, with other dabbling ducks less often seen. A few Goldeneye may accompany the Little Grebe, both species diving continuously for food. Pochard, the most numerous diving duck, often exceed 50, and perhaps 100 in some years. From time to time small numbers of other diving ducks such as Tufted appear, and American Ring-necked Duck have joined them. In severe weather all three sawbills may be present, the rarer Smew only in ones and twos.

On the lower estuary is the large creek known as Kingsmill Lake, which narrows to a saltmarsh at Landulph. At this marsh, waders, especially Redshank and Curlew, gather to roost on incoming tides. Marshy areas provide habitat for different waders; Little Stint, Curlew Sandpiper, and particularly Green and Wood Sandpipers, may be seen in early autumn in small numbers. This area is also poplar with shanks and Common Sandpiper at the same season; a few of each may remain to winter. Sometimes a Black Tern feeds here in autumn, along with a few Common Tern. Kingfisher frequent the area in both autumn and winter. A Wilson's Phalarope from America was seen feeding here recently.

In early autumn (or more rarely, spring), the Tamar sometimes plays host to an Osprey. This exciting raptor may establish temporary residence for a couple of weeks during autumn, before again setting off southward. Outside the breeding season, a Peregrine might be watched flashing over the mud pursuing a luckless wader.

Timing (all sites)

The severity of winter weather will influence variety and numbers of species; the harder the weather, the greater the numbers. Any daylight hours are suitable, but it will depend whether a high or low tide is required. For example, for watching waders across the mudflats the tide must be out, as there are no easily checked roosting points. Most waders either drop into saltmarshes at high tide, where they are impossible to see, or move away to inaccessible roosts. When the tide is out, main deepwater channels remain at all sites, used by divers, grebes and ducks.

Wader roosts at St John's Lake are also scattered and difficult to observe. Areas around Millbrook are utilised but suffer from disturbance by dogs and the public, so are not reliable.

Some shooting take place on all sites, which disrupts normal flock behaviour, especially on the Lynher and St John's Lake.

Access (all sites)

From Saltash, the *Tamar* is checked by taking A388, turning right to Landulph. Park near the church, then walk left along a narrow tarmac road until you reach a wooden gate and stile. This leads through a small rough pasture meadow, with a small marshy area to your right (which may contain interesting waders). This public path then leads to an embankment, from where you can check Kingsmill Lake area. If the tide is out (preferably now incoming), you can walk along the beach to a point which brings you level with the marshy area in the field. From here, check the saltmarsh where waders gather at its edges before dispersing at high tide. On higher tides you can, with care, walk along the concrete embankment.

The same turn off A388 for Landulph takes you to Cargreen for Avocet, this being one of their favourite feeding sites. You are likely to see at least part of the flock, if not all. Views are reasonably close and they can be seen from your car, as there are parking spaces near the waterfront.

The *Lynher* is reached from Torpoint by A374 to about 1 mile (1.6 km) past Antony; there is a well-signposted picnic area and parking place at Whacker Creek. Here you are opposite the saltmarsh and overlooking the best part of the estuary for birds. A telescope is essential, especially when checking birds on the opposite shore (where there are no public access points). Higher creeks are not easily checked; several roads pass near their edges at various points, where parking is very difficult and vision restricted by tree growth. Stretches are probably best tackled on foot.

St John's Lake is checked from Torpoint, where there are roads along the waterfront. Many birds congregate here, though mostly in mid-channel, or along the relatively undisturbed opposite shore, when a telescope will be necessary. The B3247 is taken to Millbrook village, which has waterside roads throughout its length.

Calendar (all sites)

Resident: Cormorant, Grey Heron, Shelduck.

December–February: Divers, particularly Great Northern; commoner grebes, at intervals. Possible wintering Spoonbill, occasional Brent Geese, Wigeon, small numbers of all dabbling ducks, also diving and seaducks at times. Peregrine, Turnstone, Knot, Spotted Redshank, Greenshank, Green Sandpiper, Common Sandpiper, Black-tailed Godwit, Bar-tailed Godwit; Avocet peak late December; possible Mediterranean Gull.

March–May: most of above depart from early March. By April first migrants are arriving, including a trickle of returning waders, notably Whimbrel. Sandwich and a few Common Terns. Possible Osprey.

June–July: very little other than odd late spring or early autumn passage migrants. Resident species.

August–November: early on, possible Osprey. First returning commoner waders may be in summer plumage, joined by Little Stint, Curlew Sandpiper, Green Sandpiper, Wood Sandpiper, Spotted Redshank, Greenshank; possibility of uncommon or rare waders from Europe or America; Avocet return from late November. Terns pass through, mostly Sandwich and Common, in larger numbers August–September with Arctic from mid-September to mid-October. Possible Little, Mediterranean and other uncommon or rare gulls.

21 RAME HEAD, WHITSAND BAY AND LOOE

OS ref: SX 4148 (Rame);
SX 2552 (Looe)
OS map: sheet 201

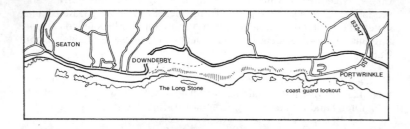

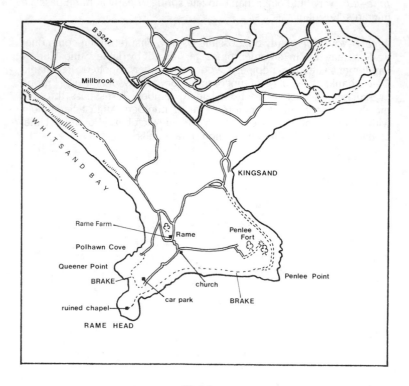

Habitat

On the southeast coast of Cornwall, Rame faces south, the closest mainland point to Eddystone Lighthouse, 6 miles (9½ km) seaward. Rame peninsula includes Penlee Point, at the western entrance to Plymouth Sound. West of Rame sweeps wide Whitsand Bay, terminating in narrow, steep-sided Looe Estuary mouth. Along the steeply sloping coastline, gorse and bracken brakes are interspersed with blackthorn, small clumps of trees and small rough grazing fields. Flatter fields above are used for arable farming. The area around Rame Church and Farm

138

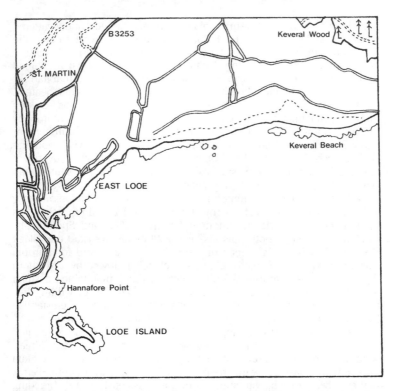

affords more shelter, with groups of trees, mostly sycamore, a few gardens, and hedgerows. A small road runs from the church to an old fortification above Penlee Point, overgrown with brambles and ash trees. Habitat along this road is varied, with a wide, dense copse, mainly blackthorn, providing shelter and cover. Alongside this lie demolished buildings, where wild flowers grow, including various umbellifers; teazels and brambles have also colonised. Adders are common. Fallow Deer from Mount Edgecumbe park may be seen from the road between the church and Penlee fort, especially in autumn and winter.

The scenic coast road from Rame to Looe, following the escarpment edge overlooking the coastline, affords panoramic views. The air in spring can be heavily scented by countless gorse flowers.

Species

The chief interest for birdwatchers visiting Rame will probably be spring and autumn migrants. Two distinct groups occur. The first is landbirds, mostly small passerines, such as Swallow and warblers; raptors, a harrier perhaps, occasionally pass through, and Honey Buzzard has been seen. A white Gyrfalcon once passed over. The second group is seabirds. Rame formerly received scant attention from seawatchers; recent years have witnessed better coverage, producing for instance a spring Long-tailed Skua, and showing that a variety of seabirds occurs in both seasons, although in smaller numbers, usually, than at some Southwest seawatching venues.

Most passerine migrants do not linger on exposed heathland, quickly working towards sheltered areas. Trees and hedgerows around the church and farm are favourite places, as are hedges and scattered groups of small trees around Polhawn Cove on the west side of the headland. Small fields among or near the brakes form yet another habitat. Resident Skylark and Meadow Pipit in the fields are joined by migrant flocks of the same species. Also sharing this habitat are common migrants, including Tree Pipit, Yellow Wagtail and Wheatear. Occasionally Turtle Dove are seen, often in cereal fields, among foraging feral pigeons. Linnets are resident, increased in autumn by migrants; a few less common finches or buntings, such as Brambling or Snow Bunting, may join them. Trees and bushes provide vital food and shelter, even if only for a few hours during early morning for overnight migrants. More common species, such as Blackcap, Whitethroat, Garden Warbler, Chiffchaff and Willow Warbler, sometimes occur in quite large numbers, and uncommon warblers such as Melodious may visit with them. Goldcrest are most numerous in autumn, as always outnumbering the brightly coloured Firecrest. Pied and Spotted Fly-catchers also visit in both seasons, as do Whinchat, Redstart and Black Redstart. A Wilson's Warbler from America, a first record for Europe, was a brief visitor to Rame one autumn, closely followed by a Northern Parula at Penlee. Dartford Warblers have at times maintained a small resident colony on the gorse slopes, although at time of writing they have died out owing to several severe winters; they could re-establish themselves if breeding colonies elsewhere produce surplus young.

When seawatching in spring, most likely species are Black-throated and Great Northern Divers, sometimes several hundred Manx Shear-water and perhaps hundreds of Gannet. A few Pomarine or Arctic Skua occasionally coast eastward in spring, or westward in autumn. Terns, particularly Sandwich, with some Common, pass east towards breeding grounds. Auks, particularly Razorbill, fly to and fro. Whimbrel and Bar-tailed Godwit also coast eastward in flocks, the former often giving their diagnostic, seven-note contact call as they pass; one or two Whimbrel often winter along this coast. In autumn all species can occur in larger numbers. Great Skua should be more evident, with more seaducks such

Black Redstart

as Common Scoter; the chance of less common species is greater, and
Sooty Shearwaters may pass.

Birds of special interest in Whitsand Bay include Great Northern and
Black-throated Divers, often in small scattered groups totalling up to ten
at a time, sometimes twice that. From late winter into spring, Black-
throated Divers gradually replace wintering Great Northerns; the few
late-staying birds may attain summer plumage. Black-necked, Slavonian,
Red-necked and Great Crested Grebes may visit in winter, usually in
ones and twos, Slavonian most frequently. Seaducks such as Eider and
Common Scoter visit in small groups, possibly attracting a Velvet Scoter.

On Looe beach in winter you can expect good views of Grey Plover,
Turnstone and Purple Sandpiper; search through rocky areas, as they
usually gather in small flocks, camouflaged among seaweed. In the
narrow estuary, especially opposite Looe railway station, gulls assemble
in large numbers, including many hundreds of Common Gull, particularly
in late winter and early spring when they accompany migrant Lesser
Black-backeds; check among them for unusual gulls, such as Glaucous
and, less frequently, Iceland. As on many of the region's estuaries,
Ring-billed Gulls have also been detected. Higher up the estuary, less
common overwintering waders may be found along marshy fringes.
These might include Spotted Redshank, Greenshank, Green and
Common Sandpipers. A vagrant Black-winged Stilt has been seen. This
area is also popular with wintering Kingfishers. In the hilltop trees,
across the estuary from the railway station, is a heronry. Activity is
visible from the station in early spring, before leaves fully clothe the
trees.

Timing

The whole area is heavily used by tourists in summer. Morning visits to
Rame area in spring or autumn, especially in southerly or southeasterly
winds during fall conditions, will almost certainly give you interesting
species among commoner migrant birds. You could try any time of day,
in any winds, in migration seasons.

Seawatching in spring or autumn could be attempted in similar
conditions to those for passerine fall arrivals, and in the same winds.
Provided there is visibility of at least 1 mile (1.6 km), winds from south
and west also give good results; neither direction has to be strong to
produce birds. Southwesterly gales have never given worthwhile results.
Onshore winds induce birds to fly close to shore. As shelter is lacking,
waterproof clothing should be taken on seawatches.

Access

From Torpoint, for Rame, take A374 to Antony. Take B3247 to Tregantle,
turning right onto the coast road to Rame. Along this route, check
Whitsand Bay and seaward brakes; there are frequent pull-ins. There is a
car park at Rame. Public footpaths along the coastline allow you to
cover all the best bird spots around Rame. From the car park, you can
follow the coast path to Penlee, or out to the headland. Another good
route is to Polhawn, where bushes surrounding the old fort (now private)
can be overlooked from the footpath. Following the above track will
bring you back to Rame Farm and Church. The narrow road from the
church towards Penlee and the overgrown fort should be checked for
migrants. A path leads from the fort to connect with the coastal track at
Penlee. From Tregantle, continue west along B3247 coast road to Port-

wrinkle; you can detour down to the village waterfront, where divers or grebes may be offshore. The main road is high above the sea, and a telescope is essential for checking waterbirds.

The next stop westward is Downderry, with the possibility of seeing any of the bay species. Drive through to adjoining Seaton. Beside the beach is a car park, adjacent to which are alder trees and sallows standing by a stream; check these for wintering Blackcap, Chiffchaff or Firecrest, or for passing migrants. Walk from the car park up the hill on your left. From this road, look seaward through groups of pines; watch in particular for Great Northern and Black-throated Divers, which gather in groups here.

Drive up this same hill, continuing along it before joining B3253 for Looe. After checking the estuary and gulls in Looe harbour, proceed to the seafront at West Looe, where parking on the waterfront road is allowed. Check the whole seashore and bay along this road, to where it becomes a dead end. Divers and grebes often shelter from winds in the lee of Looe Island, and can be seen from the road.

For seawatching from Rame Head, find what shelter you can among low rocks. Watch from near the bottom of the slope, directly in line with the old chapel at the tip of the headland.

Calendar

Resident: Cormorant, Grey Heron, Shelduck, Sparrowhawk, Buzzard, Grey Wagtail, Stonechat, Raven.

December–February: mostly Black-throated and Great Northern Divers, Slavonian and Great Crested Grebes, occasional Black-necked and Red-necked; Little Grebe Looe estuary. Eider, Common Scoter, occasional Velvet Scoter, Grey Plover, Turnstone, Purple Sandpiper, possible Spotted Redshank, Greenshank, Green and Common Sandpipers. Possible Glaucous, Iceland, Ring-billed or Mediterranean Gulls.

March–May: more Black-throated than Great Northern Divers, many fewer of each late in period; declining chance of grebes after mid-April. Glaucous or Iceland Gull possible throughout period. Terns, especially Sandwich, pass throughout, peak April when other terns coast by. Shearwaters (Manx), skuas, Whimbrel, godwits, all from April on. First migrant passerines mid-late March, e.g. Black Redstart, Chiffchaff, Wheatear; wider range of migrants later spring, including possible raptors (e.g. Hobby), hirundines, wagtails, pipits, warblers, flycatchers and Redstart.

June–July: crowds of holidaymakers. Mostly resident and breeding birds, including Fulmar, Cuckoo, Grasshopper Warbler, Blackcap, Whitethroat, Willow Warbler, Chiffchaff, Goldcrest, Spotted Flycatcher.

August–November: return passage of seabirds, birds of prey and passerines from early August. Most seabirds, e.g. shearwaters, skuas terns, late August–October. Harrier or Merlin seen mostly mid-September–October. Passerine movement peaks same months.

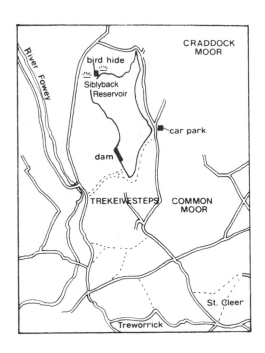

Habitat

Both reservoirs lie in wide relatively shallow moorland valleys on the southeastern edge of Bodmin Moor. Colliford was initially flooded as recently as 1985. At 900 acres (360 ha), it is one of the largest in the Southwest. Situated in a general area of Bodmin Moor where several other reservoirs already exist, its nearest neighbour is Siblyback, separated from it by about 2 miles (3 km) in a direct line.

Unlike Siblyback, no water based sports (other than angling) take place at Colliford, thus leaving this large sheet of water undisturbed, an ideal place to create a nature reserve. Known as Loveny, the reserve occupies the narrow northerly finger of water. This 340-acre (136-ha) area contains willow carr at the bottom of a shallow valley, the sides mostly rough pasture. Its most important role will be to provide breeding areas for a variety of birds such as waterfowl, waders and various passerines. Like Siblyback, Colliford's exposed location precludes the presence of high growing broad leaved trees, or lush bankside vegetation, making it suitable for birds requiring open habitat. A group of conifers forms the only tall trees within the reservoir's boundaries. Along its western margin grows a colony of at least 3,000 Frog Orchids, an otherwise rare plant in Cornwall; this is one of Britain's largest colonies. Among them are found both Greater and Lesser Butterfly

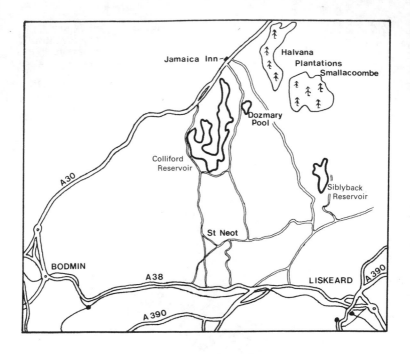

Orchids, and the rare Moonwort fern. About ten species of dragonfly breed here, unlike at the equally acidic Siblyback Reservoir, which has even fewer of their habitat requirements.

Siblyback is a much smaller water, covering 140 acres (57 ha). The flooded valley is set among moorland and rough sheep pasture. The northern shore is shallow, with mud exposed as water levels drop, becoming extensive in dry autumns. Along this perimeter are narrow areas of marshy vegetation, mostly rank grasses, bracken and bramble. As in all moorland reservoirs, the water is acidic, preventing a wider range of plants from growing. There are scattered sallows, hawthorns and rowans. Trout are the main fish stocked, the lake being extremely popular with anglers. Windsurfers and small sailing craft also use it.

Species

As the large Colliford Reservoir is too new to have produced a set pattern of occurrences of a range of species yet, the smaller, more established reservoir is described first. Siblyback is noted chiefly for autumn waders and winter wildfowl, including some scarcer species. During winter one of the most numerous birds is probably Mallard, usually 100 or so; a few breed. Coot reach 150 in most winters, with a few breeding pairs. Smew are rare visitors to Britain, little seen in the Southwest, where they are only casual visitors in severe cold. Siblyback is an exception; three to five, mostly brownheads, are virtually annual visitors. Surprisingly, other ducks are rather few, even diving ducks. Pochard may number 30, and Tufted half that. Goosander, mostly brownheads, are annual in twos and threes, and one or two Goldeneye seen regularly are also typically brownheads. Other diving ducks, usually singles, visit occasionally. The few dabbling ducks include an average of 25 Teal, perhaps 150 Wigeon, and others infrequently. Grebes have included Red-necked and, equally unexpectedly, both Great Northern and Black-throated Divers have appeared here, well inland. Small parties of Bewick's Swan very occasionally visit, as do White-fronted Geese, arrivals usually coinciding with hard weather elsewhere. Because exposed mud cannot usually be found in winter, when water level is higher, most waders are then absent, but 100 or more Snipe frequent boggy margins and field edges, accompanied regularly by one or two Jack Snipe. Flocks of Golden Plover and Lapwing crowd nearby fields, both often exceeding 1,000. Raptors wintering on the moor visit the area, no doubt attracted by the plovers; Peregrine, Merlin and Hen Harrier are regular, and Red Kite have been seen.

As spring approaches, the avian population declines and changes. There are far fewer wildfowl, although Cormorant and Grey Heron still visit. Hirundines, especially Sand and House Martins, pause on passage, often in large feeding flocks, while Swifts scream and fly over the water in hundreds. A marsh tern, usually Black, could appear in summer plumage, or some other unexpected visitor may occur.

An ornithologically quiet summer gives way to returning migrant waders; mudflats now exposed attract them to stop. Numbers are never large, but apart from regular migrants, less common (e.g. Temminck's Stint and Red-necked Phalarope, easterly species seen very little in our region), and even rare vagrants such as Wilson's Phalarope are found each year. More routine annual visitors include Ringed Plover, Little Stint, Dunlin, Curlew Sandpiper, Ruff, Spotted Redshank, Redshank, Green Sandpiper, Wood Sandpiper, Common Sandpiper, Curlew. Little Gull, usually first-winter birds with blackish 'W' markings across the wings, pass through in ones and twos. Black Tern, in dowdy grey-brown autumn plumage, also in very small numbers, sometimes include a flock of six or more.

Colliford has already shown some potential for producing interesting birds, although some are the same individuals moving between this and other nearby waters. The same can be said for birds flying across the lake's moorland surrounds, especially waders and raptors; thus both reservoirs, historic Dozmary Pool, Upper Fowey Valley, and a huge tract of surrounding Bodmin moors, now forms a relatively easily accessible area, where water and moorland birds may be encountered throughout.

Ducks tend to be in greater number here than on Siblyback, and over a period of time may possibly increase. Mallard reach over 300 in winter, with some 25 breeding pairs. Rather surprising is the regular breeding by a pair of normally coastal Shelduck. Diving Tufted Duck also breed, albeit only a pair or two, and number about 50 during winter; Pochard winter in similar numbers. Wigeon and Teal form the largest flocks, with 300–400 of each. Recently the American form of the latter, a male Green-winged Teal, visited, diagnosed by its vertical white flank stripe, instead of a horizontal one. Smew, Goosander and Goldeneye, when present, regularly move between sites, their status similar here to Siblyback. Coot are more static, about 100 occurring, and a pair or two may breed.

As already stated, moorland waders such as Golden Plover and Lapwing roam the general area in winter, changing sites as circumstances dictate. Raptors behave likewise, including perhaps a Hen Harrier gliding on wings raised in a 'V' shape. Breeding waders include a few pairs of Lapwing and Curlew, and probably Snipe. Up to 20 pairs of Black-headed Gull also breed, although numbers are sporadic as is their success; this is one of only two colonies in our region, the other being at Crowdy.

Rarities to date cannot compete with Siblyback's. Odd winter visits by divers have not yet occurred, although a Red-necked Grebe has been seen, along with a Whooper Swan. The lake and its environs appear ideal for wild swans and geese, and in future might be favoured by them on a regular basis.

Spring seems to have seen less coverage by birdwatchers; certainly interesting birds noted are few indeed, but have included Black Tern, Osprey, and three Spoonbill together.

Autumn waders have mostly been commoner species, Greenshank, Green Sandpiper, Common Sandpiper, Little Stint and Curlew Sandpiper in small numbers. Stone Curlew has visited, and any rarer water bird could well turn up.

Timing

Not critical, although mornings and evenings at Siblyback should have less human disturbance. This is usually minimal at Colliford. Hard winter weather may bring further interesting species. For waders in autumn, dry conditions expose muddy margins which in very wet years may not exist. Calm conditions allow easier viewing, and birds are not driven to seek shelter.

Access

From A38 in Liskeard, to reach Siblyback take A390 from the town centre to the outer edge of town. Branch off onto B3254 (where signposted to Siblyback Lake) for about 1 mile (1.6 km). Leave the B road and take the road to St Cleer (also signposted for Siblyback). Just past the village turn right. At the road junction, about 1 mile (1.6 km) on, take the minor road opposite which leads to the lake (again signposted). From the large car park you can scan over the lake. You can walk to the dam, continuing along this path on the opposite shore. Alternatively, walk past dinghies on the lower edge of the car park, over a stile, and continue around this boundary. Both routes lead to the shallower north end, which has difficult terrain and areas of soft mud, requiring wellington boots. A bird hide has been erected by SWW in this vicinity.

Windsurfers and boats are officially restricted from entry to the shallow end of Siblyback, but fishermen are not. Most birdwatchers approach this area, most used by ducks and waders, from the car park side. Entry permits can be otained from the warden.

Colliford is most easily approached from A30 Launceston to Bodmin road, and a minor road circles round the reservoir. Entry is directly opposite the Jamaica Inn. This entrance is very close to that taken for Upper Fower Valley. Toilet facilities at the main Simonstone car park cater for the disabled. Three car parks along the western edge, and pull-in spots along the perimeter road, also allow some coverage by the disabled. Way-marked moorland walks radiate from the main car park.

Virtually the whole of Colliford can be covered by footpaths, through rough pasture, including one path covering most of the reserve area which is restricted for use only by permit-carrying birdwatchers. Others are for use only by birdwatchers or anglers carrying permits. Towards the northern end of Loveny reserve, entry is barred to all, including those with permits for the other areas. Entry permits are obtained from the warden at Siblyback.

For access between the two reservoirs, there are several minor roads which can be taken from Siblyback signposted to St Neot, near which a minor road is signposted to Colliford. Probably the most direct and scenic route is to follow the road (see Chapter 23) through the Upper Fowey Valley to Bolventor on A30. Take the minor road from here to Dozmary Pool and the northern tip of Colliford Reservoir.

Calendar

Resident: Little Grebe, Coot, Mallard, Tufted Duck.

December–February: Geese, probably White-fronted, and wild swans in hard weather. Teal, Wigeon, Pochard, Tufted, Goldeneye, Smew, Goosander, occasional other dabbling and diving ducks, possibly a 'sea' grebe or diver. Maybe wintering raptors for moors. Snipe and Jack Snipe. In surrounding fields, Golden Plover and Lapwing. Gulls, mainly Black-headed.

March–May: winter visitors mainly depart by end March. Perhaps a stray passage diver, grebe or duck. Late April and especially May, perhaps a marsh tern, hirundines, Swift.

June–July: breeding species, including Sedge Warbler (a few pairs).

August–November: waders arrive from early August on, peak late August and September. Little Gull and Black Tern from late August. Golden Plover begin arrival from mid-September. Waterfowl return from mid-November.

23 UPPER FOWEY VALLEY, DOZMARY POOL AND MOORLAND

OS ref: SX 2174
OS map: sheet 201

Habitat

On the southeast fringe of Bodmin Moor, Upper Fowey Valley, sometimes known as Lamelgate or Bolventor, is near the head of the long Fowey river. The valley is mostly shallow-sided and forms several different habitats in miniature. Localised and uncommon wild flowers include Pale Butterwort, Lesser Bladderwort and Ivy-leaved Bellflower. The fast-flowing river is lined by alder, *Salix* and blackthorn trees. Conditions are suitable for trout. You will be extremely lucky to see an Otter, although Mink (unfortunately) are also present. Large areas of peat bog, including some small, deep pools, make walking nearby rather treacherous; sundews, including Long-leaved, thrive. Local butterflies such as Marsh Fritillaries are found. Drier areas support rank grasses, various heathers, and patches of gorse. Lichen growth (harmless to its hosts) is varied and luxuriant in the moist, clean air. Surrounding farmland is mostly rough sheep pasture. Groups of large trees in the valley are mostly beech. The huge Smallacoombe forestry plantations can be seen above the hill crest.

Dozmary Pool, over the hilltop westward, is naturally formed, circular, deep in the middle, with open perimeters. Higher moorland surrounding Dozmary has much the same vegetation as drier parts of the Fowey valley. Lower-lying areas remain wetter, with patches of *Salix* in the centre. The pool lies within sight of Brown Willy (423 m), highest point on Bodmin Moor. Across on the west side of Dozmary Pool, a few

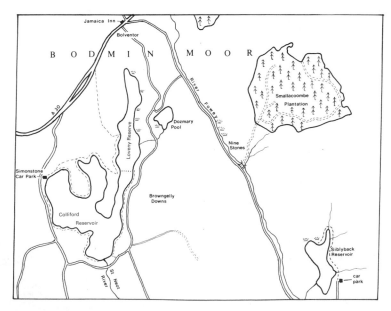

hundred metres away, is the Loveny reserve area at the northeast tip of Colliford Reservoir.

Species

There are no large numbers of birds, save for the hordes of wintering Starling noisily searching for worms and leatherjackets on short sheep pasture; they are usually joined by winter thrushes, in particular several hundred Fieldfare. Resident specialities in the valley are Dipper and Willow Tit, while Raven can be seen in groups of ten or more in winter. Kingfisher possibly breed; one or two remain through winter, but may be killed off in severe weather, when breeding may lapse for a year or two. Many common lowland passerines such as Treecreeper can be found in this moorland valley, alongside species such as summering Grass-hopper Warbler. This mix enables you to see many kinds of birds in a small area.

Male Hen Harrier

In winter fewer species inhabit the valley, but birds of prey (e.g. Hen Harrier or Merlin) might pass through on hunting trips, and occasionally a Great Grey Shrike is seen. Moorland surrounding Dozmary Pool supports interesting winter raptors, regularly including up to five Hen Harrier, a Peregrine, one or two Merlin, and a few Short-eared Owl; a Goshawk was seen recently. The pool is uninviting to most wildfowl, but small numbers of ducks come and go throughout the winter, and a dozen or so Pochard are regular, as are twice that number of Mallard. Goosander and Goldeneye occasionally visit, as do small numbers of dabbling ducks, mostly Wigeon and Teal. Tufted Duck are casual visitors, and other scarcer ducks such as Smew and Long-tailed Duck have turned up, almost certainly having moved off one of the reservoirs. Coot are often present, and a small party of Bewick's or, more rarely, Whooper Swan may visit irregularly. Snipe inhabit boggy margins and small numbers of commoner gulls usually roost; unusual for the region, there is a winter night roost of 50–100 Lesser Black-backed Gull, arriving from late afternoon. It remains to be seen how far the close proximity of the large expanse of Colliford Reservoir will affect numbers of water birds here.

Spring in the valley echoes with cascading notes of Willow Warbler song. Similar Chiffchaff are many fewer, their song enabling a ready distinction between the two. Tree Pipit, Blackcap and Grasshopper Warbler breed in quite good numbers. Spotted Flycatcher, Wheatear, Redstart and Whinchat usually breed, but are somewhat sporadic. A small number of Sand Martin may nest in suitable riverbank, while Cuckoos parasitise nesting Meadow Pipits. Snipe, present throughout the year, probably breed in ones and twos, along with Curlew and Lapwing. Some Redpoll breed in Smallacoombe plantation, ranging into the valley to feed; Siskin, which have never before been proven to breed in Cornwall, are now found annually in small numbers. Marshy areas and scrubby trees around Dozmary Pool are inhabited by Tree and Meadow Pipits, attended by Cuckoos. Willow Warbler and Chiffchaff also nest.

Late spring has recently produced one or two rarer migrants, including Black-eared Wheatear and a Red-footed Falcon.

Summer becomes quieter, as birds settle into a more secretive breeding routine; lush marsh growth aids the naturally furtive breeding behaviour of breeding waders. At the end of summer, families of young birds move around the area. Soon most summer visitors will move off, and autumn may bring a few migrants, perhaps with an uncommon raptor such as Montagu's Harrier.

Timing

For a general visit, any time of day will suffice, although in late spring and summer the earlier the better, avoiding disturbance from trippers. Birds have to be very active in the morning, ensuring for themselves and their dependent mates or young a plentiful food supply very quickly, to replace energy lost overnight, and are more easily seen then. There is also a last flurry of activity before nightfall, when the crepuscular hunting Barn Owl and singing Grasshopper Warbler are more active.

Hard weather may produce more or different birds on Dozmary Pool, such as wild swans. Raptors are best seen an hour or two before dusk, as they begin to congregate near roosting areas, becoming active again, attempting to kill and feed before nightfall.

Access

From A390 at Liskeard take the same route as for Siblyback Lake (see Chapter 22). At the crossroads to the lake, follow the road signposted to Launceston. A few hundred metres farther, a sharp turn is signposted to Draynes, Bolventor and Launceston. Follow this road until the hamlet of Lamelgate; on crossing the humpbacked bridge you have entered the valley, which is 3 miles (5 km) long. A road runs the entire length, with several pull-ins. Most of the valley can be seen from, or near, a car.

Access to Smallacombe plantation is from the track at Nine Stones bridge in the valley. The Bolventor road will also take you to Colliford Reservoir. Approach the valley from A30 to Bolventor, directly opposite Jamaica Inn public house. For Dozmary and the northeast end of Colliford Reservoir, turn off A30 at Bolventor on the opposite side of the Inn, along a minor road for about 1½ miles (2½ km) alongside rough moorland. The road skirts the pool; a rather rough track can be walked to the water's edge. Any areas allowing a good view over moors either side of the pool are suitable for passing raptors.

Calendar

Resident: Sparrowhawk, Buzzard, Snipe, Barn Owl, all three woodpeckers (Lesser Spotted very scarce), Grey Wagtail, Dipper, Marsh Tit, Willow Tit, Coal Tit, Raven, Reed Bunting, Redpoll, Siskin.

December–February: possibly wild swans. Teal, Wigeon, Tufted Duck, Pochard, possible Smew and Goosander, Hen Harrier, Peregrine. Merlin, Coot, possible Great Grey Shrike, winter thrushes.

March–May: a few of the above raptors may linger into April. Curlew, possible Lapwing, Cuckoo, Sand Martin, Tree Pipit, Grasshopper Warbler, Blackcap, Willow Warbler and Chiffchaff, Spotted Flycatcher, Wheatear, Whinchat, probable in small numbers. Chance of an unusual migrant late in period.

June–July: breeding species.

August–November: breeding species flock early in period, migrants begin departure in August. Passage migrants may occur. Towards end of period, winter visitors start to return.

24 CROWDY RESERVOIR AND DAVIDSTOW AIRFIELD

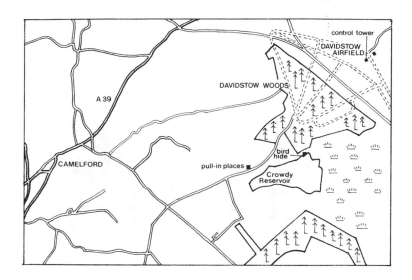

Habitat

Near Camelford town, these exposed moorland sites are close together, separated in parts by maturing Forestry Commission conifers, now being felled. The disused airfield consists of poorly drained short turf, grazed by sheep, with temporary surface water after rain. Remnants of tarmac runways are still passable, and the control tower, although ruined, still stands. The 115-acre (47-ha) reservoir has a greater area of marginal bog than other moorland reservoirs, even when water levels are high. Large areas of mud are exposed when levels are lower. There are several small islands near the shallow end (farthest from the dam) where Sundew, Long-leaved Sundew and Pale Butterwort grow in profusion. The area, prone to high winds and thick mists, is often inhospitable in winter.

Species

The main attraction to birdwatchers is the chance of good views of ducks, waders and raptors, including rarer species. During late autumn and winter flocks of up to 5,000 Golden Plover occur regularly; Lapwing (usually totalling 1,000 or more) can be equally numerous, especially when hard weather persists elsewhere. Apart from high numbers of these plovers, few waders winter, except perhaps a Ruff. This species is also a spring migrant, and five or six at a time are present each autumn. Only a few Curlew are present at any season. A winter Woodcock may be flushed from the road near the reservoir and small numbers of Snipe may be seen at most times of year. Jack Snipe occur only in ones and twos.

Little Grebe are resident in small numbers, a pair or two breeding irregularly. Other grebes and divers are very rare (fewer than Siblyback) and several years may elapse without any. Two or three Cormorant and Grey Heron are usual. Duck species and numbers are also quite restricted. Mallard and Teal both peak at about 300 in autumn (a few pairs of Mallard breed), and about 100 of each in winter. Numbers of most other ducks are tiny. Gadwall are annual with up to five present, Wigeon vary greatly from 20 to 100 or more, and other dabbling ducks visit sporadically, mostly in ones and twos. Pochard annually peak at not much more than 20 or 30, and Tufted at only half that. Goldeneye are regular, usually three to five brownheads. More casual visitors are Goosander, averaging even fewer, and Smew, occurring rarely in ones and twos. Other diving ducks are occasionally noted, including the rare Ring-necked Duck from America. Wild swans, usually Bewick's, have been recorded from time to time. Coot usually reach 100–200 in winter and two or three pairs may breed.

Unlike most reservoirs in the region, where spring sees the disappearance of most birds, several arrive and breed. The Great Crested Grebe, a scarce breeder in the Southwest, has nested recently. A few pairs of Reed and Sedge Warblers are summer residents. Most numerous breeders are Black-headed Gulls; up to 50 young have fledged at this irregular colony. Other commoner gulls bathe and preen, 200 Herring Gull being about normal most of the year. Small numbers of waders pass through in spring. Regular, distinctive and easily seen are Whimbrel. Not so regular are mountain-nesting Dotterel, small parties of which have been found on the airfield for a few days. They might also be seen on return passage in autumn in ones and twos, often among Golden Plover. Montagu's Harrier have visited on spring passage.

Autumn draws the region's more active birdwatchers, often finding interesting migrants and rarities. One of the earliest flocks of Golden Plover in the region congregates here, acting as decoys and attracting other related species. Rare, but regular in recent years, is the American Lesser Golden Plover; occurring mostly singly, difficult to identify unless you are fairly expert, they often resemble Grey Plover, which also occasionally turn up! Another American wader, the smaller Buff-breasted

Dotterel

Sandpiper, is not seen annually; when present, it often associates with plover flocks on the airfield. Unfortunately Buff-breasteds closely resemble small female Ruffs (Reeves), which also mingle with Golden Plover. An Asiatic Sociable Plover has also been seen on the airfield.

Small numbers of commoner migrant waders drop in on the reservoir's muddy margins, including a few Ringed Plover, while Dunlin attain small flocks of 30–40. Spotted Redshank, Redshank and Greenshank are seen in groups of three or four apiece, while fewer Green, Wood and Common Sandpipers, Black- and Bar-tailed Godwits occur. Little Stint and Curlew Sandpiper are noted most autumns in ones and twos, though peaks of five or six are not unusual. The reservoir has its share of American waders: Pectoral Sandpiper, Wilson's Phalarope and Long-billed Dowitcher have all graced its mud. (It should be noted that there is often interchange by many species between the two sites, if there is particular disturbance at one or conditions become more favourable at the other; birds do not necessarily stick to their normal habitat.) Black Tern are annual autumn visitors to the lake, often singly or in small numbers, and have passed through in spring.

Another group of species which ranges over both sites, as well as surrrounding moorland, is birds of prey. Food supplies, in the form of flocking birds, are an obvious attraction. All three common resident raptors are here, with others particularly during autumn and winter. Several reliable records of the often misidentified Goshawk have come from here, with adults, immatures, males and females accurately described. Hen Harrier, present on moorland around, occasionally overfly the area, wings held in a shallow 'V' as they glide; females and immatures are the more common. Peregrine arrive in early autumn and may not depart until late spring. Dashing Merlin arrive later and normally depart earlier, ranging more widely. The Hobby has been seen in spring and autumn as an irregular passage migrant. A Marsh Harrier has wintered.

Numbers of resident or breeding passerines are swollen in autumn by migrants – Meadow Pipit and Skylark for example. Other open-ground species such as Wheatear, which breed in small numbers nearby, become more numerous. Two uncommon open-ground buntings, Snow and Lapland, are occasional visitors in ones and twos in late autumn.

Timing

On fine weekends the airfield often suffers disturbance from model aircraft and gliders, so a morning visit is preferable. Individuals of smaller American waders are unconcerned; neither of these activities scares them off. Other birds move to a quieter corner, while some leave the vicinity completely, a few alighting by the reservoir. Plovers normally leave completely. Towards evening in autumn, disturbed birds, including plovers and associated species, or those which have fed elsewhere, often return to roost. This can be a rewarding time, with raptors also more active now. Vast flocks of Starling return to roost at dusk in autumn and winter.

Winds or thick mist may be localised here, or worse than elsewhere, and until your arrival you may have no real indication of conditions. Hard weather elsewhere may increase species and numbers, but, if conditions are really bad, almost certainly there will be a marked decrease. Windsurfing, towards the dam end of the reservoir, normally does not affect waders.

Access

From A39 at Camelford, minor roads lead to the site. A road runs lengthways through the airfield (with several places where you can pull off). From A30 take Altarnun turn, following minor roads after that village. From A395, several minor roads will bring you to the road running the length of the airfield; the route from A30 also leads to this same airfield road. The slightly raised road, along the flat airfield area (beware of wandering sheep), has several pull-off places on either side which lead onto the old runways across the grass; you will need these to cover the whole area adequately.

Drive along both sides of all runways slowly, stopping every 100 m or so to scan for birds; this allows close approach to species which would never permit such closeness on foot. On finding your quarry, watch from the car; you will obtain good views without disturbing them, or preventing others from seeing them. If on foot, extreme caution is needed in approaching birds, being prepared to watch most species from a greater distance. Areas near the old control tower appear favourite for many birds. Pools are attractive for some species. Raptors may be seen anywhere.

For the reservoir, from the airfield road, follow the signpost. Where the road begins to overlook the reservoir on the edge of the forestry plantation there is a pull-in. A track here leads to a hide on the water's edge at the marshy end. The reservoir can be checked from this road for waterfowl, or birds flying over, which are seen reasonably well especially with a telescope. For close access, walk to the water's edge via the track; you will need to do this when checking for waders.

Apart from use of the hide, this site, although bleak in winter, lends itself very well to visits by elderly or disabled people. The hide is kept locked; keys and permits needed for entry are available from South West Water.

Calendar

Resident: Little Grebe, Grey Heron, Sparrowhawk, Buzzard, Coot, Black-headed Gull, Coat Tit, Raven.

December–February: possibly wild swans. Teal, Wigeon, probably Gadwall, Pochard, Tufted Duck, Goldeneye, possibly Smew or Goosander. Dabbling and other diving ducks in ones and twos, sporadically. Hen Harrier, Peregrine, Merlin, Golden Plover, Lapwing, possible Ruff and Woodcock, Snipe, maybe Jack Snipe. Fieldfare, Redwing, millions of Starling roost.

March–May: most above visitors have departed by April. Wheatear from mid-March, Whimbrel from mid-April. Possible Dotterel (late April–May) and Ruff. From end of April on, possible Montagu's Harrier or Hobby, and marsh tern e.g. Black. Cuckoo.

June–July: breeding species, may include Great Crested Grebe, Black-headed Gull, Reed and Sedge Warblers, Wheatear. First returning waders, e.g. Spotted Redshank, towards end of period.

August–November: waders gradually increase in number and species; most are seen on the reservoir at the beginning, e.g. shanks and sandpipers. Early September, a few hundred Golden Plover. Most other waders begin to reach peak numbers through September. Uncommon and rare waders appear. Black Tern. Peregrine and Goshawk may appear. Early October, Merlin arrive, also Snow and Lapland Buntings, perhaps. Towards end of period, most waders have departed. Golden Plover, Lapwing and Snipe increase. Winter thrushes begin arriving, as do Hen Harrier.

24A ADDITIONAL SITE: TREGONETHA AND GOSS MOOR

OS ref: SW 9663
OS map: sheet 200

Habitat

An area of rather high, poorly drained rough ground in central Cornwall. Various bushes, small trees especially sallows, and heather, are interspersed with small fields. A small conifer plantation grows near the Tregonetha site.

Species

Tregonetha is of primary importance as a winter roost (November–March) for five or six Hen Harrier, inexplicably choosing a small indistinct area of heather-clad slope. Tregonetha also attracts other wintering raptors making last attempts to feed, or coming to roost in nearby trees. Species can include Sparrowhawk, Goshawk, Buzzard, Kestrel, Peregrine and Merlin. Barn Owl still frequent the area, with occasional Short-eared Owl.

Among marshy pools and willows around Goss Moor especially, resident Willow Tit and wintering Woodcock occur. The area could be worth a look at other seasons for those species preferring these habitats; a Great Grey Shrike stayed several weeks one spring, and a few pairs of Curlew breed.

Timing

The harriers begin arriving around the roosting area during late afternoons, though not actually going to roost until virtually dark, usually allowing an hour or so of observations down to 150 m before enveloped in darkness. Still days are the best time to visit. It is while waiting that other raptors may be seen.

Access

From A30 take the B3274, signposted to Tregonetha and Padstow; travel for about 2 miles (3.2 km), and continue over the brow of a hill. When wide valley area is in full view, park beside road, near a minor road signposted to Kernick. Harriers usually fly in from a northerly direction. Scan area from raised verges, but **do not** walk around over the ground as you will cause serious disturbance of roosting sites. Such behaviour is only practised by a tiny minority of ignorant and thoughtless birdwatchers, but would also completely undermine the credibility of the vast majority of responsible birders.

From B3274 minor roads fringe the bushy areas of Goss Moor.

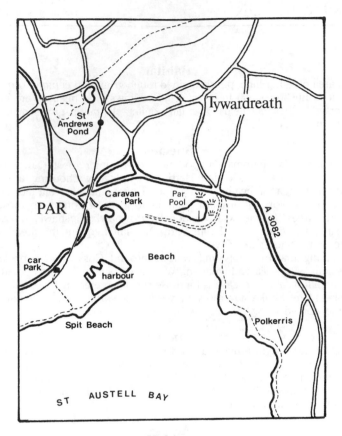

Habitat

Par Sands Beach forms part of St Austell Bay. Set within a typical mid-south Cornish coastline, it has a developed harbour waterfront on one side, the large industrial buildings projecting incongruously into the scene. Par has three main centres of interest: a relatively small freshwater pool (set behind low sand dunes), a wide shallow sandy beach, and the relatively sheltered seas offshore.

Par Beach Pool is the single most important area of fresh water here, being about 2½ acres (1 ha) in extent. The pool has mostly open banks, but with a fringe of reeds at the back and along one side. A caravan site is adjacent, with houses nearby. During summer, the area is a busy tourist resort.

One of only two known sites of Mossy Stonecrop in the Southwest region is found along the sandy margins of the pool. The general area, including the dunes, has a high botanical interest, while owing to the brackish nature of the pool, only the ubiquitous Blue-tailed Damsel breeds successfully. Eighteen commoner species of butterfly breed, including a small population of Dingy Skippers.

Species

This site offers much of interest during winter and spring, although autumn produces interesting birds especially at the pool, particularly elusive reed-bed species (mainly discovered by ringers), such as cryptically patterned Bittern and Spotted Crake, and plain-plumaged Savi's Warbler. Reed-beds, even small ones, are often invaluable as roost sites. Par is no exception, being well used by autumn's departing migrants. A thousand or more Swallow gather at dusk, along with Yellow Wagtail in varying numbers, usually 30 or so, and up to 200 Pied and White Wagtails (the latter the attractive grey-backed Continental race). Pied Wagtails stay on with a few Reed Bunting and up to 50,000 noisy Starling roosting during winter.

Apart from resident Mallard and Moorhen and a bizarre mixture of feral ducks, about ten pairs of Reed Warbler, five pairs of Sedge Warbler, and at least one pair of Cetti's Warbler breed in the reed-bed. Three Night Heron visited the poolside together recently.

As winter sets in, a wide variety of ducks arrives, mostly in small numbers. Diving Pochard occasionally reach 50, with lesser numbers of Tufted Duck. Dabbling Mallard number about 100, with up to 30 Coot. These species make up the bulk of waterbirds, with other duck only in very small numbers; perhaps ten Gadwall or Shoveler may arrive, or a few Scaup and Goldeneye. Little Grebe are watched reappearing rapidly after a short dive; up to 20 have congregated, although in recent years they have become much scarcer.

Gulls inhabit the area in very large numbers, using the pool to bathe, drink and shelter, taking advantage of a copious food supply laid on by residents – or birdwatchers trying to entice a Ring-billed Gull to feed from their hand! This American gull has been turning up in twos and threes here with regularity in recent winters. Black-headed and Herring Gulls are attracted to human environs generally, the former often exceeding 5,000, the latter about 1,000. Among them are Common Gull, up to 1,000 at times, but less than half that number of Great Black-backed Gull. Fewer Lesser Black-backed Gull stay to winter, but by winter's end start arriving back from West African waters. On the beach they assemble in many hundreds before moving off to their breeding grounds. Less common gull species appear virtually annually, including Glaucous, rarer Iceland, also Mediterranean and Little, all mostly appearing in immature plumages. They present a challenge when one or two of them may be settled among a tightly-packed flock of similar commoner birds, thousands strong.

Waders are few in winter. Surprisingly, numbers of Sanderling occurring on this sandy beach hardly attain double figures, while Turnstone usually number over 50. The most common waders are robust Oystercatcher, with over 150. Purple Sandpiper may reach ten, although rising in spring to about 25; a staging post for migrants? In autumn over 50 Ringed Plover and 100 Dunlin gather, their numbers gradually dwindling as winter approaches, when a few Grey Plover may arrive, aptly named at this season. There is a thin passage of other common waders. Unusual waders are even fewer, although several Curlew Sandpiper and Little Stint are possible; odd Wood and Green Sandpipers and Spotted Redshank may also stop over. The Little Ringed Plover has visited, and so has the rare Kentish Plover (several times) during later spring. Recently this season also produced a group of four Black-winged Stilt flying in off the sea. Spring is also the season to expect large flocks of migrating Whimbrel to drop in to rest. Terns also visit, pausing to fish, a bonus in a county not renowned for spring arrivals of this genus. Scarcer species such as Little or Roseate occur in small numbers but Common Tern can reach 50 or more, often accompanied by larger numbers of Sandwich. Autumn return passage often brings similar numbers and species.

The bay poses observation problems, being wide and not easily overlooked; however, the clifftop walk along the eastern edge offers your best chance of seeing over the further parts of the bay, with some species preferring this side. Several Red-throated Diver favour the area around Polkerris almost exclusively. Numbers of other divers, grebes or seaducks are generally low, although Great Northern Diver can reach ten. Black-throated and Red-throated Divers wander into the bay in small numbers, both species probably increasing somewhat during spring. Common Scoter can assemble in flocks of up to 50, occasional appearances being made by two or three Eider, and Slavonian or Red-necked Grebe.

Timing

At such an exposed coastal site, calm conditions are obviously an advantage to watch passive gatherings. Strong westerly or southerly winds have no history of producing instant passage in this large bay, although they could encourage birds to seek relative shelter. In rough seas any divers, grebes or seaducks may be hard to see unless close inshore. During strong easterlies, the bay is quite sheltered along its eastern (leeward) side, where waterbirds seek refuge. Southerly winds in spring might influence terns and some waders to use the British side of the English Channel while migrating through it eastward, when the bay is obviously attractive as a temporary resting place.

At Spit Beach there is a high tide roost, particularly favoured by waders and terns at the appropriate seasons. Hard winter weather usually increases both numbers and species. 'Flat' overcast light is best; glare from a low winter sun can be a problem over the sea.

Access

The A3082 passes close by Par's beaches and pool; take the minor road signposted to Par Sands Holiday Park, the entrance of which is immediately west of the Ship Inn, leading to parking places beside the pool and overlooking the beach, while allowing unrestricted access for the disabled. *Note:* public access is allowed over this privately owned road (a small charge is imposed during summer).

For roosting waders and terns at high tide at Spit Beach, park in a free public car park behind the harbour (beside A3082). A public footpath runs to Spit Beach. Birds also roost on the nearby harbour wall, and can be viewed by walking towards it on the footpath, but there is no disabled persons access; there is no public access into the busy, private dock.

A public footpath runs along low cliffs on the eastern shore, joined near the edge of the beach towards Kilmarth; the walk continues to Polkerris, about 1 mile (1.6 km). This walk in winter can produce finch flocks, and allow uninterrupted viewing over the bay.

Calendar

Resident: Mute Swan, Mallard, Moorhen; Water Rail has bred. Rock Pipit. Kingfisher, Grey Heron and Dipper have all bred nearby.

December–February: wintering Little Grebe and Coot. Duck include mostly Pochard, also Tufted. Occasional Gadwall, Shoveler, single Scaup or other species arrive intermittently. Interesting gulls could well include Ring-billed, Glaucous or possibly Iceland, the first two annual in ones and twos, as are Mediterranean. A few Purple Sandpiper among commoner waders. Lesser Black-backed Gull increase towards end January. Divers, grebes and seaducks occur in mostly small numbers.

March–May: most gulls decrease, although Lesser Black-backed may increase. Iceland and Little Gulls can arrive. Great Northern and Black-throated Divers usually increase, possibly in summer plumage, peaking later April, when terns begin arrival; scarcer terns mostly May. Whimbrel and Purple Sandpiper can arrive throughout, chance of Kentish Plover. Reed and Sedge Warblers breed.

June–July: mostly only resident species breeding, plus Reed and Sedge Warblers.

August–November: reed-bed may produce a rarity particularly up to October, and hosts roosts of wagtail, Swallow and Starling. Early part of period sees terns passing through bay. Waders can include Curlew Sandpiper, Little Stint and Green Sandpiper. Wintering species arrive in greater numbers on pool and in bay towards end of period.

26 GERRANS BAY AND NARE HEAD

OS ref: SW 9038
OS map: sheet 204

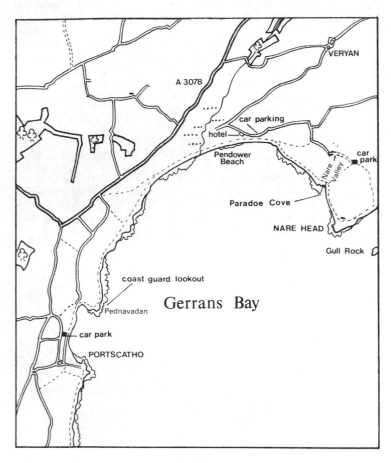

Habitat

A southerly-facing bay on the south coast of Cornwall, east from Carrick Roads waterway system (near Falmouth). The bay has no apparent unique habitat features; a rocky coast extends its length, unprotected from heavy seas from most wind directions. Gerrans Bay runs from Nare Head at the east end west to Portscatho. The exposed and scenic Nare headland itself is under National Trust control with public footpaths. These paths run eastward far beyond Nare, and are continuous westward to Portscatho and beyond.

Nare Head has a good range of commoner butterflies including a strong colony of Green Hairstreaks, found near the mouth of Nare Valley. A variety of habitats encompassing many wildlife requirements is found in a fairly compact area, offering the chance of a good natural history walk combined with dramatic views.

Species

The bay's real claim to fame emanates from one species, the Black-throated Diver. The area holds numbers unequalled anywhere else in Cornwall, peak counts occasionally exceeding 50. The population can fluctuate wildly throughout winter and spring months, even during the period when they are traditionally present in good numbers. This may arise through genuine absence or because they have moved farther out to sea; some may move to another area (they visit adjacent Veryan Bay).

Red-throated, Black-throated and Great Northern Divers

The Black-throated usually form several groups, scattered across the area. At times they feed very close to shore, among rocky gullies densely covered in seaweed, searching out small crabs and fish. Later in April a few may attain immaculate summer plumage; the white foreneck is lost, as are the white flanks, but they still lack any trace of tail, an important distinction from either Shag or Cormorant.

The next most numerous diver, Great Northern, struggles to muster ten individuals at a time, five being average. The Red-throated Diver, as elsewhere in South Cornwall (apart from passage birds at one or two localities), is a scarce, irregular visitor, usually singly. Grebes are annual winter or early spring visitors, most numerous being Slavonian, for which this is possibly the best site in Cornwall, with ten normally present, reaching double this figure quite often. The Black-necked Grebe, confusingly similar, and the larger Red-necked Grebe, which has a diagnostic yellow-based bill, are annual but scarce; only ones and twos are normally recorded, staying usually only a week or two. Great Crested Grebe are very spasmodic in occurrence. Seaduck are poorly represented, only groups of up to 20 Common Scoter visiting with any regularity. There is a possibility of the odd Velvet Scoter, or a few Eider, usually brown females or pied immature males. Most surprisingly, a female King Eider, a northern species which never usually reaches our region, has been recorded close inshore off Portscatho. Guillemot and Razorbill breed on Gull Rock (off Nare Head), although numbers of both fluctuate each year; up to 30 or so pairs of Razorbill may nest, with Guillemot sometimes attaining over 75 pairs; a few individuals of both species are present throughout the year. Several pairs of Lesser Black-backed Gull also breed. Sandwich Tern can be watched heading eastward from early spring, or west in autumn. Other terns, such as Common or Arctic, are also seen, but less predictably. Whimbrel pass, usually in small flocks, and Fulmar cruise by *en route* to nearby breeding ledges.

Nare Head is very underwatched and under-rated with respect to a very wide range of migrants; the few watchers who visit enthuse over its potential. Were it visited on a regular basis it would certainly offer many avian rewards. Good numbers of all the commoner migrants are recorded, especially during spring, possibly less so in autumn. One notable rarity was a Red-rumped Swallow. Other, unexpected visitors to the general Gerrans Bay area have included Bonaparte's Gull, Least Sandpiper (an unusual midwinter record), and a Lesser Grey Shrike, at Portscatho.

Timing

Any daylight hours should suffice. Flatter light reduces glare and shadow caused by low winter sunlight. An incoming tide may induce birds to drift closer to shore. Calmer seas enhance chances of picking out smaller birds such as grebes. Calm conditions are virtually assured with northerly biased winds. During westerlies, water birds often move to Portscatho. During the last hour or so of winter daylight, up to 300 Shag fly eastwards from the St Anthony Head area to roost at Gull Rock, about which time divers cease feeding, remaining on the surface; often highest counts are then made, whereas grebes continue diving almost until dark.

Access

Leave A3078 when signposted to Pendower Beach and Hotel. The road runs beside the hotel, and adjacent to the cliff edge (more or less beside the hotel) are roadside parking spaces for several cars. This is probably the best vantage point in the bay, with at least a few divers and particularly grebes always present in winter; it is not unusual to find the largest flocks off here. From Pendower, rejoin the A road at the point where you left it. Next checking place is at Pednavadan (near the village of Rosevine). Park carefully, beside the narrow road, taking care not to block farmers' access into fields. Walk out to the point along public footpaths. A concrete bunker marks an appropriate place to stop and look. The coastline here is low, thus reducing distance between you and the sea, with close divers often an added bonus.

To check around Portscatho, park near the western edge of the village. At the west point of the village, watch from along coastal public footpath. Divers, grebes and seaducks are recorded, especially during prolonged stronger westerlies when numbers often increase as birds seek shelter. Some rare visitors have also occurred here. The bay here can be overlooked from a car, useful for the less physically mobile, by watching from the National Trust car park above the village; a telescope is essential from here.

For Nare Head, about 2 miles (3 km) south of Tregony just past the Roseland Garage, turn left off A3078 following signs straight on to Veryan, turning left at signpost to Carne, straight across cross roads, following the Carne and Pendower signs. After a few hundred metres turn left (still heading towards Carne); on a bend a National Trust sign reads Nare Head. Bearing right, pass over a cattle grid to the car park. The distance from Roseland Garage turn off to Nare Head is about 4 miles (6½ km). The so-called 'circular' walk around the Head comprises the high plateau clifftop some 100 metres above the sea, following a path down to within 10 m of the sea, a stiff incline. Our suggested route runs clockwise. From the car park, follow a farm track southwards for ½ mile (0.8 km) in the direction of Lemoria Rock with sea vistas and Gull Rock as a focal point. Turn northwards downhill (towards Pendower), to the mouth of Nare Valley at Paradoe Cove. Turn northeastwards up the valley amid bushes and some trees (good for migrants); the steep path leads onto a field edge and back to the car park.

Calendar

Resident: Cormorant, Shag, Guillemot, Razorbill.

December–February: up to early February, low numbers of Black-throated and Great Northern Divers, Slavonian Grebe; Common Scoter often present. Possible Red-throated Diver, Black- and Red-necked Grebes. Divers increase towards end.

March–May: March–early April, peak numbers of Black-throated Diver, especially beginning April. Late April, most divers and grebes have left, few remaining early May, perhaps in summer plumage. Sandwich Tern from early April, Common Tern and Whimbrel from mid-April, possibly Arctic Tern May.

June–July: breeding species.

August–November: from end May–November, little normally present; late October, first divers, probably increasing by late November; from November, grebes and seaducks.

27 FAL ESTUARY–
CARRICK ROADS COMPLEX

OS ref: SW 8336
OS map: sheet 204

Habitat

The Truro and Fal Rivers, joining to form Carrick Roads waterway have their combined entrance at Falmouth Bay, between the headlands of St Anthony on the eastern side and Pendennis on the west. Nearby is Falmouth town (see next chapter). Although tidal, deep water remains in the Roads, which at the widest point are about ¾ mile (1.2 km) wide; there are no sand or mud banks. On the eastern side of Carrick Roads a high steep bank, forming a brake, terminates in a low rocky cliff,

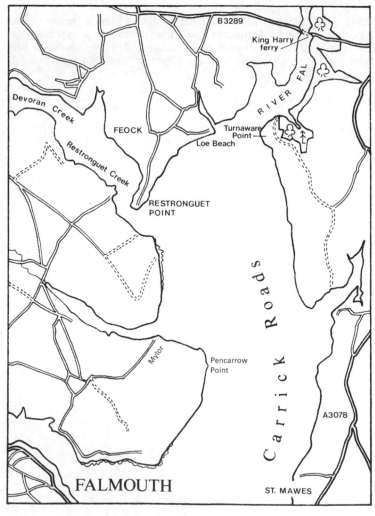

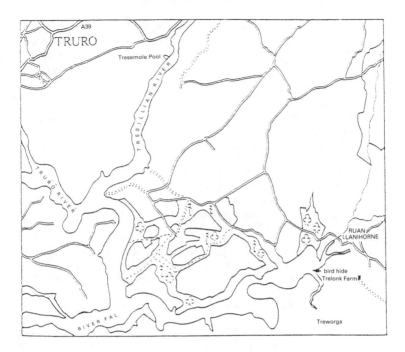

shelving abruptly into deep water. On the western side, land is more level, and villages such as Mylor, or individual houses, are scattered along.

Extensive creeks lead off on both sides of the Roads, the largest being Restronguet, sheltered from rough weather. It is mostly narrow, however, and suffers from human disturbance along both banks; there is a quieter, very narrow area towards Devoran. Tresillian is a very narrow, tree-lined river with a small saltmarsh; it is extremely sheltered from high winds. Many of the trees lining the banks are alder. Ruan Lanihorne is the wide upper reaches of the Fal estuary; here the surroundings are more open, and with human habitation lacking, much less disturbance occurs.

Species

The habitat and underwater-diet preferences of diving ducks are reflected by their concentrations on the Roads; Goldeneye regularly peak at more than 40, while the Red-breasted Merganser average is higher, often exceeding 50. This is the two species' stronghold in Cornwall. Females predominate, especially in Goldeneye. All three divers visit, Great Northern being most frequent, with two or three present for much of the winter, and often six or more together. Black-throated tend to appear later in the winter, when three to five is not unusual. Although recorded annually, the smaller Red-throated Diver is least common, very irregular, and usually seen singly. Grebes are regular visitors, most frequently Great Crested and Slavonian, with at least five of each present at a time most years; Black-necked and Red-necked Grebes are annual but irregular, in ones and twos. Eider and Common Scoter visit most winters, with up to ten of each sometimes, and single visits are occasionally made by Velvet Scoter, Long-tailed Duck and Goosander. Among the few Razorbill and Guillemot seen in winter are now almost annual sightings of single Black Guillemot; later sightings may find them in full black and white summer plumage. Why this largely sedentary northern auk should turn up here is a mystery. Both Shag and Cormorant are common, their preferred habitats overlapping in the Roads.

Restronguet Creek seems to attract only unexceptional numbers of commoner waders, many of which feed along deepish freshwater channels which flow across these mudflats. When the channels are filled by the incoming tide, waders begin to fly to Devoran roost, as remaining mudflats are rapidly covered. Up to 500 Dunlin and 200 Redshank form the bulk of birds at the roost. A few Greenshank and Spotted Redshank pass through in autumn, as do Little Stint and Curlew Sandpiper. Two or three of both migrant shanks stay to winter. Little Grebe frequent the main stream, remaining in the creek even when the tide is out. Surrounding sheltered gardens and hedgerows provide habitat for a few overwintering Blackcap, Chiffchaff, Firecrest and Black Redstart.

Tresillian River, with dense bush and tree cover in places, provides winter quarters not only for the same passerines as those found at Restronguet, but also for small flocks of Siskin which find here their favourite food, alder seeds. Grey Heron are resident and several pairs breed, as do Shelduck. Probably two pairs of Kingfisher also nest. Autumn brings a good passage of Spotted Redshank and the larger Greenshank, with more than 25 of each some years at peak times; about six of each may overwinter. Greenshank have slow, graceful wingbeats, their dark upperwing contrasting with white underparts; their ringing 'choo-choo' call also readily identifies them. Green and Common Sandpipers pass through in small numbers in autumn, but neither appears to stay regularly in winter. Black-tailed Godwit peak at about 50 most autumns, some still with rich chestnut underparts of summer plumage.

On the ornithologically important mudflats at Ruan Lanihorne, waders attract most attention. Apart from high numbers of common waders in autumn and winter, small numbers of less common visitors to Cornwall are regularly noted, mostly in autumn. These include Wood Sandpiper, and rarities such as American waders: Baird's and Pectoral Sandpipers have been seen. Among commoner waders, both Dunlin and Curlew can attain 1,000 each; Curlew usually peak in autumn, when about 800 is normal, whereas Dunlin numbers remain high throughout winter, sometimes reaching over 2,000. Oystercatcher may exceed 300. Black-tailed Godwit in autumn are over 200, one of the region's larger gatherings of this localised species, but only about 100 overwinter. Ringed Plover often reach 100 or so in autumn, but, as usual in south-west England, few remain to winter. A regular feature in early autumn is the number of Spotted Redshank which gather, up to 30 or more at a time in some years. Elegant birds, they wade belly-deep while sweeping their long, straight bills sideways through the water; several of the earliest arrivals may still be in their jet-black and silver-spotted breeding plumage. Greenshank can reach a similar number in autumn, and up to five of each species regularly winter. Little Stint and Curlew Sandpiper are annual autumn visitors, but numbers are never much over five apiece, often not even that. Ruff and Green Sandpiper are annual in ones and twos, as are Avocet, which sometimes stay to winter. Gulls roost and loaf in the area, Black-headed often exceeding 5,000, especially in autumn. Common Gulls average about 100 during winter. From late

Little Egret

winter the largest gatherings of Lesser Black-backed Gull take place, with several hundred sometimes present.

On the Fal complex, dabbling ducks are generally restricted to the most common kinds. Average peak numbers around Ruan area, where most are seen, are 200 Teal and Mallard, 400 Wigeon and about 100 Shelduck. Other ducks visit, sporadically in ones and twos, and include all diving species.

Grey Heron, like Mallard and Shelduck, breed near Ruan, where up to 20 nests have been counted. One or two pairs of Kingfisher also breed. The Osprey, usually singly, passes through in autumn, often staying several days, sometimes weeks. Peregrine are frequent visitors which menace and panic Ruan's avian occupants throughout autumn and winter. A Spoonbill may arrive during autumn or early winter, possibly staying for a month or two. Other exotic heron visitors have been Little Egret, a species more frequently recorded on the region's sheltered estuaries in recent years, and a Great White Egret once.

Timing

Low or incoming tides are required for waders on mudflats such as Devoran Creek and Ruan; rising tides concentrate previously scattered birds, and those feeding in deep channels, into reasonably defined areas. There is no one consistent high-tide wader roost at any of the sites. Very high tides (over 5 m) cover all mud and saltmarsh, and waders are forced into fields or split up to roost until tides begin to drop, exposing some mud.

From the hide near Ruan, waders are best seen an hour or so after the tide begins to rise, driving them out of gullies and main channels (which fill first) across still-exposed mudflats. This enables you to watch waders for several hours, before high tide moves them off altogether. At high water in winter, diving ducks, such as Red-breasted Merganser and Goldeneye, may follow the tide up, swimming close to the hide. If tides are not particularly high, waders at Ruan will roost towards the right-hand side of the hide.

It is pointless checking Devoran at low tide. As with Ruan, waders are forced out from deep channels and other hidden areas by rising tides. For about three hours before high tide, waders fly into Devoran Creek, and close views are obtained. On very high tides (over 5 m), roosting areas are flooded, and the birds disperse. Greenshank and Spotted Redshank do not usually appear until almost high tide. At low tide on Carrick Roads, some birds drift downstream towards the mouth, returning when waters rise; many, however, stay around the wider middle reaches at all times. Hard weather, as with other similarly sheltered areas in the Southwest, brings a short-term increase in many species as they flee worse conditions elsewhere. Boating activities in the Roads become quite busy from April onwards and this, combined with a traditionally early departure by many waterfowl wintering in southwest England, means that few birds remain from that date.

Access

To check Carrick Roads, leave A39 Truro–Falmouth road at St Gluvias and drive to Mylor village, where there are parking facilities. Walk along the beach on the south side of the creek to Pencarrow Point overlooking the Roads. This widest area is usually one of the best for concentrations of most species. A good telescope is essential for a complete check.

For the best area at Tresillian, mostly for close views of waders at low tide, leave A39 where signposted to Pencalenick, north of Truro as you leave towards St Austell. Leave your car beside the road at Pencalenick as near as possible to the public footpath. Take this good path, which follows the riverbank to St Clement, just outside Truro. The track passes Tresemple Pool, which often provides first-class views of Kingfishers. This walk is about ¾ mile (1.2 km).

Access to Devoran Creek is gained by taking a right turn from the direction of Carnon Downs on A39 south of Truro, along Greenbank Road, just before the main road crosses the creek and before reaching a garage. After entering Quay Road, drive at least 50 m past a very sharp bend (for safety), parking beside the road. Walk along this narrow road, adjacent to the creek. After about ¾ mile (1.2 km), you can obtain close views of assembled waders, before and after high tides.

Access to the hide near Ruan Lanihorne is by leaving A3078 Truro–St Mawes road at Ruan High Lanes. Drive a couple of hundred metres along the road signposted to Philleigh, then take a minor road to Trelonk Farm. (Please note: the hide is on private farmland. Access throughout the Fal complex is difficult, often impossible, because of private land, so please respect this farmer's stipulations.) Near the farm entrance the farmer has provided car-parking space which is marked, or enquire at the farm. Follow two fields leading from the car park to the hide. As there are no hedges or other cover near the hide for further concealment, the farmer insists that the hide **must** be used if a visit is made. Keys are obtainable only from Mr. G.C. Jackson, Curgurrell Corner, Portscatho, Truro; all enquiries should be addressed to him.

Calendar

Resident: Cormorant and Shag present all year. Grey Heron, Sparrow-hawk, Buzzard, Kingfisher, Raven.

December–February: divers of all three species; Little, Black-necked, Slavonian and Great Crested Grebes, probably Red-necked Grebe; Teal, Wigeon and other dabbling or diving ducks visit irregularly; seaducks – Eider, Common Scoter, possible Velvet Scoter, Long-tailed Duck – and Goosander. Goldeneye, Red-breasted Merganser, Dunlin, Spotted Redshank, Redshank, Greenshank, Black-tailed and Bar-tailed Godwits, Curlew, Snipe, probably Avocet, possible Spoonbill. Lesser Black-backed Gull numbers rise from February. Probable Blackcap, Chiffchaff, Firecrest, Black Redstart, Siskin.

March–May: by mid-April, most waders and waterbirds have departed. Possible rare species, e.g. Little Egret, from mid-April.

June–July: breeding species. By mid-July returning waders, including Spotted Redshank and Green Sandpiper.

August–November: most wader numbers and species increase through August and September, including Ringed Plover, Greenshank and Black-tailed Godwit. From September–October, waders include Little Stint, Curlew Sandpiper, probably Wood Sandpiper, Ruff; also raptors – possible Osprey, probably Peregrine. By end of period divers, grebes and seaducks returning.

28 FALMOUTH, THE BAY AND ROSEMULLION

OS ref: SW 8031
OS map: sheet 204

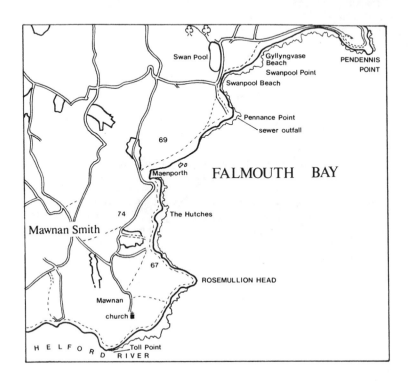

Habitat

On the west side of the large Carrick Roads–Fal estuary complex, at the mouth, lies the town of Falmouth. Eastward, docks face back towards Carrick Roads (see previous chapter); southwards, the town looks onto a deep but sheltered bay. A mile (1.6 km) of mainly rocky shoreline with small shingle beaches extends between Pendennis Castle promontory, by the estuary mouth, and wooded Pennance Point at the west. The tip of Pennance Point has a sewer outfall. A marshy wooded valley runs down the west side of the town, culminating in Swanpool, a ¼-mile (400-m) -long park lake with reedy fringes and alder trees immediately behind the beach. The town has large gardens with mature trees and bushes, including palms and other exotics. Water Voles are common in Swanpool.

West of Pennance Point, the high rocky coast of Falmouth Bay curves south towards the Lizard peninsula, interrupted by the deep mouth of Helford River (known as the Passage). Overlooking the Passage is the open downland National Trust property of Rosemullion Head, with wide coastal views, projecting eastward into the bay. The only gap in the cliffs between Falmouth and Helford Passage is at Maenporth, a deep sheltered cove and stream valley 1 mile (1.6 km) south of Pennance Point.

172

Species

Falmouth has gained a reputation in recent winters as a feeding area for large numbers of gulls, including regular occurrences of scarcer species, making it one of the better areas in our region for studying this group of birds. The town has overwintering warblers in the sheltered valley behind Swanpool, with the chance of an uncommon migrant at the lake.

The sharp rise in gull sightings off Falmouth is probably due partly to increased careful watching, and especially to large trawlers and fish-factory ships which may base themselves in the bay for periods during the winter. Thousands of gulls wheel screaming over the ships, generally too distant to watch, or rest in large numbers along seafront rocks, where they can be checked closely. Swan Pool and Maenporth Cove serve as drinking, bathing and preening areas, with a steady stream of gulls commuting in and out to boats. The majority of gulls following trawlers are Herring Gull, with brown immatures numerous. The more slender Iceland Gull, with long white wingtips, might be picked out among a resting flock; often they sit on flat rocks just east of Swanpool beach. Iceland Gulls can be as regular here as anywhere in southern Britain, especially in late winter. Care should be taken in distinguishing them from the other northern gull, the burly thick-billed Glaucous, also a regular visitor, often seen resting on Maenporth beach where many larger gulls including Great Black-backed gather. Wind and tide drift fish scraps onto the seashore, giving a chance for agile Black-headed Gulls hovering over the tideline, sometimes joined by a Little Gull. The smaller gull species can also be seen feeding at Pennance sewer. Mediterranean Gull are present most winters, particularly late in the autumn, with a chance of further individuals passing through, in a variety of plumages from young birds resembling patchy young Common Gull to white-winged winter adults. Common Gull move through in flocks towards spring. Kittiwake, normally oceanic feeders in winter, gather in thousands to feed on easy food sources here when the fishing fleet is present.

In early spring, most larger gulls soon move off, but one or two Glaucous or Iceland may linger late, fresh individuals appearing with passage groups of gulls moving up the coast. Black-headed and Common Gulls move through, with the chance of a rare transatlantic visitor such as a Bonaparte's Gull, or the now increasingly detected Ring-billed Gull, among them. Identification of the varying plumages of the many gulls present requires patient and meticulous watching.

Although most birdwatching visitors expect to see gulls, other species of interest may be found. Parties of several Great Northern and Black-throated Divers, and one or two Slavonian Grebe, are seen offshore. Small groups of Eider are irregular off the rocks, where Turnstone and Purple Sandpiper forage busily; a Black Redstart is likely in a sheltered corner of the shoreline or around seafront buildings. Auks are scattered on the sea in small numbers, and the rare Black Guillemot has been reported in the bay several times. The deep waters off Rosemullion and Helford Passage may also be used by feeding divers, seaducks, often including a Velvet Scoter or two, and auks. A Red-necked Grebe is seen most years, seeming to favour deep, rocky bays more than other grebes; this species and Velvet Scoter are also seen intermittently off Falmouth front, presumably the same individuals moving along the coast. Sometimes coastal ducks such as a single Long-tailed take up residence, along with Pochard and Tufted Duck, on Swan Pool, where close views are possible; Water Rail lurk in the margins.

Moving inland, sheltered trees near the stream behind Swan Pool often hold a wintering Blackcap, Firecrest or Chiffchaff, also seen in well-vegetated gardens around the town. Chiffchaff can be quite numerous, over 40 wintering birds having been counted in the district. Siskin in twos and threes use the waterside alders.

Early spring warblers and hirundines appear in sheltered coves. Groups of up to half a dozen Black-throated Diver pass through the bay, where the odd Slavonian Grebe may linger and acquire breeding dress, and Sandwich Tern are seen in small numbers. A variety of passerine species may be seen around Swan Pool, including one or two Sedge and Reed Warblers later in spring, which are likely to stay and breed, as do Little Grebe most years. Other 'marsh' species have included over-shooting rarities such as Little Bittern, surprisingly hard to see when not in flight, even in this thin fringe of reeds.

In later spring, and through to early autumn, seawatching off Rose-mullion promontory can be worthwhile, with a chance of Manx Shear-water, skuas and terns passing south offshore after being pushed into Falmouth Bay in poor weather. Although numbers have not been high (three or four skuas in a watch) and few birdwatchers spend time here, interesting observations, such as feeding parties of tiny Storm Petrel or a non-breeding summer flock of Pomarine Skua, have been made. Falmouth is busy with tourists throughout the summer and relatively little visited by birders until the end of the year, when gull numbers start to build up again. One winter, Britain's first Forster's Tern, from the Americas, spent several weeks fishing off the seafront. Late autumn gales may blow in a tired Grey Phalarope or Little Auk to rest on Swan Pool. Warblers around the lakeside at this season have included Yellow-browed and Pallas's.

Timing

In peak winter periods, gulls are constantly moving in and out from the beaches to ships, so give yourself time to wait (two or three hours at least) at strategic points such as Swanpool and Maenporth for incoming birds. Falling tides attract birds, mostly smaller gulls, to Pennance sewer, where larger species may be seen passing *en route* to favoured areas. For resting gulls on shoreline rocks and beaches, a dropping tide leaving more exposed landing space is best. Time of day is not critical; afternoon is usually best at Swan Pool for gulls, but avoid very late afternoon when fading light will not permit detailed watching. Easterly and southeasterly winds bring most fish debris onto the beaches.

Swanpool valley is most likely to hold interesting spring migrants and overshoot species when they funnel in on southerly and southwesterly winds. Wintering passerines are most numerous in years without heavy frost. Seawatching at Rosemullion seems best in winds between south and east in early morning, tending to drift seabirds nearer shore, and in poor visibility or drizzle, especially after anticyclonic spells. Strong depressional southwesterlies do not seem to produce much here, but may force individuals in to shelter on Swan Pool in late autumn.

Access

Falmouth lies at the south end of A39 from Truro.

Swanpool district: follow signs to Swanpool and Gyllyngvase beaches along a right fork as you enter Falmouth. (There is only a short gap between Penryn and Falmouth towns along the main road.) Continue along a suburban B-class road for 1½ miles (2½ km), then take a signposted right turn downhill past the cemetery. Arriving at the top end of the pool, stop to check marginal vegetation and trees behind. (*Note:* do not trample down reeds as some irresponsible birdwatchers have done in the past.) Drive down to the seafront car park, from which gulls are clearly visible flying in to bathe. Spend time here but also try walking east (left) along the tarmac footpath overlooking the shore rocks, round to Gyllyngvase beach (½ mile/0.8 km), or farther if large groups of gulls are visible ahead. Most scarcer species, however, are seen near the Swanpool end of the bay. Also try walking up past the cafe right from Swan Pool and along the muddy ½ mile (0.8 km) track to Pennance Point for close views off the sewer.

Maenporth is reached by following Swanpool beach road over the hilltop past the cafe, then forking left, about 2 miles (3 km) by minor road, or by coast footpath beyond Pennance.

Rosemullion and Helford Passage: continue beyond Maenporth for 2 miles (3 km) to Mawnan village, parking near the old church. On the coast path, turn left for ½ mile (0.8 km) out to Rosemullion for passing seabirds, or right for a few hundred metres to view the bay for divers, grebes and seaducks in winter.

Calendar
Resident: little of note, apart from Little Grebe, Shag.

December–February: Great Northern and Black-throated Divers, Red-necked and Slavonian Grebes, Tufted Duck, Pochard, seaducks, Water Rail, Turnstone, Purple Sandpiper. Gull flocks peaking February, including Glaucous, Mediterranean and Little among commoner species. Auks, Blackcap, Chiffchaff, Firecrest, Black Redstart, in small numbers.

March–May: wintering divers, grebes and gulls present to early April, with further migrant groups arriving, but total numbers drop from mid-March. Possibly a rare gull March–April, Sandwich Tern, early hirundines and singing warblers end March, summer migrants and maybe an overshooting rarity from mid-April. Manx Shearwater, Arctic, Pomarine and maybe Great Skuas, Sandwich and 'Commic' terns all possible off Rosemullion, especially May.

June–July: breeding Reed and Sedge Warblers. Off Rosemullion possibly seabirds, including Manx Shearwater, Storm Petrel, skuas, auks. Fulmar breed.

August–November: quiet period. Maybe skuas or terns off Rosemullion August–September, Grey Phalarope or Little Auk at Swanpool in November.

28A ADDITIONAL SITE: ARGAL AND COLLEGE RESERVOIRS

OS ref: SW 7633
OS map: sheet 204

Habitat

In the hills immediately west of Falmouth lie these two adjacent reservoirs. Argal (65 acres/26 ha) and College (35 acres/14 ha) lie on a north-south line, College being the more northerly. Argal has mostly open banks, but College has surrounding woodland. Both sites are steep-banked, lacking marsh or adjacent wetland. They are heavily used by anglers.

Species

The main interest is a variety of ducks, mostly diving species, and occasional interesting migrant waders. Water birds are likely to interchange with the Stithians Reservoir population, especially when human disturbance drives them from here. Duck numbers are perhaps higher on Argal than on College, with up to 60 Tufted and 20 Pochard on occasions; other sporadic diving visitors have included Goosander, Scaup and one or two Ruddy Duck. Goldeneye can often be seen in ones and twos in midwinter. Rarer visitors have included a Ferruginous Duck on College Reservoir. Dabbling ducks are not particularly attracted to these reservoirs, but apart from the expected Mallard, once a rare Blue-winged Teal arrived. Winter visitors to the reservoirs might see groups of bathing and roosting gulls; this is less noted as a gull site than the nearby coast, but there have been records of Mediterranean and Ring-billed, so it is worth checking. A Kingfisher may be present along the banks, and College Wood holds a cross-section of common woodland passerines and woodpeckers, often easier to see on leafless trees. There is little of note on spring passage usually, although recently a Night Heron was recorded. Great Crested Grebe have bred and might do so again, although this is isolated from other breeding sites. Interest changes as water levels drop in late summer, bringing sandpipers to the margins, including Green and Common; College tends to be more favoured. Other less regular migrants which might appear during autumn include Little Stint, Curlew Sandpiper, Wood Sandpiper, Ruff, in ones and twos. As with most Cornish lakes, there have been a few sightings of American wader vagrants, including Pectoral and Least Sandpiper; Black Tern are also noted occasionally.

Timing

The major factor is human disturbance, especially at College, so early morning or weekday visits are advised. Cold winter weather will increase duck numbers and dry autumns will increase mud available for waders, which might include American species after westerly gales.

Access

From Falmouth, take A39 to Penryn, turning left on B3291 towards Gweek and Helston. After 2 miles (3 km), turn right onto a minor road which takes you between the two lakes. A footpath, with a marked

Nature Trail, leads around College, which has open access; at Argal a permit is required to walk the banks, although it can be viewed from the car park and picnic area. Permits, if needed, can be obtained from the SWW Ranger at Little Argal Farm, Budock, near Penryn (tel. 0326-72544).

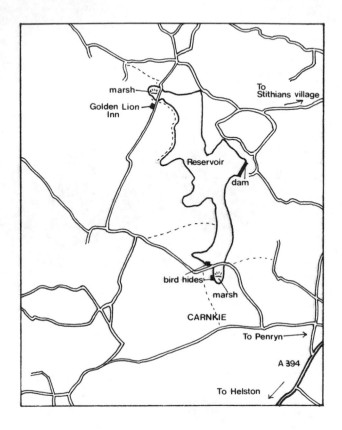

Habitat

At 274 acres (111 ha), this reservoir, south of the large town of Redruth, is the largest in the western half of Cornwall. It lies within a large area of high, rough ground, much of it semi-moorland covered by bracken and heather, reaching 250 m altitude. This setting produces weather conditions far removed from those on the sheltered south coast. Even on otherwise warm days, a chill wind often blows across this exposed water.

The reservoir is quite shallow over large areas, having steeper sides only towards the dam, and a margin of mud is quickly exposed at its further perimeters when water levels drop. No islands break up the lake's expanse. There is only minimal human habitation immediately surrounding the reservoir.

Species

This is the region's most important reservoir for birds, although the completion of the very large reservoirs at Colliford and Roadford may eventually alter the balance. As ducks and waders are the main species, most interest centres on autumn and winter. The surrounding rough open terrain is attractive to small numbers of birds of prey, which also hunt near and over the reservoir, providing added value for birdwatchers. Winter is particularly bleak here, so few of the waders which typically winter on the region's sheltered estuaries remain at Stithians throughout. Conversely, autumn wader counts for some species are the highest for either county, and many rarities have been found.

There are more dabbling ducks than diving species, possibly owing to the shallow grassy margins which they favour. Numbers, however, are not that large, and variety of species is limited. Teal and Wigeon are approximately equal in number, averaging 100 each and sometimes reaching double that, while Mallard total only about 50. Up to five Gadwall are usually present, but can reach 20 in some years. Few other species occur regularly, and then only in ones and twos. The most numerous diving duck is Tufted, with about 50 usually present; Pochard are less common, reaching only about 20. Counts of four or five Golden-eye, mostly females, can rise to more than 20 for short periods some years. Scaup are almost annual, visiting from late autumn on, often in twos and threes, and may include grey-backed males. Goosander do not arrive annually, but two or three might be present, usually brown-heads. Probably because of the reservoir's expanse and relative solitude, various wandering grey geese sometimes visit. The region as a whole is poorly served for grey geese, so any occurrences are noteworthy. White-fronted Geese predominate, and once a group of the Greenland form, which winters in large numbers in Ireland, was identified; Pink-footed and Greylag Geese have also been seen. Occasionally Bewick's Swan have also visited, in very low numbers.

Two or three pairs of Little Grebe breed. In winter up to 15 are seen, but other species are almost non-existent, with just a couple of sightings of Great Crested on record. Divers, although only ever accidental on our inland waters, also shun this locality, but a few single Black-throated have been reported. Cormorant fly far inland to feed, and four or five are not unusual. Coot can muster over 100 from late autumn onwards, and five or six pairs breed. Moorhen, which visit in small numbers, are not known to breed. Few uncommon species of gull are seen, and gull numbers here are fairly low, but the odd Mediterranean Gull has been identified among Black-headed Gulls.

As spring approaches, wintering ducks and other species are quick to depart. A combination of high water levels and poor spring wader passage generally in Cornwall means that very few pass through here at this season. If Stithians does not stand out as a 'hot spot' for spring waders, the same certainly cannot be said in autumn; indeed, waders pass in high numbers from late summer. Most of those early high numbers are created by Green, Wood and Common Sandpipers. This reservoir is certainly the best venue in both counties for these three birds. Green Sandpiper tend to disappear into narrow gullies, and hug grassy margins; over 20 may be seen at once. Wood Sandpiper are much less common, but here ten or more have been seen together, four or five being more normal. More elegant in stature, they feed more in the open. Soon a wide range of other waders appears, the plover family being well represented. Ringed Plover, reaching over 30, are found more on this reservoir than any other in Cornwall. Another plover which passes through with reasonable regularity is Little Ringed, and one or two may be watched among their similarly-marked chubbier cousins. Lapwing congregate early, over 1,000 spending winter in the general area. Golden Plover, too, return early, one of the few places where they do so, numbering perhaps less than 100 at first, although they may reach several thousand later. This small early flock is enough to lure one of Stithians' specialities; often one of the autumn's first major rarities is the American Lesser Golden Plover, here almost annual, and two or three are identified in some autumns; in flight their underwings are dusky grey, as opposed to the commoner bird's white. Dotterel have also been recorded.

Greenshank reach over 20 at a time, but few Redshank occur. Dunlin average 30, and Ruff can be equally common in some years, although ten is more usual. Each year at least two or three Ruff overwinter. As the autumn advances, more species arrive, including Little Stint and Curlew Sandpiper from Russia. In years when numbers are generally good, 15 or more of each may be seen together; such large numbers do not usually stay more than a week, and about five of each is more usual.

By now rarities, either extreme or semi-rare, will have shown up. One of the more regular comes into the latter category; Pectoral Sandpiper is almost an annual visitor, and seven together have been recorded, but one or two are seen most often. Long-billed Dowitcher is another fairly regular American species, visiting singly, and has been known to stay the winter. Lesser Yellowlegs, which resembles Redshank but has long, slender, yellow legs and lacks white on the wings, has turned up more than once. Baird's Sandpiper has been seen recently and Wilson's Phalarope has occurred. Solitary Sandpiper and Semipalmated Sandpiper are two other Americans which have been found here, all extremely rare anywhere in Britain. Snipe, on the other hand, reach over 200 in late autumn and winter, possibly accompanied by a Jack Snipe or two.

Teal arrive back early, and attract other closely related species. Garganey have visited here in spring, but this is one of the very few places in southwest England where they are seen more often in autumn, a careful search revealing one or two in most years. Two American teal have also been found among their European relatives: Cornwall's first record of Blue-winged Teal came from here, and the European Teal's New World subspecies, the Green-winged Teal, has stayed.

One or two Little Gull, often immatures with black-marked wings, and similar numbers of Black Tern pass through, both typical of reservoir habitats. The much-hoped-for White-winged Black Tern has also been seen.

As with any good birdwatching spot, the variety of different species seen, sometimes quite accidentally, heightens interest. Birds of prey other than the residents are seen quite often. Probably most regular are Peregrine, mostly single immatures, clumsily chasing whatever comes their way. The moorland attracts small numbers of Skylark and Meadow Pipit, and contains many small rodents. Merlin have specialised their feeding techniques for chasing small passerines over open ground; these tiny falcons have on several occasions been watched hurtling and twisting among panic-stricken flocks. There have also been sightings of the opportunist Hen Harrier, dropping into bracken after prey. Rodents are probably of most interest to the one or two Short-eared Owl which are seen most winters and often stay through to spring. Dead sheep are more to the liking of the few Red Kite which have drifted over. Lucky, and brief, sightings of Osprey and Hobby have been made of birds moving through. Recently the hirundines feeding over the water in summer were joined briefly by Britain's first Crag Martin.

Timing

Factors are few. If winds are high elsewhere, they will be worse here, from whatever direction. This makes observation difficult for the watcher, and encourages birds to huddle together or seek whatever shelter is available. Windsurfers use this water and disturbance is probably worse on weekend afternoons; this sport does not normally disturb waders but can disrupt waterfowl.

Access

The nearest A road is A394, from Helston to Penryn, from which you take Stithians sign north (left). The reservoir is reached by a minor road signposted to Carnkie. Roads run beside the lake at several points. Most people watch from these, which happen to be the most important wader spots, providing good views.

A road cuts off a small marshy part of the reservoir's southern tip, and here two hides have been erected, one either side of the road. From here, views are also gained of a large stretch of open water, often used by ducks. At the northern boundary of the reservoir, near the roadside Golden Lion Inn, a road again divides a small marshy area from the main lake. Here access around the western perimeter of the reservoir, generally the best side for waders, can be gained; open water is also seen from here. A road runs from this area to the dam. Keys for both hides, and access permits, are available if required from SWW.

Calendar

Resident: Little Grebe, Coot.

December–February: possible Bewick's Swan or grey geese, e.g. White-fronted; Teal, Gadwall, Wigeon, Pochard, Tufted Duck, possible Scaup and Goosander, Goldeneye, possible Hen Harrier, Merlin or Short-eared Owl. Golden Plover, Lapwing, Ruff, Snipe, possible Jack Snipe and Mediterranean Gull.

March–May: most waterfowl leave by end March. Light wader passage possible, including Ruff. Possible Short-eared Owl March–early April.

June–July: breeding species. By beginning of July first returning waders, especially Green, Wood and Common Sandpipers.

August–November: from early August, first Golden Plover and Lapwing, Ringed Plover, Dunlin, possible Lesser Golden Plover and Pectoral Sandpiper. From late August through September, Teal, maybe Garganey, Peregrine. September–October, probably Little Ringed Plover, Little Stint, Curlew Sandpiper, Ruff, Greenshank, possible Long-billed Dowitcher and other American rarities, Little Gull, Black Tern. Most waders left by end October. Lapwing, Golden Plover and Snipe increase. Most waterfowl begin returning November.

30 THE LIZARD

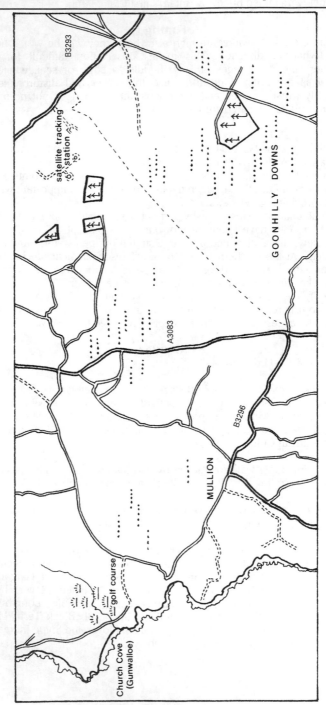

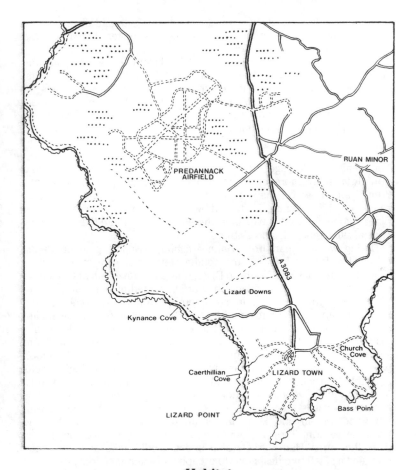

Habitat

On Cornwall's south coast, this is the most southerly peninsula in England. It is flat-topped, with few trees, and large areas inland are not particularly scenic, but with high cliffs (of serpentine rock in places) the coastline is spectacular, wave-lashed and rugged. Coves such as Kynance have superb scenery; their valleys often contain little dense cover, as soil is sparse, with a few wind-blown bushes, bramble and bracken. Church Cove offers more shelter than Kynance, with Cornish elms towards the valley head. Cottage gardens scattered through the valley provide further shelter. Toward the mouth, the bushes peter out to bracken and bramble. A brook runs through the valley. Another small bushy valley runs parallel about 100 m to the north. Gunwalloe valley has trees towards its head, but the valley bottom consists of reed-bed and marsh, lacking open water; a golf course flanks the south bank.

Towards the tip of the Lizard are very large tracts of wet maritime heathland, a habitat of European conservation importance. Most is owned by the National Trust; a large, especially interesting stretch lies above Kynance Cove. Predannack Downs Nature Reserve is renowned for its specialised habitat. Here, lilac-coloured flowers of normally rare Cornish Heath are abundant. A wide variety of heathers mingles with bright yellow flowers of Western Gorse. Open heathland also predominates on the west side of the Point, the nearest sheltered area from the tip being small Caerthillian Cove.

Among other interesting plants on the Lizard are Lesser Quaking Grass, both Dwarf and Pygmy Rushes, and several unusual clovers, including Upright and Twin-flowered Clover. High populations of Adders and Common Lizards are found on the heaths. Among a variety of butterflies, such as skippers, are Dark Green Fritillary and Grayling, as well as migrants such as Painted Ladies.

Species

The peninsula, a huge area, deserves more watching for birds and doubtless many more occur than are reported, especially migrants. Some parts, however, have difficult access, requiring long walks over rough or steep terrain, and land-ownership denies access to other places good for birds. We have therefore concentrated on southerly coastal sites, relatively accessible.

During winter, apart from Gannet fishing or passing in hundreds, especially off Bass Point on the southeastern corner, or an infrequent Black-throated or Great Northern Diver, only a few Razorbill or Guillemot, commoner gulls and abundant Shag are expected at sea. Purple Sandpiper and Turnstone feed in small groups among seaweed-covered rocks. On land, too, interesting birds are few, with little suitable shelter from winter storms. The Lizard is home to small numbers of the locally distributed Corn Bunting; it forms small flocks in winter, often harder to see than in summer when the male, perched on posts or telegraph wires, endlessly repeats its jingling song. Jackdaws, breeding in clefts and holes in rock faces, flock in thousands from late autumn onwards. Most common woodland species, however, are very scarce in this relatively treeless area. Birds of prey hunt over open expanses, with Peregrine, Merlin and Hen Harrier all present annually outside the breeding season. The fast, agile Merlin hunts largely over heaths, as does the larger Hen Harrier, also unexpectedly agile at times when pursuing a small bird desperate to escape its snatching talons. Peregrine range more catholically, often choosing for their prey a white-plumaged feral pigeon from a flock of more darkly marked birds. Two or more of each raptor usually winter. There is a light spring passage of Merlin, and a small autumn passage of all three species. Much rarer is the Red Kite, but several have passed through, and one or two have wintered. During spring further species of migrant raptors occur, including annually a few Hobbies. Increasingly rare in Cornwall, slim Montagu's Harrier are still noted some springs, now only singly. At least two or three Short-eared Owl arrive in spring, often staying a week or so before moving on; few, if any, regularly overwinter. There are recent spring records of the lovely little insectivorous Red-footed Falcon, a true rarity.

Early spring brings the first passerine migrants, a group of chestnut-tailed Black Redstart, a Wheatear or two, and less often but equally early a white-gorgeted Ring Ouzel, nervously perched atop a high boulder. A few Firecrest are also early arrivals. In general, high numbers of migrant passerines are not the order of the day. Throughout spring a scattering of short-staying migrants passes through in small groups; Chiffchaff, and rather more of the later Willow Warbler, arrive in parties of ten or more. Later still, Whitethroat come, and Wheatear numbers increase; some Wheatear breed, with up to ten pairs around the Kynance area alone.

Woodchat Shrike

Whinchat pass in groups of two or three throughout later spring. Far more Hoopoe are usually reported by the public than found by bird-watchers, but a few are seen annually in this area, including one or two in autumn when they are less expected. Other exotic overshooting migrants in spring have included Subalpine Warbler, Woodchat Shrike, Golden Oriole and the white-bellied Alpine Swift. Other commoner migrants are regular in spring, but in tiny numbers (only two or three Redstart or Spotted Flycatcher at a time). A few Turtle Dove pass in late spring and in autumn.

Seawatching in spring may provide a few coasting skuas, including perhaps a Pomarine or two. Passage of all seabird species, including Sandwich Tern, appears very light, although auks and Gannet are often in hundreds. Fulmar and Kittiwake breed nearby, including a colony of about 80 pairs of Kittiwake near Kynance. Occasionally in spring, Manx Shearwater pass by in hundreds. Oddly, in spring as well as in autumn, the majority of movement is westward for all species. Common Scoter and Puffin occurrences peak here in summer, with up to 15 Puffin and 50 or so Scoter passing in a day. Rather more skuas are seen in autumn than in spring. Sooty Shearwater are annual in very small numbers, while both the rare Great and Cory's Shearwaters have occurred. Gannet can pass at 1,000 per hour, and Kittiwake peak in late autumn, when hundreds include many black-marked first-winter birds.

Some passerine migrants are far more numerous in autumn than in spring, and probably more unusual species also occur then. Up to 50 Wheatear per day may be seen, and more than ten Whinchat at a time. Spotted Flycatcher, the less common Pied Flycatcher, and Tree Pipit all occur more than in spring. Small groups of both Yellow and White Wagtails pass through, and coasting Grey Wagtail head westward, sometimes a steady trickle of ones and twos through the day, for several weeks. A long-tailed Tawny or Richard's Pipit may be found among wagtail and pipit flocks.

Less common migrants which appear almost annually, often in early autumn, are Wryneck, and Icterine and Melodious Warblers. Although the first is a woodpecker, it often creeps along low stone walls in search of food. The two stout warblers, both possessing a long dagger-like bill, require experience to tell apart. Swifts, late arriving and early departing, pass through in hundreds per day in both seasons. During this earlier autumn period, Red-backed and Woodchat Shrikes sometimes arrive. All shrikes are uncommon, and colourful adult males are a lucky find, but grey-brown immatures are also likely. Among major autumn rarities in recent years was an Upland Sandpiper, an American wader of grassland, seen on extensive heathland around Kynance.

From late autumn a few Ring Ouzel, Black Redstart and Firecrest replace the early migrants. One or two Lapland or Snow Bunting may appear on open ground towards the close of autumn. Finches and buntings are always among the last large-scale passerine arrivals. Chaffinch form the bulk, with many hundreds moving through; among them the similar but distinctively white-rumped Brambling occurs, picked out by nasal 'tchaek' calls overhead.

Timing

Correct weather conditions are always important for migration-watchers. Spring passerine migration in Cornwall is generally small, and conditions need to be very favourable. Fall conditions are ideal, but any winds off the Continent, particularly south or southeast, will bring birds across; even in clear weather, a small proportion of the birds passing over will land. Before travelling on, these less-fit birds will need to seek food and possibly rest; they often take only a couple of hours after dawn if they have arrived overnight, especially in later spring, and by mid-morning, an area which held a scatter of interesting migrants at dawn can be almost empty. Exceptions are day-flying migrants such as Swift and Swallow, which leave the French coast at first light, arriving here four or five hours later; in mid-spring they begin to arrive about mid-morning.

During autumn, movements are much more protracted and, although quiet mornings are still often best, many birds remain throughout the day, perhaps for several days. For new arrivals the same conditions apply as for spring.

Although the Lizard appears a very good seawatch point, it is useless unless winds are in the southern half of the compass; even if winds are only light from southerly quarters, passage may occur. In spring a seawatch between dawn and mid-morning is essential; after this time migration usually ceases. The same applies in autumn unless winds are gale force, when migration can last all day. Sea mist and poor visibility, causing birds to hug the coastline, can also bring results.

For winter landbirds, choose a fine day without high winds, when birds will not shelter and raptors can hunt over moors.

Access

By A3083 down the peninsula from Helston. The first cove off this road is Gunwalloe, also called Church Cove; we have used the former name to avoid confusion with Church Cove near Lizard Point, which is described above. For Gunwalloe, follow a good road taken opposite the far end of Culdrose Airfield, through Gunwalloe village, following signs to Church Cove where there is a large car park. Try tamarisk bushes along car park hedges, and around adjacent farm buildings, for migrants. Among reeds and marsh are high breeding populations of Sedge Warbler and Reed Bunting. Cetti's Warbler almost certainly breed, but are far more often heard than seen. Public footpaths follow the coastline left and right of the cove. Among the cove's sandy-topped cliffs Sand Martins breed. Public access to the lower part of the reed-bed is by walking along the golf-course edge.

Kynance Cove is reached via a private toll road; at the bottom is a car park. Walk right a few hundred metres to the steep, quite small valley. For Predannack Downs, continue up the steep valley slope. Another, more direct, access to Predannack Downs is by parking in a pull-in opposite Kynance road. Walk towards Helston for about ½ mile (0.8 km), where there is a wide track through a gap in the hedge, level with the road, on the left. Small grassy fields on its perimeter are favoured by pipits; open areas are used by raptors.

For Church Cove near the tip, taking the road forking left just before Lizard town, immediately past the private Kynance road. Follow signs until the church, where there are limited parking spaces. Walk down through the village after searching through the elms and churchyard areas. The tarmac road becomes a rough track near the cove. A National Trust footpath is taken on the left, and another small bushy valley leads back to the church.

To reach Bass Point, best for passing seabirds, walk from the head of Church Cove along a concrete path to the lifeboat station, then continue to the Point along a narrow clifftop path about 1 mile (1.6 km) to the Coastguard station.

Caerthillian Cove is not signposted anywhere. Park in Lizard town square, following the public footpath beside it, signposted to Kynance Cove and Pentreath Beach. Walk for about ¾ mile (1.2 km) along a wide track, alongside a row of houses; the last house overlooks the small shallow valley. It contains no trees. Cover for small migrant birds is blackthorn bushes, bramble, and gorse especially towards its head; although sparse, this is the only cover within 2 miles (3 km) this side of the exposed Point, and surrounded by equally exposed land.

Flat Goonhilly Downs are reached through the middle of Culdrose Airfield, on B3293. Scan moorland around the satellite-tracking dishes. Minor roads left and right, which dissect the open ground, can be taken. Raptors use this area and a few pairs of Curlew breed; use your car as a hide. The B road continues to Coverack Cove.

Calendar
Resident: Shag, Sparrowhawk, Buzzard, Cetti's Warbler, Curlew, Corn Bunting, Raven; Gannets offshore all year.

December–February: seabirds including Black-throated or Great Northern Diver, Guillemot and Razorbill, Hen Harrier, Peregrine, Merlin, Purple Sandpiper, Turnstone, possible Short-eared Owl, winter thrushes.

March–May: a few Firecrest and Black Redstart by early March; mid–end March, Chiffchaff and Wheatear, possible Ring Ouzel. Early April, Willow Warbler, possible Hoopoe; mid-April, Merlin, Short-eared Owl, Whitethroat, hirundines. End April–early May, Swift, higher numbers of above warblers, other commoner warblers, Whinchat, Redstart, Spotted Flycatcher, possibly Hobby, Turtle Dove; perhaps southern overshoots from mid-April. Manx Shearwater, possible Arctic or Pomarine Skua.

June–July: breeding species, including Wheatear, Whitethroat, Sedge

Warbler, Sand Martin. Common Scoter and Puffin passage peaks mid-June–end July.

August–November: seabirds, including a few Arctic, Great or Pomarine Skua, possible Great or Cory's Shearwater, probably Sooty Shearwater especially early in season. Later in season (October–November) Kittiwakes peak. Commoner passage migrants through September, especially Wheatear, Whinchat, Tree Pipit, Yellow Wagtail, coasting Grey Wagtail. Possible Woodchat or Red-backed Shrike. Mid-October through November, Firecrest, Black Redstart, Ring Ouzel, possible Snow or Lapland Bunting. Chaffinch flocks contain Brambling; winter thrushes arrive.

30A ADDITIONAL SITE: LOE POOL

OS ref: SW 6424
OS map: sheet 203

Habitat
At 125 acres (51 ha) and only 1 mile (1.6 km) long, this relatively small water is nonetheless the largest area of naturally occurring fresh water in Cornwall. Situated near the town of Helston, it is separated from the seas of Mount's Bay by a massive shingle bank, known as the Bar. Towards the further end from the sea is Loe Marsh. Small woods on either side give shelter from 'sea breezes'! Loe Pool lies amid the National Trust-owned Penrose Estate; there is no shooting, and bank fishing is limited.

Species
Some interest may be sustained throughout the estate all year if watching the many kinds of common woodland passerines, although autumn through to spring provides opportunities of greatest interest on and around the pool. Autumn's muddy margins produce only small numbers of commoner waders. Common Sandpiper can reach 20, Green Sandpiper peak at half that, one or two regularly wintering. Several Little Stint, Greenshank, or Wood Sandpiper may pass through. Before the construction of several large reservoirs in the county, this site was regarded as one of the better places for wintering duck, particularly diving species (albeit in small numbers). Tufted Duck average 50, Pochard can exceed 150; no other diving duck attains anything like these numbers. Up to ten Goldeneye are annual. Both Long-tailed Duck and Scaup are less common, but regularly turn up in ones and twos. Rare American Ring-necked Duck have appeared several times. Dabbling duck are chiefly Mallard, of which about 250 winter and several pairs breed. Teal may number up to 100. Gadwall, Shoveler and Pintail can attain double figures, while Wigeon flocks increase dramatically in hard weather. Other species of duck are attracted irregularly in small numbers. The pool shelters an occasional diver, more regularly grebes, although only a few Little are regular. Great Crested and Slavonian are most frequent of the other grebes in ones and twos, plus infrequently a Red-necked or Black-necked. Coots vary between 50 and 200, depending on winter severity, and two or three pairs attempt breeding. Moorhens are well represented, joined by furtive Water Rails in winter, when you may chance upon a Bittern.

Wintering Great Black-backed Gulls form flocks of 300–500. Transient Lesser Black-backed in spring or autumn may reach 200 or so; among them may be a Glaucous or Iceland Gull.

Breeding species are curiously few, but there is a small colony of Reed Warbler. Unexpected migrants might turn up at any time, having included Hobby, Osprey, Hoopoe and Green-winged Teal.

The sea off here is not very productive, most birds preferring more sheltered and probably shallower areas of Mount's Bay, but small numbers of divers, grebes and seaducks are occasionally recorded.

189

Timing

Considerations are few, although harder winters increase numbers and species present. Calmer conditions will allow easier viewing over the pool, with birds not attempting to seek shelter. Time of day can decide which side of the pool you walk if looking into the sun, which can be a problem especially with low winter light.

Access

From A394 in Helston take B3304. Near where the River Cober adjoins this road there is a National Trust car park. Of several surrounding National Trust car parks, only this one is adjacent to the footpath leading the length of the valley, skirting Loe Marsh. Left-hand paths (estate drives) lead to the bird hide (not now suitable for disabled persons).

It is now possible to walk the entire 5 mile (8 km) perimeter of the pool and marsh. Access is year round without restrictions.

31 MARAZION MARSH, MOUNTS BAY AND WATERFRONT TO NEWLYN

OS ref: SW 5131
OS map: sheet 203

Habitat

Penzance is probably the best-known locality here, and the last large town on the south coast of Cornwall. The harbour entrance leads out into Mounts Bay, at the east side of which lies St Michael's Mount, a steep, rocky, privately owned island. Marazion Marsh is opposite the island, just inland from the sandy beach.

Penzance harbour and adjoining Newlyn contain most of west Cornwall's fishing fleet, mainly small inshore trawlers, although large trawlers from farther afield have operated offshore in recent winters. The bay's seabed is largely sandy, with the greatest area of rocks around St Michael's Mount; several freshwater streams drain across the broad beaches. As the bay faces south, it is sheltered from all winds from northerly quarters.

Marazion Marsh is not large, covering only some 85 acres (35 ha), but it is the largest reed-bed in Cornwall. A main road runs along the seaward side, a major railway line crosses the marsh, and houses are adjacent on one side. The marsh comprises an expanse of dense

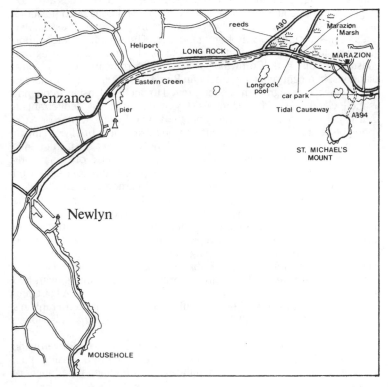

Phragmites reed, relatively small areas of open water, and a larger area of low sedges and Flag Iris, in which clumps of willow grow. There is a small stand of pines at the rear. Negotiations are under way to make the marsh an RSPB reserve.

Species

Geographical position makes the marsh and bay one of Cornwall's most important sites for birds. Winter is very interesting in each habitat within this area. The bay regularly attracts divers, grebes and a few seaducks, while unusual gulls and several wader species are found along the shoreline. Great Northern Divers appear from early winter and decrease from early spring. In good years up to ten might be present at a time, but four or five is more usual; often they cruise close to shore in search of small crabs, finding them on almost every dive. One or two Black-throated Diver may occur through the same period, generally increasing from late winter as passage migrants gather; numbers vary, usually fewer than 15. Slavonian Grebe may be present in twos and threes, later birds perhaps attaining summer plumage. Black-necked and Red-necked Grebes are only rare visitors, but one or two a year are expected. Seaducks are irregular in occurrence, and only commoner species are generally seen – two to three Eider perhaps, or a small flock of Common Scoter, which may contain a large-billed Velvet Scoter with wedge-shaped head profile more reminiscent of an Eider. Dowdy immature or female Long-tailed Duck have visited, usually singly.

Large numbers of gulls are found throughout the district. Freshwater outlets running across the beaches towards the sea at low tides are used by gull flocks to bathe, preen and drink. From semi-concealed positions behind rocks nearby, extremely good views may be had of assembled birds. Unusual gulls occur here regularly. The standard uncommon gulls are the same four that occur reasonably regularly throughout coastal Devon and Cornwall: Little, Mediterranean, Iceland and Glaucous. In recent years the American Ring-billed Gull, once considered an extremely rare vagrant, has been proved to occur at least as frequently as the Iceland Gull, with individuals staying long periods. Mediterranean Gull of all ages appear in ones and twos, with a late winter or early spring peak as different birds moving through stop here briefly. A similar pattern of occurrences exists for the Iceland Gull, but most frequently seen are pale-fawn-speckled immatures. Glaucous, also often similarly marked and coloured immatures, arrive less predictably, but Little Gull tend to be more numerous towards spring. Common Gull are found in quite high numbers, which rise as more than 300 late-winter immigrants arrive. Gull flocks are further increased by passages of Lesser Black-backed Gull in similar numbers to Common, while a few Kittiwake are also present. Other gull species reported in recent years have included further American vagrants, stopping off at this, the first resting and feeding area they reach on the British mainland; Bonaparte's Gull has become almost a regularly occurring rarity in recent winters, with two together seen on several occasions, and three together once! A Laughing Gull has stayed to winter. The particularly rare, dark-backed Franklin's Gull has strayed here and the high-Arctic Ross's Gull has also been recorded.

Other irregular visitors to the bay might include a storm-driven Little Auk or Grey Phalarope, possibly a Red-throated Diver or a passing skua. There is no skua passage as such, although that traditional harbinger of

Sanderling

$9TEVE BIRD$ 90

spring, the Sandwich Tern, is normally a particularly early arrival and a small but steady passage ensues. Later, small numbers of Common and a handful of Arctic Terns pass by, with one or two Roseate and Little Terns. In autumn, especially earlier, terns are the only seabirds of interest regularly seen, although, as in spring, numbers are small.

Waders are generally low in number, the sandy beach habitat being responsible for several omissions. One wader specialising in sandy conditions is the pale grey and white Sanderling, uncommon in many parts of Cornwall. Over 100 may gather here, its stronghold on the Cornish mainland. Sprinting along the tideline, they follow receding waves down the beach. Never fewer than 40 in winter, counts at migration seasons are erratic, peaks occurring in spring in some years and autumn in others; some stay to early summer at least, moulting into bright-brown-spangled summer plumage. Ringed Plover also like this habitat and are scattered throughout. In spring the rare Kentish Plover might be seen. Bar-tailed Godwit and Grey Plover share the beaches, usually small numbers although up to 50 of the latter have been counted. Turnstone will turn seaweed and even tin cans when searching for food, and so are found all along the shore, over 50 being usual. At high tide they often sleep on moored trawlers. Purple Sandpiper flocks, on the other hand, remain loyal to rocky outcrops, especially around Penzance and Newlyn; 20 or more is not unusual and over 50 occur at times.

Marazion Marsh has an interesting and regular wintering population, annually supplemented with unusual visitors. No species of bird is present in very large numbers, although gulls visit in higher numbers for short periods to bathe and preen and may include individuals of scarcer gull species. Ducks are probably most common, Mallard and Teal often totalling well over 50 apiece. More interesting are Shoveler, the gatherings of 30 or more being unusually large for Cornwall. Other dabbling ducks turn up occasionally, mostly in ones and twos, and regularly include Gadwall. A small number of diving ducks consists mainly of Pochard, with ten or so usual, about the same counts of Tufted, and occasional Scaup. Several Little Grebe and both Coot and Moorhen are present, but only the latter breed. Water Rail are also present at this season, too secretive for their numbers to be estimated realistically but probably under ten. In some winters, particularly in hard weather, a Bittern may briefly take up territory, although such quick sightings as might be gained will be provided reluctantly by this reticent

193

species. Snipe may be 50 strong, remaining largely unseen until they fly. Completing a group of species less likely to be seen than most is a fairly recent immigrant to this country – newer still to Cornwall – Cetti's Warbler; this vocal species has now become a breeding resident, though probably no more than two or three pairs nest.

Grey Heron are far more obliging residents, ten or more of which may be seen at once. Five or six pairs breed, some in traditional habitat high among topmost branches of nearby pines; each year, however, two or three pairs nest on the ground among reeds, a much less usual situation in Britain. During irruption years, when breeding of Bearded Tit has been exceptionally good in East Anglia (or even Holland) with as many as three broods raised in the season by each pair, and five or six young per brood, the species visits reed-beds far outside its normal range in search of food; Marazion is no exception. Every autumn and winter, up to 20,000 babbling Starling use the reeds as a night roost.

On average each year, the marsh probably produces some of the earliest returning hirundines in Britain. Sand Martins are by tradition early, but at Marazion a few Swallows and sometimes a House Martin may equal them; later their numbers increase substantially. Other migrants well known for making early landfalls also visit, such as Wheatear, shy Garganey swimming close to reeds fringing the pools, and perhaps a Hoopoe. Further exciting visitors usually occur later in spring – a white-plumaged Spoonbill or Little Egret perhaps. A Citrine Wagtail was a recent surprise visitor. Common waders passing through early, such as Dunlin, are supplemented by a few Ruff, sometimes only two or three at a time. Among them may be rarer visitors such as Little Ringed Plover. Whimbrel are annual migrants, often counted in hundreds through a season. Sparrowhawk and Buzzard regularly hunt the marsh, joined rarely by a Marsh Harrier quartering the reeds. Also hawking over the reeds one recent spring was a White-winged Black Tern in full summer plumage. Yellow Wagtail pass through in small numbers in spring and autumn, and a pair or two have bred in past seasons. Among their numbers birds of differing geographical races sometimes appear, 'blue-headed' most frequently. Migrant parties are joined by a few White Wagtail, and at the same period, or perhaps earlier, the uncommon pale Water Pipit may be seen by freshwater margins. Sedge and Reed Warblers arrive to breed in the marsh; in autumn juveniles of the former can be mistaken for the more brightly marked Aquatic Warbler, one of the earliest autumn rarities that appears almost annually.

During autumn it may be possible to see many species which were noted in spring. Others are restricted to autumn and include the highly elusive Bluethroat; on the rare occasions when this species is reported, it is often by a ringer who has extracted one from a mistnet. Difficult, but not impossible, to see is the intricately marked Spotted Crake; patience and silence pay off when from out of deep cover the buffish crake steps nervously, warily picking insects from a muddy pool. Some years three or four may be present together. Interesting waders may include a few Little Stint, Curlew Sandpiper or Spotted Redshank. American rarities are expected, though not necessarily annually; the most regular among them is the Dunlin-like Pectoral Sandpiper, but Long-billed Dowitcher have also been seen several times.

Hirundines once again begin to mass, joining large groups of Swift feeding before departure. Swallows roost at night in the reeds, where over 1,000 may assemble. This late activity attracts another migrant, the

Hobby, preying on the Swallow tribe at this time of year. Among the Swallows and martins feeding on the myriad insects, especially flying ants over the marsh, there may be one or two Little Gull or Black Tern, and always something very special may appear.

Timing

Gulls gather at the beach freshwater outflows when the tide is out. They also throng the tidelines, joined by waders. During rough weather, especially from late autumn through to spring, a wide variety of species may seek the bay's comparative shelter, particularly if winds are from northerly quarters. The beaches are popular with local inhabitants as well as tourists, but may be less disturbed in winter. If possible, early morning or midweek visits are advised, on ebbing tides in good weather. When trawlers unload in the harbour, gulls are drawn from widely scattered areas and this greater concentration may contain unusual species.

Even in very early spring, a spell of settled weather with winds from southerly quarters off the Continent may produce early migrants of a wide range of species, including land- and waterbirds and waders. The marsh is far less disturbed, and most species adapt to interruption from trains and cars. Lower water levels encourage waders to visit and stay, while hard weather may increase numbers of more common birds and produce the odd rarity. Westerly winds from the Atlantic are mostly responsible for the arrival of American waders. Calm winter days are best for views of Bearded Tit if present.

There is much interchange of birds between here and the Hayle Estuary complex; conditions, if rough at one site, are often sheltered at the other. Although the two localities are quite close, they are on opposite coasts and there is a slight difference in tide times of which many birds, particularly gulls, take advantage. Also note that some gulls fly inland to bathe at Drift Reservoir (see next chapter).

Access

A30 runs alongside Mounts Bay, and through Penzance, beside the waterfront. From the marsh to Newlyn is about 3 miles (5 km). There are car parking facilities throughout the area. Public roads fringe harbours and fish quays, where public access on foot is allowed. The beaches can be walked full length, from Marazion to Penzance. Alternatively, the beach named Eastern Green, immediately east of Penzance, may be reached on foot via a level crossing over the railway line (almost opposite the Heliport entrance). This area is a favourite with gulls, as also is the sewer beside the outer wall at Newlyn fish quay.

Marazion can be viewed easily from the roadside pavement. Arriving on A30 from Hayle side, turn left at Longrock before Penzance and drive east along the front to the marsh. If access onto the marsh is necessary, there is a path opposite the small grassed car park at its eastern end. Please do not enter the marsh carelessly and disturb birds. Careful approach and concealment is made easier by low clumps of bushes.

Calendar

Resident: Cormorant, Shag, Grey Heron, Cetti's Warbler, Reed Bunting.

December–February: divers, especially Great Northern, and grebes, mostly Slavonian. Unusual gulls, Glaucous in earlier part, Little, Mediterranean and Iceland mostly towards end of period, when Common and Lesser Black-backed Gulls and Kittiwake arrive. Possible Eider, Common Scoter or Long-tailed Duck, Sanderling, Purple Sandpiper, Turnstone, Grey Plover, Ringed Plover, Snipe, Teal, Shoveler, probably Gadwall; Pochard and Tufted Duck. Water Rail. Possible Bittern and Bearded Tit. Black-throated Diver mostly towards end of period.

March–May: unusual gulls may occur throughout, mostly March, when Ring-billed possible. Black-throated Diver often peak early April. From mid-March, first Sandwich Tern, Garganey, Ruff, Sand Martin, Wheatear, maybe Water Pipit, possible Swallow or Hoopoe. From mid-April, Whimbrel, Common Tern, Arctic, possible Roseate or Little Tern. Possible Little Ringed Plover, Kentish Plover, Spoonbill, Little Egret or other southern overshoots.

June–July: breeding species, including Reed and Sedge Warblers.

August–November: from mid-August to end September, possible Aquatic Warbler, return tern passage. Light passage of common waders, including high Sanderling numbers. Unusual waders; Little Stint, Curlew Sandpiper, possible Green and Wood Sandpipers, maybe American waders. From September through October, probable Spotted Crake, Black Tern, Little Gull, Swallow roost to end September, possible Hobby. Starling roost from early September. Divers, grebes and sea-ducks begin to return November.

Habitat

This most westerly English reservoir, set in the hills between Mounts Bay and Land's End, is 64 acres (26 ha) in extent. It contains shallow water, with broad muddy margins exposed to a greater extent and for longer periods than deep-sided reservoirs, thus attractive to both waders and diving ducks (which prefer not to dive too deeply for prey). Wooded at its northern end, it is for the most part surrounded by open farmland. Although used by many bank anglers, it has no watersports.

Species

This water's proximity to Penzance seafront encourages some species to move between sites freely, for example gulls, which consistently flight from Mounts Bay, especially at high tides or during stormy weather. Some gulls roost here. Rarer species are frequent; if missed along the shoreline, an errant bird may well turn up here. Mediterranean Gulls are seen most often, but Glaucous, Iceland and Ring-billed are all attracted; even a Bonaparte's has been seen.

During autumn this reservoir has a reputation for producing rarer waders. Wader passage in west Cornwall is poor compared with other areas of the region, but among small numbers of commoner waders less common species may occur, such as Ruff, Little Stint, Curlew Sandpiper, Wood and Green Sandpiper. Virtually annually it produces an American wader, often a Pectoral Sandpiper. Lesser Yellowlegs and Spotted Sandpiper have also been found.

During winter, Drift may host a sheltering diver or two, while grebes are a more frequent sight. Little Grebe only reach about ten, others occur only in ones and twos irregularly. Coot average 50. Duck numbers are unremarkable, Pochard being the most common diving duck, attaining 100 or so. Goldeneye, Scaup and Goosander arrive in very small numbers most years. Among dabbling ducks, typically Mallard, Teal and Wigeon are commonest, at times 150 plus. Other duck species or maybe a wild swan will visit at times.

Breeding species are few, but include a small colony of Sedge Warbler. Lack of surrounding varied habitats reduces occurrences to those attracted to the reservoir's open environs, such species being chiefly present through autumn, winter and to a lesser extent, spring.

Timing

Gales may induce birds to shelter, high tides can cause gulls to arrive. Hard winters increase numbers and species. Strong westerly winds are responsible for autumn arrivals of American waders. Calm conditions allow easier viewing.

Access

The A30 passes through the village of Lower Drift; here take the minor road on your right (if heading west towards Land's End) signposted to Sancreed. Opposite the dam is a car park just off the road. Elevated above the reservoir, it offers extensive views, thus useful for the disabled, although from here a telescope is essential. A check from the car park around nearby fields could be worthwhile if gulls are gathered. From the car park a path leads past the warden's building to the water's edge. No entry permit is required.

CBWPS have recently erected a public hide (no key required) on the western side of the reservoir; follow the track along the left bank from the dam car park.

32 PORTHGWARRA–LAND'S END AREA

OS ref: SW 3722
OS map: sheet 203

Habitat

Porthgwarra valley, and adjacent south-projecting Gwennap Head, lie only about 3 miles (5 km) from Land's End. Birdwatchers include the whole vicinity south of a line from Carn-les-Boel cliffs to, and including, St Levan church to the east. This coastal site is exposed to winds from most directions, except for the lower valley and areas around St Levan church, and in higher winds even gardens and more sheltered areas become affected. At the head of the valley is a small bush-fringed pond, shallow and usually dry from late spring to late autumn. There are small fields of rough pasture and arable land on the landward side of the valley. Above the more luxuriant growth in the valley lies an expanse of more exposed heathland. Gorse and heather, including Western Gorse and Cross-leaved Heath, grow in profusion. The 'moors' in late summer are a mixture of blazing purple and gold. In the stream valley, groups of

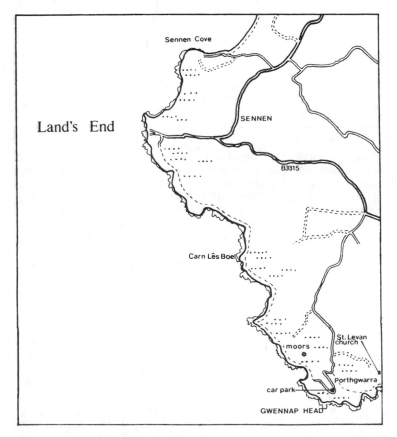

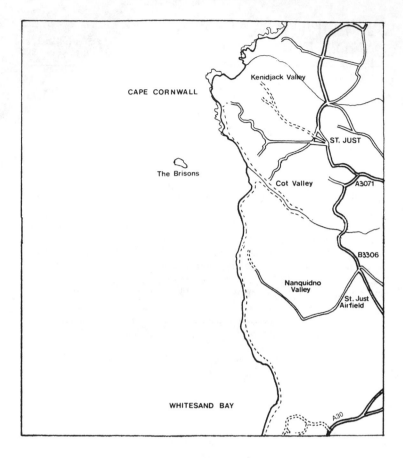

trees, mostly sallow, are kept low by salt-laden winds. Stands of Cornish elm are now virtually nonexistent due to the ravages of Dutch elm disease. Royal Fern grows in boggy patches near the stream. Dense areas of bracken, bramble and blackthorn are also found. The magnificent cliffs contain huge, rounded granite boulders, the heath extending to cliff-edge sea turf. Among this fine, short grass grow blue carpets of Autumn and Spring Squill, Rock Sea Lavender and Golden Samphire. Around St Levan church are sheltered groups of trees, gardens and hedgerows. A brook runs through the centre. Looking seaward on a fine clear day, the outline of the Isles of Scilly can be seen 28 miles (45 km) offshore. One mile (1.6 km) offshore, from Gwennap Coastguard lookout, lies Runnel Stone reef, marked by a bell-buoy. A powerful tiderace flows past the headland.

Interesting butterflies are seen on land. Graylings are common, some still flying to early October. This is a good spot for migrant butterflies; among Clouded Yellows, a few Pale Clouded Yellows are noted. Some years in early autumn, thousands of migrant day-flying Silver-Y Moths drink from heather flowers. Adders and Grey Seals are common; Killer Whales and dolphins have been watched offshore.

North of Porthgwarra are other, less-known sheltered coastal valleys adjacent to Land's End. Nanquidno valley, near St Just, has a stream flowing through, lined by bushes and hedges. The small Cot Valley, little visited by birdwatchers until recently, deserves to be better known; many interesting or uncommon migrants are seen in spring and autumn. This picturesque valley, steep-sided and gorse-covered, with rubble from disused mine workings spread over valley sides, has most cover including trees and cottage gardens towards its head. Some sallow and elderberry bushes grow beside its stream. Seaviews are panoramic, facing Brisons Rocks 1 mile (1.6 km) distant. Kenidjack, just north of Cape Cornwall, is another sheltered valley. On flat land overlooking the bend of the valley is St Just Airfield, an open area of short turf. Further inland east and north along Land's End peninsula, an exposed bank of moorland and hills with heather, brambles and rough pasture rises to 200–300 m, overlooking the cultivated coastal plain and extending some 12 miles (19 km) to St Ives.

Species
Porthgwarra is visited by birdwatchers seeking migrants – preferably rare! – for which this beautiful area is nationally known. Because of the exposed habitat, residents are few, but include Little Owl. Occasionally woodland birds wander into the area, when in autumn or winter foraging birds extend their travels. Lengthening spring days herald traditionally early migrants; a scatter of Wheatear, Chiffchaff and Willow Warbler. They are often backed by an arrival of five or six Black Redstart from early March, including attractive males in black, white and red summer plumage. Goldcrest, calling almost incessantly, may be present in high numbers, perhaps with a Firecrest among them calling more deeply, less often. The outside chance of a Hoopoe increases slightly a month later, when more migrants arrive. Porthgwarra does not seem normally to attract large spring falls; small arrivals of up to ten birds are more likely, often a handful of breeding-plumaged birds, including Blackcap, Whinchat, Redstart and Ring Ouzel. Later in spring, commoner species such as Whitethroat and hirundines pass through in groups of ten or so of each at a time. Sedge Warbler appear as migrants and three or four pairs stay to breed in the valleys, as do up to 20 pairs of secretive Grasshopper Warbler on the moors and hills. This latter species also appears as a coastal migrant, together with Spotted and Pied Flycatchers, Cuckoo and Turtle Dove in twos and threes.

Only in later spring are rarer migrants expected; every year, two or three at least are found in Porthgwarra district. The red-capped Woodchat Shrike has turned up on several occasions, although not annual, and has also been seen in early autumn; it is more frequent here than the declining Red-backed Shrike. The exciting bird may be a raptor, drifting overhead; not only has a Red Kite done so, but also the really rare Black Kite. Honey Buzzard, Montagu's and Hen Harriers and Hobby have all been seen on several occasions. Among commoner *Sylvia* warblers, naturally skulking, was once an even more skulking Subalpine Warbler.

Off the headland, small groups of Whimbrel pass eastward close to shore. The casual watcher will almost certainly see Gannet, and Fulmar just a few metres offshore, but a more sustained watch is required to see more interesting seabirds. The best months to see divers passing are April and May, but probably only two or three in a morning. Most commonly seen is the large Great Northern, with slow wingbeats; next most numerous is the slightly smaller Black-throated with faster wingbeats, showing strongly contrasting black upperparts and white underparts; least numerous, as always in south Cornwall, is the smaller, browner, fast-beating Red-throated. A few Common Scoter flying past close to the sea in single file are the only regular ducks. There is very light skua passage; Arctic travel singly, perhaps two or three a day, but rarely a pack is seen, signalling Pomarine. Tern passage is also light, mostly Sandwich, often in small groups of up to ten; a few Common pass, but Arctic or Roseate are less likely. Skua and tern passage is eastward, usually within a mile (1.6 km) range. Seawatching in summer can still be rewarding, with ocean-going Kittiwake breeding towards Land's End. About 100 pairs of Razorbill breed on Brisons Rocks. Feeding parties of Manx Shearwater, probably from the Isles of Scilly or Welsh islands such as Skomer, pass by quite frequently, sometimes thousands in small groups in a few hours. Strings of auks, constantly passing to and fro, often include a few Puffin. Hard to observe, Storm Petrels are often seen singly, but a group of three or four may 'dance' over the water; only very rarely do higher numbers of 50 or more occur.

HARRISON 83

Cory's Shearwater and Great Shearwater

Rare Cory's Shearwater, straying from breeding grounds farther south, can be looked for; unlike Manx, which they dwarf, they do not continually bank from side to side, but glide, often on bowed wings, giving a few languid flaps before another extended glide.

Towards late summer, commoner seabird migrants such as terns begin to pass westward and the chance of a Cory's, along with two large shearwaters from the south Atlantic, Sooty Shearwater and the rare Great, increases slightly. Care should be taken when claiming Sooty, as sightings of the browner Mediterranean form of Manx, the Balearic Shearwater, also increase. Through early autumn, seabird numbers and variety improve. Skua numbers are higher, although often only three or four Arctic or Great per day may pass by; Pomarine, now travelling singly, are the least frequent of the three commoner species. Lesser Black-backed Gull, including many first-year birds, pass westward in hundreds. At sea off here one expects to see unusual or rare birds; apart from those already mentioned, Soft-plumaged Petrel, Black-browed Albatross and Little Shearwater have all been reported.

Passerine migrants return from early autumn; average numbers are higher than in spring, and birds stay longer. Expected early birds are Spotted and Pied Flycatchers, *Phylloscopus* warblers and Whinchat, which stand out from resident Stonechat by their off-white eyebrow-stripe. Among the first unusual warblers may be a Melodious; although virtually annual, only one may be identified in a season. Icterine Warbler are less regular. Open-ground species favour the heath and pasture; 20–30 Wheatear, White and Yellow Wagtails and 100 or so Meadow Pipit gather; among them a few Tree Pipit are often heard calling. The larger, long-tailed Tawny Pipit may visit from the Continent. Looking like a very pale juvenile Yellow Wagtail but larger, it has a similar call, plus a sparrow-like 'chirrup'; one or two are seen each autumn. The Asiatic Richard's Pipit, with rich brown coloration, is similar, but its 'shreep' flight call is distinctive; formerly at least five or six occurred in some years, but recently only the same number as its European relative. Sharing the moorland habitat with pipits and wagtails may be a Dotterel, occasionally two or three, although not every autumn. Whimbrel also stop to feed among the heather, where the 'quip' call of Ortolan Bunting has been heard. Single Corncrake, now rare migrants, are occasionally flushed from the same habitat. Grassland-feeding species are also attracted to St Just Airfield, where Dotterel and the rare larger pipits have been recorded on a number of occasions; other plovers, and waders such as American Buff-breasted Sandpiper, have visited here in autumn. On the short grass those birds present may be easier to see than at Porthgwarra, although slight undulations in the ground can conceal even Dotterel when sitting. Sometimes, however, particularly if flights have taken place, the airfield is deserted by birds.

Raptors are regular autumn visitors to the area, one or two Peregrine, Merlin and Hobby passing over the coastal valleys; other less frequent birds of prey include Osprey, Red Kite, Honey Buzzard and Montagu's Harrier.

As the season progresses, numbers and species of birds begin to dwindle. Replacements are likely to be more unusual or rare species. Regular, though only ones and twos per autumn, are exquisite and intricately marked Wryneck. Barred Warbler, large, grey and white with few markings, are also found most years. Migrants which traditionally arrive late and in larger numbers include Robin, of which 50 or more may be present, and Goldcrest in similar numbers. Firecrest peak at about ten in Porthgwarra, but three or four is more likely. Up to ten Black Redstart are normally seen at a time, but perhaps over 20 towards late autumn. Other later migrants, visiting in ones and twos, are the harrier-like Short-eared Owl, Hen Harrier and Ring Ouzel. Lapland and Snow Buntings, feeding on heather seeds on the heath above the valley, are difficult to see on the ground; they may also turn up on the airfield. Rare, usually seen only once per autumn, are Red-breasted Flycatcher and the tiny hyperactive Yellow-browed Warbler, both preferring valley trees; such species may also turn up, along with small numbers of Firecrest, Goldcrest and other passerine migrants, in the other valleys. Arctic and Greenish Warblers have also been seen.

If conditions are right, large movements of finches pass over the valleys. Thousands of Chaffinch, hundreds of Brambling and dozens of Siskin are involved. When such movements take place, with hundreds of Skylark and flocks of Stock Dove passing, a Twite or Serin may be recorded.

By the end of the season most migrants have departed, but a few individuals linger into early winter. Some may even stay, such as Water Rail, Firecrest, Black Redstart, Snipe or perhaps Jack Snipe, and Wood-cock. Short-eared Owls and other predators may also be encountered; two or three of these day-flying owls, plus one or two Merlin and often four or five Hen Harrier, west Cornwall's largest concentration, arrive to winter on the peninsula's higher moorland slopes. By now Porthgwarra will have produced another major rarity for Cornwall, perhaps Pallas's Warbler or a Tree Sparrow! Like the Scillies, this area has an enviable record for producing American vagrant landbirds; three seen here, and nowhere else in Britain before, were American Redstart, Veery and two Chimney Swifts together. A Blackpoll Warbler and an Asiatic Radde's Warbler were both first records for the Cornish mainland. Other neighbouring valleys have shared in these surprise arrivals; recently, Europe's first Varied Thrush, a Pacific coast woodland bird, was found at Nanquidno. Kenidjack may also share interesting migrants (once an American Redstart, recently a Yellow-throated Vireo), while Cot Valley has produced a Swainson's Thrush.

Timing

For seawatching off Porthgwarra, a southeasterly or southwesterly wind, light to moderate, is best. Mist at sea could be an advantage, as long as you can see 1 mile (1.6 km) or so out. Strong or gale-force south-westerlies, or offshore strong winds, are least productive, but birds may appear soon after these have abated, or travel before a front passes. Mornings, late afternoons and evenings through spring and summer, and very early autumn, have been good. During autumn migration, seawatching at any time of day will probably be rewarding in the right conditions. Strong sunlight causes problems, as everything is in silhouette for much of its travel; eyestrain can be a problem. When the sun has moved around later in the day, conditions improve a little. Best is when there is no direct sunlight on the water.

For landbirds in spring, any wind from a southerly quarter, light to moderate, can produce a few migrants; the valleys are adversely affected by high winds. If conditions are clear, most soon depart. Mist or drizzle, of the type associated with wet southeasterlies, may delay them, and produce more birds. The same conditions in autumn are responsible for some of the best bird days. In autumn light easterlies are also excellent, especially if cloud or rain causes birds to land. As a rule birds move off less quickly in autumn, but not always. Strong winds from any direction, funnelling through valley bushes, make the area inhospitable; on such days few migrants are seen. St Levan may be more sheltered, and could be worth checking. Strong northerly winds make visiting largely a waste of time.

Watch St Just Airfield when it is not in use (best early mornings, evenings or weekdays). Fine days are best for moorland raptors in winter; late afternoon, when Short-eared Owls start hunting and harriers or Merlin strive to make a last kill before nightfall, can be interesting. Two or three hours' watch is needed, ideally over an open stretch, to see raptors coming and going, as they range widely.

Access

For Porthgwarra, from A30, after leaving Penzance towards Land's End, take B3283 through St Buryan. Follow this road to B3315 and continue towards Sennen; at a sharp bend to the right, turn off left on a minor road signposted to Porthgwarra village and car park.

Check for passerines at the base of Porthgwarra valley, among trees and sheltered gardens, especially tamarisk bushes. You can follow a steep path from the cove cliffs, or walk up the road to the Coastguard cottages and heathland. There are good paths from here to the cliffs or across the heath. From these paths, search carefully through bushes and trees in the valley.

For seawatching, sit left of the Coastguard lookout, more or less opposite the reef marked by Runnel Stone buoy. Seabirds often feed around the reef and over the tiderace. You can walk to St Levan Church via a highly scenic coast path. Check among the trees and bushes for small birds, and the fields for pipits, etc. A coastal public footpath extends from Mousehole around the entire Land's End peninsula to Hayle.

From B3315 past Porthgwarra, to reach Nanquidno and St Just, continue west towards Land's End, turning north on A30 then B3306 towards St Just. Before reaching the village, you pass the airfield to the left. Immediately afterwards, turn left down a minor road along the airfield boundary towards Nanquidno. Good views of the airfield are possible from this roadside. There are several vergeside pull-offs for cars down the valley, but it is better to park and cover the whole valley on foot.

To reach Cot Valley take road signposted to Cape Cornwall, situated in the middle of St Just village, near the clock tower; within about 200 m take a minor road on the left, signposted to Cot Valley. There is limited car parking beside a narrow road at the head of the valley (this road runs the length of the valley, with further limited parking). On sunny weekend afternoons you may have to park in St Just, as this is a popular tourist spot; but few birds will be seen at these times anyway. Follow public footpaths around gardens at the valley head (good for flycatchers and warblers). An elevated path on the left (facing sea) runs the length of the valley. Check lower rocky areas for such species as Wheatear and Black Redstart. *Note:* there is a Youth Hostel in the valley.

For Kenidjack, after leaving St Just northwards towards St Ives, take the first left-hand turning at bottom of hill. Limited parking available.

Several good minor roads intersect the high moorlands, and all could probably produce interesting raptors. A particularly high vantage point with the widest possible vista is required to enable sightings of more distant raptors. One of the better places is near Trewey Hill. Turn right off B3306 when heading from St Just to St Ives, along the minor road signposted to Newmill and Penzance; this rather steep road begins to level out, with views over a wide area of moor. Pull off on to the verge and scan the area. Other minor roads near Trewey should also be tried.

Calendar

Resident: Gannet, Cormorant (both non-breeders); Shag breed, Sparrow-hawk and Buzzard breed inland. Razorbill and Guillemot constantly passing. Little Owl, Green Woodpecker, Rock Pipit, Stonechat, Reed Bunting, Raven.

December–February: few interesting birds winter regularly on the coast. Possible wintering passerines. Hen Harrier, possibly Peregrine, Merlin, Short-eared Owl inland on hills, occasional on coast.

March–May: early part of period, Fulmar and Kittiwake return. First passerine migrants may be Black Redstart early–mid-March; end March, first Chiffchaff and Wheatear; by April, Willow Warbler and Goldcrest. Mid-April onwards, Blackcap, Whinchat, Redstart, Ring Ouzel, possible Hoopoe; hirundines pass through. End April–May, Whitethroat, Grass-hopper Warbler, flycatchers, Cuckoo, Turtle Dove, Whimbrel. At sea in April–May, all three divers pass, Manx Shearwater, Sandwich and Common Terns. Mid-May, Arctic and possible Pomarine Skuas. Rarer landbirds expected through May.

June–July: breeding species, possible late arriving migrants, and spring overshoots. Seabirds throughout period include Manx Shearwater, possible Cory's, Storm Petrel, Common Scoter, Puffin.

August–November: seabirds may now include Great, Sooty and Balearic Shearwaters; Pomarine and Arctic Skuas, Great Skua, Lesser Black-backed Gull, Sandwich and Common Terns. Early August on, common *Phylloscopus* and *Sylvia* warblers, especially Whitethroat. Wheatear, Whinchat and Redstart, Spotted Flycatcher, possible Melodious Warbler or Woodchat. From September, the above plus Whimbrel, Turtle Dove, Tree and Meadow Pipits, possible Osprey, probable Dotterel, Wryneck, Barred Warbler, or Tawny Pipit; White, Grey and Yellow Wagtails; other less regular or rare species. From October, Goldcrest, Firecrest, Ring Ouzel, Hen Harrier, Peregrine, Merlin, Short-eared Owl; towards end October to November, Black Redstart, Robin, flocks of finches, Skylark, and Stock Dove, Water Rail, Woodcock, Snipe, possible Jack Snipe, Lapland and Snow Buntings, possible Yellow-browed Warbler and Red-breasted Flycatcher. Moorland raptors arrive to winter from end October. *American vagrants*: waders mostly through September, passerines largely October.

32A ADDITIONAL SITE: SENNEN BAY

OS ref: SW 3526
OS map: sheet 203

Habitat
This wide, deep, sandy bay, normally located on maps as Whitesand Bay, is situated between Land's End and Cape Cornwall, flanked by high cliffs on either side. On the southern edge a rather flat-topped rocky outcrop stands just offshore. Facing westwards, the bay is exposed to all westerly and most southerly winds, which here are frequently strong. It is, however, sheltered from any easterly-based winds. A major tourist area, the beach is also popular with surfers.

Species
The bay is mainly interesting for wintering divers and grebes in small numbers; seaducks are scarce, normally confined to a few Common Scoter, although Long-tailed Duck have visited intermittently, reaching double figures some years. Great Northern Diver and Slavonian Grebe are most common, usually about six of each being present, while other divers and grebes visit occasionally in small numbers. Recently an oiled White-billed Diver was found alive here. Gulls are mainly the local breeding species, including Kittiwake, but after autumn gales the bay may harbour a Sabine's or Little Gull. Terns pass through in small flocks, mostly Sandwich, with some Common in both seasons, and occasionally scarcer tern species are seen. Few waders visit, mainly Purple Sandpiper, Turnstone or Oystercatcher in small numbers, and a few Grey Plover. All gulls, terns and waders may use the rocky outcrop as a perch.

Timing
Visit on calmer days for water birds, or during sheltering easterly winds. Westerly winds can induce passing seabirds to fly closer, or attempt to find some shelter.

Access
The A30 passes through Sennen village; the minor road marked to Sennen Cove leads down a very steep hill. The bay is overlooked from two rather low-set car parks. One directly overlooks the rock outcrop.

Checking the often productive area around Aire Point is impossible without a telescope. Aire Point is on the eastern edge of the bay, about halfway along towards Cape Cornwall.

33 THE ISLES OF SCILLY

OS ref: SV 9011
OS map: sheet 203

Habitat

Twenty-eight miles (45 km) beyond Land's End, and visible from Cornish mainland cliffs on a clear day, the Scillies are a world apart from the rest of the region. Of 100 or so rocks forming the archipelago, only five are regularly inhabited, the largest St Mary's, with a length of 2½ miles

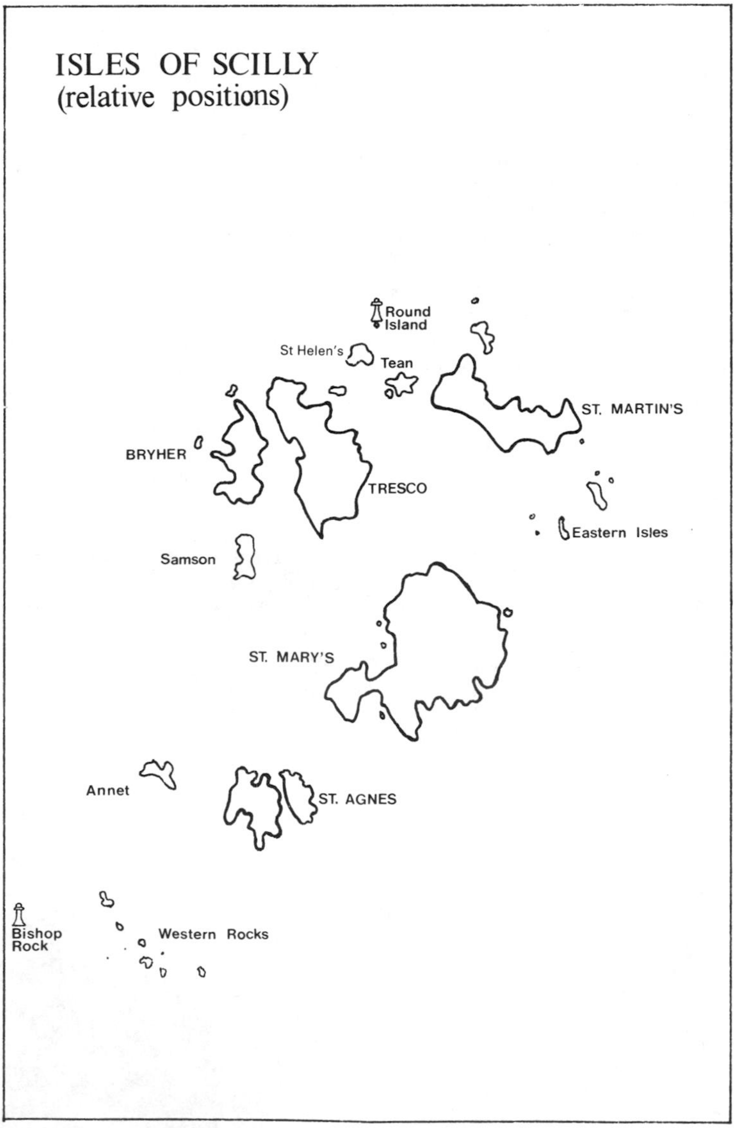

ISLES OF SCILLY
(relative positions)
Round Island
St Helen's
Tean
ST. MARTIN'S
BRYHER
TRESCO
Eastern Isles
Samson
ST. MARY'S
Annet
ST. AGNES
Bishop Rock
Western Rocks

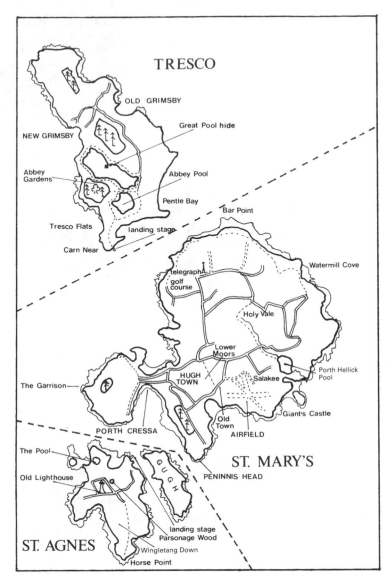

(4 km) and the major portion of the inhabitants. Within this highly scenic island group, no more than 10 miles (16 km) from corner to corner, the variety of habitats includes rocky and sandy shores, cliffs, farmland, heaths, open downs, sea turf, marshes, lakes and woods. The land is characterised by lush vegetation in sheltered areas, which responds to the mild oceanic climate and lack of frost. Light snowfall is seen every 20 years or so on average. The main limiting factors for vegetation are high winds and blown sea spray. High windbreaking hedges of salt-resistant *Pittisporum* around small flower-growing fields are a characteristic landscape feature on inhabited islands. Other introduced subtropical plants such as tamarisks and palms form a

substantial addition to the native flora of the main islands. A recent severe frost has, however, caused considerable damage to these. Island wildlife includes the Scilly Shrew, while Porpoises are often seen in channels between islands; Grey Seals are resident, often seen basking on rocks in fine weather, and breeding on quieter outer isles. Many rare wild flowers or rare local forms of commoner plants are found. Autumn winds have brought large orange Monarch butterflies from America, and Clouded Yellows in groups from southern Europe. Although Rabbits are common, most other animals found on the mainland are unknown here; snakes, Foxes, Badgers, Stoats and Weasels are entirely absent.

The main islands and rock clusters are:

St Mary's: contains Hugh Town, port and main town for the islands, with over 2,000 inhabitants. Although chiefly agricultural, the island has two major boggy south-facing valleys, Lower Moors and Holy Vale–Porth Hellick, with water and sheltered bushes. Areas of open downland with heather and granite boulders face the coast. The turf expanses of the airfield and golf course occupy prominent positions on the higher slopes of the island. West of Hugh Town is The Garrison headland, with coniferous trees and bracken, from which wide scenic views can be gained across the sounds to all other main islands.

St Agnes: separated from the others by deep and sometimes rough water, this island, little over 1 mile (1.6 km) long, is the last inhabited outpost of Britain, excluding Bishop Rock lighthouse 4 miles (6½ km) to the west. The island is dominated by the disused lighthouse in the centre, surrounded by a few cottages. Bracken-covered Gugh islet is connected to the east flank of the island at low tide by a sand bar. The windswept south (Wingletang Down) and west of St Agnes are open downland, rocks and bracken, but the centre and east contain tiny hedged bulb fields. The little Parsonage Wood near the old lighthouse is a very sheltered area of elm trees. Beyond this lies a small marshy pool near the north end of the island, which looks out towards Annet. This low uninhabited ½-mile (0.8-km) island of rocks and turf, a seabird sanctuary in summer, faces onto open ocean westward.

Tresco: across the relatively shallow, sandy sound north of St Mary's lies privately owned Tresco, with its abbey, subtropical ornamental gardens, lakes and sand dunes. The northern end of the 2-mile (3-km) island, relatively little visited, is mostly open downland, but pine clumps and dense rhododendrons grow on the sheltered eastern side of the ridge. Lush subtropical gardens surrounding the abbey are bordered by tall mixed woodland. This overlooks the ½-mile (0.8-km) -long shallow Great Pool, fringed by reeds and willows, which runs across the southern half of the island. In front of the abbey, separated from the Great Pool by a narrow twisting isthmus of bracken, is round, sandy Abbey Pool. West of Tresco lie open bracken-clad Samson (uninhabited), with twin hills, and Bryher (a little agriculture and a hotel), which has a small pool on the west side.

St Martin's: east of Tresco, the 2-mile (3-km) -long ridge of St Martin's overlooks extensive white shell-sand beaches facing back across the sound towards St Mary's. Although mainly agricultural, the top of the island is relatively open fields, lacking deep cover; the eastern end near

Daymark beacon is open downland. Most of the sheltered hedged fields are along the southern side of the island above the beach. To the northwest lie rocky Round Island with a lighthouse, St Helen's and Tean.

There are two other main groups of uninhabited rocks and islets: Western Rocks, a series of jagged reefs and stacks in deep water 3 miles (5 km) west of St Agnes; and Eastern Isles, between St Martin's and St Mary's. These more sheltered isles are covered with grass, Giant Mallow and gorse, with sandy bays between them. The islands, visited by thousands of tourists in summer, play host to hundreds of birdwatchers, especially in autumn.

Species

The Scillies have built up a reputation as probably *the* place in Britain to see stray autumn migrants from all over Europe, Asia and North America. This is probably due to their position on the outer fringe of the European landmass, acting both as a last resort for birds blown across from the east, and as a first landfall for birds which have made accidental ocean crossings from America. Some of these intercontinental wanderers, although very rare on the British mainland, have become regarded as 'regulars' on the Scillies at certain seasons.

Resident species on the islands are few (Song Thrushes seem to replace most other passerines), and many familiar mainland birds, especially woodland types such as woodpeckers, Jay, Nuthatch and Treecreeper, are absent; even Carrion Crow and their close relatives are scarce. The bird population is augmented by important seabird colonies on several islands in summer.

Few birdwatchers visit Scilly in winter, when silver Sanderling scurry along windy beaches, Turnstone and Purple Sandpiper pick among the rocks, and occasional Merlin wander between islands in search of small passerines. Great Northern Diver are often seen in the sounds between the islands, where Gannet and Kittiwake shelter from gales. Parties of Tufted Duck and Pochard gather on Tresco pools, Pochard usually most noticeable with peaks of 30 or more, while Tufted may not reach double figures. At the same locality the American Black Duck which was resident here for several years, hybridising wth Mallard, has left a legacy of assorted puzzling offspring. Water Rail are confiding, often entering gardens, where Chiffchaff winter. Black Redstart are present most winters in sheltered coves, where dead seaweed encourages insect life. There is always a chance of a rarity 'left over' from the previous autumn, particularly a wader. The orange-rumped Killdeer, a plover from America has turned up several times in late autumn and winter, staying for several weeks on open damp grassland.

Spring is the less-known of the migration seasons on the islands, with room for further discovery, although many rare birds, such as overshooting Mediterranean herons and warblers, which have been found, have often moved on within a few days. Fewer watchers are present at this season, although this is starting to change. As with most coastal points in the region, characteristic early spring arrivals are Chiffchaff, Firecrest, Wheatear and Black Redstart. Hoopoes are expected annually, usually several and sometimes two or three together, on coastal downland. Later in the spring, large falls of warblers, especially Willow, can occur, as well as smaller numbers of all common migrants. Exotic overshoots, which increase later in spring, may well include a

Woodchat Shrike. Recently a Caspian Plover was a first record for Britain this century. No spring passes without the liquid warbling of Golden Oriole in sheltered trees on one or more of the main islands, especially St Martin's, although even brilliant yellow and black males can be hard to spot in thick cover. Sometimes loose parties of several birds arrive in warm weather and stay for weeks.

Among the seabirds, Fulmar and auks (apart from Puffin) tend to arrive early in spring, while the screaming terns do not arrive until up to two months later. Although the seabird colonies are small in comparison with some on the Scottish and Irish coasts, numbers such as 500 pairs of Kittiwake, 200 or so pairs of Razorbill and over 100 of Puffin (the latter mostly on Annet) are greater than those remaining on the mainland coast of our region. More important regionally is southwest Britain's only regular tern colony, with over 100 pairs of Common Tern in sandy areas of Tresco and Eastern Isles. This species is vulnerable to disturbance, and visitors are aksed to keep away from roped-off areas to give them a chance of success. Good views can be obtained of these graceful birds flying over to feed on sand-eels in the shallow sounds and bays. With luck one of Scilly's specialities, the delicate Roseate Tern, may be seen flying past; a handful of pairs of this rare and decreasing seabird still breed among Common Terns. A few Sandwich Tern may also be seen. Out in the sounds there are usually dozens of Shag fishing, and at times 200–300 gather to attack fish shoals.

In contrast to the eastern isles, which shelter terns suited to feeding in shallow seas, the more rocky northern and western sides of the archipelago support deepwater feeders, with most Fulmar and auks in Men-a-vaur, St Helen's and Round Island area, north of Tresco and St Martin's. The most dramatic seabirds are on the reserve island of Annet, on the outer western edge of the main island group, which supports breeding populations of Manx Shearwater and Storm Petrel. These elusive breeders are hard to census, as they avoid gull attacks by approaching their colonies from the ocean only after nightfall, spending the day either well out to sea feeding or under the ground in burrows and crevices. Recent estimates have given 500 pairs of shearwaters, small by national standards, and perhaps 2,000 pairs of Storm Petrel, an important colony. Both species, particularly shearwaters, tend to flock near the isle towards dusk, but in daytime there is no sign except for corpses of unwary birds killed by the abundant Great Black-backed Gull, which exceed 1,000 pairs in the island group. The concentration of Lesser Black-backed Gull, with 500 pairs on Annet and 2,500 total, is the largest in our region.

Breeding landbirds are limited. The best chance is in damp areas of cover, such as near Tresco pools, where a few Reed and Sedge Warblers nest. Gadwall are regular nesters on Tresco, where Shoveler and Teal may also raise broods in the reed-beds. One or two pairs of Whitethroat or Chiffchaff might be found in well-vegetated areas of St Mary's. Absence of almost any breeding summer migrant passerines on the Scillies means that new arrivals are easily noticed when migration starts. One influential factor in the number of unusual birds found here is probably the intense scrutiny given to any migrant in autumn, because watchers are always on the lookout for the unusual. Perhaps similar detective work would pay off in mainland areas where many rarities seen on Scilly have never been found. One strange feature of migration on Scilly is that, while numbers of ordinary migrants are often very small, the counts of rarer arrivals can be equal to or even greater than those of 'common' species!

Early autumn is not a peak period for migrants on Scilly, but is probably best for wader variety. Low water levels on Tresco pool margins leave mud, which attracts European migrant waders such as Curlew Sandpiper, Dunlin, Little Stint and Greenshank in small numbers. Likely American species include the stout Pectoral Sandpiper, virtually annual and sometimes in twos and threes, and other rarer visitors such as a pale, slender Wilson's Phalarope. The pool on St Agnes and Porth Hellick Pool on St Mary's may also come up trumps. Along rocky bays, birds resembling Common Sandpiper are checked carefully for that species' very similar transatlantic cousin, the Spotted Sandpiper. The very rare dark-winged Solitary Sandpiper has also been seen on several occasions. At the same time, watchers on open ground may find the autumn's first Dotterel from the mountain tops of northern Europe. Early passerine migrants tend to include several larger Melodious and Icterine Warblers among commoner species, perhaps an Ortolan Bunting, and very often a Red-backed Shrike hawking bees from a gorse or bramble perch, a rare bird now on the mainland.

The pace quickens rapidly from mid-autumn as tourists are replaced by birdwatchers from all over Britain. Those crossing by ferry from the mainland often report Sooty Shearwater and skuas passing close by the boat, or occasionally a raft of dark-capped Great Shearwater on the sea. St Mary's becomes one of the nation's ornithological centres of communication, with scores of birdwatchers meeting to exchange news; an evening bird log and discussion takes place at Porthcressa Restaurant. From now on rare birds are the order of the day, with groups of observers hurrying from island to island to catch up with the latest arrivals. Birds become more varied and numerous through mid and late autumn, even common summer visitors continuing to pass through here when nearly all have left the mainland. Next on the list are waders and pipits, turning up on open turf and down such as St Mary's golf course and airfield; Buff-breasted Sandpiper have reached up to half a dozen sprinting around the seaward side of the airfield on occasion, and some are seen virtually annually. Almost certainly there will still be one or two Dotterel, standing unconcerned while being watched from point-blank range, and a Lesser Golden Plover might drop in with a group of Golden. The same areas may hold a long-legged Richard's or Tawny Pipit, or perhaps a sandy little Short-toed Lark. The inconspicuous Lapland Bunting may also feed in this habitat, although this regular visitor is perhaps more likely on coastal heath such as Peninnis Head on St Mary's or Wingletang on St Agnes. The extra birds arriving will generally attract a few Merlin and probably a Peregrine. 'Lost' larger raptors such as Osprey, Red Kite, Honey Buzzard or a harrier may spend two or three weeks wandering from island to island between favoured feeding spots.

On the edge of the ocean, the Scillies are battered most autumns by at least one severe depressional gale. High winds, rain and sea spray usually prevent much effective birding for a day or two; some people try to seawatch, although numbers of birds passing the islands are low. With luck a passing oceanic migrant such as a Great Shearwater, petrel or scarcer skua may be noted. Observations have been made from Tresco north cliffs, or, more usually, southern points of St Mary's and St Agnes. Passengers on MV *Scillonian* may have better luck, if seasickness permits, with a chance of many larger shearwaters or a Sabine's Gull following the boat and sometimes a flock of Grey Phalarope sitting on the sea in the lee of Eastern Isles. The real excitement on the islands is in searching for American landbirds when the weather abates; Scilly is Europe's best centre for seeing these lost wanderers. Although numbers of individual birds are irregular, depending on strength and timing of gales, a few are swept across every year. A sighting such as that of an American Nighthawk weaving around St Agnes lighthouse at dusk, or a tiny striped Black-and-white Warbler scrambling head-first down a tree trunk on St Mary's, is one of the year's high points for many keen watchers. Many 'first sightings for Britain' have been made here at this period. Multiple arrivals of Grey-cheeked Thrush and Blackpoll Warbler have taken place, while Red-eyed Vireo are found virtually every autumn. Apart from the dumpy little Grey-cheeked Thrush, other New World thrushes have included Swainson's, Wood and Hermit Thrush. Other American rarities in recent years have included first records of American Pipit, Tree Swallow and Cliff Swallow. Crowds of hundreds of watchers have gathered to see some of these birds.

Black-and-white Warbler

In favourable conditions, a wide variety of interesting European migrants may be encountered. Spotted Crake are glimpsed regularly in marshy valleys and poolsides. Firecrest are frequently seen, sometimes amounting to dozens across the islands, and there will usually be several Yellow-browed Warbler, often lingering in waterside trees and thickets where insects are plentiful. Icterine Warbler are still seen and the Red-breasted Flycatcher is another regular, often seen flicking white tail-patches in wooded areas. Towards late autumn almost anything from the northern hemisphere might be found, setting identification puzzles when little-known Asiatic warblers such as Paddyfield and Booted are reported. Green and Two-barred Greenish Warblers have been recent 'firsts' detected by close observation on these islands; Asiatic thrushes, like their New World counterparts, can produce some surprises, which have included Black-throated and Eye-browed Thrushes. Weedy fields prove attractive to elusive small buntings such as Rustic, and perhaps rare pipits including Olive-backed from the Far East. Most seasons a pale young Rose-coloured Starling is found in similar habitat. Black Redstart can be astonishingly numerous around coves and buildings at this season, with falls estimated at several hundred in the whole island group. A Woodcock or Short-eared Owl may be flushed from coastal bracken, and one or two northern wildfowl such as Barnacle Geese appear most years, usually not staying for long.

Birds can continue to arrive right through to the end of autumn, while mild weather encourages some exhausted vagrants which arrived earlier in autumn to stay on. Every year the Scillies turn up a Pallas's Warbler, or even several, at the last moment. Then the flood of birdwatchers returns to the mainland, leaving us to speculate on what might still arrive.

Timing

Most people on pre-arranged visits will be unable to alter timing according to weather conditions. Warm southerly winds are most likely to produce spring exotic overshoots and falls of commoner summer migrants. Deep depressions which have originated off the American coast in autumn, especially those which start as hurricanes off the Florida and Gulf of Mexico coasts, will tend to move east and affect the Scillies a few days later. Look for American vagrants on the first bright day after the gale, as they come out to feed. In windy weather, sheltered trees such as Holy Vale on St Mary's or the eastern side of St Agnes are likely to be productive, or perhaps Tresco (if birds can be found in thick cover). In southerly or southwesterly gales, try seawatching off southerly points such as Porth Hellick or Peninnis on St Mary's and Horse Point on St Agnes. Porth Hellick Point should be the first landfall for birds moving west past the islands. Results are probably best in bad visibility, rather than gales which push birds towards the Cornish mainland. In strong northwesterlies, shearwaters and skuas have been seen from Tresco north cliffs. For breeding shearwaters and petrels coming to Annet, a dusk visit by boat will give a chance of seeing birds gathering nearby. For European and Asiatic migrants, a southeast wind, even if light, usually brings good watching in autumn. Surprisingly, however, the passing over of a deep depression can funnel in birds from both east and west, bringing a complete mix of rarities.

In early morning sun, the trees around the sunken east-facing 'tennis court' area on Garrison Hill, or the east side of the battlements path, are good places from which to start on St Mary's. Parsonage Wood on St Agnes can also be very good.

Access

By boat on MV *Scillonian* from Penzance to St Mary's, a two-and-a-half hour journey and sometimes very rough, although possibly interesting for seabirds. Details of sailings from Isles of Scilly Steamship Co., Penzance Quay, telephone Penzance 62009. Day trips to St Mary's (four hours ashore) are possible.

By helicopter from the British International Helicopters heliport at the Eastern Green end of Penzance to St Mary's Airfield, a 20-minute crossing. Telephone Penzance 64296.

By aircraft from Plymouth (Roborough) Airfield in Devon at peak holiday periods, via Brymon Airways (telephone Plymouth 707023); or from

Land's End Airport, St Just, by Skybus Air Service, telephone Penzance 787017.

Note that the boat may be unable to sail in exceptionally severe gales, and *all* services may be suspended in fog.

Most birdwatchers base themselves on St Mary's, where guest houses and flats are available; contact Isles of Scilly Council offices in Hugh Town for accommodation lists for this and other main islands. St Mary's, as well as holding many good bird spots, is the most central from which to take boats to other islands. *Inter-Island Boats* leave Hugh Town quay at about 10.15 most mornings; details are chalked on the notice board outside the shipping office in the main street. You can usually return in mid or late afternoon. Groups can often arrange by request to charter boats for special outings.

Some visitors may prefer to keep out of the autumn 'ornithological rat-race' and conduct their birdwatching at a quieter, more leisurely pace. Those more attracted by this idea could consider basing themselves on St Martin's or Bryher, which are less visited, probably cheaper, and still provide plenty of scope for seeing birds. For an economical stay on St Mary's (Garrison) and St Agnes, there are basic camp sites, but these are exposed in rough weather.

Note: on all the islands, there are lanes, public paths, nature trails or coast walks which enable birdwatchers to search the ground thoroughly. Most fields are small and can be scanned easily from the edge; if a bird fails to appear, wait until it does. There is no reason to enter fields without the farmer's permission. In the past, a few irresponsible rarity-hunters have clashed with local residents over access to cultivated land, causing bad relations all round. Muddy boots can bring soil parasites such as nematodes (eelworms) from an infected area into a healthy field, ruining crops and putting the farmer's livelihood at risk. **Please** keep to paths! Note also that stone walls may collapse if leant on.

Migrants, including unusual birds, can turn up anywhere but some of the best-known watching areas are:

St Mary's: Garrison trees for warblers; Lower Moors for raptors, crakes or warblers (hide available); Peninnis Point for larks, pipits, Lapland Bunting, and possibly passing seabirds; Porth Hellick Pool for herons, ducks, waders; Holy Vale for warblers, flycatchers and other passerines, probably crakes; airfield and golf course for Dotterel and other waders, pipits and Lapland Bunting; Salakee Farm area between the airfield and Porth Hellick for various small passerine migrants; fields east of Telegraph Hill for rarer buntings and pipits.

St Agnes: Parsonage trees for warblers and flycatchers; the pool and surrounds for waders and crakes; Troytown fields for warblers, pipits and buntings; Barnaby Lane and Covean for warblers; Wingletang Down for Merlin, Short-eared Owl, pipits and Lapland Bunting; Horse Point for seabirds passing.

Tresco: Great and Abbey Pools (hide available by Great Pool) and surrounding vegetation for ducks, raptors, waders, warblers; north cliffs for passing seabirds.

Bryher: weedy fields across the island centre and near the pool for warblers and buntings.

St Martin's: fields across the top of the island for pipits, buntings and other open-ground birds; also sheltered fields just up from the landing stage.

Access to some parts of Tresco, Eastern Isles and the whole of Annet in summer is restricted to permit-holders only, by agreement with the Nature Conservancy Council, to protect breeding seabirds. From St Mary's, special boat trips, which do not land, take visitors out past seabird colonies and seals in season, or near dusk to Annet.

Calendar

Resident: Cormorant, Shag, Gadwall, Kestrel, Moorhen, Oystercatcher, Ringed Plover, Great Black-backed Gull, Raven, Carrion Crow, Rock Pipit, Stonechat. Passing Gannet and Kittiwake all year.

December–February: Great Northern Diver, Wigeon, Teal, Shoveler, Tufted Duck, Pochard, possibly Goldeneye, Long-tailed Duck, Merlin, Water Rail, Golden Plover, Grey Plover, Turnstone, Sanderling, Purple Sandpiper, Short-eared Owl, Grey Wagtail, Chiffchaff, Blackcap, Firecrest, Black Redstart. Possible geese and Woodcock.

March–May: Fulmar and auks have arrived back. Hoopoe, Chiffchaff, Firecrest, Wheatear, Black Redstart passing through from mid-March. Manx Shearwater, Storm Petrel, terns arrive April; commoner passerine migrants peak late April. Overshooting southern species mostly May, best month for Golden Oriole.

June–July: breeding seabirds, ducks and Ringed Plover; occasional late migrants and overshoots remain from spring; a few warblers breed.

August–November: breeding shearwaters, petrels and auks have departed. Wader movement including American species peaks mid-September. Beginning of passerine movement with chance of Icterine or Melodious Warbler and Ortolan (mid-August on). Red-backed Shrike (early September–mid-October). Seabirds on *Scillonian* crossing (mostly early September–mid-October), including Manx and Sooty Shearwaters, Great Shearwater (irregular, mainly September), possible Cory's Shearwater, Gannet, Grey Phalarope (mostly October), skuas, occasional Sabine's Gull. On islands, American waders including Buff-breasted Sandpiper (mid–late September), European plovers including Dotterel (late August–mid-October); raptors from early September. Wide range of passerines from mid-September including warblers, flycatchers, chats and pipits, with chance of Richard's and Tawny Pipits; Melodious and Icterine Warblers, Red-breasted Flycatcher, Lapland Bunting all regular. Peaks for rarer species; American landbirds late September–end October; European and Asiatic birds, e.g. rare pipits, warblers and buntings, early October–early November. Short-eared Owl arrive mid–late October, Black Redstart often abundant end October–early November. Late summer visitors and a few vagrants stay into November, when Pallas's Warbler may still arrive.

33A   ADDITIONAL SITE: PELAGIC SEABIRD TRIP

Habitat
At the Western Approaches to the English Channel, approximately 70 miles (112 km) west-southwest of the Isles of Scilly, lies an area of rich fishing waters at the outer edge of the Continental Shelf seas.

Species
In late summer and early autumn of recent years, several pioneering charter boat trips have taken birdwatchers out to the deep water fishing grounds near the edge of the Continental Shelf. Here, several hours' voyage out of sight of land, many seabird species, including some rarely glimpsed from mainland watchpoints, can be viewed in quantities milling around feeding and following fishing trawlers. Use of 'chum', a smelly fish oil mixture thrown overboard, lures birds close to watchers' vessels, allowing spectacular views of skuas, Storm Petrel, Great, Sooty and perhaps Cory's Shearwaters, within photographic range at times a few metres off. One or two Wilson's Petrel, formerly almost unknown off British coasts, have been identified on most trips, pattering low over the sea with Storm Petrel. Other extremely rare petrels and shearwaters have also been reported and photographed. Dolphins and porpoises following the boat can be an additional attraction.

Timing
Voyages have been between one and three days long; there is little point in going without adequate time to search the trawler area thoroughly. Fares can be expensive and seasickness is common; conditions can easily become very rough.

Access
Enquire from Isles of Scilly Steamship Co., Penzance, or look for advertisements in bird magazines to find out who is planning to run trips. These will usually require pre-booking some months in advance. Most have started from Penzance or Falmouth, between end July and mid-September.

34 ST IVES ISLAND AND BAY

OS ref: SW 5241
OS map: sheet 203

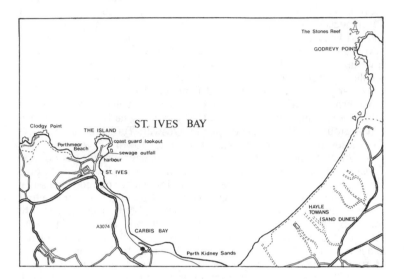

Habitat

St Ives is in far west Cornwall, on its north coast. The 'Island' is a 20-m high rocky headland with a Coastguard station on top, from which you can look across the bay to Hayle Sands and Godrevy Point lighthouse, 2½ miles (4 km) away; directly seawards off Godrevy is a long narrow reef, the 'Stones'. Running in a semi-circle from the edge of St Ives town, Carbis Bay is a particularly sheltered section of the larger St Ives area, the whole of which remains sheltered from most easterly and all southerly winds, including prevailing southwesterlies. Overall it has a sandy bottom, with long stretches of wide sandy beaches, backed towards Hayle Towans by high sand dunes. Some parts have a more rocky shoreline, like that found near the Island.

Just below and behind the Island, which forms the western corner of the main bay, is a sewage outfall. (There are plans by South West Water to reposition it farther out.) As the bay and headland face north, strong opposing sunlight is not such a problem as at many coastal points, except perhaps in early mornings. The high light values in the far west produce perfect colour and detail.

Species

This area is famous chiefly for large spectacular passages of seabirds off the Island, especially in autumn gales when birdwatchers from many parts of Britain come here to see pelagic birds, normally rarely seen from land.

In winter and early spring, St Ives Bay is noted mainly for diving birds, especially when sheltered from rough seas. Most numerous of the interesting species are divers and grebes. Two or three Great Northern

Diver are almost always present, sometimes ten or more. Recently a rare White-billed Diver from the high Arctic joined them for a few days in late winter. Smaller and more snake-necked, Black-throated occur quite often singly, but there can be five or more; numbers tend to rise from late winter and by early spring ten or more may be present. Red-throated Diver are only occasional single winter visitors. Typical of the region, Slavonian is the most common grebe, although fewer than five is normal. Black-necked are uncommon, most years bringing one or two. Red-necked Grebe, as elsewhere, are scarce, and not even seen annually. A very light scattering of seaducks come and go through winter; perhaps a group of three or four female or immature Eider is present, diving for shellfish off rocky areas, with similar numbers of Common Scoter, once an American Surf Scoter; the odd Long-tailed Duck which visit prefer small fish. None of the above diving species competes for food with the 50 or more Shag and dozen or so Cormorant regularly seen in the bay. Small groups of Purple Sandpiper forage with Turnstone along rocky foreshores, often below seafront houses in the town.

When spring arrives, ducks leave quite quickly as a rule, as do most Great Northern Diver and grebes; as is normal in Cornwall, however, Black-throated Diver often increase in spring. Lingering individuals may attain summer plumage. Up to five Glaucous Gull might appear together, frequenting especially the harbour and fishing boats. They may also be joined by the smaller, slimmer Iceland Gull, but only irregularly. The largest male examples of Glaucous can be larger than the largest Great Black-backed Gull, while smallest females may be little bigger than a Herring Gull. Very early spring is a good time for unusual gulls, especially Little Gull. These begin appearing in groups of three or four, gradually increasing, sometimes to 15. Mediterranean Gull, like Little, tend to hover over wave crests and sewer outfalls, picking scraps from the surface; only two or three may visit, sometimes joining together. Rarities such as American Laughing Gull have been found at this season.

Soon the first migrant terns appear in the shape of excited Sandwich Terns, loudly proclaiming their arrival while diving for fish; this is the most common tern in spring. Later small flocks of ten or more, moving through the bay, may be joined by two or three Common or Arctic Tern.

Seawatching from the Island is possibly worth a try year-round in any conditions, on the off-chance that an interesting species may fly past. From March prospects become more certain, and if conditions are favourable, a scattering or even sustained passage may occur. True movement is usually eastward, up the coast, as opposed to seabirds milling around the general sea area, such as a few Gannet. One species present in the general area, as well as passing through, is the Fulmar, but hundreds, even thousands, streaming past the headland indicate real movement. Manx Shearwater and Kittiwake are also involved, in similar numbers, heading towards breeding colonies; 2,000 or more of each may pass in just a few hours. Among the Manx may be a few browner Balearic Shearwater. If divers are passing (usually only in twos and threes), they are most likely Black-throated. A few Bar-tailed Godwit or Whimbrel may fly past later in the season, and there is always the chance of a skua or two, or even a few Storm Petrel. Sightings of the latter are well on the cards throughout late spring and summer, and small feeding parties occasionally wander close to shore. If winds blow strongly from the right direction, even in high summer, especially in early mornings, odd non-breeding birds of several interesting species may be seen; these may include a stray from southern oceans spending its winter here, possibly an albatross!

As late summer approaches and depressional Atlantic gales become likely, the chance arises for the first major seawatch. Really high numbers of seabirds do not occur early on, but some will already have left their natal colonies to begin their westward journey. All true passage will now be westward. *Note:* all numbers quoted below are on a per-day basis. Shearwaters, skuas and terns make up the bulk of early passages, if conditions cause them to occur. Fifty or more of each of Common and Sandwich Terns pass, perhaps accompanied by two or three Roseate, Little or Black Tern; terns use the bay regardless of winds, small groups fishing or gathering along quieter sandy beaches. Skuas may be present, in ones and twos, skilfully harrying feeding terns; early ones will be predominantly Arctic, maybe 30 or more, with four or five stocky Great Skua (frequently known by their Scottish name, 'Bonxie'). Groups totalling up to 150 Shag and 50 or so Cormorant move westward. Manx Shearwater can pass in very high numbers early on; the more usual counts of 10,000 have occasionally risen to well over 20,000, among which may be 20–50 Balearic-race birds. Sooty Shearwater speed through, attaining peak numbers early; often 30–40 may be seen, rarely over 200; small numbers are also seen outside their main season. Storm Petrel appear off the headland in variable numbers; passing throughout autumn, they may be absent on some days, flit low over the waves in twos or threes, or occur in hundreds.

As the season progresses, tern and skua numbers increase and the two most common terns, Sandwich and Common, can pass in hundreds, although Roseate may not increase from two or three and rarely move through in double figures. Never are there more than a handful of Little Tern. Black Tern usually pass in twos and threes, but more than 30 may be seen. Arctic Tern, later migrants, are usually seen only in numbers up to ten. Both Arctic and Great Skuas can now reach 50 plus. Bonxies have the longest season, and are not up to peak numbers here until after other skuas have reached their southern destinations. Daily counts of over 100 for either of these commoner skua species are unusual. Pomarine Skuas, more heavily built than Arctic although similarly shaped, fly with slower, more measured wingbeats, resembling their larger Bonxie cousin. Usually only in ones and twos, certain weather conditions can bring this ocean-going migrant closer to shore, producing ten or more per day; odd ones are seen both very early and very late. The rarest skua to pass is the smallest, usually now seen annually – the Long-tailed Skua – which has the most oceanic migration, taking it far from the coast; this lovely skua remains rare at St Ives, in very good years perhaps four or five in a season. Recently Britain's first South Polar Skua, a southern hemisphere relative of the Bonxie, were identified here.

From mid-autumn, earlier and later migrants merge, numbers gradually increasing. The St Ives speciality is now most likely to be recorded. The dainty, fork-tailed Sabine's Gull has been recorded here more frequently than anywhere else in Britain. Even so, only four or five pass in some years, while in stormy autumns groups of this number may occur, sometimes amid throngs of similarly-marked first-winter-plumaged Kittiwake. Kittiwake can number well in excess of 30,000! Such figures are recorded mostly late in the season. Little Gulls, on the other hand, pass in twos and threes, occasionally reaching 20 or more. Few Leach's Petrel are seen early in the season, and in some unfavourable autumns

Sabine's Gull – adult (top) and juvenile

they are absent; rather like Storm Petrel occurrences, some apparently good days produce none, or two or three, while on other days 50 or more may move past. Gannet, in hundreds even on quieter days, are easily capable of reaching 25,000, although up to 5,000 is more usual.

As the season moves on, and tern and shearwater numbers decline, other birds come to the fore. Replacing black-and-white hordes of Manx Shearwater are auks, in even greater number. They appear to be mainly Razorbill, but distance often precludes accurate identification. The flocks passing on whirring wings act as a backdrop to more exciting species. Counts are made of over 50,000 (average numbers per hour passing, multiplied to give a day figure). Puffin, strangely, are almost non-existent, while Little Auk appear only at the very end of autumn. The latter, too, have good and bad years, in some barely seen, while in others 50 pass a day; up to ten is more usual. Least common, not surprisingly as most populations are non-migratory, are Black Guillemot, one or two being noted some years. Another later species is a sea-going wader, the small greyish-white Grey Phalarope, often stopping to rest on the waves; numbers are similar to Little Auk, but over 50 is exceptional.

Divers come through in higher numbers later on. This is one of the few places in Cornwall where substantial numbers of Red-throated are seen. In fact St Ives probably records most, with daily totals of 20 or 30 attained, as well as at least as many Great Northern although rather fewer Black-throated. No real passage of grebes occurs, but occasionally one passes by. Later in the season, a few other ducks may attach themselves to small parties of Common Scoter, which pass throughout

222

autumn; perhaps a larger Velvet Scoter showing distinctive white wing-patches, a Red-breasted Merganser, or an Eider or two. Geese, uncommon in the far west, have been seen in small flocks, usually 'black geese' (Brent or Barnacle). A thin scattering of northern white-winged gulls, such as Glaucous, occurs. Once an adult Ross's Gull was seen in an exceptionally fierce gale. Herring Gull can pass in thousands, whereas Lesser Black-backed Gull, which move in autumn and early winter, reach only 200–300. Keeping birdwatchers company later in autumn may be two or three Snow Bunting on the Island slopes, while Black Redstart confidingly join forces with Rock Pipit feeding among turf and Sea Pinks.

The most notable omissions from the species list are Cory's and Great Shearwaters, which regularly gather in thousands to feed at the entrance to the Western Approaches, off Ushant, Brittany. Fairly frequently following cold-water currents, and associated food, they visit the sea area around Land's End, albeit in quite small numbers; only rarely are they seen from the Island, usually singly and a long way out.

St Ives Island has produced some of Britain's highest totals of migrating seabirds, as well as some of its rarest species. Apart from the few already mentioned, recent sightings include Little Shearwater, Wilson's Petrel, Bridled Tern and Black-browed Albatross. These unexpected, but hoped-for, birds make ten-hour watches in howling gales, squalls and freezing conditions well worthwhile.

Timing

More or less any time could justify checking the headland or bay if you are in the area. Conditions conducive to large passages past the Island are highly critical, although birds such as terns pausing to feed in the bay or semi-resident winter divers and grebes may be seen in varying conditions. In incorrect conditions, however, actual passage off the Island will be little or nothing.

For substantial seabird movement to be seen, winds should ideally be between westnorthwest and north. An Atlantic depression from the southwest will have just passed through, preferably with its centre not much higher than Northern Ireland. As it passes, the wind veers from southwest towards northerly; at this point seabirds begin to pass. The larger, more vigorous, faster-travelling and more rain-bearing the depression is, the greater a seabird passage will result.

There are many variations, but results then become more uncertain. Sometimes a strong front of northerly air alone will produce good results. At other times, days of southwesterly gales which fail to veer (therefore no birds pass) finally do so, but abate to a breeze; either few birds then pass, although they may include a rarity, or a good passage may take place as tired birds merely track with the wind. On the day of a major gale, those species able to cope pass through. The next day (or morning), provided winds are still from the right direction, smaller species such as terns, small gulls, etc. come through when strong winds have decreased. Strong winds from due west usually produce little or no *close* passage; the moment they flick north of west, especially if the weather system contains frequent squalls, the bay can be seething with birds, all of which were passing by, unseen, further out! Sometimes ideal conditions start early in the morning; heavy passage takes place, the wind then dies, or backs to southwest, and passage ceases, perhaps by midday. Conversely, passage may not start until late afternoon, frustrating if you have been watching an empty sea for five hours, knowing what you are missing. Very occasionally correct winds will blow for two or three days, during which passage will be sustained. Until these critical conditions arrive, some years for only three or four days, major passage is non-existent.

Although most passage occurs within a mile (1.6 km) – often very close – it should be remembered that perhaps less than five minutes may elapse between initial sighting and brief views before a moving seabird is lost to view round the headland; the sheer numbers can also cause bewilderment. It is better to learn basic seabird identification elsewhere if possible, or visit on a quieter day, if you are inexperienced.

Access

St Ives is reached by A3074 from Hayle. For the Island, head to the northern tip of the town, following signs to the car park. This car park lies immediately below the steeply rising headland; a tarmac path leads to the top. Watch from areas sheltered from the wind (if possible), around the outer walls of the Coastguard lookout. From the edge of the car park very close views of the sewer and its gulls are gained. The sewer can also be seen well from the Island.

The outer part of the bay is also checked from this car park or from the harbour walls, as well as from roads adjacent to the bay. Check the harbour for unusual gulls. Public footpaths lead from the town, remaining close to shore, extending to the mouth of Hayle estuary at Porthkidney beach (part of Carbis Bay), where terns often rest. A branch railway line from London–Penzance main line runs from St Erth to St Ives all year round, daily except Sundays, giving panoramic views *en route*.

Calendar

Resident: Gannet and Oystercatcher (do not breed but seen all year). Cormorant, Shag, Razorbill and Guillemot breed nearby. Rock Pipit.

December–February: Black-throated and Great Northern Divers; Red-throated mostly pass the Island. Slavonian Grebe. Possible Black-necked and Red-necked Grebes, Eider, Common Scoter. Turnstone, Purple Sandpiper. Possible Grey Phalarope past Island, Great Skua, Little, Mediterranean and Glaucous Gulls, possible Iceland Gull and Little Auk.

March–May: Apart from Black-throated Diver and uncommon gulls, all above species gradually decline. Fulmar, Manx Shearwater, possible Storm Petrel, especially towards May. Bar-tailed Godwit and Whimbrel pass from mid-April. Possible odd skuas throughout period. Sandwich Tern from mid-March, a few 'Commic' from April.

June–July: breeding species. Chance of seabird movement, particularly Manx Shearwater or Storm Petrel. End of period, terns reappear in bay.

August–November: early part of period, August–early September; Fulmar, Sooty, Manx and Balearic Shearwaters. Terns including Black, Sandwich, Common and Roseate often peak now. Whimbrel, skuas (mainly Arctic), Little Gull, Lesser Black-backed, possible Sabine's Gull. Middle period, mid-September–mid-October; all the above, some peaking now, e.g. Arctic Skua. Leach's Petrel, Common Scoter, Great and Pomarine Skuas, possibly Long-tailed Skua, Mediterranean Gull, Arctic Tern, Grey Phalarope. End period, end October–November: three species of diver past Island. Many species decline past October, except: Grey Phalarope, Great Skua may peak now. Possible Glaucous Gull, Kittiwake and auk passage increases, perhaps including Little Auk.

34A ADDITIONAL SITE: PENDEEN WATCH

OS ref: SW 3836
OS map: sheet 203

Habitat

Pendeen Watch lies at the far northwestern tip of the exposed Land's End peninsula, some 12 miles (19 km) west by road from St Ives. It is the last north-facing point on the coastline. The watching area is an open grassy clifftop beside the lighthouse.

Species

Pendeen complements St Ives as a seabird migration watch point; all aspects affecting movement at that site apply here (even the same individual birds being seen, often within an hour or so of leaving St Ives!)

Differences between the sites are perhaps ill defined, but basically are: seabirds tend to be a little further out, and do not linger as they sometimes do in St Ives Bay. Greater numbers of 'large' shearwaters (Great, Cory's and Sooty) are often recorded off Pendeen; occasionally bigger counts of other seabirds are also reported. Smaller species, e.g. terns and petrels, often allow vital closer scrutiny at St Ives, however. Attributes shared with St Ives include wide, uninterrupted vistas, and superb light. At this site a nearby reef helps as a focal point, most movement on a good day taking place about equidistant to it.

Access

The A3074 runs from A30 to St Ives; take B3306 which passes through the village of Pendeen some 10 miles (16 km) westwards. A minor road signposted to the lighthouse for about 1 mile (1.6 km) allows parking where the road ends beside the light. Steps lead down the right-hand side of the light. A position near the base of the eastward-facing wall affords some shelter from northwest winds, allowing good views over the sea. Watching from the small car park to the right of the lighthouse is not very practical, with a more restricted viewing area and greater distance between you and the birds.

35 HAYLE ESTUARY (INCLUDING CARNSEW POOL AND COPPERHOUSE CREEK)

OS ref: SW 5436
OS map: sheet 203

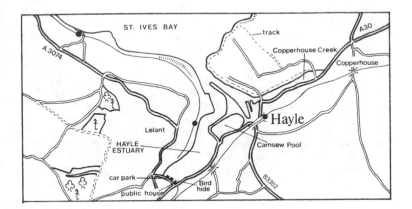

Habitat

This estuary and adjoining areas are adjacent to Hayle town in west Cornwall, on the northern side of the peninsula. The area is important as the only estuary in the far west, and very sheltered from the sea. The mouth lies at a different angle from the main basin, separated by a long curving channel cutting through a barrier of dunes. The lower estuary is predominantly sandy, becoming muddy higher up. A freshwater channel flows at low tides. At the bottom of the estuary, an embankment encloses an artificial tidal area known as Carnsew Pool, where a large sheet of water is retained even at low tides, when soft mud is exposed. Running alongside the town centre is another muddy tidal area, Copperhouse Creek, less than half the size of the main estuary.

· Winter temperatures in low, sheltered areas of the far west at times bear little resemblance to those even in eastern Devon. Apart from exceptionally cold years, far fewer days are below freezing, and snowfall is not annual.

At low tides fishermen bait digging can disturb the estuary's birds, especially off the lower parts around Lelant. However, there is no shooting over this relatively small 220-acre (90-ha) but nonetheless very important estuary, which is a Site of Special Scientific Interest.

Among other interesting fauna is found a centipede which inhabits the shore edge around Lelant, so rare it occurs nowhere else in England. Several locally rare plants grow including Sea Aster, while four species which are deemed nationally rare are: Ivy Broomrape, Wild Cabbage, Purple Ramping Fumitory and Round-fruited Rush, the latter growing near the reeds at Copperhouse.

It remains to be seen how extensive future developments planned for the area will affect the complex; it is hoped the main estuary basin will become an RSPB reserve.

Species

Although well known to most birdwatchers for migrant waders and wintering ducks, the first sight as you glance over the estuary in winter is of large flocks of gulls. They congregate mainly towards the middle and upper sections. This estuary does not attract extremely high numbers, perhaps no more than 1,500 Herring Gull at a time. Black-headed Gulls, which flock in nearby fields, often number less than 1,000 on the mudflats. Normally about 500 Great Black-backeds gather. The two most numerous migrant gulls, Lesser Black-backed and Common, achieve highest numbers in late winter–early spring. Paradoxically, Common Gulls are not at all numerous in Cornwall until fresh migrants (mostly adults) appear, swelling the small winter population; flocks of 500 and more then become commonplace. The build-up of Lesser Black-backed Gull is even more noticeable, as many fewer remain through early winter; being so far west, concentrations of over 200 soon appear in late winter, reaching 1,000 or more later; autumn passage peaks at around 300.

Uncommon gulls are relatively frequent visitors at any time during non-breeding seasons, but more occur from late winter through spring. Normally present as single birds, some species such as Glaucous, Mediterranean and Little Gulls may total five or more individuals a year. Least frequent are Iceland, normally one or two a year. Apart from odd appearances of truly rare gulls such as Bonaparte's, in recent years Ring-billed Gulls have been identified with increasing regularity, mostly in late winter and early spring. Almost certainly they arrive with migrating Common Gulls, which they closely resemble in all plumage stages.

When conditions are severe elsewhere, weather movements bring higher numbers of ducks and waders to the milder far west. Groups of up to ten Brent Geese may arrive. Average winter populations are not large, nor particularly varied. Wigeon are the most numerous duck, at about 800 (American Wigeon have occurred, including several together). Teal peak at little over 300, and sometimes the American subspecies, Green-winged Teal, visits. Mallard and Shelduck reach about 50 and 30 respectively; one or two pairs of each breed. Gadwall are annual, usually six to ten. Other common dabbling ducks occur annually at irregular intervals. The most common diving ducks are Goldeneye, usually females (brownheads), perhaps reaching 20, although half of this is normal. Goosander visit most winters, when two or three brownheads may be seen. The closely related Red-breasted Merganser is also seen in groups of three to five, again usually brownheads. Tufted Duck often occur, in parties of under ten.

Wintering flocks of waders are rather low. Dunlin fluctuate, averaging 500. Curlew reach 500 in winter, and up to 700 are often counted in autumn. Lapwing use the estuary as a temporary roost, several thousand sharing local fields with Black-headed Gull; only a few hundred of these plovers visit the estuary at any one time. Grey Plover keep to the estuary, totalling about 100 birds. Only about ten Knot stay the winter, although in autumn twice as many are seen. Fifty Bar-tailed Godwit arrive in autumn and stay throughout winter. Black-tailed Godwit visit only irregularly in ones and twos, while Oystercatcher gather in almost static numbers of 100 for much of the year. During autumn a heavy passage of Ringed Plover peaks at over 300, occasionally as many as 50 over-wintering. Whimbrel, often heard before being seen, stop off briefly; small groups of ten or more behave similarly in spring. Redshank, long called 'sentinel of the marshes' from their loud ringing calls, are present in most months of the year; autumn flocks build up to about 300, and 100 normally winter. Turnstone gather in groups of up to 25 in autumn, also staying in winter.

Small numbers of less common waders regularly occur on autumn passage. Both Little Stint and Curlew Sandpiper are annual. Subject to their migration patterns, numbers fluctuate from year to year, though not often over ten; a party of five of either species can be reasonably expected. Higher numbers are more regularly achieved by Curlew Sand-piper, with 12–20 in good years. Flocks of up to ten Ruff may pass through in autumn, with two or three at a time in spring. Greenshank and Common Sandpiper appear in similar numbers to Ruff, but one or two may overwinter. Spotted Redshank are less numerous, perhaps only three or four visiting at a time in autumn, often only singles. Little Ringed Plover are now more or less annual, occasionally with two together; in some years they are recorded in both migration seasons.

Rarities turn up annually. Pectoral and White-rumped Sandpipers and Long-billed Dowitcher are American species seen several times over the years. Every year the area is certain to produce a number of such birds. Probably this is due largely to its geographical position, being both the first and last estuary most migrants will see in Britain. In one recent spring a Broad-billed Sandpiper, a rare European wader, was identified – the first ever recorded in Cornwall. Occasionally a Spoonbill makes a spring visit, and Black-winged Stilt has been recorded; Gull-billed Tern and Wilson's Phalarope are recent rare sightings.

Grey Heron and Buzzard are resident, but, whenever either flies over, gulls and waders take flight in alarm. Peregrine have the same effect, with better reason, and often visit through autumn and winter. One or two Kingfisher are present throughout the same period.

HARRISON 83

Peregrine Falcon

A small passage of terns uses the estuary, either as a temporary roost or to pause a short while to feed. Having followed the main channel up from the sea, they find shelter especially in rough weather. Most common is Sandwich, among the first spring migrants to reach us; later groups of 20 or more may gather and higher numbers are normal in autumn. Arctic, Roseate and Little Terns occur in flocks of fewer than five in spring and autumn. Up to ten Common Tern come through in spring, often many more in autumn. The rare White-winged Black Tern has occurred on several occasions.

In the quiet winter waters of Carnsew Pool, an exhausted diver may be sheltering; single Black-throated and Great Northern Divers are not uncommon. One or two Slavonian Grebe are annual, but apart from up to ten Little Grebe, all other grebes are rarer visitors, though single Great Crested and Black-necked are recorded most years. Red-breasted Merganser and Tufted Duck favour the pool rather than the estuary, as do the occasional Long-tailed Duck which appear. Many birds which use the main estuary, including most smaller waders, also habitually visit Carnsew.

Copperhouse Creek, more open to disturbance, is also quite narrow, and less attractive to wary species. The gull flocks which congregate should be checked for uncommon species, which regularly occur, including up to five 'tame' wintering Ring-billed Gull often representing all age groups, one or two of which have now become virtually resident. They feed largely on scraps found in the adjacent car park, and copiously added to by many birders. Mute Swan reach over 30 through autumn and winter. Among the many fewer waders are some which prefer this area; Little Ringed Plover and Wood and Green Sandpipers in spring and autumn, for example, are less often seen on the main estuary. Pectoral Sandpiper tend to frequent this spot. In an area of grassy wasteland in hard weather, up to 50 Snipe may flock; among them a Jack Snipe may be flushed. The same area in autumn may have standing pools which attract interesting waders, once a Temminck's Stint. Behind this small grassy area is an equally small stand of *Phragmites* reed, probably most important as an autumn roost for about 150 Pied/White Wagtails, and several hundred Swallows.

Timing

A visit at any time of day, through all seasons, could prove worthwhile with the chance of occasional late passage or non-breeding birds and strays moving through. Low winter sunlight is not much problem here, as you can face away from the sun most of the time. For waders the tide must be out to some degree. A rising tide, or one just starting to fall, forces many waders to alight on relatively small areas of mud at the head of the estuary when close views are obtainable; there is no central high-tide roost. Hard winter weather may increase numbers and species, while rough seas will induce some species such as terns to shelter. Strong westerly airstreams in autumn are responsible for American vagrants.

Access

The main estuary is just west of Hayle town. The main road through Hayle runs beside the sites (the old A30, before the Hayle bypass was created). There is car parking in the town. At the head of the estuary, beside the main road, a publican has kindly allowed his car park to be used when checking here. The car park is a good vantage point. The RSPB has erected a public hide (again on the publican's land) giving close views of the main channel. A log of watchers' records is kept inside. The estuary is flanked on the north side by a branch railway line, but the main road along the opposite shore allows checking along its length. The hide is near the A30/A3074 junction to St Ives, at the west end, on the right as you turn off towards St Ives from Hayle town.

Access to Carnsew Pool is by a public footpath located from the road, near the site of some small industrial units beside the lower end of the estuary. From this path, on three sides of the pool, extremely good views are obtained. In addition to the main road, public paths run along the remaining three edges of Copperhouse Creek, including alongside the grassy areas at its head (i.e. on the right as you enter Hayle town from the east off A30).

Calendar

Resident: Grey Heron, Oystercatcher.

December–February: probable Black-throated and Great Northern Divers; Slavonian Grebe, Little Grebe, possibly other grebes. Possible Brent Geese; Teal, Gadwall, Wigeon, Tufted Duck, possible Long-tailed Duck, Goldeneye, Red-breasted Merganser, occasional Goosander, possible Peregrine. Ringed and Grey Plovers, Lapwing, Turnstone, Dunlin, Knot, Redshank, possible Spotted Redshank, Greenshank, Common Sandpiper, Bar-tailed Godwit, Curlew, Snipe, possible Jack Snipe; possible Mediterranean, Ring-billed, Little, Iceland and Glaucous Gulls, particularly towards end of period. Lesser Black-backed Gull passage from late December, may peak at end of period. Common Gull arrive from mid-February. Kingfisher.

March–May: most grebes, ducks and waders begin departure from early March. Sandwich Tern arrive from second week of March. Common Gull peak first half of March. Uncommon gulls continue to pass through. Mid-April, Whimbrel arrive. Late April and May, Common, Arctic, Roseate and Little Terns. Possible Ruff, Little Ringed Plover, Wood Sandpiper and Black Tern late spring.

June–July: first returning waders end July, including Green Sandpiper. Possible Roseate Tern. Shelduck and Mallard breed.

August–November: most common waders gradually increase throughout period. Exceptions are: Whimbrel pass through early period, Ringed Plover peak in September, Little Stint and Curlew Sandpiper arrive from early September (leave by early November), Ruff, Spotted Redshank, Greenshank and Common Sandpiper peak early September. Possible Little and Mediterranean Gulls through period. Lesser Black-backed Gulls peak September. Black, Sandwich, Common, Arctic and Little Terns, August to October. From mid-September, Wigeon and Teal begin to return, other ducks towards end of period.

Habitat

Halfway down Cornwall's exposed north coast, the tourist resort of Newquay stands on open clifftops, with high open turf and rock headlands on either side. Sandy beaches intermingle with cliffs. At the northwestern side, Towan Head, with a large sewage outfall immediately on the north flank, projects seaward. The bay north of the headland, known as the Gazzle, forms a slightly sheltered area of sea even in rough weather. The south side of the town is bordered by the sandy Gannel estuary, subject to human disturbance, with a small area of saltmarsh on the upper reaches. Beyond this southward lie extensive National Trust areas around West Pentire and Kelsey Heads, separated by sheltered Porthjoke stream valley; behind the clifftops lies open arable land, left as stubble in autumn. Immediately west of Porthjoke lies rolling Cubert Common, a National Trust area of botanical interest, covered with Cowslips in spring. The Porthjoke stream is lined with Irises in summer, then tends to flood in autumn into small pools in the hollow between the upper stream and Cubert Common.

Two miles (3 km) inland to the east of Newquay, set in a steep-sided farmland valley, lies 40-acre (16-ha) Porth Reservoir, formerly known as Melancoose. SWW maintain the area furthest away from the dam as a Bird Sanctuary. Copses border the lakeside and there is a small area of marsh and damp woodland at the top end.

Coastal areas are heavily used by holidaymakers in summer.

Species

Newquay district's varied habitats provide a good list of migrants and seabirds, plus one or two localised breeding species. It is, in particular, one of the region's best seawatching stations away from St Ives, although only receiving 25–30 per cent of the overall passage numbers of most species recorded at that more famous site. Certainly it has the advantage of being less crowded with birdwatchers than St Ives Island can become at peak periods.

In winter, strong gales blowing in off the Atlantic may bring very large westward movements of seabirds off Towan Head, the point from which most observation is carried out. Passages can include thousands of Gannet, auks and Kittiwake. Occasionally a Grey Phalarope, Little Auk or even a Puffin may accompany them. The presence of the large sewage outfall here produces a regular share of the scarcer gulls, including one or two Glaucous most winters; Mediterranean and Little Gull are also recorded quite regularly and singles may stay for weeks. Iceland Gull, with single records most years, is the scarcest of the regular interesting gulls. Small parties of Purple Sandpiper and Turnstone, probably no more than 10 or so of each, scurry about the rocks below the headland. Two or three Eider or Common Scoter are often driven into Gazzle bay north of Towan by rough conditions. Small numbers of all three diver species are seen off this point in winter, although Black-throated are scarcest, perhaps only seen as late autumn migrants. Shag feed commonly on the sea across the whole district.

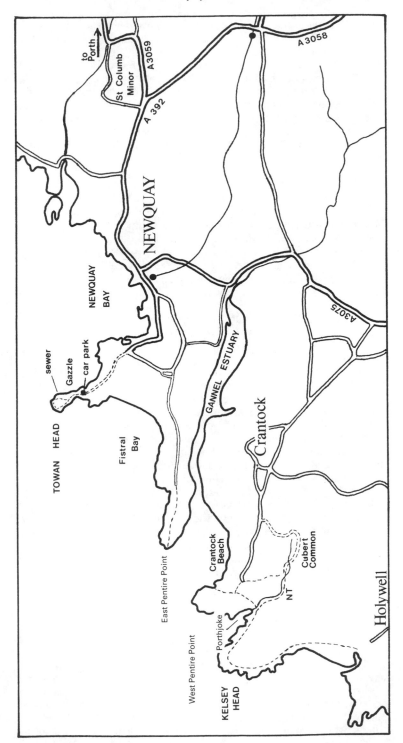

The Gannel estuary does not attract any regular or substantial population of most waders, owing to its disturbed position and open sandy bed with little food content. A few Oystercatcher are most likely to be present in daytime, accompanied by scattered Curlew. Up to 500 Curlew which have fed in nearby fields will, however, drop in to roost at dusk; this is one of Cornwall's larger flocks. More prominent on the estuary are gull flocks, resting and bathing; over 1,800 Herring Gull and 2,000 Black-headed Gull form the bulk, with a few dozen Great Black-backed. In late winter as gull passage commences, up to 800 Lesser Black-backed and 300 Common Gulls may join them. All the area's scarcer gulls might be seen here or at Towan. The saltings harbour an occasional Jack Snipe, along with a few of its commoner relatives the Snipe, and Rock Pipits may be joined by one or two pale Water Pipit. Ducks are not numerous, but usually include 20–30 Wigeon, together with ones and twos of other dabbling ducks at times, including Gadwall. The upper estuary may attract one or two Little Grebe and perhaps a Red-breasted Merganser. In some recent winters one or two Grey Heron fishing here have been joined by a conspicuous white Little Egret, a bird whose occurrences in our region have increased greatly in recent years.

At the edge of the town near the estuary is open-banked Trenance Park lake, inhabited by ornamental ducks; in winter wild Tufted Duck and Pochard join them, although probably each in single figures. Gulls fly in to bathe in the fresh water, and at this closer range identification of more difficult species such as Ring-billed has sometimes been possible, although the other uncommon gulls have all been seen flying in occasionally.

Sandy Crantock Bay, off the Gannel estuary mouth, flanked by East and West Pentire Heads, holds a regular flock of Red-throated Diver in the coldest winter months, reaching 20–30 most years. Single figures of Black-throated and Great Northern may also be seen, plus one or two Slavonian Grebe and Eider. The open downland overlooking either side of the bay may hold one or two wintering Snow Bunting, shuffling along low while searching for seeds. Other passerines which might be seen along the coast beside the ubiquitous Rock Pipit, are Stonechat and occasionally a Black Redstart. The stubble fields towards Kelsey Head contain flocks of Skylark and Meadow Pipit, plus parties of up to 10–15 stout streaky Corn Bunting, a local resident with a declining range. The flocks form a target for one or two wide-ranging Merlin; Peregrine overfly the entire area and can even be seen over the main seafront at times. The small Porthjoke cove beach acts as a refuge for gull flocks disturbed off the main beach, and Mediterranean Gull have been found here.

Porth reservoir is not a major duck habitat, but up to 40 each of Tufted and Pochard may gather, joined by up to 150 Mallard and perhaps 200 Teal; odd ones and twos of other dabbling ducks visit, plus the odd Goldeneye. Goosander, Smew and Scaup are all hard-weather specialities in very small numbers, as have been wild swans in the past, although these have been scarce in recent seasons. Occasionally a Bittern may occupy the tiny marsh at the top end of the reservoir in cold spells. Singles of all three diver species have been seen when storm-driven, as have various grebes, including a number of records of Great Crested. Two or three Cormorant are often present on dead trees, flying down to the upper end of the lake to fish, while a Kingfisher may flash past low over the water. Dippers have been found just below the dam in winter, where small groups of Siskin may gather to feed on lakeside trees which contain all three species of woodpecker, although Lesser Spotted is typically hard to see.

The jingling song of male Corn Bunting in the clifftop fields is a typical spring sound at the south end of the district. Up to 500 pairs of Kittiwake return to breed on the cliffs just below Newquay's Atlantic Hotel, also gathering at the sewer to feed. Shag and Herring Gull breed widely along the coastlines, while Little Owl might be found in the Cubert/Porthjoke area along trackside telegraph posts at dusk; this species is rare and probably decreasing as a Cornish resident. Spring migration of small passerines can be noticeable around Porthjoke, with varied falls in the streamside bushes; a Hoopoe or Quail might be reported in the valley, and a Sardinian Warbler was a recent vagrant from southern Europe. One or two singing Sedge and Grasshopper Warblers stay to nest. Passing flocks of Curlew and Whimbrel drop in to feed in clifftop fields and occasionally a noteworthy wader stops off at the Gannel; a Black-winged Stilt has been recorded. Wader numbers, however, remain low as usual here. Hirundines gather over Porth Reservoir and commoner warblers sing in the surrounding trees, but no major passage occurs; odd records over the years have included Osprey and White-winged Black Tern visiting. The flat rattling song of one or two Lesser White-throat, an expanding population although still small, might be heard in hedgerows near Porth and the Gannel river. The sea may be quiet, although gulls, which have started to pass through early, may still provide a scarcer species. A few Sandwich Tern pass north at sea, and with the onset of the breeding season, seabird flocks from Britain's West Coast colonies start to pass by southward on a daily basis *en route* to feeding grounds. Manx Shearwater are seen commonly, up to 10,000 having been recorded some days. Gannet and auks, which later on may include a few Puffin, pass by in large parties. The summer season, when Newquay is full of tourists, sees the start of occurrences of one of Newquay's specialities; the tiny ocean-going Storm Petrel is seen on a frequent and at times daily basis from now through to autumn, with up to 200–300 at times hovering to feed over Towan sewage outfall. Rough weather may drive them in, or a passing flock may be attracted into the bay to feed around a fishing boat, coming close inshore at times; the sewer provides best views generally, as birds may stay fluttering over the water for hours. This is one of mainland Cornwall's best sites for petrels, elusive ocean birds seldom otherwise seen from land. There is also a late summer southward movement of Curlew and Whimbrel down the coastline, the latter reaching 50 per day at times, an unusual autumn count for our region.

As water levels start to drop in later summer and early autumn, exposed mud at the upper (east) end of Porth Reservoir, in common with many such sites in Cornwall, can start to attract interesting waders. Numbers here are never large, but species regularly include Green and Common Sandpipers, Greenshank, Ringed Plover and Dunlin. The American Pectoral Sandpiper has occurred here and scarcer European waders have included Little Ringed Plover and Wood Sandpiper. Cornwall's only record of Terek Sandpiper came from here in the 1960s. After strong autumn gales, a Grey Phalarope might be blown in; one or two terns might also occur here or on the Gannel in similar conditions, and have included Common, Arctic and Black. A few waders also occur on the Gannel, and have included a Lesser Yellowlegs; the pools between Porthjoke and Cubert have also attracted varied waders, which have

Storm Petrel and Leach's Petrel

included an American species occasionally, such as Pectoral Sandpiper.

Passerine migration, apart from widespread Wheatear on clifftops, can include reasonable falls in valleys such as Porthjoke, although numbers do not match those farther east in Britain, warblers for instance being counted in dozens rather than hundreds on a good day. Firecrest are expected in later autumn, and scarcer species have included Red-backed Shrike and Red-breasted Flycatcher. In late season visible migration overhead can be interesting, with winter thrushes and pipits dropping in to rest in the valley; a Richard's Pipit has also been seen. Five Stone Curlew, rarely seen anywhere on passage, were once found in a nearby field! Large flocks of larks, finches and pipits may accumulate on stubble fields towards Kelsey Head, including one or two Snow and Lapland Buntings. These flocks may attract passing raptors, including a Hen Harrier or Short-eared Owl; Merlin which arrive often stay through to the year's end.

At sea, Sandwich Tern which start to pass at the end of summer and early autumn may be pursued by a few Arctic Skua. Numbers of both predator and prey build up as autumn continues; all four skua species have been recorded in recent autumns. Gales have produced up to 50–60 Arctic Skua per day and up to 100 Great Skua, although Pomarine are generally in single figures and Long-tailed are rare, a record of four together here being very exceptional. Terns pass in dozens, mostly Sandwich and Common, with a few Arctic. Roseate and Little Terns are very scarce. Flocks of up to 20 Black Tern may occur, often congregating in a flock in the Gazzle bay. Terns, in common with waders and some-times skuas, tend to fly across the narrows by the lifeboat slip behind Towan Head rather than around the end, especially in high winds. A Mediterranean Gull is often seen off the sewer; up to three have occasionally gathered, and Little Gull might pass in small numbers through autumn, although most frequent in late autumn when 10–15 might be seen. The strikingly-marked Sabine's Gull, a Cornish autumn speciality, is seen mostly passing in ones and twos, but single birds at the outfall may linger for days, providing excellent views. Storm Petrel continue to be recorded through autumn, with hundreds at times – occasionally a thousand or more – accompanied by a few larger, browner Leach's Petrel; up to 10 of the latter may pass, sometimes close off the rocks, when their forked tails may be noted. The Fulmar is an abundant migrant, reaching counts of over 1,000. Manx Shearwater are joined by a few of the Balearic race from late summer; Sooty Shearwater, flying swiftly without lingering in the bay, have an extended passage period, ones and twos being routine most autumn days; over 70 have been recorded exceptionally. Great and Cory's Shearwaters are much rarer, with no regular passage, although a few storm-driven birds do move through. Gannets are a familiar and common migrant, although peak counts of 1,500 per hour have not been reached until winter. Late autumn and early winter can produce maximum passage of Kittiwake, reaching 2,500 per hour at times. This period brings some passage of divers and ducks; all three diver species may fly past in small numbers. Seaducks, such as Scoter, may be joined by scarcer species such as Velvet Scoter (once even a Surf Scoter) and a few dabbling ducks may pass. The Grey Phalarope is a storm-blown later autumn migrant, sometimes reaching 15, with long stays recorded at the sewage outfall. Little Auk may pass at similar times, although usually not more than 2–3 per day. At this season watchers often see a few Black Redstart flitting around seafront rocks.

Timing

Seawatch conditions for maximum passage off Towan Head are similar to those at St Ives, peak passages being recorded on the same dates. There may, however, be sheltering birds in Gazzle bay in westerly or even southwesterly winds. Such conditions can also blow in a stray tern or phalarope to Porth reservoir, and possibly transatlantic vagrant waders to freshwater margins. Storm Petrel require little wind to pass in summer, especially if fishing boats are present in the area, although gale days can bring good numbers. Manx Shearwater summer feeding parties are seen mostly in early mornings and evenings. Black Tern in autumn are seen mostly in southerly winds and rain. Sewage outfall is at its maximum at ebbing tides, although there is always some emission. Passerine migrants are, as usual, seen mostly in easterly and south-easterly winds, when many birds seem to pass straight across from south to north Cornish coasts, especially in fine anticyclonic conditions. Wader passage at Porth depends on dry conditions, increasing exposed margins of mud. Gannel estuary is best watched for gulls and waders when mudflats are exposed; weekdays or early mornings might bring less human disturbance. If watching westward off Towan, later afternoon light can be poor against the sun, although most observations will be of birds coming in from north.

Access

Newquay, a major coastal resort, is well signposted on A-roads. Leaving the town eastward on A392 towards Bodmin, after 2 miles (3 km) turn right (south) on a minor road signposted to the reservoir. After 1 mile (1.6 km), turn left into the reservoir car park. Footpaths lead along both north and south banks; the top end is best for waders. There is no permit requirement.

In Newquay itself, follow signs north past the harbour towards Fistral beach for Towan Head. Turn right at the lane opposite Carnmarth Hotel, and down to the small free car park at the end, on the narrow neck of land just behind the Head. The sewage outfall is directly in front of you. You can watch from the public shelter overlooking the rocks, or even from the car window in bad weather, also suited for watching by the disabled. Some seabirds fly south directly over the car park in bad weather, and birds circle the bay in front. A footpath also leads around the front of the headland; you can shelter behind rocks in bad weather. For some species, e.g. shearwaters, this may be a better watchpoint than the sewage outfall side.

Follow the signs for A3075 towards Redruth and Truro south from the town centre, passing Trenance Park lake on the right. At a mini-roundabout 100 yards (100 m) later, turn right along the flank of the Gannel Estuary. After ½ mile (0.8 km), having passed Medallion Court flats on the right, pull off on the left at a parking area to view the estuary. From here you can walk downriver on foot to check gull flocks. From here, drive on through Pentire area, parking in the free car park at the end of Pentire Avenue to view across Crantock Bay for divers in winter; walk across the open down headland to East Pentire Point.

To check Porthjoke and Kelsey Head, continue from the mini-roundabout for 1 mile (1.6 km) farther on A3075, turning right towards Crantock. Follow signs on towards West Pentire, then left on a minor road past Treago Farm. Pass the farm and through the gateway past National Trust Cubert Common sign. Remember to shut the gate after entry. The stream to the left widens 200 yards (200 m) upstream; this is the area where waders may occur if ground is flooded. Down-stream lies the first section of streamside bushes used by migrants. Drive on down the sandy track; Little Owls might be found in this area. The point where the track branches right to a group of buildings is a particularly sheltered area of bushes for migrants. Keep left on the track to National Trust car park. Walk on down the valley from here; reaching the cove, go up left onto the coast path for Kelsey Head. Watch from the coast path; do not cross stubble fields.

Calendar

Resident: Shag, common raptors, Great Black-backed Gull, all three woodpeckers, Rock Pipit, Stonechat, Raven, Corn Bunting.

December–February: divers, all three species but chiefly Red-throated, peaking end January–February; occasional Slavonian Grebe, Cormorant, Eider, Scoter; gale passages of common seabirds, maybe a Grey Phala-rope, Little Auk or Puffin. Possibly a Black Redstart wintering on coast. Merlin and Peregrine seen over area. Coastal flocks of larks and pipits, maybe Snow Bunting. Tufted Duck, Pochard, Wigeon and Teal flocks, occasional other ducks on freshwater areas. Kingfisher, Dipper, Siskin likely at Porth. Chance of wild swans. Gull flocks in coastal areas include Mediterranean, Little, probably Glaucous. Curlew assemble on Gannel; Water Pipit or Jack Snipe might be seen. Grey Heron, Purple Sandpiper, Turnstone.

March–May: residents breeding, Kittiwake arrive at colony. Manx Shear-water start feeding passages from April. Gull passage peaks early; Mediterranean or Little possible throughout. Lesser Black-backed and

Common Gull build up into March. A few Sandwich Tern from end March. Some early passerine migrants from early March but peaking from mid-April, especially Porthjoke. Whimbrel pass through, Sedge and Grasshopper Warblers singing, a few Lesser Whitethroat. Occasional scarcer migrants throughout.

June–July: residents continue breeding, Manx Shearwater feeding, maybe a Puffin with passing auks; Storm Petrel often seen. Towards end of period, Sandwich Tern and first Arctic Skua might be seen; chance of Balearic and Sooty Shearwaters. Common and Green Sandpipers, Greenshank may start to pass; Whimbrel and Curlew fly south.

August–November: freshwater margins attract waders mostly in August–September, with chance of a Pectoral Sandpiper or other rarer species September. Seabird passage increases in volume and variety, probably greatest variety September, when Leach's Petrel, Sabine's Gull and phalaropes start passing; after mid-October less variety but greater numbers of Gannet, Kittiwake, auks, with chance of phalaropes and Little Auk. Divers and seaducks pass from late October mainly. Passerine movement may include occasional rarer species September–October; finches, larks and pipits mostly October with attendant raptors and chance of Snow and Lapland Buntings.

37 CAMEL ESTUARY AND AMBLE MARSHES

OS ref: SW 9874
OS map: sheet 200

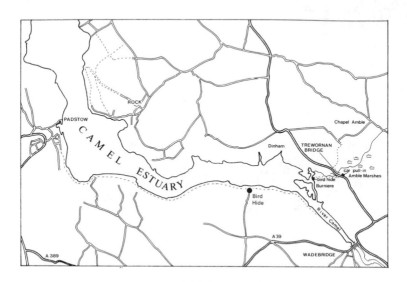

Habitat

On Cornwall's north coast, near the town of Wadebridge, this very interesting diverse habitat combines marshy meadows, mudflats on the upper Camel estuary, and a sandy lower estuary around Padstow and Rock towards the sea. Near the river mouth are extensive high sand dunes along the north shore. At low tide two very large sandbanks and several smaller ones are exposed.

Along these lower estuary shores few trees grow, unable to survive salt-laden Atlantic winds. Farther up the estuary, sand gives way to mud, trees grow on the more sheltered margins, and the estuary forms a much wider basin towards the head. The River Camel meets the smaller River Amble at the head of the flats; the Amble flows through the marshy ground around Chapel Amble, which is now, in part (about 50 acres/ 20 ha), Walmsley Sanctuary. There is little human habitation over much of the area, which therefore remains relatively undisturbed.

Among interesting plants on the sand dunes is Storksbill, which attracts Brown Argus butterflies. Marbled White, Large and Small Skippers are all found on the north side near Rock and Daymer Bay.

Species

The varied habitat results in a good selection of species, the area being particularly important for waders and wildfowl. During winter, Amble marshes attract a couple of hundred Snipe, often difficult to see as they crouch among rough grass; one or two smaller Jack Snipe may associate with them. Walmsley Sanctuary was created mostly to protect a regular wintering flock of White-fronted Geese, which formerly attained 100 or so individuals each year. In recent years, either the flocks have not arrived or 20 or less have visited briefly. During very hard weather their numbers increase as the geese home in on this traditional site. Unusual species include other geese, mostly in ones and twos, perhaps a Barnacle Goose, or the odd Greylag or Bean Goose; the orange-billed Greenland White-front has been recorded on several occasions, in addition to the normal Russian form. Bewick's and Whooper Swans, mostly the former, occur in small groups from time to time, but neither is annual. The marshes here support huge concentrations of Lapwing and Golden Plover; in normal winter periods both species can easily exceed 1,000 apiece, but with prolonged hard weather numbers become quite phenomenal, exceeding 10,000 of both. Dabbling ducks, mostly Wigeon and Teal, use both estuary and marshes, flighting to and fro, when Wigeon can be heard giving their high-pitched whistling 'wheeoo' calls; over 1,000 of each may gather (nowhere else in Cornwall receives this number of Teal). Pintail are seen in small flocks, over 20 at times. Among these regular visitors a few Gadwall or Shoveler may stop over. On the higher estuary, diving ducks are few. Most numerous is Goldeneye, about 15 usually, nearly always brownheads. A few Tufted Duck can occur, but more interesting are one or two Smew, seen most winters. In harder weather very small numbers of other ducks may visit, including Goosander. Other unusual birds seen around the estuary's upper reaches and marshy areas have included Bittern. Green Sandpiper often overwinter, and recently a Cattle Egret frequented the area.

Through winter on the lower estuary, and around the mouth to where it meets the sea at low tide, interesting waterfowl are expected. Three or four Great Northern Diver are often seen, and both Black-throated and Red-throated Divers in ones and twos. Up to five Slavonian Grebe at a time is not unexpected, and one or two Red-necked and Black-necked Grebes occur most years, along with a few Great Crested Grebe. Sea-ducks are not infrequent, but only in small numbers. Most numerous are Common Scoter and Eider, the latter mostly brown females and patchy black and white immature males; both species reach small groups of about ten. Red-breasted Merganser rarely attain this figure, three or four being more usual. Only one or two Velvet Scoter or Long-tailed Duck occur. In the lower estuary Shag are common, but fail to penetrate further upriver, the Cormorant occupying this niche; here the division in habitat between the two is clearly marked. Along this lower sandy stretch, ten or more white and pale grey Sanderling run along the tidelines.

Farther upriver the waders mass, as usual little grey-brown Dunlin being most common with over 1,000 probing the soft mud. More than 500 Curlew winter here and 1,000 may occur in early autumn. Oyster-catcher, however, average only about 400. Ringed Plover tend not to winter in large numbers in the southwest, but 100 or so have been counted here, often favouring sandy lower reaches. In winter plumage Grey Plover are well named, having only a jet-black patch at the base of their off-white underwing (a diagnostic field mark) as a noticeable marking; over 200 can sometimes be seen.

Quite high numbers of gulls use the estuary in winter, over 5,000 Black-headed Gull being most common; Herring Gull average 2,000, often with 500 Greater Black-backed. Some 100 Common Gull winter, looking rather like miniature Herring Gull but adults differing in their greenish bill and legs, and darker grey upperparts; by late winter, northbound migrants can increase their numbers greatly, and 1,000 have been counted. Lesser Black-backed Gull arrive at about the same time, and up to 500 may assemble for a week or two before moving on. Recent sightings around Padstow harbour have included Glaucous, Iceland and Ring-billed Gull.

The Camel is well known for terns, seen from the estuary mouth and flying up to the highest reaches to feed. High numbers are recorded in spring as well as autumn. As always Sandwich Tern are first to arrive and most numerous, with up to 50 in both seasons. In spring only two or three each of most other tern species are seen, although Common may reach ten or more. Arctic are also seen, and the rosy-breasted Roseate, whose long tail-streamers and graceful flight help make this uncommon bird the loveliest of sea terns. The Little Tern is diminutive, and a decreasing species in Britain. Black Tern are seen practically every spring, resplendent in summer plumage; their autumn and spring numbers are roughly similar, as with other tern species (although in autumn over 50 Common Tern may flock). Terns greatly favour sand-banks which become exposed and on which they settle, or where they dive for sand-eels among the shallows; as incoming tides submerge this habitat, they follow the rising tide up the estuary.

Whimbrel constitute by far the strongest spring wader migration, with sometimes over 100 passing in flocks overhead giving their distinctive multiple whistling calls, or resting for short periods; there is also a strong autumn passage. As autumn approaches, waders begin to gather. Among the first to arrive are Greenshank; very high numbers pass through in some years, in excess of 50 in loose flocks, one or two staying to winter. Common Sandpiper may also be seen, about 20 at a time, again two or three spending winter on sheltered stretches. Each autumn one or two Wood Sandpiper pass through. About ten Spotted Redshank join over 300 shorter-billed Redshank, and may stay on with them. Up to 15 Ruff are seen and a couple stay through winter, while two or three at a time may also pass in spring. Both godwit species use the estuary, perhaps no more than ten of the larger Black-tailed, but Bar-tailed can reach 80, as can Knot; godwit numbers usually decrease by half in winter. Only about four or five Curlew Sandpiper are usual, with about the same number of Little Stint; the latter species has a history of one or two birds passing winter here. When all the other waders which sometimes winter on this estuary are present together, there are more unusual wintering waders here than on any other estuary in southwest England. Rarer waders visiting on migration have included Collared Pratincole, Lesser Golden Plover and Semi-palmated Sandpiper.

In addition to common breeding raptors, two others regularly hunt through the non-breeding seasons, a third less regularly. Peregrine, often inexperienced juveniles, chase the estuary's waders, and spec-tacular displays of aerial skill are demonstrated as the hunted attempts to outmanoeuvre the hunter. They are seen from late summer, with two or three different birds during autumn and winter. The Merlin is much less regular but favours this area, appearing from late autumn, and one or two prey on small waders and passerines through winter. A single individual of the magnificent fish-catching Osprey may pass through some autumns, possibly staying several weeks. A few Hen Harrier and a couple of Goshawk have also appeared briefly.

One of the largest heronries in Cornwall is situated among the estuary's bankside trees; about a dozen nests are occupied each year. Little Egret may join their commoner relatives occasionally in spring or

Grey Heron

autumn. Kingfisher are resident and one or two pairs breed, along with two or three pairs of Mute Swan. A few Mallard also breed, but their numbers here are rather low. Perhaps six or more pairs of Shelduck breed, and in winter their numbers may rise to over 200.

Timing

Low tides are essential to see waders on the estuary mud, and for terns gathering on sandbanks or feeding in shallows near the river mouth. High, or rising, tides encourage terns to fly upriver. A rising tide, or one just ebbing, is best for watching waders from the CBWPS hide at Amble Dam outflow overlooking the estuary head and at Tregunna, also near Wadebridge. From midwinter, especially if there is a hard spell, geese and wild swans can occur on the marshes. Numbers of other species also rise, both there and on the estuary.

Access

A39 north out of Wadebridge leads to B3314 left, just after leaving the town. The B road crosses Trewornan Bridge across Amble marshes, and on to St Minver. At the bridge there is roadside parking. From here good views are obtained over the marshes (Walmsley Sanctuary) on the right; access there should be unnecessary and could seriously disturb the birds. On the left just before crossing the bridge is a gate leading into a field. Follow a footpath, keeping close to the hedgerow so as not to damage farm crops. Continue through another field to Burniere Point at Amble Dam, where the CBWPS hide is situated. While walking along the fields there is marshy ground on the right, and looking through gaps in the hedge might produce something of interest such as Green Sandpiper. Views from the hide are very good, covering the head of the mudflats where many ducks and waders assemble. Gaps in the hedge near the hide allow good views if keys to the hide are not obtained. In the summer of 1983 a new hide was erected at Tregunna. From A39 at Wadebridge take a minor road to Edmonton (to the right, on a sharp left-hand bend). Take right-hand turn to Tregunna, down narrow lanes, where there is limited parking near the farm. Follow a lane about ¼ mile (400 m) to estuary and hide. Alternatively follow the public path along a now disused railway track from Wadebridge; the track runs close to the hide. This track continues along the whole length of the estuary to Padstow, giving excellent views throughout.

To reach the lower estuary continue from the bridge to St Minver, and take a narrow but good road signposted to Rock. At Rock there is a car park. From the road good views of this part of the estuary are possible. When the tide is out the sandbanks are well seen. A main channel continues to flow and often contains all the same birds, such as divers and grebes, as when the area is flooded by the tide. At low tides you can walk to the mouth, where other waterbirds, especially terns or Sanderling, are seen. Access onto the dunes is from the car park. From Amble marshes to river mouth is about 4½ miles (7 km). For Padstow, take A389 for good views of terns, divers, grebes and gulls off the harbour, near the mouth, opposite Rock.

For keys to the bird hides, contact CBWPS (Hon. Treasurer, 33 Treworder Rd, Higher Redannick, Truro, TR1 2JZ).

Calendar

Resident: Cormorant and Shag present all year and breed nearby. Grey Heron, Mute Swan, Shelduck, Mallard, Oystercatcher, Kingfisher.

December–February: Great Northern and probably other divers, Slavonian, Little and probably other grebes, probably White-fronted Goose, Teal, Wigeon, Pintail, Tufted Duck, Eider, Common Scoter, possible Velvet Scoter and Long-tailed Duck, Goldeneye, possible Smew, Red-breasted Merganser, Peregrine, Merlin, Ringed Plover, Grey and Golden Plovers, Lapwing, possible Little Stint, Dunlin, Knot, Sanderling, probable Ruff and Spotted Redshank, Redshank, probable Greenshank, Green Sandpiper, godwits, Curlew, Snipe, possible Jack Snipe. Commoner species of gull, with Lesser Black-backed and Common Gull migrants arriving from February.

March–May: most above waders and waterfowl begin to leave by early March. End of March, first Sandwich Tern, Ruff pass through. Mid-April on, Whimbrel and other tern species, probable Roseate and Black Terns.

June–July: from mid-July, commoner waders start returning, also Green Sandpiper.

August–November: most wader species and numbers increase throughout early autumn. Late August–October, Little Stint, Curlew Sandpiper, probable Wood Sandpiper, Whimbrel. All terns reoccur in same period. Peregrine, maybe Osprey. From end September, probable Merlin. Waterfowl return from end of period.

38 TINTAGEL–BOSCASTLE, NORTH CORNWALL

OS ref: SX 0689
OS map: sheet 200

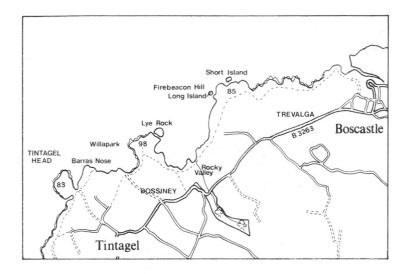

Habitat

This 5-mile (8-km) stretch of the north coast incorporates some of the most rugged and spectacular cliff scenery in the region. Off the 100-m high mainland cliffs and coves lie a number of rock pinnacles and islets, surrounded by Atlantic surf, a few dozen metres from the mainland. The coast is backed by high, open farmland, but much of the coastal strip is covered by heath, bracken and sea turf. Tintagel Head at the south end of the area projects farther out to sea than the series of promontories which stretch towards Boscastle, with deep water close offshore. Much of the coastline is owned by the National Trust and the views attract numerous visitors. Single Grey Seals often appear offshore.

Species

This is the best seabird breeding area on the mainland coast of the two counties. Winter is relatively quiet except for a few passing groups of Gannet, auks and Kittiwake. On fine days, however, parties of Guillemot may fly in to look over nest sites, while Fulmar are often back on nest ledges after only a few weeks' absence at sea in early winter. Spring proper brings a great deal of activity on the cliffs and islets as birds jostle for nesting space in favoured sectors. Scattered pairs of Shag and Cormorant are found all along the area, while Oystercatcher nest on inaccessible rocks. In recent years Fulmar colonies have expanded to occupy amost all available sites; scores of pairs now breed along this stretch of cliffs. Herring Gull are here in hundreds, with many nests on offshore islets. Great Black-backed Gull also breed, a scourge to other species as they search for exposed nests and young. The smaller Kittiwake does not breed here, but large flocks often feed offshore, or

245

move past with Manx Shearwater and Gannet flying down from Welsh colonies.

This area, in particular Long and Short Islands halfway to Boscastle, now holds the largest Cornish mainland colony of breeding auks. Parties of dozens sit on the sea offshore or whirr past swiftly to land on concealed ledges. In good light the browner backs of Guillemot and black backs of Razorbill can be distinguished. Puffin can also be seen without too much difficulty, sitting in rafts of up to 20 on the sea or standing near their nest burrows on offshore islands; their smaller, more dumpy outline and white cheek-patches usually stand out before the multi-coloured beak can be seen. All auks breeding here are difficult to census, but a watch along the entire area described might reveal up to 70 of the two commoner auks, although Puffin now reach only 10–15 pairs.

Puffins

A local oddity is a cliff-nesting colony of House Martin near Tintagel Head, a habit seen in few other parts of Britain.

Although much bird activity is down under the cliffs, with excellent views at times of seabirds passing below, it is worth looking in other directions. Peregrine can be watched frequently, often circling high over the clifftops to obtain a wide view of approaching prey along the coast. An Alpine Swift also passed over recently. Raven are a common sight, and the jingling song of Corn Bunting may be heard from posts and hedgerows.

By late summer auks have left, although gulls still have young in the nest.

Timing

The seabird colony can be seen at any time of day during the breeding season. The number of tourists using the area makes little impact. Strong onshore winds with high seas should be avoided if you want parties of off-duty auks sitting on the sea. Such conditions, with west or northwest winds, could, however, force in other seabirds moving down the coast. The clifftop viewpoints lack any cover and watching breeding seabirds is difficult in very wet weather.

One problem caused by the summer tourist influx is that parking can be difficult if you arrive after mid-morning, especially on warm weekends.

Access

A39 from Bude to Wadebridge runs past here well inland. Turn off west on one of several B-class roads to Tintagel and Boscastle; B3263 is the main coast road between the two villages, passing through the small settlements of Bossiney and Trevalga *en route*. There is a coastal footpath all along this stretch of cliffs and the full walk from Tintagel to Boscastle is worthwhile for those with time and energy. If unable to do this:

Tintagel itself is the most visited by tourists. Not the best point for auks, although Fulmar are numerous. The outer headland is a possible sea-watching point. Look at the sea caves just west of the head for House Martin breeding. *Bossiney* car park is a good central starting point. Walk down the valley footpath which starts at the road bend just east of the village. Near the bottom, turn left onto the steeply sloping coast path. Continue up left to overlook Lye Rock area, which gives good views and often Puffin on the sea (about ½ mile/0.8 km walk). Alternatively, walk right from the cove for 1 mile (1.6 km) to reach Long and Short Islands just offshore, with breeding Puffin and other auks.

Calendar

Resident: Shag, Oystercatcher, Great Black-backed Gull, Stonechat, Raven, Corn Bunting.

December–February: occasional passing seabird flocks. Fulmar begin arriving back at sites, Guillemot and Razorbill prospect ledges inter-mittently.

March–May: Fulmar, passing Manx Shearwater and Gannet, Cormorant, Kittiwake, Razorbill, Guillemot, Puffin, House Martin, all best seen late spring although auks may flock offshore in April.

June–July: main period of breeding activity, but auks depart to sea from mid-July. Manx Shearwater, Gannet and Kittiwake passing may be joined by other migrant seabirds towards end.

August–November: most breeding seabirds departed by late August. Chance of migrant shearwaters or skuas passing with commoner species at sea.

Habitat

The small tourist town of Bude faces west towards the Atlantic, in the centre of a long line of jagged cliffs and high coastal downs leading towards North Cornwall's border with Devon. Maer Downs are the open clifftop areas just north of the town. A small river drains down into the sandy Bude Haven bay; the river valley just east of the town centre has damp meadows and a small area of reed-bed which is a Local Nature Reserve. A disused canal runs inland adjacent to the reeds and continues for another 2 miles (3.2 km). Immediately north of the town, within a few metres from housing in the Flexbury district, is low-lying Maer Lake. This semi-permanent area of inundated meadow, with muddy freshwater pools and ditches, extends in the wet season into a shallow lagoon of several acres; in midsummer it almost dries out.

Five miles (8 km) north of Bude is Cleave Camp, an area of high coastal downland occupied by prominent satellite tracking radar dishes; coastal footpaths lead across the slopes of the down, which has extensive gorse thickets, and down into sheltered hollows leading towards Coombe Valley on the south side. A mile (1.6 km) south, back towards Bude, high farmland overlooks tiny Sandy Mouth inlet; the fields above are often left as stubble in autumn. Five miles (8 km) south of Bude, along a straight open stretch of coast fully exposed to wind and surf, lie Widemouth Bay sands; at the south end the rocky Millook Haven bay is a little sheltered.

Species

Although it has no species unique in the region, Bude district has a combination of habitats which can produce a good variety of birds for most of the year.

Winter brings more floodwater to Maer Lake, with the likelihood of some dozens of Teal and Wigeon; other ducks are relatively scarce in the area, except for tame Mallard hybrids along the canal banks. A Goosander or seaduck might arrive on the sheltered waters of the canal, while an Eider or two spends periods off the harbour mouth some winters. In the reed-bed a Cetti's Warbler occasionally bursts into song and Water Rail squeal; one or two Chiffchaff often winter here. In sustained cold a Bittern or a group of agile Bearded Tit may arrive in the reeds. Snipe can occur in dozens at the reed-bed, but are more abundant at Maer Lake, where over 500 have been recorded on occasions. Curlew can often be seen feeding on lakeside fields, which are also visited intermittently by flocks of Golden Plover. The windswept beach can only boast a few Oystercatcher and Purple Sandpiper.

Gulls are present, although not in very large numbers; gales offshore may drive up to 5,000 to fly in to roost at Maer Lake, where a scarcer species such as Mediterranean or Iceland might be picked out by thorough searching among Black-headed and Herring. Black-headed are usually the majority; a few Lesser Black-backed and Common are also expected. Some gulls also bathe in the river mouth, particularly larger species, which have included Glaucous. Other seabirds offshore

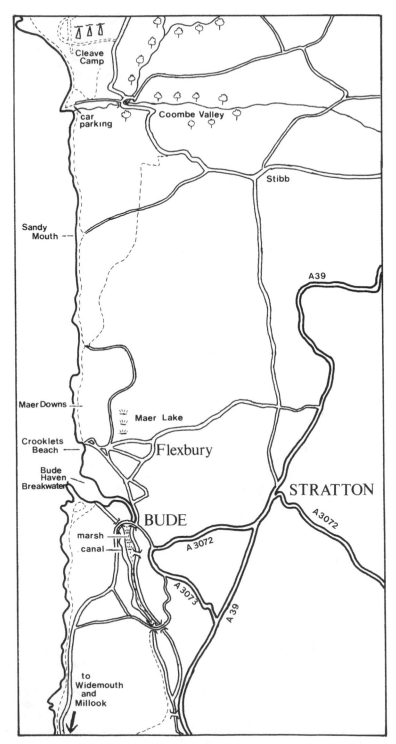

may include passages of Gannet and Fulmar down the coast in gales; Kittiwake are relatively scarce in winter except for storm-blown or oiled individuals which may fly in to Maer Lake to shelter. Divers, however, may be seen offshore most days; as at Hartland to the north, most are identified as Red-throated. Up to 30 are seen at times in the southern half of Widemouth Bay and Millook Haven; they seem to fly north along the coast past Bude, presumably to join the large concentrations reported off Hartland Point tide race, then fly back south after feeding.

Passerines on land in winter are variable in interest; some winters when stubble fields on high coastal downs are left unploughed, large flocks of Skylark gather, perhaps accompanied by a few Snow or Lapland Bunting, often picked out by call notes when a flock flies up. The rattling 'tick-tick-tue' calls of Lapland are distinctive once heard, but sightings need careful distinction from Reed Bunting which may also fly to stubble to feed in winter. Fields above Sandy Mouth are a possible location for these flocks, which may attract a wide-foraging Merlin, also hunting occasionally at Maer Lake. A Black Redstart may stay in seafront gardens in Bude, where Stonechat come down from the clifftops to shelter, and Grey Wagtail feed with many Rock Pipit. The pale-fronted continental Water Pipit can sometimes be detected around the edges of Maer Lake and one or two probably stay through most winters.

Spring can bring some large flocks of dozens of Whimbrel moving north along the coast, or occasionally resting by Maer Lake along with godwits and other common waders. Occasionally a flock of Arctic Tern is blown into the bay; Black and Little Terns have also been recorded several times in recent springs, although Sandwich is the most regular. Auks pass offshore on feeding movements from colonies, and very soon the mass southward movements of Manx Shearwater commence; as at Hartland, these are chiefly an early morning phenomenon, with thousands passing in a few hours. Views off Bude itself are not very close and a telescope may be needed; headlands to the north of Bude may give better results, although perhaps less than Hartland.

Passerine migration is not particularly known in this area, but high headlands such as Cleave Camp may have resting parties of north-bound migrants, such as Wheatear, with commoner warblers in the surrounding gorse and scrub. The nearby valleys such as Coombe may be productive; few birdwatchers visit them. Birds of prey, including the occasional harrier, may circle over, and Raven breen on nearby cliffs. At the reed-bed Sedge and Reed Warblers arrive in good numbers, this being one of very few north Cornish breeding sites for Reed; singing birds may extend inland along overgrown canal fringes. Recently a Squacco Heron was seen in a flooded water meadow nearby and Little Egret have occurred. A Garganey may drop in on Maer Lake marsh. Other spring migrants seen in the general district in recent years have included a vagrant Alpine Swift and a Sardinian Warbler.

Summer is not a particularly good time of year for birdwatching here, with large numbers of tourists using the coastline. Offshore, however, feeding movements of Manx Shearwater and other commoner seabirds continue on a daily basis. In late summer–early autumn the movements start to contain more variety, with the odd skua, or a Balearic or Sooty Shearwater. When autumn gales start, seabird species passing may reflect those recorded off Newquay and St Ives, although numbers this far back up the coast are much smaller, with less chance of a major rarity. Wader migration at Maer Lake can be interesting by now, with a

Wheatear

chance of less common species; European migrants such as stints and sandpipers are recorded, and the stint-like Semi-palmated Sandpiper from America was detected once recently. The small reed-bed, as all habitats of this type, attracts hundreds of Swallow and Starling roosting from early autumn.

From mid-autumn the downs and sheltered valleys around Cleave Camp are watched for passerine migrants; this area has had a good share of passing species (maybe attracted at night by the bright illumination around the radar station?). Scarcer continental migrants such as Icterine Warbler, Wryneck and Red-backed Shrike have been recorded in nearby thickets. Later in the season, large-scale finch and pipit movements take place each morning, birds coasting southwards low along the edge of the downs; this is a good time to check for oddities, Richard's Pipit having been reported, while Snow and Lapland Buntings pass through quite regularly. Coombe Valley and areas near the camp are still worth checking with a chance of scarcer warblers such as Yellow-browed, and outstandingly, once a Dusky Thrush.

Timing

Activity at Maer Lake is largely governed by water levels; in summer it may be too dry to support birds, while winter floods attract ducks and force waders out onto the edges to feed. Onshore gales bring in sheltering gull flocks. Westerly gales in autumn might bring an American vagrant wader. The tiny reed-bed nature reserve is likely to be most productive in early morning, or at dusk when roosting species are gathering. The regular feeding movements of shearwaters and other seabirds offshore are chiefly in the first three hours or so of daylight. Autumn gale sea-watching requires sustained rough weather, to force oceanic birds this far up towards the mouth of the Bristol Channel before they pass back southwards. The second day of a gale may be more productive than the first. Winds required are much as at St Ives, with depressional south-westerlies and rain followed by clearing weather from the west and northwest.

251

Passerine migration at Cleave Camp is much as at other coastal migration points, with winds from the east bringing scarcer night migrants, while the 'coasting' movements on late autumn mornings are chiefly into light–moderate west or southwest winds.

Access

Bude is reached by turning west off the main A39 North Cornwall–North Devon coast road at Stratton; it is well signposted. On entering the town, turn left at a mini-roundabout to the large car park by the Tourist Information Office to view the adjacent canal and reed-bed; a 'trim track' (for joggers) runs around the marsh. A hide, suffering vandalism, overlooks the reeds from the canal bank. This is a flat area which would suit those unable to walk far. It is possible to continue inland along the canal bank to view the water meadows at the rear.

For the seafront and breakwater, walk to the right from the car park along the canal towpath, crossing over at a lock gate and walking down the west side; at the end, a footpath leads up to the left overlooking the shore and river mouth. At the breakwater, walk left until you come to a series of brick shelters inset into the rock face, a convenient sheltered seawatch point in bad weather (a telescope may be needed).

Maer Lake (also known as Maer Marsh) can be reached by continuing from the roundabout first reached, on through the town centre and left at the top, across the golf course; the road reaches Crooklets Beach car park. Stop here and park. Turn inland on foot for 100 yards (100 m); a sign points up a lane northward towards Bude holiday park. From this lane after 100 yards (100 m) Maer Lake is obvious on the right (whether it is actually a lake or just a muddy expanse depends on season and rainfall). There is nowhere to park along the lane; watch on foot from the verges. There is no access to the marsh, the perimeters being private farmland; closer approach would anyway only frighten off the birds using the area.

Cleave Camp is not actually marked as such on current O.S. maps; it is the area between Morwenstow village and the Coombe Valley. The radar dishes are marked on maps. Drive north on A39 from Stratton for about 4 miles (6.4 km) then turn west down a minor road to Coombe. Park at car park at the end of this road; check streamside vegetation for warblers and walk north along coastal footpaths, exploring thickets. The public footpath leading into a sheltered hollow on the south side of the radar station boundary (aim towards the middle radar and adjacent buildings) is also worth checking for migrants. Sandy Mouth can be reached by turning off left halfway along the minor road to Coombe; it is also signposted from other junctions along the main road. Park at sea edge car park and walk back up to the hill crest; public paths run across fields to the north and south. Look for stubble fields to find lark flocks with attendant species.

From Bude car park, turn left to reach Widemouth Bay by a minor coastal road with viewing points; at the south end towards Millook, about 5 miles (8 km) from Bude, the road becomes narrow and winding with steep inclines. A high car park overlooks the rocky Millook cove.

Calendar

Resident: Shag, common raptors, Raven, Rock Pipit, Stonechat, Cetti's Warbler, Reed Bunting.

December–February: divers (mostly Red-throated), Fulmar, Gannet passing, Teal, Wigeon, occasional Eider, maybe Merlin, Water Rail, Oystercatcher, Curlew, Snipe, Golden Plover, gull flocks including scarcer species, Black Redstart, Grey Wagtail, Water Pipit, Skylark, possible Snow or Lapland Bunting.

March–May: gulls passing from start with further chance of scarcer types; Wheatear on downs late March on, chance of Garganey on marsh. Warbler migration from April with Sedge and Reed from mid-month arriving to breed. Possible raptor over downs April–May, when Manx Shearwater and other seabirds pass. Terns and waders move north from mid-April. Whimbrel, Godwit and sandpipers may drop in at Maer Lake.

June–July: least interest; seabirds, mostly common species, pass off-shore, occasional Balearic or Sooty Shearwater late July.

August–November: possible unusual waders with common species at Maer Lake (mostly August–September), variety of seabirds passing including a few less common species (mostly August–October), reed-bed roost, warblers and other passerines on downs (September–October), pipits, finches and buntings moving south October–November with occasional oddities.

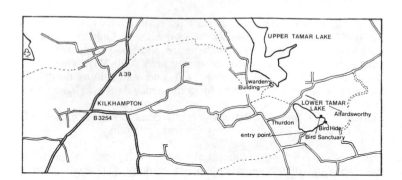

Habitat

Straddling the North Cornwall/Devon border, these two neighbouring man-made reservoirs with natural banks lie among high rolling farmland in a sparsely populated district. The 40-acre (16-ha) Lower Lake, tree-fringed with shallow marshy areas and rushes at the top end, is now used for recreation only, since completion of the 81-acre (33-ha) replacement Upper Lake, with more open banks. Both lakes, stocked with trout, are used extensively for fishing, and sailing is regular on the Upper Lake. Wildlife includes occasional otters glimpsed on the banks on quiet mornings.

Species

These two reservoirs have suffered neglect from birdwatchers, partly because of lack of resident watchers nearby. Scarcer migrants, particularly waders and ducks, have been reported in the past, and the lakes, although comparatively small, attract a good variety of ducks, waders and waterside species, there having been no comparable habitat in this corner of the region; it remains to be seen whether the large new Roadford reservoir nearby will lure birds away from here.

An attraction at the beginning and end of the year is the fairly regular occurrence of small parties of wild swans and grey geese, both quite scarce and irregular visitors to most of the region. Hardly a winter passes without a visit by a small tightly-knit group, probably a family, of Bewick's Swan, relatively slight in build beside resident Mute. Sometimes longer-billed Whooper Swan, more on a size par with Mute, are also reported. The swans can be seen on either lake, but the grassy banks of the Upper Lake may be more attractive for a grazing party of half a dozen White-fronted Geese. None of these larger wildfowl stays through winter, although Bewick's Swan have been seen for two- or three-week spells. A smaller winter visitor, found in twos and threes regularly, is the grey-brown Little Grebe. Great Crested, the only other grebe at all likely, was formerly a passage migrant, odd singles turning up in spring or autumn; there has, however, been a recent breeding pair or two, noteworthy in a species which breeds at less than half a dozen sites in our region. Four or five Cormorant usually fish on the lakes.

Dabbling ducks, although not found in huge numbers, are attracted by the relatively shallow muddy banks, enabling a range of species to find suitable feeding. They often include over 100 Mallard, and varying numbers of up to 200 or more Teal often concealed among marshy vegetation. With careful observation, both Green-winged and Blue-winged Teal from the Americas have been found among their commoner cousins. Flocks of 100–200 Wigeon might be seen at peak periods grazing on grassy banks, the male's yellow crown-stripe conspicuous, while one or two Pintail may join them irregularly. Shoveler are regular, this being one of their most established winter haunts in the region, although numbers are not large; up to 30 have been seen, but often counts are in single figures, chestnut-and-white-sided drakes usually in the majority. Another local speciality is Gadwall, the females often overlooked as slim Mallard but for their white speculum-patch on the wing; up to 15 have often been seen on Lower Lake, and this rather unevenly distributed species is rarely absent in winter. Diving ducks are not present in exceptional numbers, but winter counts of 40–60 Pochard and about half that number of Tufted are normal, with often half a dozen brownhead Goldeneye feeding in deep stretches. The larger American Ring-necked Duck has been seen among the Tufted. A Goosander may call in, and 'coastal' species such as single Scaup or the dark-winged Long-tailed Duck have spent long periods here through winter, especially on Upper Lake, perhaps staying into spring.

Waders tend not to winter in numbers on reservoirs, where water levels are too high for edge feeding, but Green and Common Sandpipers have been flushed from quiet bays, where several dozen Snipe and occasionally a Jack Snipe can be found. Flocks of several hundred Lapwing, often accompanied by 100 or more Golden Plover, gather on nearby farmland. These, and reservoir ducks, may attract a passing Peregrine to try its luck, but hundreds of Fieldfare and Redwing feeding in the vicinity may be more to the taste of Merlin, seen dashing overhead at irregular intervals most winters; these raptors may be the same as those seen at other sites in north Cornwall and northwest Devon. One or two ringtail Hen Harrier also seem to wander large expanses of north-west Devon in winter, and may beat low over the reservoir banks for a day, although they are by no means predictable. Another smaller but no less fierce predator, the Great Grey Shrike, has been seen several times among bushes in open land near the reservoir banks. Gull flocks often bathe and preen, but the totals of 400 or so Black-headed and Herring Gulls are unexceptional, and, apart from 20–30 Common Gull, occurrences of this family are not usually noteworthy.

Warmer weather brings activity among residents. Two or three hissing cob (male) Mute Swan defend territory vigorously, while a pair or two of Coot and Moorhen nest. A pair of Kingfisher usually breeds in the area and singles may be disturbed from waterside trees, darting off low and straight across the lake. Usually nasal 'buzzing' calls of nesting Willow Tit can be heard in trees by the Lower Lake. Up above, Rooks are busy nesting, and several pairs of Grey Heron build bulky treetop nests nearby. Spring migrants, although less varied than autumn, can be numerous, with hundreds of hirundines and Swift massing to feed low over the water on their way north. In most springs, probably late on, they are joined briefly by a breeding-dress Black Tern or two, scarce in our region at this season, which benefits similarly from hordes of midges just over the lake surface. At the same time, a few pairs of Reed and

STEVE BIRD 90

Willow Tit

Sedge Warblers join smart, black-headed Reed Bunting singing in the fringe vegetation of the Lower Lake. Wader migrants usually include Ruff, Green and Common Sandpipers (once a Spotted Sandpiper), and one or two noisy Greenshank. Ringed Plover are regular inland passage migrants in single figures on both migrations, and the flat 'peeo' calls of a slim-winged Little Ringed Plover have been heard. Curlew, which breed nearby, are also likely to be seen.

In autumn, when water levels have dropped, waders are present for longer periods. The marshy end of Lower Tamar Lake is favoured. Four or five Green Sandpiper are expected, joined by varying numbers of Wood Sandpiper with pale-spangled upperparts, from singles to (more exceptionally) half a dozen birds or more according to early autumn migration conditions. Similar numbers of Little Stint peck at titbits on open mud, and may stay for several weeks with groups of Dunlin, which reach 30 birds at times. Usually one or two Greenshank, Ruff and long-legged Spotted Redshank feed for periods off-passage at this season, along with probably the first few Teal in the shallows. Black Tern are, as in spring, a regular feature, seen through early and mid-autumn, with one or two pale winter-plumaged and juvenile birds present almost continuously, although more than four or five is rare. A White-winged Black Tern has been reported: other migrants noted have included Spotted Crake, venturing out from waterside vegetation. American visitors have included single Pectoral Sandpiper, and Long-billed Dowitcher, looking somewhat like very large greyish Snipe.

Timing
This type of habitat repays regular visiting rather than one-off visits, as birds filter through over a period. Black Tern and large hirundine flocks are most likely on humid, cloudy days, possibly with drizzle, especially in winds from southerly or easterly quarters. Dry autumn periods with falling water levels leaving mud margins are best for feeding waders. American species are, as usual, most likely after strong west winds. Disturbance from fishing and sailing is normally less on weekdays or early mornings. Wild swans or geese are seen mostly in cold weather, but geese may soon depart because of disturbance.

Access

Although the A39 Bude–Bideford road lies only 4 miles (6½ km) to the west, the reservoirs might easily be missed; the erection of brown tourist singposts to them may help. From the Bideford direction, turn left (east) off the A39 at Kilkhampton on B3254 towards Launceston, turning left after ½ mile (0.8 km) on minor roads towards Bradworthy and Holsworthy. For the Upper Lake, turn first left after 1 mile (1.6 km), then take a left turn signposted to the reservoir car park. For the Lower Lake, continue towards Holsworthy, turning second left after leaving the B road, then pulling into the lower car park. A footpath connects the two. The marshy end of the Lower Lake, overlooked by a bird hide, is maintained as a bird sanctuary from August to April; permits for the hide are available from the SWW warden's office by the Upper Lake dam. At other times there is open access to the lake banks and the other parts of the lake can be viewed at any time. Visitors to the Upper Lake banks also require a SWW permit. A bird logbook is kept at the warden's building and information centre.

Calendar

Resident: Grey Heron, Sparrowhawk, Buzzard, Coot, Barn Owl, King-fisher, Willow Tit, Reed Bunting.

December–February: Little Grebe, Cormorant, probably wild swans or geese, Teal, Wigeon, Gadwall, Shoveler, Tufted Duck, Pochard, Goldeneye, maybe Scaup or Long-tailed Duck, occasional Goosander, irregular Hen Harrier, Peregrine and Merlin, possible Green or Common Sandpiper, Snipe, maybe Jack Snipe, commoner gulls, possible Great Grey Shrike, winter thrushes.

March–May: a few ducks, especially diving ducks, e.g. Tufted or a Long-tailed, stay through April. Migrants including Sand Martin from mid-March, most species from mid-April including commoner warblers, Reed and Sedge, hirundine flocks, waders e.g. Ringed Plover, Ruff, Green and Common Sandpipers, Greenshank; probably Black Tern late April–May.

June–July: breeding species, including probably Great Crested Grebe and Curlew, a few Sedge Warblers. Migrant waders, including Ringed Plover, Dunlin, Ruff, Green Sandpiper, from late July.

August–November: protracted wader migration peaking end August–September, with Ringed Plover, Ruff, Spotted Redshank, Greenshank, Dunlin, Little Stint, Common, Green and Wood Sandpipers, maybe scarcer species; most left by late October. Probably Black Tern August–early October; winter visitors arrive back during November, except some Teal from early autumn.

40A ADDITIONAL SITE:
ROADFORD RESERVOIR

OS ref: SX 4290
OS map: sheet 190

Habitat

In mid-west rural Devon, in a sparsely populated farmland environment underlain by the Culm Measures, the dam which will impound the region's largest reservoir has recently been completed (1989–90), and the River Wolf valley is starting to flood. Eventually the lake, in a 'Y' shape, will extend to cover 738 acres (299 ha). It will be the only 'mud-bottomed' major Devon reservoir, the county's existing larger waters being generally on acidic moorland areas poor in natural food supply.

Amenity development at the site will include facilities for angling and sailing; the upper arms of the 'Y' away from the dam will be kept as nature reserves.

Species

It is too early to say what will be attracted, but there is expectation of large duck flocks; already commoner dabbling ducks such as Mallard, Wigeon and Teal have been seen in dozens, and both Tufted Duck and Pochard have arrived in good numbers, the latter exceeding 100 at times. Smaller numbers of other ducks including Pintail and Goldeneye have started to use the area. A Ring-necked Duck was the reservoir's first transatlantic vagrant, soon followed by a Green-winged Teal within the first winter when less than half full. Flocks of prey-species may attract passing raptors; a Peregrine has been sighted already.

The shallower 'arms' of the reservoir will be likely to attract passage waders, especially when late summer and autumn bring muddy margins; with a large lowland reservoir at last, Devon's list of rarer waders may improve considerably, bringing American species already seen annually at Cornish waters.

This previously out-of-the-way part of Devon's countryside has always held one or two breeding specialities; Barn Owl, for instance, still find a home in a few derelict buildings. It must be hoped that increased development and use of the area associated with public access and amenities will not drive them out. A characteristic small bird of the Culm Measures damp farmland is the Willow Tit, which is likely to be present in thickets and copses around the reservoir banks.

Timing

Dry conditions leaving mud areas freshly exposed are always an attraction at reservoirs; this reservoir is still filling, however, so such conditions cannot be predicted yet. Sailing and angling activities on the main body of the lake could clearly cause some disturbance to wildfowl, particularly at weekends. This may cause them to retreat into side bays, where they may be difficult to view without a long walk, or towards the north end.

Access

Approach from A30 between Okehampton and Launceston, turning north at Portgate on a minor road towards Broadwoodwidger village; do not turn left towards the village but drive on. The lake is signposted on the right as you approach, about five miles (8 km) from the main road. You arrive at the dam first, with parking on the right. A network of paths is to be constructed around the lake, giving good viewing; the area can also be viewed from the large car park near the dam, or from various minor roads around the perimeter, especially to the east and northeast where smaller car parks are being constructed overlooking bays and inlets. On the northeast side at Southweek Viaduct, on the Germansweek road, a narrow marshy arm of the lake will eventually extend under the road, creating a good watching area. Turn left out of the dam car park and follow a network of lanes towards Germansweek. The lake is in view intermittently on the left, with stopping places; after about 3 miles (4.8 km) you reach the viaduct. From the lay-by on the left, a footpath leads around the entire eastern lakeshore; there is no restriction on access. Shortly after the viaduct, a lane on the left marked as a 'no through road' can be driven down to a car park overlooking the northwest arm of the lake. A path leads across to the right; an island in the middle may prove attractive to resting ducks or waders, perhaps even breeding species eventually.

With such a large expanse of water, birds may be a long way from a convenient access point, making a telescope essential. The various car parks and roads circling the lake enable some coverage by those confined to a vehicle.

41 HARTLAND POINT AND DISTRICT

OS ref: SS 2327
OS map: sheet 190

Habitat

On the corner where the North Devon coastline turns sharply southward towards Cornwall, the high jagged cliffs of Hartland face across deep water towards Lundy Island 12 miles (19 km) away. On a ledge below the cliffs stands a lighthouse, overlooking a strong tiderace offshore. Grey Seals might be seen and dolphins or porpoises may leap in the tiderace. The surrounding gorse-clad coastline, backed by high farmland, includes many small coves and rocky promontories. A sheltered, bushy stream valley lies just west of the Point. Eastward towards the tourist village of Clovelly 6 miles (9½ km) away, the cliffs are heavily wooded. Inland, 4 miles (6½ km) south of Hartland village, lie the dense conifer plantations of Hartland Forest, and nearby open heaths such as Bursdon Moor. Other forestry plantations lie further inland. Farmland in parts of northwest Devon, part of the poorly drained Culm Measures, is a patchwork of fields and damp rushy hollows, areas overgrown with willow scrub, and uncultivated heathy areas a few hundred metres in size.

Species

The Point is well placed for seeing birds moving across from Wales and the Bristol Channel coastline. The powerful lighthouse also acts as a focus for nocturnal migrants. Early in the year the area is very windswept, and the most obvious birds are parties of Raven foraging along clifftops. Flocks of up to 300–400 divers at times gathering on the sea have, however, created surprise and some identification discussion among the region's birdwatchers. Most of the birds, which are present in variable numbers through the winter period, are slim and grey-backed, now accepted as Red-throated; it is possible, however, that flocks of other species pass through, and clearly more watching and research is needed to gain the full picture. The peak numbers quoted above are only reported once or twice a year; peaks of 70–100 are, however, quite regular. These are by far the largest concentrations of divers in the region, dwarfing most other regular wintering groups; birds appear to commute in to feed from various parts of the north Cornwall and north Devon coastline. Divers feeding in the tiderace may fly in at the top end of the race, let themselves be drifted through as they dive repeatedly for fish, then fly back across to the start when they have drifted too far past. This intense activity, presumably because of an outstanding food supply in a small area, can make watching individual birds difficult. A telescope is often needed as birds may be scattered well out to sea. A few auks also feed in the area, while Fulmar are rarely absent and Gannet pass offshore.

The rough farmland and heaths inland are hunted over by raptors in winter, although the numbers of individual birds involved are small and they may cover a large area. Hen Harrier and Merlin are the main winter visitor species, although Peregrine are also seen intermittently; the main ways to see raptors are at food prey concentrations or as the hunters

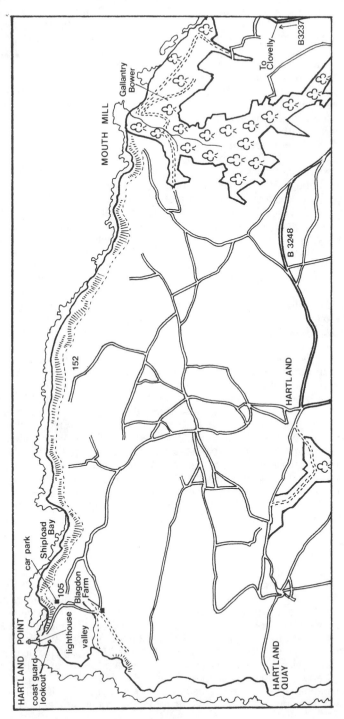

themselves go to roost. Starlings mass in winter roosts of hundreds of thousands, a spectacular sight as they gather; roosts may change every few years, but recent large gatherings have been at Hardsworthy Plantation, a forestry area about 10 miles (16 km) southeast of Hartland village, which may attract raptors including resident Sparrowhawk. Hen Harrier and Merlin which have hunted the inland districts, or even as far south as Tamar Lakes, have been seen returning to roost at Bursdon Moor; singles of both species are often seen, but up to three of either occurs at times. A Barn Owl may still be seen patrolling silently over the heaths, sometimes joined by a Short-eared. A Goshawk once wintered nearby.

Small passerine migrants arrive early in spring at Hartland Point if the weather is fine with high barometric pressure, first dates being even earlier in some cases than on the south coast. Possibly the birds have flown through Devon without stopping, coming to rest on the north coast before making another sea crossing towards Wales. Wheatear are often the first arrivals, and passerine migrants later in the season include all the commoner warblers. Among these may be a dozen or more Grasshopper Warbler, the males detected by their high 'reeling' song, some staying to breed in coastal scrub. Most other transient species, including a few Lesser Whitethroat (scarce this far west), occur in thick bushes along the stream valley on the west side, where they can be hard to watch. Sedge Warbler stay to nest in the damp undergrowth. Groups of diurnal migrants such as Swallow may often be seen circling up over the Point in early mornings before departing northwards, probably via Lundy; several Marsh Harrier have circled northward and an Alpine Swift passed over recently.

On early mornings in summer, Manx Shearwater pass westward in long strings, flashing black and white as they bank low over the waves. Numbers often run into thousands (15,000 have been counted in a morning), believed to be breeding adults from Skokholm and Skomer Islands in Pembrokeshire, *en route* from the colony on a daily journey to feeding grounds. Some returning birds are confused by the lighthouse beam on dull nights and become injured in collision with buildings. Single Storm Petrel have been recorded fluttering in the lighthouse beams, but have never been seen in daylight. Other seabirds flying past on summer days include feeding parties of Gannet, Kittiwake and auks. Bunches of non-breeding Common Scoter are frequently seen passing. Fulmar are abundant breeders, heckling each other noisily on cliff ledges, together with Herring Gull. Great Black-backed Gull nest in small numbers on isolated rocks. Several pairs of Oystercatcher raise young in quiet coves, while coastal passerines include Stonechat and Whitethroat in thickets.

For those wishing to see woodland species, there are breeding season records on a variety of birds in Hobby Drive woods above Clovelly. Singing Pied Flycatcher have started to occur in recent seasons and several Wood Warbler are likely to be heard, while Grey Wagtail flit along the damp woodland tracks. Breeding birds of the inland area are not well known, but Curlew and Grasshopper Warbler are found on open heathland. One or two pairs of Turtle Dove, and some years churring Nightjar, have been reported in the main forestry area. The dull sooty-capped Willow Tit is a thinly scattered local resident.

In autumn, westward movement of seabirds off the Point is still poorly known, but appears to be sporadic, chiefly in rough weather; there is

Firecrest

still scope for more regular observation, and few birdwatchers live close
enough to the Point to study it. There are annual records of Arctic and
Great Skuas, usually no more than half a dozen of either in a day, with
most years a scarcer species such as a Sooty Shearwater, or a Sabine's
Gull beating past in a gale. Morning coasting movement of landbirds
may be interesting, with flocks of thousands of Chaffinch and Meadow
Pipit in later autumn, perhaps pursued by a Merlin or Peregrine.
Brambling, Siskin and Redpoll may also be passing over in good
numbers; a scarcer migrant such as Lapland Bunting might be found
among them. As warbler movement slackens after mid-autumn, a few
Firecrest arrive, often two or three giving hoarse 'zip' calls from sheltered
bushes. Large movements involving thousands of Fieldfare, Blackbird
and other thrushes have been seen, with the chance of scarcer warbler
species during these falls. Red-breasted Flycatcher and Yellow-browed
Warbler have been seen, but so far not the major rarities recorded
on nearby Lundy; again, there is scope for future discovery. A Black
Redstart is often present around rocks and buildings at the start of
winter, while flocks of a dozen or more Purple Sandpiper pick over the
tideline rocks. A flock of up to 200 Common Scoter is often present off
Clovelly at the end of the year, and perhaps through to spring.

Timing

To see wintering diver flocks, calm seas are helpful; greater numbers
also seem to occur then. Birds may move up the coast to gather off the
Point at high tides. Terns and Arctic Skua have been seen on early
autumn anticyclonic easterlies with haze. The most likely conditions for
numbers of other seabirds would be a strong westerly or northwesterly
gale, after a period of southwest winds has driven birds up towards the
Bristol Channel (compare with St Ives in Cornwall). Summer feeding
movements of Manx Shearwater take place early after daybreak each
morning, but farther out in calm weather. The largest arrivals of thrushes
and warblers take place in typical autumn conditions, overcast with east

winds, but clear mornings (first three or four hours of daylight) with an opposing breeze are best for diurnal passage, especially finches.

On the heaths and plantations fine weather is needed to see raptors; they may be encountered hunting at any time of day but in the last hour's light they will be seen approaching their roosting areas. Fine summer evenings are necessary for crepuscular species such as Nightjar and Grasshopper Warbler singing, and in late summer with hungry broods to feed, Barn Owls might be active before nightfall.

Access

From A39 between Bideford and Bude. For the Point and lighthouse, take signs towards Hartland, bypass the village and follow separate signs down lanes to the Point. The road bends down past a farm entrance and terminates in a clifftop car park. From the car park a lane leads down to the lighthouse compound. Access to the compound is not normally permitted outside daytime visiting hours, but you can seawatch from the lane near the lighthouse entrance. A coastal footpath runs across the clifftops westward above the lighthouse, and eastward past the radar station into the next bay. Westward the path runs across the mouth of the sheltered stream valley, worth a look for migrants. Alternatively, walk down the track into the valley past the farm buildings, on the corner of the road.

For Clovelly woods, take the signposted turn off A39 4 miles (6½ km) east of the Hartland road. Drive to the main tourist car parks. Walk right along wooded Hobby Drive, which can be followed for 2 miles (3.2 km) until it rejoins the main road. For the plantations and Bursdon Moor, continue west towards Bude on A39 past the Hartland turn. From the Forest Office on the left (east) side of the main road as you reach the plantation, signposted woodland walks can be taken. Over the next 2–3 miles (3–5 km) southward, heaths can be seen right of the main road; Bursdon, one of the largest, is opposite the south end of the plantation. Pull over by the entry to the wood and scan across the road for raptors; **do not** cause disturbance by walking on the heath. The woodland walks leading from the adjoining plantation edge may produce Nightjars in summer. At the south end of Bursdon Moor, a small poorly-signed turning on the right takes you northwest towards Tosberry Moor, giving another chance to scan for raptors. Hardsworthy Plantation, for Starling roosting and attendant predators, can be reached by turning off on a minor road eastward 2 miles (3 km) further south down A39, then following signs towards Bradworthy; after another 2 miles (3 km), turn left towards Northmoor; you pass the plantation on the left.

Calendar

Resident: Shag, common resident raptors, Oystercatcher, Great Black-backed and Herring Gulls, Barn Owl, Raven, Willow Tit, Stonechat, Rock Pipit, Grey Wagtail.

December–February: diver flocks mainly Red-throated, peaking late January–February, common seabirds e.g. Fulmar, Gannet, auk; raptors, particularly Hen Harrier and Merlin over heaths; Common Scoter (Clovelly), Purple Sandpiper, Starling flocks, winter thrushes, maybe Black Redstart.

March–May: Fulmar, Manx Shearwater (from end March), Wheatear and

Chiffchaff from mid-March, other warblers including Lesser Whitethroat, Sedge and Grasshopper mostly from late April, common summer visitors from April. Potential for further migrant watching. Curlew arriving on breeding heaths and wet farmland; possible Turtle Dove and Nightjar (late May on); singing woodland passerines at Clovelly.

June–July: offshore Manx Shearwater, possibly Storm Petrel, Fulmar, Gannet, Kittiwake, auks, Common Scoter. Breeding species including Whitethroat, Sedge and Grasshopper Warblers; warblers, flycatchers, common woodland passerines at Clovelly. Curlew breeding inland, still maybe Turtle Dove or Nightjar.

August–November: Fulmar, Arctic and Great Skuas, occasional scarce seabirds (September–October mainly), warblers, chats and flycatchers peaking end August–September, Firecrest (mainly October), Black Redstart (late October–November), winter thrushes (late October–November), finches, pipits, raptors mainly October–November; not intensively studied, but considerable potential for rarer migrants turning up throughout.

Habitat

Twelve miles (19 km) north of Hartland Point, between the northwest corner of Devon and the Welsh coast, lies the rugged granite mass of Lundy. The island, about 3½ miles (5½ km) long from north to south and ½ mile (0.8 km) wide, has a near-level plateau top about 100 m above sea level. Much of the top is boggy and stony moorland, except in the slightly wider southern quarter where there are a few fields, mostly rough pasture. Stone walls cross the island to mark quarter, half and

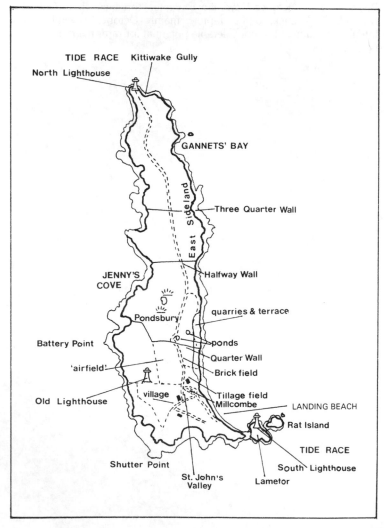

TIDE RACE   Kittiwake Gully

North Lighthouse

GANNETS' BAY

East Sideland

Three Quarter Wall

JENNY'S
COVE

Halfway Wall

Pondsbury

quarries & terrace

Battery Point

ponds

Quarter Wall

'airfield'

Brick field

Old Lighthouse

village

Tillage field
Millcombe

LANDING BEACH

Rat Island

TIDE RACE

South Lighthouse

Shutter Point

St. John's
Valley

Lametor

threequarter points northward from the south end. Permanent standing water is found at Pondsbury depression, almost halfway up, and at tiny pools near Quarter Wall and scattered across the southern quarter.

The north and west of the island are flanked by deep gullies, spectacular cliffs and rock buttresses, but the east side is a little more sheltered, with steep slopes clothed in places by rhododendron thickets and bracken. At the south end is the partly detached block of Lametor, with a lighthouse. There is also a working lighthouse at the north end, but the old light-tower, a prominent landmark across the top of the island, is no longer used; its accomodation was used for a bird observatory from 1947 to 1973, and is now visitor accomodation. Nearby, at the southeast corner of the plateau, stands the small collection of inhabited houses, farm buildings and Marisco Tavern. Between village and sea is the steep, sheltered Millcombe valley with walled gardens, a little mixed woodland (chiefly Turkey oak, sycamore and Monterey pine) and thickets; at the foot is the stony Landing Beach. Off the beach the 'Roads' form a calmer, sheltered expanse of sea in prevailing and often strong west winds. Strong tideraces occur off both ends of the island.

Apart from the limited expanse of farmland in the south of Lundy, largely surrounded by stone walls, much of the island is too exposed and barren to support stock. A few sheep, bullocks and ponies graze the turf. Flocks of feral Soay Sheep from Scotland, primitive goat-like brown creatures, spend a hardy existence feeding on steep slopes and crags. Offshore, Grey Seals are a frequent sight, and their moaning breeding calls can be heard from sea caves at several points in the northern half of the coastline. Botanical interest includes the unique Lundy Cabbage. No snakes are found, nor larger mammals such as Foxes or Badgers, although Rabbits are quite plentiful. The island is owned by the Landmark Trust and preserved as a national heritage; the waters around the island are a Marine Nature Reserve.

Species

Lundy has a long tradition of bird observations, encompassing accounts of both its seabird colonies and of many rare and exotic migrants noted over the decades. Since the demise of the full-time Bird Observatory it attracts less systematic ornithological attention, but must be rated as one of the region's top bird migration watching areas. Those who wish to search for a variety of migrants, including the chance of unusual finds, but do not wish to join the throng on the Scillies in autumn, may find Lundy an alternative; like all islands, however, in unfavourable winds it can have quiet weeks, when few birds are present.

The barren, windswept nature of much of the island prevents many species from living here all year, although Raven are often in view as several resident pairs soar over the steep sidelands. Shag, common breeders, can still be seen in small numbers in other months, although the less marine Cormorant is only a passing migrant. In stony coves Oystercatcher are always present in small numbers, several pairs staying to nest, while Turnstone and Purple Sandpiper are seen occasionally on weedy rocks in winter. Lapwing are commonly met on the rough grassland; winter influxes of a couple of hundred may occur, joining dozens of Golden Plover feeding with Snipe, Starling and winter thrushes on the pasture. Even Skylark and Meadow Pipit, typical summer residents of open terrain, may move away partly in winter. The population of common woodland passerines is very limited; tits, even Blue and Great, are not normally resident here.

Some breeding seabirds return early to the island. Fulmar and Kittiwake loiter in the area from late winter, coming ashore intermittently, although not fully occupying ledges until late spring. Manx Shearwater return to burrows on the south and west slopes, although the status of this visitor, which does not fly to land until darkness covers its movements, is hard to determine. Certainly the species is seen at sea in daytime around the island in late spring and summer, often zigzagging low over the tideraces or flying south in lines past the west cliffs; many of these, however, are presumed to be from the scores of thousands breeding on Skokholm and Skomer Islands in Pembrokeshire. Flocks of thousands seen from the boat, resting in masses on the sea between Lundy and the Devon mainland on calm summer mornings, are thought to be of similar origin. The wailing cries of incoming birds circling low over the island at night, and occasional remains of an unwary shearwater killed by gulls, prove that some stay to breed, or at least summer, here. Detail is similarly lacking for the dainty Storm Petrel, believed to breed in small numbers along the wildest rocky west cliffs, but rarely seen in daylight except when gales drive small flocks in to patter over Lundy Roads bay or when one is glimpsed from the boat crossing. Gannet are seen frequently feeding offshore, although counts of more than a few dozen are unusual. Most of the seabird breeding population is concentrated on the higher cliff slopes of the west and north. The Lesser Black-backed Gull's summer breeding population fluctuates annually, but reaches several dozen pairs. Herring Gull are typically abundant, with well over 1,000 pairs. Great Black-backed also breeds, more solitarily, often 20–30 pairs or more on the island. The delicate Kittiwake is particularly conspicuous around the island's north end, the total of pairs perhaps exceeding 1,000.

Many visitors to Lundy's cliffs seek out the island emblem, the rotund Puffin, most commonly seen around Battery Point on the west coast, or near the north end. Numbers of this very localised seabird have, sadly, decreased until no more than a few dozen pairs can be expected, peaking in late spring. Other auks are scattered around the island, Razorbill taking advantage of crevices and fissures between granite rocks to support a population of perhaps 700 pairs (the region's largest). Guillemot nest on sheerer cliffs in similar numbers. All the auks, however, disappear swiftly to sea once chicks have fledged. A Peregrine might be seen hunting over the seabird colonies. Recently an astonishing discovery was an Ancient Murrelet, a small North Pacific auk, summering with the Guillemot.

Spring migration can be heavy and concentrated, Millcombe valley bushes in particular holding scores of fluttering yellowish-brown *Phylloscopus* warblers in early mornings with 'hooeet' calls from all directions. Many warblers, and other small passerines such as Goldcrest, flycatchers and a few Redstart as spring progresses, feed in East Sidelands thickets as they work their way northward. Sheltered level areas such as the disused quarries and Terrace with water and bushes, high up on the east slopes, tend to concentrate small migrants. As at the region's other migration points, the main passage is often preceded by a good scattering of Wheatear, which may number scores later, early Chiffchaff and Goldcrest, with perhaps a couple of Firecrest in the bushes or Black Redstart on the rocks. The short turf in the south of the island is ideal for a probing Hoopoe, likely to turn up most years. The most noticeable bulk of spring passerine movement consists of commoner warblers, which may be present in mixed aggregations of several hundreds on fall mornings (Willow Warbler being most abundant), and hirundines, which pour northward overhead particularly from mid-spring. A very wide range of small birds passes through annually, with always the chance of a really rare sighting, especially towards the end of spring or in early summer. The high, repetitive song of a Greenish Warbler has been heard in Millcombe valley, and one recent year a visiting party of naturalists was entertained by a superb black-hooded Ruppell's Warbler (Britain's second ever) singing in bushes on East Sidelands. Lundy shares with the Scillies the distinction of late spring visits by the beautiful but elusive Golden Oriole, sometimes two or three together, and its fluting 'weela-weeoo' song has been heard a number of times in Millcombe trees. Some late arrivals stay for long periods in thick cover; Common Rosefinch might even have bred here.

Up on the plateau there is a steady spring passage of open-ground species, including departing groups of winter thrushes and Starling, along with Pied/White Wagtails and Meadow Pipit. A Merlin may be attracted in pursuit and a passage Short-eared Owl might be flushed. Small parties of bronze-winged Ring Ouzel often stop to feed in habitat resembling their moorland haunts. Golden Plover often pass through in small flocks, and resting groups should be inspected for one of Lundy's regular specialities, the Dotterel. Smart breeding-dress birds with white supercilium (eyebrow) stripes and breast-band are virtually annual, sometimes in small groups, *en route* northward to high mountain haunts. Walls and telegraph wires near the village, or up on the east side, may attract a perching migrant shrike, very occasionally the declining Red-backed, but nowadays perhaps more likely an overshooting south European Woodchat. Occasionally a raptor such as a Montagu's Harrier may also drift over.

In summer an occasional pair of migrant warblers, perhaps White-throat or Willow, stays to breed. A surprise southern vagrant could still turn up at any stage. Breeding Curlew (usually two or three pairs present) bubble in song over boggy tracts of moor, joining two or three dozen Lapwing diving in nesting display overhead; a pair of Wheatear may nest on drier ground. In some years late summer has brought an influx of ten or more Continental Crossbill, these stout pine-feeding birds looking strangely out of place here, where they may glean a temporary living from eating seeds at ground level; such arrivals, however, are very irregular and unpredictable.

Waders are among the first migrants to indicate the end of summer; a small party of Dunlin, a shank or Green Sandpiper may drop in beside Pondsbury, or at tiny pools in the south of the island. As autumn progresses, these miniature habitats are worth watching for a variety of waders, although usually no more than a handful of birds. Towards mid-autumn, American Pectoral Sandpiper have been recorded often enough to be almost predictable, and any tiny stint-like waders should be carefully inspected for signs of other transatlantic visitors such as Least or Semipalmated Sandpiper, which have both been identified here. Mid-autumn usually brings another chance to see the scarce but often tame Dotterel, with small parties most years on open spaces such as the 'Airfield'.

Autumn passage movement is often less concentrated than in spring as far as small night migrants such as warblers and flycatchers are concerned, although a few very large arrivals (over 1,000 birds coming in overnight) are on record. The normal daily trickle of migrants may include a heavier-built Melodious Warbler among Willow Warbler and Chiffchaff. Lundy is one of the region's few localities where skulking East European breeding birds such as the grey Barred Warbler have been found on a number of occasions; ringing has helped to reveal this and other unobtrusive species, such as the rare Thrush Nightingale recently recorded. Intensive watching of the East Sidelands bushes and Millcombe is needed to discover warblers and flycatchers, often busy feeding under cover; the casual observer may see little without searching, unless there has been a recent sizeable fall.

Lundy's high top attracts large numbers of passing open-ground birds such as pipits, larks and buntings to stop off in autumn. Numbers of early migrants such as Yellow Wagtail and Tree Pipit may not exceed a couple of dozen per day, but Meadow Pipit pass in many hundreds, and occasionally a rarer pipit such as the heavily streaked Red-throated or larger Richard's, which often hovers indecisively if disturbed from the ground, is seen for a few days on the farmland. Seed-eating species include annual occurrences of Ortolan Bunting in the fields, a very scarce migrant in our region. There have been a small number of occurrences of Little and Rustic Buntings from the sub-Arctic. The stripe-headed northeastern Yellow-breasted Bunting was also recorded recently. Often a few Lapland Bunting are seen in moorland habitats, recognised by the hard 'tick-tick-teu' call as they fly up, and Snow Bunting may also be encountered. Other migrants in open areas may include a dull immature Red-backed or Woodchat Shrike, or a passing raptor such as Hobby or Merlin; the latter often stays for a week or two to take advantage of resting migrant passerines in the pastures. Most surprisingly, a Rough-legged Buzzard which arrived one autumn became resident on the island for many months. Late in autumn, flocks of finches coast high overhead; Chaffinch, sometimes thousands a day, form the bulk, but Siskin, Redpoll and Brambling are also heard calling as they pass over. There may still be a surprise in store, such as the American Robin which foraged for worms with Redwing flocks one recent autumn. Lundy has a long list of American rarity occurrences over the years, including the distinctive Yellow-billed Cuckoo, sadly seldom surviving long, several Red-eyed Vireo, and the thrush-like Veery (second record for Europe; also a first for Devon, like many other of Lundy's rarities). It is perhaps surprising that none of these species has been detected on nearby mainland headlands, although birds always tend to stay longer and be easier to find in a restricted island area.

Timing

As with all islands, most watchers find themselves contrained by access, which makes timing a visit for special conditions difficult. Birds may 'filter through' here, between the land-masses of Wales and Devon, so it cannot always be assumed that birds will tie in exactly with expected arrival weather. Nevertheless, larger numbers of warblers, flycatchers, thrushes and other insect-eating passerines are seen in classic overnight fall conditions after high pressure, and east or southeast winds are, as at all migration points, the most interesting, especially in autumn. Most finch and pipit movements in autumn are against light headwinds. Open ground species such as wagtails, wheatears and Whimbrel may be 'held

Yellow-billed Cuckoo

up' on the bare north end in spring if weather conditions prevent them from continuing their northward journey. Hirundines and other diurnal migrants arrive in the very early morning in spring, having roosted on the nearby Devon mainland, in contrast to arrivals on the south coast of the region where arrivals of diurnal migrants take place 4–5 hours after a dawn departure from France. Larger species such as raptors take time to soar up and may not arrive on the island until later in the day. Fine spells of weather with light southerlies have brought many scarcer birds, including spring exotics. Most American rarities have occurred after strong Atlantic depressions with westerly gales. Such winds have not proved very good for seawatching, except for common species and the odd sheltering Storm Petrel. Few seabirds seem to pass here on migration, but poor visibility may bring those that do (e.g. occasional skuas) closer. For Manx Shearwater or Storm Petrel landing, a night search with flashlights on the west or south cliff slopes would be needed, but great care should be exercised; cliff accidents have claimed lives here.

Note that Landing Beach is not sheltered from east winds; a strong easterly may prevent visitors from landing by boat, although proposed construction of a pier may ease this. Gales from any direction may cause sailings to the island to be cancelled.

Access

By boat from Bideford in North Devon, by the M.V. *Oldenburg*. Tickets from Lundy Oldenburg Office, Bideford Quay, North Devon, tel. (0237) 470422. Additionally, steamer excursions may be arranged for tourists, although time ashore on Lundy is limited. Steamers cannot unload passengers direct at the shallow landing area, and there may be a delay while small boats ferry passengers ashore. Lundy Field Society and various other organisations such as RSPB and DBWPS run excursions advertised through their membership. Lundy Field Society, which publishes news letters and an Annual Report, can be contacted via their Secretary at 2 Beaufort Close, Reigate, Surrey, RH2 9DG, tel. (0737) 245031.

For details of regular transport to Lundy, and accommodation including cottages, camping field and hostel, contact the Landmark Trust, Shottesbrooke, Maidenhead, Berks, SL6 3SW, tel. Littlewick Green 5925. Most bird news is exchanged in the Marisco Tavern, where a bird log is kept, although on a small island like this, with only a couple of dozen regular inhabitants, 'bird events' are general knowledge.

If time ashore is limited, most visitors usually concentrate on Millcombe valley (and St John's Valley, which branches left near the top) for migrants just arrived; the Terrace and East Sidelands for migrants feeding and filtering along; or main seabird colonies such as around North Light or the projecting Battery Point halfway down the west coast, the latter probably best for Puffin. If visiting the north end, try Kittiwake Gully, reached by railed steps right of the lighthouse, for close views. The main track from Landing Beach winds up very steeply through Millcombe to the village; there is a well-marked track north past the Airfield and other pasture and cultivated areas, through the centre of the island past Pondsbury and to the north end. From the far end to the village is about an hour's walk.

Calendar

Resident: Shag, Oystercatcher, Lapwing, Herring and Great Black-backed Gulls, Rock Pipit, Raven.

December–February: reduced winter numbers of residents. A few Water Rail, Golden Plover, Snipe, Woodcock. Possible weather influxes of open-ground species such as plovers and larks, or winter thrushes. Probably Teal. Fulmar, Kittiwake, Guillemot, Razorbill start to return at end. Occasional Peregrine, probably Purple Sandpiper and Turnstone.

March–May: from mid-March, Wheatear, Black Redstart probable, Chiffchaff, Firecrest probable, Goldcrest; passing winter thrushes, Golden Plover and maybe Jack Snipe, maybe Peregrine, Merlin or Short-eared Owl; most departing winter species have passed by late April. Chance of Hoopoe from mid-March, a few Manx Shearwater from end March. Main passage of small migrants from mid-April, including hirundines, pipits, Yellow Wagtail, all commoner warblers, a few Pied Flycatcher, Redstart, Whinchat, Ring Ouzel. Probably Dotterel late April–May; maybe southern rarities, e.g. Woodchat, Golden Oriole or vagrant warblers, chiefly May. Many Whimbrel pass April–May. All seabirds here by May.

June–July: chance of late commoner migrants, maybe a vagrant. Breeding Lapwing, Curlew and seabirds. Manx Shearwater and maybe Storm Petrel seen on crossing. Chance of wader passage, sometimes Crossbill, and first warblers by end July. Auks leave late July.

August–November: Warblers, flycatchers, other small migrants increase through August, peak usually early–mid-September, maybe Melodious Warbler August–September, possibly a shrike late August–September. Thin wader passage mostly August–September, e.g. Dunlin, Whimbrel, shanks, Common and Green Sandpipers, with maybe American species, especially September; chance of Dotterel mostly late August–early October. Probable Ortolan Bunting late August–September; through September–October, probably Merlin, Peregrine, Lapland Bunting, maybe Snow Bunting October. Scarcer eastern migrants mostly late September–October. Pipit passage peaking late September–October. Finches coasting mid-October on, peak end October, winter thrushes arriving, maybe a rarity end October-early November, when Firecrest and Black Redstart arrive. Probable Short-eared Owl and remaining Merlin into November.

Habitat

The exposed, rocky coastline of North Devon is interrupted by only one substantial river system, the combined estuary of Taw and Torridge. This wide, sandy basin is fringed by high sand dunes and low-lying rough grazing marshes. On the north side of the estuary mouth lies the 3-mile

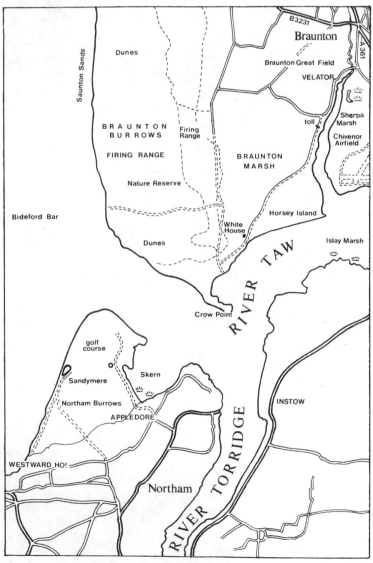

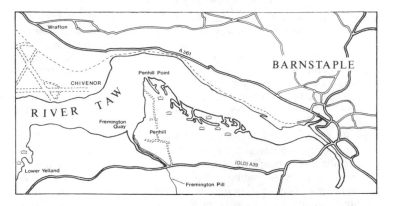

(5-km) expanse of Braunton Burrows, with dunes up to 29 m high, part of which is a National Nature Reserve. On the south side of the estuary system is the smaller Northam Burrows area, a Country Park, with a high pebble ridge along its seashore. Skern saltmarsh lies on the upriver side of Northam Burrows; a municipal rubbish tip is near the outer end. Between these two peninsulas is the relatively shallow river mouth into Bideford Bay. The estuary's sandy nature creates a less rich intertidal fauna than is found on some of the region's muddy estuaries, but its value is increased by the wide area of scantily populated bordering marshland, especially on the Taw. Areas of saltmarsh occur in the Taw's south bank at Penhill Point and Islay Marsh bay; the latter, which has deep sheltered muddy channels, is now an RSPB reserve covering 85 acres (34 ha).

Main population centres are Bideford on the Torridge and Barnstaple on the Taw, both at the head of the rivers concerned. On the northwest side of Bideford, adjacent to the built-up zone, is the small area of pools and bushes at Kenwith Valley, a 20-acre (8-ha) nature reserve administered by DBWPS.

Wildlife on the marshland still includes an occasional elusive otter, mainly in winter, and salmon pass up the rivers. Braunton Burrows is of exceptional botanical interest; rarer plants include Sand Toadflax and Water Germander. Other flora of interest include coastal species such as Sea Holly and Sea Stock, or orchids such as Early Marsh, and Marsh Helleborines. In early summer the dunes can be a mass of flowers. Water Germander is also found at Northam, together with Sea Stock and Dune Pansies.

The beaches at Northam Burrows and neighbouring Westward Ho!, as at Saunton Sands fronting Braunton Burrows across the river, are popular with summer holidaymakers and water sports are increasing around the estuary mouth; both create disturbance to wildlife. Parts of the lower estuary, especially around Braunton Burrows, are used for military exercises at times.

Species

This large area supports the area's third largest wader population after the Exe and Tamar, although it has large numbers of certain species rather than variety. Peripheral dunes and marshland attract a number of species of interest, including some uncommon winter visitors.

Low-lying Braunton marshes, on the upriver side of the dunes, may hold huge flocks totalling several thousand each of Lapwing and Golden Plover early in the year, perhaps accompanied by a few Ruff; over 200 Snipe are regular, scattered around marsh dykes and rushy areas. The large flocks of plovers are often targets for a wintering Peregrine circling overhead while Merlin are also likely, hunting larks and pipits over the fields, or swerving over saltings after small waders such as Dunlin. Smaller flocks of the same waders, again attended by raptors, may be expected at Northam Burrows. Around estuary mouth beaches, there are often over 100 silver-white Sanderling running along tidelines; muddier stretches hold up to 2,000 Dunlin, and flocks of up to 200 Ringed Plover are among the southwest's largest winter gatherings of this species. Large waders are conspicuous, midwinter counts of Oystercatcher and Curlew both easily exceeding 1,000. Main roost for estuary waders are on either side of the estuary mouth, at Crow Point on the north side at the tip of Braunton Burrows, or at Northam Burrows on the south side by sheltered Skern saltmarsh. Other waders may be seen; up to 500 Redshank, perhaps 100 Grey Plover and half that number of Turnstone, together with usually a few Knot and Bar-tailed Godwit.

Wildfowl population of the 'Two Rivers' estuary, although perhaps as with the waders lacking in variety, may be considerably enhanced by cold weather. Grey geese, usually White-fronted, may arrive in scores, or perhaps a family party of Whooper or Bewick's Swan, the smaller Bewick's being probably the more frequent. Brent Geese were formerly almost unknown in North Devon, but, as this small blackish goose has increased elsewhere, it has become regular on the saltmarshes; up to 200 might now be encountered, including occasional individuals of the pale-breasted race which normally winters further north. At the beginning or end of winter they may be joined on the estuary for a few days by a small party of white-faced Barnacle Geese, particularly after northerly winds; this other 'black goose' does not normally winter anywhere in our region except for a few tame individuals escaped from wildfowl collections (several arriving together probably indicate wild stock). Shelduck are widespread, reaching late winter peaks of well over 100 most years. Regular ducks include up to 1,000 Wigeon, mostly on the lower estuary basin, and often 200 or more Teal, which may be scattered in groups over the marshes. Shoveler gather on muddy pools, groups such as 20 together on Northam Burrows being among the largest in Devon. Flocks (perhaps the same birds) also occur on outer Braunton marshes, where there is standing water, or at Kenwith valley pools, along with a range of other dabbling ducks. Other wildfowl such as Pintail and Gadwall turn up in the area sporadically in small groups, generally less than half a dozen. Kenwith pools are a likely habitat for Gadwall to use if around. Diving ducks are limited on the open estuary, although two or three Goldeneye and single-figure counts of Red-breasted Merganser may occur; the sheltered waters of Kenwith attract small flocks, up to a dozen or so Tufted and Pochard being expected, plus an occasional rarer visitor such as a Scaup, once a Ring-necked Duck. Common Scoter are often present in dozens in Bideford Bay, perhaps seen off Westward Ho! front, or Downend rocks beyond Braunton, habitats where a few Purple Sandpiper may be discovered feeding inconspicuously on the shore. One of the outstanding local wildfowl is Eider, of which a non-breeding flock (variable, often 20–30 birds) is habitually present around the lower estuary or mouth; a recent record count was of 84 summering. Most are brown female or immature birds,

Eider

some with a confusing pattern of black and white blotches appearing as smart adult male colours show through; full adult males are a small minority.

Rough weather offshore may force a Great Northern Diver to feed in the estuary mouth, where one or two Slavonian Grebe are present most winters. The browner Little Grebe, a marshland breeder here in very small numbers, may also be found diving on the tideway in winter. Colder months can bring increased interest to the marshes and freshwater pools, where a streaky-brown Bittern may lurk camouflaged in reedy margins, joining Water Rail. At sheltered spots such as Wrafton Pond east of Braunton Marsh, the 'ping' calls of small parties of Bearded Tit have also been heard.

Further upriver, in side creeks and bays, Grey Heron fishing may be joined by rarer relatives. Single Little Egret have wintered several times, often in the deep sheltered saltmarsh channels at Islay Marsh, where they may be hard to watch. Spoonbill have been present for long periods in recent winters, up to three being on view at times; they are likely to be seen roosting at a sheltered saltmarsh bay such as Islay, but at lower tides might be watched sifting through the shallows anywhere on the wide middle reaches of the estuary. Some are immatures, picked out in flight by the black wingtips. One winter a Crane was found feeding on Northam Burrows. Sheltered areas may also hold wintering Greenshank, totalling up to half a dozen around the area, but Spotted Redshank found in similar habitats are much scarcer, only one or two being normal. Kingfisher are also regular visitors to the upper estuary, and the muddiest creeks or the riverside marshes above Barnstaple and Bideford may hold a Green or Common Sandpiper staying through. Gulls also use the marshes, including Black-headed with an estuary total which may approach 10,000. Herring Gull, usually under 2,000, are not exceptionally plentiful compared with other parts of the region, but coastal gales may drive in several hundred Great Black-backed to the estuary mouth. The area has only recently been watched intensively for rarer gulls; single Glaucous and Iceland are now recorded each winter, particularly around Northam Burrows, and Ring-billed has been seen. Records of Mediterranean and Little Gull are not yet as regular as on the south coastal estuaries, but may prove so with more observation.

Spring wader passage is conspicuous, with dozens of whistling Whimbrel and many scattered Common Sandpiper stopping off. Sometimes migrant parties of 30 or more pale grey-backed White Wagtail are seen on marshes near the estuary mouth. Sedge, Reed and occasional Grasshopper Warblers sing in the marsh dykes, although breeding numbers of these 'waterside' warblers are not large here. Whitethroat singing in thickets on Braunton Burrows are joined by one or two dark-faced Lesser Whitethroat, an increasing species here on the edge of its breeding range; two or three pairs of Turtle Dove are likely in similar habitats. Later, in the ancient Great Field area near Braunton, Quail may be heard calling, probably invisible in the cultivated land; this is a long-established site for the scarce and diminutive gamebird. More common, but perhaps unexpected at sea level, are breeding Wheatear in the shingle and dunes around the estuary mouth, utilising Rabbit burrows and man-made pipes or debris for nest holes; good views can be obtained especially along Northam Burrows ridge, where a dozen or more pairs may breed. Several pairs of Oystercatcher and Ringed Plover lay their well-camouflaged eggs on quieter stretches of the estuary.

Autumn brings varied, although not intensively watched, wader passage. Sheltered bays and creeks where streams flow in, known locally as 'pills', may hold Little Stint or Curlew Sandpiper, generally fewer than six of each; they are seen particularly at muddy feeding areas near the estuary mouth, such as Northam Burrows tip road pool or the River Caen outlet at Braunton Pill behind the Burrows. Occasionally an American vagrant such as Pectoral Sandpiper or Long-billed Dowitcher is reported in these habitats. Passerine migrants move through the dune-slack bushes, where damp conditions encourage rich insect life, and among commoner warblers a scarcer bird such as Wryneck might be seen. Icterine and Yellow-browed Warblers have both been reported in Kenwith Valley bushes. Feeding hirundines, often in hundreds over the marshes, may attract a passing Hobby. A few Sandwich, Common and Little Terns feed out around the estuary mouth, but numbers on this coast are small, rarely exceeding a dozen of any species, although Sandwich may peak at 20 or so. An encouraging trend in recent years has been an increase in Little Tern records, with small flocks regularly present in spring, late summer and autumn. Common Tern, if seen closely, may be checked for individuals of the scarcer Arctic Tern, seen most years in autumn. The lower estuary also attracts considerable gatherings of noisy Greenshank, with frequent counts of over 20, and perhaps a group of passing Bar-tailed Godwit.

Late autumn is often interesting. When Peregrine and Merlin return to harry wintering flocks, there is often a Short-eared Owl in the coastal dunes, and a Hen Harrier, usually a brown ringtail, may quarter the marshes, staying to winter in years when voles are plentiful. Late season also brings specialities such as regular Snow Bunting, seen flashing white wing-patches particularly along Northam pebble ridge, sometimes in parties up to a dozen although twos and threes are more normal. Parties of other uncommon northern visitors such as Twite, Shorelark and Lapland Bunting have also arrived on the estuary edges and dunes in some years. A gale at sea may bring in an exhausted Grey Phalarope to spin on one of the pools. Descending winter sees Raven circling over Northam rubbish tip, and maybe a Barn Owl floating white across riverside pastures.

Timing

At low tide, the vastness of the estuary system defeats close watching of ducks or waders; there is a very large tidal drop on this coast. Saltmarsh areas such as Islay, which can be productive, are hardly worth visiting at low tides, when waders are hidden in deep muddy channels out of sight. An incoming tide, particularly about halfway into creeks and bays, is more likely to bring success, or a visit to the main roosts on either side of the estuary mouth two hours or so up to high tide as birds fly in. Snow and ice in other regions are likely to increase considerably flocks of open-ground species and probably bring White-fronted Geese. Look for American waders after strong, persistent autumn west winds, and Grey Phalarope after northwest or northerly gales have forced them into Bideford Bay in late autumn. Quail are more likely if the summer is hot and dry.

Water sports may disturb the lower estuary and mouth on sunny weekends; public use of Crow Point beach and Braunton Burrows is increasing at weekends. See Access section for Army restrictions. Some motorcycle scrambling is also carried out on the dunes, mostly at weekends. Northam rubbish tip is used by gulls particularly on week-days when council tipping is in progress.

Access

Barnstaple, reached by A377 from Exeter, is the usual starting point at the head of the Taw estuary. It is linked by A39 west to Bideford on the Torridge. (Note that the old A39, which ran along the estuary-side route between the two towns, is now a secondary road; the new A39 takes a more direct hilltop route between the two, crossing the Torridge Estuary on a high bridge just east of Bideford.) Large areas of estuary are difficult to approach, but probably not outstanding for birds. The local council has recently allocated old branch railway tracks on both banks of the Taw estuary as public amenity areas for walking and cycling; they run from Barnstaple along the south bank through Instow towards Bideford and on the north bank past Chivenor airfield. They may not be worth walking throughout unless you have a large amount of time to spare but form convenient access points for some of the sites below. The south bank walk can be started in the Sticklepath area, just south of Barnstaple Bridge on the *old* A39 signposted towards Fremington and Instow; footpath signs lead off the main road. It may be better to start the north bank walk midway, near Ashford, from which a wide view of the estuary can be gained, then walk in either direction. Those wishing to leave their car and do a circular walk can pick up a bus on the main roads past the access points.

The following are probably the best bird areas:
NORTH SIDE –

Braunton Burrows: drive west on A361 from Barnstaple, signposted towards Ilfracombe, then turn left at Braunton town centre towards Saunton and Croyde. After 1 mile (1.6 km), take a minor road left (not conspicuously signposted) to the Burrows. The Great Field area, surrounded by minor roads, is on your left. Drive down the lane behind the dunes; you can stop in signposted Nature Conservancy Council car parks, complete with map boards, or continue down a rough track (driveable with care) towards the estuary mouth. The NCC signs detail National Nature Reserve areas and regulations for those who enter; there is normally access for visitors except when Army exercises take place. Further details from the Warden, tel. Braunton 812552. After 2 miles (3 km) of dirt track, park and walk ahead towards Crow Point at the tip for resting waders and views up the estuary; or right across the dunes by a duckboard path to the beach and river mouth. Snow Bunting might be in the area in late autumn or winter. Given time, a walk along the last 2 miles (3 km) of track with stops to check the bushes may be profitable, especially at migration periods. Eider may be in sight off either beach or river side of the dunes.

From here you can take a driveable track leading around the perimeter of Braunton grazing marshes behind the Burrows, with the tidal flats and pill across a seawall to the right. Reaching a tarmac road, continue back through Velator tollgate towards the main road. A complete circuit of the dune and marsh peninsula gives chances to see varied ducks, waders and perhaps hunting raptors; do not forget to look in the pill for autumn passage waders.

Sherpa Marsh: across the pill from Braunton lie further extensive grazing marshes, less disturbed by public access. A path leads along the seawall on the eastern side of the pill. Geese may use the fields, and the reedy Wrafton Pond can shelter marsh birds such as rails or Bittern.

Downend: by continuing past Braunton Burrows another mile (1.6 km) towards Croyde Bay, you reach exposed Downend, on a sharp corner with parking on the left. A wide view of the shallow sea off the Burrows can be obtained. Common Scoter are often seen from here and Eider might be visible; seabirds are sometimes seen from here in rough weather. Purple Sandpiper may be on the end rocks in winter.

Ashford/Heanton Court: good views of the central part of the Taw estuary can be obtained from a roadside pull-in just before Heanton Court, 5 miles (8 km) along A361 west from Barnstaple towards Braunton. Do not block the hotel car park entrance. Penhill Point marshes lie across the river; views are long distance, requiring a telescope. Duck flocks may be located from here and feeding Spoonbill may be visible in winter especially at lower tides. For closer views, walk back 300 metres east until opposite the minor turn marked to West Ashford. At this point a footpath leads down across a stone bridge onto the disused railway embankment, now a public track. Walk 100 metres west until you reach a stone lookout hut adapted by DBWPS for birdwatchers, but subject to vandalism.

SOUTH SIDE –

Penhill/Fremington: drive west on the old A39 road from Barnstaple. Between Bickington and Fremington villages, a small lane leads off right towards the disused rail halt. Park by main road and walk down the lane by the creek for feeding waders (maybe Greenshank or Spotted Redshank), then turn right along the estuary bank to view Penhill Point bend after 1 mile (1.6 km). Alternatively this can be used as an access onto the railway embankment path, but the estuary is rather distant in places.

Islay Marsh: at the west end of Lower Yelland village, a lane runs 300 yards (300 m) north towards the estuary; formerly this led to a power station, now demolished. Industrial traffic goes to a small oil terminal and factory estate; a housing development will take over the old power station site. At present it is probably best to leave vehicles on the main road in the village, walk down the lane and access the railway line footpath to the right. Islay Marsh bay lies adjacent to the rail bank after 100 yards (100 m). Either view the area from the path by walking on eastward, or, as you reach the bay, cross a stile to the left and take a coastal footpath around the western perimeter of the bay on a raised bank (the power station waste tip, now grassed). Parts of the tip may still be unsafe; keep to the path. Do not walk onto the marsh, which is now an RSPB reserve.

Northam Burrows: drive to Bideford and cross the bridge, turning right on A386 for Northam and Westward Ho! For the road past Skern salt-marsh and freshwater pools, with views over the rubbish tip, turn right towards Appledore then second left (Broad Lane) off the main road. Continue across minor road junctions, and on down the mile-long (1.6 km) tip road with close views of marshes on the right (car window views) and freshwater pools on the left. Golden Plover flock on nearby turf. The tip is at the far end on the left.

For Northam pebble ridge, follow signs towards Westward Ho! and turn right past holiday camps to Country Park entry points. Drive past golf course and pastures, watching again for plovers, out to Sandymere Pool depression beside the pebble ridge. Wheatear and perhaps Ringed Plover are here in summer, probably Snow Bunting in late autumn–winter.

Kenwith Valley: driving through Bideford town centre towards Westward Ho!, turn off sharp left at Raleigh Garage, then pass the reserve notice after 200 yards (200 m) on the right; park ¼ mile (400 m) along this road (Northam Road) and walk back. Public paths are laid out around this small area; walk past the first lake to the public hide overlooking the sheltered second lake.

Calendar

Resident: Little Grebe, Cormorant, Grey Heron, Sparrowhawk, Buzzard, Oystercatcher, Ringed Plover, Lapwing, Barn Owl, Raven; generally some Eider stay through although numbers vary.

December–February: Great Northern Diver (sporadic), Slavonian Grebe, possible wintering Spoonbill or Little Egret, maybe Bittern or grey geese, and wild swans (hard weather only), Brent Goose, Shelduck, Teal, Mallard, Wigeon, Shoveler, probably Gadwall, Tufted Duck, Pochard (Kenwith), probably Goldeneye, Red-breasted Merganser, Eider, Common Scoter, Hen Harrier some winters, Peregrine, Merlin, Water Rail, Grey and Golden Plovers, Snipe, Bar-tailed Godwit, Green and Common Sandpipers, shanks, Sanderling, Dunlin, Turnstone, Purple Sandpiper, Knot, maybe Ruff, Kingfisher, possible Snow Bunting especially early winter.

March–May: Wheatear arrive to breed; later wader passage (especially from mid-April) including Whimbrel and shanks, a few terns especially

Sandwich but chance of Little flocks from mid-April, White Wagtail mostly April; a winter Spoonbill may still be present. Commoner warblers arriving mostly from mid-April, including Lesser Whitethroat. Winter visitors mostly left before then. Glaucous or Iceland gulls may still appear. Turtle Dove arrive May; perhaps a scarcer migrant e.g. Hoopoe in dunes.

June–July: breeding species, including Shelduck, maybe Water Rail some years, Lapwing, Ringed Plover, Oystercatcher, possibly Quail, Turtle Dove, Reed and Sedge Warbler, Wheatear; returning Black-headed Gull and first waders, e.g. Dunlin, Common Sandpiper, shanks and Whimbrel from late July. A few terns may stay through.

August–November: hirundines feeding August–September, perhaps Hobby; Yellow and White Wagtails pass. Possibly terns August–September, including Arctic and Little; perhaps a Mediterranean Gull; passage of commoner *Sylvia* and *Phylloscopus* warblers; passage wader peak September, with possibly Little Stint and Curlew Sandpiper, perhaps an American, e.g. Pectoral Sandpiper. Peregrine and Merlin from late September, maybe Grey Phalarope, and probably Snow Bunting, late October–November; chance of Twite or other northern passerines; chance of Hen Harrier or Short-eared Owl.

44 NORTH DEVON COAST (MORTE POINT–LYNTON)

OS ref: SS 5248
OS map: sheet 180

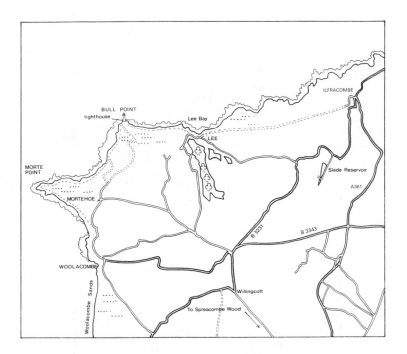

Habitat

A highly scenic exposed coastline of cliffs and a few rocky coves runs directly east-west from the Bristol Channel coast until an abrupt southward turn at long, jagged Morte Point on the edge of Bideford Bay. Coastal resort towns such as Ilfracombe, Combe Martin and Lynton are encircled by steep, rocky slopes and backed by high ground, rising especially to the east, on the fringe of Exmoor. Over much of the area, although sheer cliffs are limited and often under 50 m, the land rises very fast, reaching 300 m within ½ mile (0.8 km) inland.

Inland behind the high, open coastal downs, steep sheltered valleys (combes) hold belts of mainly deciduous woodland. Spreacombe Wood in the west of the area is an RSPB reserve. Arlington Court estate (National Trust), farther east, has a 6-acre (2.4-ha) lake set in mature mixed wood and parkland. On the edge of Exmoor nearby, 43-acre (17.4-ha) Wistlandpound Reservoir is extensively used for sailing and fishing. The whole area is heavily used by summer holidaymakers.

Species

Although much of this area is not regularly looked at by birdwatchers, it offers attractive birdwatching territory with a variety of typical Devon breeding birds, seabird colonies and coastal migration potential.

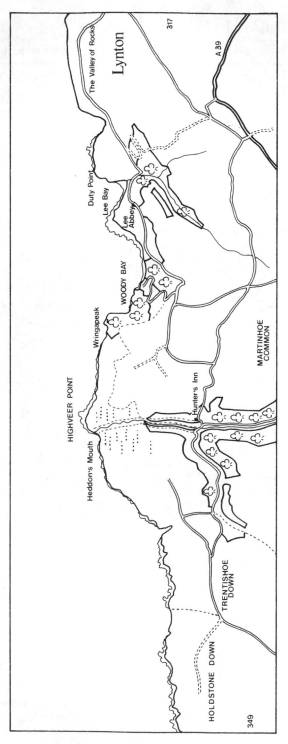

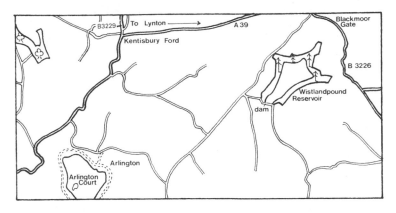

Through spring and summer, the coastline is occupied by large numbers of breeding seabirds, with countless widespread Herring Gull, and a number of Great Black-backed Gull nesting on rocky promontories. Fulmar have spread enormously and are now one of the commonest coastal species, with total counts of hundreds sitting on cliff ledges or veering past on stiff outstretched wings. Breeding Razorbill are scattered along the eastern half of this coastline, particularly around Heddon's Mouth–Martinhoe–Woody Bay district, where small groups gather off the towering coastal downs from early spring. The population is almost impossible to census, but up to 400 pairs have been estimated, the region's largest mainland colony. Guillemot are also present but less widespread, with counts of up to 200 individuals in the nesting period around Woody Bay. Kittiwake, less common, have small colonies of two or three dozen pairs at Bull Point, farther west, and Woody Bay. All through summer, lines of Manx Shearwater can be seen passing west from protruding headland lookout points, and in onshore gales there is often a Storm Petrel or two pattering low over wave troughs off Ilfracombe or Combe Martin.

Breeding species include one of Devon's larger heronries, of up to 30 nests, at Arlington Court, where a mix of common woodland passerines may also be found. Coastal valleys, and even scrubby trees on steep clifftop slopes, also hold small populations of interesting summer migrant passerines such as Redstart and Wood Warbler. The Pied Fly-catcher, increasing here as elsewhere, has recently become established in nestboxes at Spreacombe Wood, and smart cock birds turn up to sing in clifftop copses. Heath and bracken valleys overlooking the sea hold a few breeding Whinchat and regular 'reeling' (singing) Grasshopper Warbler, unobtrusive and usually unseen. Spring migrants passing through can include a party of Ring Ouzel pausing to feed on coastal downs on their way north. Falls of commoner migrants might be attracted by Bull Point lighthouse, while exotics such as Hoopoe have been reported on Morte Point's turfy slopes. The high line of downs may prove a suitable thermalling path for an occasional migrant raptor; indeed, less common birds such as the intricately-marked Honey Buzzard have been watched soaring over. Some of the region's characteristic breeders are particularly common inland. Raven breed in many woods such as Spreacombe, often choosing large old conifer trees and sometimes competing for territory with mewing Buzzard. Sometimes a dozen or more of the latter can be seen in the air at once. The attractive tail-flirting

Grey Wagtail, flashing sulphur-yellow underparts, is a frequent sight by hill streams, many of which have a resident pair of Dippers.

Although migration has not been particularly studied, westward offshore movements of seabirds have been noted, including longer-distance migrants such as skuas and terns, especially in autumn. An occasional Arctic Skua and a trickle of terns, usually Sandwich, might be seen in spring. The Capstone at Ilfracombe has proved a suitable lookout point in summer, autumn and winter, but Morte Point on the corner of the coast might be good, especially in spring. Astonishingly, considering how much seawatching takes place elsewhere, Devon's only accepted record of Black-browed Albatross was at Morte Point. Movements of over half a dozen skuas, mostly Arctic with a few stocky Great in autumn, and over a couple of dozen terns, mostly Sandwich or Common, normally moving west, are unusual even in autumn; spring up-channel movements probably amount to no more than a quarter of this. Scarcer species such as the oceanic Sooty Shearwater are more likely through late summer and autumn, when a handful of birds probably pass westward each year, although, surprisingly, this wanderer has also been seen off the coast in spring. Brownish Balearic Shearwater are probably also annual in varying numbers moving west, but are less frequent than off the region's southern and western extremities. Divers of all three species have been noted moving past in winter and especially spring, although (as usual) Black-throated is least often certainly identified and over half a dozen of any species in a day is unusual. Divers appear not to feed regularly along this stretch, although some-times in winter a Great Northern has arrived unexpectedly on Wistland-pound Reservoir. Recently Morte Point produced another 'first for Devon' when a White-billed Diver paid a short visit.

Autumn brings large coasting movements of hirundines along the clifftops, followed later in the season by other diurnal migrants concentrated into a stream by the straight coastal escarpment. Passages of finches are a well-known feature, although little watched recently. Sometimes several thousand move west in a day in late autumn, the vast bulk being Chaffinches, perhaps bound for Ireland although some flocks certainly continue down the North Cornwall coast. At any point along the coastal downs the flocks can be seen passing over. The 'pinking' calls of Chaffinch are accompanied by a few harsher-calling Brambling and other finches or buntings. Cold weather may bring a party of Snow Bunting to rest and feed on open down or moorland, such as Holdstone Down near Trentishoe, and predators such as Merlin often pass down the coast in pursuit of the travelling flocks of passerines.

Winter does not bring major gatherings of birds inland, but, depending on disturbance levels, ducks (mostly diving species) visit Wistland-pound Reservoir, with up to 30–40 Pochard, a dozen Tufted, and four or five Goldeneye at times; small groups also appear on nearby Arlington Lake. Less common diving ducks such as Scaup are seen singly on either lake in most winters (probably the same individual); and an American Ring-necked Duck, as usual a prominent drake with high crown and grey-shaded flanks, has wintered among the Tufted Duck. The small wooded areas bordering Wistlandpound are also worth a look if undisturbed; harsh nasal calls draw attention to Willow Tit, and a Woodcock may burst out from ground cover.

Timing

At any time of day, highly scenic wood and coastal walks can bring views of characteristic local birds. Most woodland bird song in spring–summer will be in mornings, which are also best for coastal migrant passerines. Fall conditions might leave resting migrants at dawn around Morte or Bull Point; autumn coasting movement of hirundines and finches, commencing soon after daybreak, is most prominent up to mid-morning, especially in westerly winds. Northerlies bring the northern birds such as Snow Bunting. Occasional larger raptors circling over the coast are most likely on warm anticyclonic days, later in the morning than other migrants, when thermal currents have had time to develop. At this time of day, local Buzzard and Raven will be seen in strength.

Seawatching is best when seabirds are confused or pushed in against the coast by mist, rain or onshore winds. Strong northwesterlies are often interesting, and likely to produce numbers of passing birds, mostly early in the day. Seabirds breeding locally pass to and fro at any time of day.

Wistlandpound Reservoir, vulnerable to disturbance, is best visited at off-peak periods such as weekday mornings.

Access

A-class roads, such as A39 Barnstaple–Lynton and A399 through Ilfracombe and Combe Martin, serve main holiday resort towns. Minor roads cross the hinterland, running south through wooded valleys towards the Taw valley and Barnstaple; relatively few minor roads give access to the larger expanses of coastal down and cliff. Public footpaths are the best way to cover these areas; west from Lynton, for example, good signposted paths lead from Heddon valley woods near Hunter's Inn, either way along the clifftops, for views of seabirds breeding far below and clifftop passerine migrants. This area can be reached by leaving Lynton southward on A39 and taking narrow right turns to Martinhoe and Hunter's Inn. Park by roadsides near the Inn (can be congested later on summer days), and choose your path beside the Inn; west takes you across high ground towards Holdstone Down; east leads back towards Lynton via Woody Bay. Worth at least two or three hours' walk in either direction.

The Capstone seawatching point is clearly visible as a high, grassed headland beside Ilfracombe seafront. From this town, B3231 and B3343 lead west towards Woolacombe and little-watched Morte Point – worth a try. South of Morte–Woolacombe area, a left turn (eastward) off B3231 ½ mile (0.8 km) before Georgeham village takes you to Spreacombe Wood, a small RSPB reserve. Entry is by permit; contact RSPB regional office or the Warden, Mr C.G. Manning, Sherracombe, Raleigh Park, Barnstaple (please send s.a.e.).

No permit is needed to visit Wistlandpound Reservoir. The lake can be reached off A39 Barnstaple–Lynton road, turning south at Blackmoor Gate junction on the edge of Exmoor, on B3226 towards South Molton, then right on a minor road after ½ mile (0.8 km).

Calendar

Resident: Sparrowhawk, Buzzard, Oystercatcher, Great Black-backed and Herring Gulls, Grey Wagtail, Dipper, Rock Pipit, Stonechat, Willow Tit, Raven.

December–February: a few divers passing. Possible Hen Harrier, Peregrine or Merlin over downs. Diving ducks – Tufted, Pochard, Goldeneye, maybe Scaup – at Wistlandpound, maybe Woodcock. Teal and Wigeon irregular. Fulmar, Grey Heron and Raven start breeding cycle at end of period.

March–May: passerine migration along coast, Wheatear and probably Ring Ouzel from mid–late March. Summer breeding visitors and passerine migrants, including warblers, Pied Flycatcher, Redstart from mid–late April. Seabirds at colonies from mid-April (Fulmar earlier), maybe raptors or other overshooting migrants especially from late April. Manx Shearwater pass from April, maybe Storm Petrel from May. Divers passing, Sandwich Tern, maybe Arctic Skua.

June–July: summer breeding passerines and seabirds, including Fulmar, Kittiwake, Razorbill, Guillemot. Passing Manx Shearwaters, occasional Storm Petrel, Gannet offshore, a few Sandwich and Common Terns from July. Woodland birdsong decreasing from late June. Auks leave mid-July.

August–November: summer breeding passerines depart from August. Possibly migration 'falls' on coast (little known). Possible Balearic and Sooty Shearwaters, Arctic and Great Skuas, terns with possibly Black (mainly August). Chance of waders at Wistlandpound, e.g. Greenshank or Green Sandpiper, August–September. Coastal movement of finches and northern migrants, finches peak late October–early November. Winter visitors returning November.

Purple Sandpiper

45A MOLLAND COMMON AND
TARR STEPS, WEST EXMOOR

OS ref: SS 7932
OS map: sheet 180

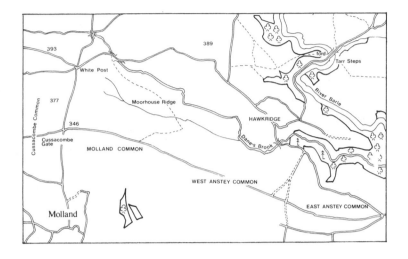

Habitat

Molland Common is a ridge of heather moorland rising to about 400 m on the south edge of Exmoor; we have included neighbouring commons towards Hawkridge and East Anstey, which form a continuation of Molland. Hill farms and sheltered bushy combes at a lower altitude border the ridge. The open common is frequented by moor ponies, and with luck a herd of Red Deer might be spotted; they may lie in long heather or bracken and sometimes only the spreading antlers of a stag are visible. To the northeast of the ridge, the River Barle, a tributary of the Exe, flows through a steep wooded valley and under the stone clapper bridge at Tarr Steps, a popular tourist feature in summer.

Species

Molland ridge holds a selection of moorland birds, but the speciality is wintering and passing birds of prey. Hen Harrier are always in the district in winter; open views along the ridge mean that hunting birds can soon be located as they beat low across the common. Two or three, often including a smart grey male, may be found in the vicinity, together with a small number of Merlin, which occur in most months outside the breeding season, pursuing small passerines in low, swerving flight. Peregrine occasionally fly over, and common breeding West Country raptors also use the area, giving a variety of species although total numbers of birds are small. Short-eared Owl, hunting diurnally on long buzzard-like wings, also winter some years when voles are plentiful, or after a good breeding season when their numbers are high. Other birds can appear scarce, but a walk through the heather might put up a Red Grouse and there are sometimes large finch flocks, including Brambling, on adjacent agricultural land. Fieldfare are often present in chattering

Buzzard

flocks. Great Grey Shrike have been seen several times along the edge of the common and may be regular visitors.

The prominent position of Molland ridge, facing south at the edge of the moor, means that migrant raptors may circle over it on spring passage; a Montagu's Harrier or Hobby, for example, could be seen on a fine day. The summer breeding population of the ridge is not outstanding, but the bubbling song of Curlew may be heard overhead, while a few Snipe breed in the boggy hollows. Wheatear and Whinchat breed in small numbers along this side of the moor, and Meadow Pipit and Skylark are plentiful. At this season the oakwoods and waterside of Tarr Steps may be rewarding, with a good selection of woodland species including Pied Flycatcher singing close to the bridge, Redstart and numerous trilling Wood Warbler. There is a good chance of Grey Wagtail and Dipper along the riverbanks.

Timing

Winter raptors are most likely to be active on fine, clear mornings after a frosty night. Hen Harrier, however, will hunt in most weathers. In spring, high pressure with fine weather and winds between south and east is most likely to bring passage birds. Breeding waders are most active in early morning and evening. Avoid peak summer weekends at Tarr Steps when tourist congestion is likely, or visit early in the day.

Access

Turn north off *old* A361 between South Molton and Bampton (a new A361, known as the North Devon Link Road, has just been completed, which runs further south). Follow minor roads to Molland village. Turn right in village centre, then left uphill onto the common. Explore minor roads across open land; the road east towards Hawkridge gives views over most of the area and raptors might be seen from the roadside. Public footpaths and bridleways (see 'stag's head' National Park emblem) cross the area. For Tarr Steps, turn north through Hawkridge from the east end of the common and continue on a very narrow road down into the valley. Cars can cross the Barle only by a deep ford beside the clapper bridge.

Calendar

Resident: Sparrowhawk, Buzzard, Kestrel, Grey Wagtail, Dipper, Raven.

December–February: Hen Harrier, Merlin, maybe a Peregrine or Short-eared Owl, Red Grouse, maybe Great Grey Shrike, winter thrushes, finches.

March–May: Hen Harrier leave by early April, Merlin may occur later. Possibly migrant raptors late April–May. Summer woodland visitors from late April. Breeding waders arriving.

June–July: breeding residents, waders, moorland and woodland summer visitors.

August–November: summer visitors depart August; migrants and winter visitors appear mostly from mid-October.

45B ADDITIONAL SITE: RACKENFORD, KNOWSTONE AND HARE'S DOWN

OS ref: SS 8521
OS map: sheet 181

Habitat

In the northeast corner of Devon, flanking the southern edge of Exmoor, lies a strip of rough hill farmland and wet heath which represents some of the original Culm Measures habitat of mid and north Devon. The areas of heathland have been encroached on and fragmented in recent years by agricultural improvement and road building. Rackenford Moor (137 acres/55 ha) has recently been acquired as a DWT reserve.

Species

The birds of the heaths include some specialised breeders of marginal agricultural land, and visitors from the nearby moorland areas including predators. In winter, the heaths can appear bleak and birdless; a Hen Harrier or Merlin may come down from the moors to hunt, however, and the wet areas may hold both a scattering of Snipe and one or two scarce Jack Snipe. Woodcock might be flushed from nearby copses. Flocks of 200–300 Golden Plover and winter thrushes feed on nearby farmland. Resident Willow Tit are present in trees and encroaching damp scrub on the edge of the heaths. Occasionally a Great Grey Shrike (perhaps connected with occurrences on nearby Molland Common) is reported. Summer brings a wider range of interest, with Curlew a regular breeder, this being one of its most regular breeding sites on the Devon mainland, while a few pairs of Lapwing are also found in the district. Nightjar have also been recorded. Small passerines arriving as summer visitors include a few Grasshopper Warbler, Whinchat and Tree Pipit.

Timing

In open areas such as this, fine bright days produce maximum activity, and the likelihood of raptors hunting in winter; Grasshopper Warbler and Nightjar are most likely to be singing at dusk in summer.

Access

The new A361 North Devon link road can be joined at the roundabout at the north end of Tiverton. From here Rackenford village is signposted as 9 miles (14½ km) on to the west. After 5½ miles (8 km) on the main road, turn left towards Rackenford onto B3221. *Do not* turn left off B3221 at Rackenford village entrance; continue on west for another mile (1.6 km) to Knowstone Cross, turning right to Knowstone and Molland. After ½ mile (0.8 km), passing open heath areas on the left, cross a flyover over the A361. Stop at a layby immediately on the right; the entry to Rackenford Moor DWT reserve (contact DWT for entry permit) is through the gate. The area can be scanned from the roadsides for larger birds. The open unfenced heath to the left of this road is part of Hare's Down area. By continuing on this road and taking left turns back through Roach Hill hamlet you pass Knowstone Moor to the left, immediately before arriving back on A361. Alternatively, by continuing straight on from Rackenford Moor, through East Anstey village, after 6 miles (9½ km) you can continue onto the Molland ridge (see previous chapter). Follow signs to Hawkridge from East Anstey village, turning left to explore along the ridge.

45C ADDITIONAL SITE: WINKLEIGH AIRFIELD AND DISTRICT

OS ref: SS 6209
OS map: sheet 191

Habitat

In the sparsely populated interior of mid-Devon, amid fields heavily used for sheep pasture, the Culm Measures have still left a few areas of unimproved boggy grazing, damp heath and uncultivated land. North of Winkleigh lies an area of flat ground at about 160 metres altitude, the site of an old wartime airfield, crossed by roads; recently, unfortunately, industrial development has started to sprawl across this site. Similar, smaller areas lie to the north.

Species

The attraction of such areas is chiefly for seeing winter flocks of open-ground species and passerines, which also attract occasional predators. Although not usually visited as a specific birdwatching excursion, they can be fitted easily into a journey to or from North Devon. Birds may move between similar areas when disturbed.

Winkleigh has a reputation for attracting very large flocks of Golden Plover and Lapwing in particular; close roadside views can be obtained of birds feeding. Totals of Golden Plover in the general district have exceeded 4,000 and often top 1,000, although this number may be fragmented between several groups moving around the area. Plover from here are believed to range all over central Devon at times. Birds start gathering from mid-autumn, but leave early in spring. Lapwing often gather in hundreds, and when the fields are wet, parties of Snipe totalling several dozen may be spread across the airfield. Other species seen in good numbers are likely to be Starling, Redwing and Fieldfare, the latter two species often seen in flocks of 200–300 at a time. The presence of these prey species may induce a Merlin to hunt over the district intermittently in late autumn–winter, or more occasionally a Peregrine visits. Raven are common in the surrounding sheep farming land, and at times dozens have been seen gathered together at Winkleigh. Buzzard are also well represented. Other breeding species are not outstanding, but small numbers of Willow Tit occur.

Comparison with similar areas such as Davidstowe Airfield in Cornwall leads one to assume that scarcer visitors might be attracted to join in the wader flocks; indeed, an American Lesser Golden Plover, Devon's first, was seen at Winkleigh. Closer scrutiny of this district might pay off, although movement of the flocks over a wide area might make it very difficult to keep track of an individual rarer bird, and industrial development at Winkleigh means the main site is becoming less attractive to large flocks. Other uncommon visitors have included occasional Snow Bunting, and good Brambling flocks have occurred.

Timing

Heavy rainfall making flood pools in the grass will attract waders; cold weather further north is likely to give a general increase in numbers. Early mornings and late afternoons, with less disturbance, may be better; some species seem to roost at Winkleigh then fly off for the daytime. Weather can be wet and windy, with mist or low cloud, at this exposed site.

Access

A377, signposted towards Barnstaple, leads west from Crediton onto B3220 for Torrington. The road bypasses Winkleigh village itself; 1 mile (1.6 km) afterwards, the road crosses the flat hilltop Airfield area, with views from the verges. A minor road also leads left towards Dowland. Try also checking the next 5 miles (8 km) north on B3220 towards Beaford village, stopping on verges to check rough wet pastures on either side of the road where plover feed. These sites can be checked by car-bound birdwatchers.

45D ADDITIONAL SITE: SHOBROOKE PARK, CREDITON

OS ref: SS 8501
OS map: sheet 191

Habitat

The market town of Crediton lies in the Creedy valley 9 miles (15 km) northwest of Exeter, surrounded by rolling agricultural land; Raddon hills rise to over 250 m to the east. Immediately northeast of the town is Shobrooke Park estate, with two ornamental lakes totalling 12½ acres (5 ha) set in open parkland with mature deciduous trees.

Species

This is a convenient area to see a range of woodland and waterside species, including some localised breeders. It may have general bird-watching interest all year, although winter visits are most productive for a range of species including residents, winter visiting passerines and waterfowl. The lakes are dominated by the large population of feral Canada Geese, the region's largest, reaching over 400 birds at times; flocks from here travel all over east and south Devon. Wooded islets in the lower lake provide nesting refuges for a number of pairs. The geese act as a decoy for various other geese which may spend several weeks at a time accompanying the flocks; such stragglers have included Bean, White-fronted, Pink-footed and Greylag Geese, usually single individuals, whilst Barnacle Geese have become regular, sometimes two or three. The origin of these birds is unknown, but some are likely to be escapes. Other wildfowl include midwinter counts of up to 70 Tufted Duck and 40 Pochard; the only other duck normally present in numbers is Mallard, which may approach 200 in number, including feral hybrids. Several pairs normally breed here. Other dabbling ducks such as Teal, Wigeon and Shoveler may visit in small parties, especially when driven by cold weather; such conditions may produce a visit from a Goosander, Smew or Goldeneye. Ducks and geese resting on the undisturbed west bank of the lakes may be joined by up to 80 Coot, a few of which will stay to nest, together with Moorhen.

Shobrooke is one of the region's few localities where Great Crested Grebe breed most years, although it only supports a single pair; often at least one stays through the year. Little Grebe may also breed, although not always present at other seasons. Lack of lowland freshwater lakes severely limits the region's population of these two species. Cormorant are a far more conspicuous visitor, especially outside the summer breeding season, resting on the west banks when not fishing, or roosting in tall trees on the islets. 10–20 birds can be expected regularly, some white-bellied immatures; breeding has, however, been attempted on at least one occasion. Grey Heron are similarly conspicuous, with an old-established heronry of 15–20 pairs in the park, and often a line of birds resting along a quiet stretch of lake bank, although breeding birds feed widely along the river valleys from here.

The parkland hosts a good range of commoner species characteristic of Devon lowlands; Green and Great Spotted Woodpeckers are often seen and heard, while Buzzard and Sparrowhawk pass over. Little Owl are usually present in the area although not often seen. Stock Dove and Jay frequent the old oaks, while a Raven may fly over, and there is an active Rookery on the edge of the park. Small birds may include up to 50 Siskin in waterside trees in winter, when flocks of Redwing and Fieldfare are usually present, and Brambling are often found among Chaffinch. Grey Wagtail are often flushed from the waterside, where a Kingfisher may sit outside the breeding season. Spotted Flycatcher and commoner breeding *Phylloscopus* and *Sylvia* warblers are in good numbers through summer. Passage is not very marked this far inland, although a Common or Green Sandpiper may stop off by the lakes. In late summer a Hobby may dart in to attack feeding hirundines which gather over the water.

Timing

Freezing weather elsewhere brings more ducks to the lakes. Fine bright days give the best winter watching conditions, all day being suitable, although there will probably be more activity in the mornings. Sunny weekends may bring public visiting and more disturbance.

Access

Crediton is reached by A377 from Exeter; turn right in the town centre towards Tiverton (A3072). After a mile (1.6 km) turn right following Shobrooke sign. After 100 yards (100 m) park in a layby on the left, and walk through the gate into the park following public footpath signs. The path follows the right (east) bank of both lakes. Sheep may be grazing and dogs should be kept on leads.

GLOSSARY OF TERMS USED
AND USEFUL ADDRESSES

For ease of use of the text, and to enable the reader to understand what other birdwatchers are discussing, we have used a number of words and expressions which may need explanation. We have avoided 'jargon' for its own sake, but the terms listed below serve the double function of making a clear ornithological point and being in familiar use by experienced watchers in the region. They fall into four categories: terms used to describe birds, or groups of birds, and their actions; weather phenomena; geography; and initials of relevant organisations.

Bird Terms

Activity Times:
Crepuscular – Active in dim light at dawn and especially dusk, e.g. Nightjar.
Diurnal – Active in full daylight.
Nocturnal – Active at night, e.g. most owls; many small insect-eating passerines are nocturnal fliers (navigating by stars) when migrating.
Auk – A seabird of the Guillemot–Razorbill family.
Brownhead – A female or immature of certain northern ducks, usually Goldeneye, Smew, Red-breasted Merganser, Goosander.
Coasting – Diurnal movement against the wind by groups of migrants, e.g. Swallows and pipits, following major landmarks and coastlines. Most noticed on autumn days with a light–moderate wind from southwest or west.
Commic Tern – A sea tern, Common or Arctic, not specifically identified.
Common Woodland Passerines – Those small birds resident in most English woods, e.g. Dunnock, thrushes, tits, Nuthatch, Treecreeper, Wren.
Ducks, Dabbling – Surface-feeders such as Mallard and Teal.
Ducks, Diving – Species which seek food entirely by swimming underwater, e.g. Tufted Duck, Pochard.
Fall – Mass arrival of night-flying migrants, e.g. warblers, flycatchers, along the coastline when conditions prevent them from continuing their journey. Winds from fine high-pressure weather areas on the Continent, combined with cloud, mist or drizzle at our end, are most likely to cause this, as large numbers of birds set off in the fine conditions and are then forced down.
Feral – Introduced here by man and now living in the wild state, e.g. Canada Goose, Ruddy Duck.
Hirundine – A bird of the swallow–martin family.
Irruption – An arrival of certain specialised feeders from the Continent, e.g. Waxwing and Crossbill, when their population is high and food runs short in their native areas. Irruptions vary greatly in size from year to year and are more marked in eastern Britain; only larger arrivals extend to our region.
Movement – A long-distance purposeful journey, e.g. migration or search for food, rather than a routine local activity.
Movement, weather – Mass movement of wintering species, e.g. wildfowl, open-ground species such as Lapwing, winter thrushes, into our region when ice and snow prevent feeding in other parts of Britain and the adjacent Continent.
Off-passage – Used to describe a migrant which makes an extended stop-over to rest and feed, maybe for weeks, before resuming its journey.
Open-ground Species – Species which tend to use treeless expanses, open fields, moors and downs, e.g. plovers, larks.
Overshoot – In spring and early summer, 'exotic' species such as Little Egret, Hoopoe and Golden Oriole migrating into southern Europe from Africa may overshoot their normal range and be carried to Britain by high pressure with following winds.
Passage Migrant – A bird which occurs only when passing through on migration between summer and winter quarters.
Passerine – 'Sparrow-like', small perching birds; used to describe all small landbirds.
Pelagic – Feeding over areas of deep sea and not normally seen near the coast except when visiting nest sites, e.g. small petrels, or when displaced by gales.
Raptor – A diurnal bird of prey, e.g. Kestrel, buzzards; excludes owls.
Ringtail – Female or immature Hen or Montagu's Harrier.
Sawbill – A duck of the Red-breasted Merganer–Goosander–Smew group, with a serrated bill edge to grasp fish.

Seabird – One of the mainly pelagic or coastal species or groups of birds, not normally seen inland, e.g. shearwaters, Gannet, skuas, most gulls.

Seaducks – Marine diving ducks not normally seen on fresh water, e.g. Eider, scoters.

Seawatch – A prolonged watch over an area of sea through binoculars or telescope from a coastal headland, scanning to pick out passing seabirds. Views can be distant and considerable skill is needed to make accurate identifications. Most likely to be productive in poor visibility or onshore winds. In wrong conditions can be unrewarding, but on good days thousands of birds may pass.

Shank – A medium-sized wader of the *Tringa* genus, e.g. Redshank, Spotted Redshank, Greenshank.

Vagrant – A rare, accidental visitor from other countries, mainly at migration times.

Wader – A bird which feeds in mud, water or marsh, e.g. Dunlin, Curlew, but including some plovers and Woodcock which have adapted to drier ground.

Warbler, Phylloscopus – A 'leaf warbler', e.g. Willow, Wood, Chiffchaff and scarcer related species. For quickness, often shortened by birdwatchers in the field to 'Phyllosc.'

Warbler, Sylvia – One of the larger scrub-haunting warblers, e.g. Blackcap, Whitethroat. (Note: the other main warbler groups have fewer species and we have named these individually in the text.)

Wild Swans – Whooper or Bewick's Swan, uncommon winter visitors to our region, rather than the introduced Mute Swan.

Winter Thrushes – Those which come across from northern Europe in winter, chiefly Fieldfare and Redwing flocks, but Blackbirds and Song Thrushes also arrive to join local birds.

Wreck – An arrival of exhausted and hungry seabirds, e.g. petrels, Little Auks, after prolonged severe gales at sea, occasionally driven far inland.

Weather Phenomena

Anticyclonic (or high) – An area of high barometric pressure, where fine clear conditions predominate, from which winds flow out to neighbouring regions. High pressure is defined as over 1,000 millibars, sometimes reaching 1,040 in strong anticyclones. Such conditions encourage migrants to start off.

Depression (or low) – A system of low pressure, generally originated over the Atlantic and drifting eastward towards Britain unless pushed back by high pressure over the Continent. As it drifts, with winds revolving in an anticlockwise direction and strong at times, water is drawn in to create an unstable weather zone with rain and cloud. Low pressure is defined as under 1,000 millibars and may drop to 950 (rarely lower) in deep depressions, with strong gales.

Front – A sharp division between two air masses of different temperature and humidity, drawn together in a depression. Fronts passing overhead are often accompanied by rainfall and poor visibility. They usually herald a change in temperature, wind direction and humidity as the new air mass arrives. Passerine migrants tend to land and seabirds may fly close inshore to avoid the front. A *cold front* precedes the arrival of cold, clear polar air, often with intermittent heavy showers, and characteristically with west or northwest winds. A *warm front* brings milder, cloudy and damp conditions, often with southwest winds. In a normal depression, warm fronts arrive first, and the wind veers towards northwest when cold fronts arrive later.

Thermal – A rising current of warm air over land, often used by soaring raptors to gain height without exertion.

Geographical Features

Brake – A dense area of trees and bushes, often on sloping ground.

Carn (Cornwall) – An open hilltop vantage point.

Combe (or Coombe) – A steep-sided valley, often wooded.

Dyke – An embanked marsh-drainage ditch.

Escarpment – A prominent edge of a hill or ridge from which the land drops away steeply.

Leat – Artificial freshwater channel fed off a stream to supply water to a village.

Pill – A very narrow creek or channel.

Tor (chiefly Devon) – A protruding mass of granite boulders standing on a moorland hilltop.

Useful Organisations

CBWPS – Cornwall Bird Watching and Preservation Society. Current Secretary: M. Lawson, Fieldfares, St Giles Drive, Wadebridge, Cornwall. Recorder: S. Christophers, 5 Newquay Road, St Columb Major, nr Newquay, Cornwall.

CTNC – Cornwall Trust for Nature Conservation Ltd. Conservation Officer, Five Acres, Allet, Truro, tel. Truro 73939.

Dartmoor National Park. Office: Parke House, Bovey Tracey, South Devon, tel. Bovey Tracey 832093.

DBWPS – Devon Bird Watching and Preservation Society. Current Secretary: N.L. Trigg, Hawthorns, 8 White Park, Moreleigh nr. Totnes TQ9 7JL. Recorder: P. Ellicott, 34 Maple Road, St Thomas, Exeter, Devon.

DWT – Devon Wildlife Trust. 35 New Bridge Street, Exeter, Devon, tel. Exeter 79244.

Forestry Commission. Contact: Head Ranger (Conservation), Forestry Commission, Bullers Hill, Kennford, Exeter, Devon EX6 7XR, tel. Exeter 832262.

Nature Conservancy Council (NCC) (controls National Nature Reserves). Regional Office: Roughmoor, Bishops Hull, Taunton, Somerset, tel. Taunton 283211

National Trust. Regional Office: Killerton House, Broadclyst, Exeter, tel. Exeter 881691. (For Cornwall, enquiries to Lanhydrock House, Lanhydrock PL30 4DE, Cornwall.)

RSPB – Royal Society for the Protection of Birds. Regional Office: 10 Richmond Road, Exeter, tel. Exeter 432691.

Royal Society for the Prevention of Cruelty to Animals (RSPCA). See telephone directory.

SWW – South West Water (issues reservoir permits and information leaflets). Contact: Recreation Office, South West Water, Peninsula House, Rydon Lane, Exeter, Devon EX2 7HR, tel. Exeter 219666.

CODE OF CONDUCT FOR
BIRDWATCHERS

Today's birdwatchers are a powerful force for nature conservation. The number of those of us interested in birds rises continually and it is vital that we take seriously our responsibility to avoid any harm to birds.

We must also present a responsible image to non-birdwatchers who may be affected by our activities and particularly those on whose sympathy and support the future of birds may rest.

There are ten points to bear in mind:

1. The welfare of birds must come first.
2. Habitat must be protected.
3. Keep disturbance to birds and their habitat to a minimum.
4. When you find a rare bird, think carefully about whom you should tell.
5. Do not harass rare migrants.
6. Abide by the bird protection laws at all times.
7. Respect the rights of landowners.
8. Respect the rights of other people in the countryside.
9. Make your records available to the local bird recorder.
10. Behave abroad as you would when birdwatching at home.

Welfare of birds must come first

Whether your particular interest is photography, ringing, sound recording, scientific study or just birdwatching, remember that the welfare of the bird must always come first.

Habitat protection

Its habitat is vital to a bird and therefore we must ensure that our activities do not cause damage.

Keep disturbance to a minimum

Birds' tolerance of disturbance varies between species and seasons. Therefore, it is safer to keep all disturbance to a minimum. No birds should be disturbed from the nest in case opportunities for predators to take eggs or young are increased. In very cold weather, disturbance to birds may cause them to use vital energy at a time when food is difficult to find. Wildfowlers already impose bans during cold weather: birdwatchers should exercise similar discretion.

Rare breeding birds

If you discover a rare bird breeding and feel that protection is necessary, inform the appropriate RSPB Regional Office, or the Species Protection Department at the Lodge. Otherwise it is best in almost all circumstances to keep the record strictly secret in order to avoid disturbance by other birdwatchers and attacks by egg-collectors. Never visit known sites of rare breeding birds unless they are adequately protected. Even your presence may give away the site to others and cause so many other visitors that the birds may fail to breed successfully.

Disturbance at or near the nest of species listed on the First Schedule of the Wildlife and Countryside Act 1981 is a criminal offence.

Copies of *Wild Birds and the Law* are obtainable from the RSPB, The Lodge, Sandy, Beds. SG19 2DL (send two 2nd class stamps).

Rare migrants

Rare migrants or vagrants must not be harassed. If you discover one, consider the circumstances carefully before telling anyone. Will an influx of birdwatchers disturb the bird or others in the area? Will the habitat be damaged? Will problems be caused with the landowner?

The Law

The bird protection laws (now embodied in the Wildlife and Countryside Act 1981) are the result of hard campaigning by previous generations of birdwatchers. As birdwatchers we must abide by them at all times and not allow them to fall into disrepute.

Respect the rights of landowners

The wishes of landowners and occupiers of land must be respected. Do not enter land without permission. Comply with permit schemes. If you are leading a group, do give advance notice of the visit, even if a formal permit scheme is not in operation. Always obey the Country Code.

Respect the rights of other people

Have proper consideration for other birdwatchers. Try not to disrupt their activities or scare the birds they are watching. There are many other people who also use the countryside. Do not interfere with their activities and, if it seems that what they are doing is causing unnecessary disturbance to birds, do try to take a balanced view. Flushing gulls when walking a dog on a beach may do little harm, while the same dog might be a serious disturbance at a tern colony. When pointing this out to a non-birdwatcher be courteous, but firm. The non-birdwatchers' goodwill towards birds must not be destroyed by the attitudes of birdwatchers.

Keeping records

Much of today's knowledge about birds is the result of meticulous record keeping by our predecessors. Make sure you help to add to tomorrow's knowledge by sending records to your county bird recorder.

Birdwatching abroad

Behave abroad as you would at home. This code should be firmly adhered to when abroad (whatever the local laws). Well behaved birdwatchers can be important ambassadors for bird protection.

This code has been drafted after consultation between the British Ornithologists' Union, British Trust for Ornithology, the Royal Society for the Protection of Birds, the Scottish Ornithologists' Club, the Wildfowl Trust and the Editors of British Birds.

Further copies may be obtained from The Royal Society for the Protection of Birds, The Lodge, Sandy, Beds. SG19 2DL.

INDEX TO SPECIES BY CHAPTER

Index to Species by Chapter